APPROACHES TO GRAMMA

TYPOLOGICAL STUDIES IN LANGUAGE (TSL)

A companion series to the journal "STUDIES IN LANGUAGE"

Volumes in this series will be functionally and typologically oriented, covering specific topics in language by collecting together data from a wide variety of languages and language typologies. The orientation of the volumes will be substantive rather than formal, with the aim of investigating universals of human language via as broadly defined a data base as possible, leaning toward cross-linguistic, diachronic, developmental and live-discourse data. The series is, in spirit as well as in fact, a continuation of the tradition initiated by C. Li *(Word Order and Word Order Change, Subject and Topic, Mechanisms for Syntactic Change)* and continued by T. Givón *(Discourse and Syntax)* and P. Hopper *(Tense-Aspect: Between Semantics and Pragmatics)*.

Volume 19:1

Elizabeth Closs Traugott and Bernd Heine (eds)

APPROACHES TO GRAMMATICALIZATION

APPROACHES TO GRAMMATICALIZATION

VOLUME I

FOCUS ON THEORETICAL AND METHODOLOGICAL ISSUES

edited by

ELIZABETH CLOSS TRAUGOTT
and BERND HEINE

JOHN BENJAMINS PUBLISHING COMPANY
AMSTERDAM/PHILADELPHIA

1991

Library of Congress Cataloging-in-Publication Data

Approaches to grammaticalization / edited by Elizabeth Closs Traugott and Bernd Heine.

p. cm. -- (Typological studies in language, ISSN 0167-7373; v. 19)
Contents: v. 1. Focus on theoretical and methodological issues -- v. 2. Focus on types of grammatical markers.
Includes bibliographical references and index.
1. Grammar, Comparative and general -- Grammaticalization. I. Traugott, Elizabeth Closs. II. Heine, Bernd, 1939- . III. Series.
P299.G73A6 1991
415--dc20 91-3650
ISBN 90 272 2901 5 (set)/90 272 2895 7 (Vol. I)/90 272 2899 X (Vol. II) (Eur.; hb; alk. paper)
ISBN 90 272 2902 3 (set)/90 272 2896 5 (Vol. I)/90 272 2900 7 (Vol. II) (Eur.; pb; alk. paper)
ISBN 1-55619-404-8 (set)/1-55619-400-5 (Vol. I)/1-55619-402-1 (Vol. II) (US; hb; alk. paper)
ISBN 1-55619-405-6 (set)/1-55619-401-3 (Vol. I)/1-55619-403-X (Vol. II) (US; pb; alk. paper)

Table of contents

VOLUME I

VOLUME II

ABBREVIATIONS

ABL	ablative
ABS	absolutive
ACC	accusative
ACT	active, actor
ADV	adverb
AF	actor focus
AGR	agreement
AOR	aorist
ART	article
ASSOC	associative
ASP	aspect
AUX	auxiliary
BEN	benefactive
CAUS	causative
COMP	complementizer
COMPL	complement
COMPAR	comparative
COND	conditional
CONJ	conjunction
COP	copula
DAT	dative
DEC	declarative
DEF	definite
DEM	demonstrative
DET	determinator
DIR	directional
DO	direct object
DS	directional subject
DU	dualis
DUB	dubitative
DUR	durative
EMPH	emphatic
ERG	ergative
EXCL	exclusive
EXCLAM	excalamative
FEM	feminine
FIN	finite
FOC	focus
FUT	future
GEN	genitive
GEN.OBL	general oblique preposition
GER	gerund
IMP	imperative
IMPERF	imperfect
IMPFV	imperfective
INCL	inclusive
INCONS	inconsequential
INDEF	indefinite
INF	infinitive
INFL	verbal inflection
INT	intensifier
INTR	intransitive
IO	indirect object
IRR	irrealis
LOC	locative
MASC	masculine
MED	medial
MID.VCE	middle voice

ABBREVIATIONS

NEG	negative
NOM	nominative
NOMI	nominalizer
NONFUT	nonfuture
NONPAST	nonpast
NP	noun phrase
OBJ	object
OBL	oblique
PART	particle
PARTCP	participle
PARTV	partitive
PASS	passive
PAST	past
PERF	perfect
PFV	perfective
PL	plural
POS.PURP	positive purpose
POSS	possessive
PRE	verbal prefix
PREC	precaution/ negative purpose
PRED	predicate
PREP	preposition
PRES	present
PROG	progressive
PROH	prohibitive
PURP	purposive
Q	interrogative
QUOT	quotative
REAS	reason
RED	reduplicative
REFL	reflexive
REL	relative clause marker
REP	repetitive
SEQ	sequential
SG	singular
SS	same subject
STAT	stative
SUB	subordinate
SUBJ	subject
SUBJUNCT	subjunctive
TNS	tense
TOP	topic
TRANS	transitive
VB	verb
VOC	vocative
1SG	first person singular
1PL	first person plural
2SG	third person singular

Foreword

The papers in these volumes grow out of a symposium on grammaticalization organized by Talmy Givón, and held at The University of Oregon at Eugene in May 1988. The purpose of this symposium was to "present and discuss ... a broad range of empirical and theoretical issues concerning the genesis of morphosyntactic structure". We wish to acknowledge the inspiration provided by Talmy Givón's leadership of the symposium.

Many people helped bring these volumes into final shape. Especial thanks are due to John McWhorter and Gillian Ramchand for their assistance in commenting on and copy-editing papers, and to Ulrike Claudi and Friederike Hünnemeyer for preparation of the final materials.

Introduction

Elizabeth Closs Traugott and Bernd Heine
Stanford University and University of Cologne

1. INTRODUCTION

Although not everyone who uses the term would agree, "grammaticalization" as we define it refers to that part of the theory of language that focuses on the interdependence of langue and parole, of the categorial and less categorial, of the fixed and the less fixed in language. Grammaticalization is the linguistic process, both through time and synchronically, of organization of categories and of coding. The study of grammaticalization therefore highlights the tension between relatively unconstrained lexical expression and more constrained morphosyntactic coding, and points to relative indeterminacy in language and to the basic non-discreteness of categories.

These volumes present a number of diverse theoretical viewpoints on grammaticalization and give some detailed insights into specific grammaticalization phenomena in a number of languages. However, no attempt is made at completeness; for more comprehensive studies of the field of grammaticalization as a whole, see Lehmann (1985), Heine and Reh (1984), Hopper and Traugott (In progress), Heine et al. (1991). The diversity of perspectives is manifest in a number of ways. For example, disagreement about how to approach the subject starts with disagreements about what to call it. Some authors prefer "grammaticization" or even "grammatization" to "grammaticalization". There is more significant disagreement about whether grammaticalization is primarily a diachronic phenomenon to be studied from a "source and pathway" perspective, or primarily a syntactic, discourse-pragmatic phenomenon, to be studied from the point of view of fluid patterns of language use across time or at a synchronically segmented moment in time. In so far as there is any correlation between perspective and terminology, those who espouse the latter view of the subject tend to call it grammaticization. However, since the majority of participants used "grammaticalization", whatever their perspective, we have chosen to use this term in the title and in this introduction. We have not imposed uniform terminology on the contributors, and both terms will be found in the volumes.

Together the papers suggest answers to a number of questions, some of which focus on testing the boundaries of grammaticalization, others of which test the assumptions of linguistic theory in general. We outline here some of the models of grammaticalization that the authors use, challenge, or develop, and some of the main issues that the papers highlight.

2. THE LEXICAL ITEM > MORPHEME MODEL

Early work on grammaticalization viewed it as a diachronic phenomenon. Although many examples were discussed by nineteenth century scholars (e.g. Bopp, 1816; Humboldt, 1825; Gabelentz, 1891), the term was apparently first used by Meillet (1948 [1912]). He defined it as the evolution of grammatical forms (function words, affixes, etc.) out of earlier lexical forms, and much subsequent work has been conducted within this framework. Later researchers have emphasized that morphemes may also arise out of other morphemes. For example, Lehmann, acknowledging Kuryłowicz (1965), says: "Under the diachronic aspect, grammaticalization is a process which turns lexemes into grammatical formatives and makes grammatical formatives still more grammatical..." (1985:303), and Heine and Reh define grammaticalization as: "...an evolution whereby linguistic units lose in semantic complexity, pragmatic significance, syntactic freedom, and phonetic substance..." (1984:15).

In the present volumes papers by Abraham, Bybee et al., Campbell, Carlson, Craig, Greenberg, Heine et al., Keesing, Lehmann, Matisoff, Rude, Traugott and König owe much to this perspective, although all have also been influenced to greater or lesser degree by the discourse > morphosyntax perspective outlined in 3.

3. THE DISCOURSE > MORPHOSYNTAX PERSPECTIVE

Alongside the lexical item > morpheme tradition which derives from Meillet, there has been a more recent tradition associated with Talmy Givón, Charles Li, Sandra Thompson and others that focuses on the "packaging" of discourse and evolution of syntactic and morphological structure through fixing of discourse strategies. For example, Givón (1979:209) characterizes the process as one of cyclic waves involving

Discourse→Syntax→Morphology→Morphophonemics→Zero

cf. also Bybee (1985), Hopper (1988), Li and Thompson (1974), among others.

Papers in these volumes that develop this morphosyntactic perspective particularly clearly are those by Genetti, Givón on the development of dependent clauses in Hebrew, Haiman, Herring, Hook, Hopper, Lichtenberk, and Shibatani. It should be noted that in many cases the source item or items discussed by these authors is not lexical but morphological (a possibility clearly permitted by the definitions of grammaticalization cited in 2.).

4. THE GRAMMATICAL CODING PERSPECTIVE ON GRAMMATICALIZATION

So far we have reviewed issues of grammaticalization that are one way or another issues related to language change. Yet another perspective on grammaticalization asks not so much how grammatical coding comes into being, but what grammatical coding is possible typologically in a language or in languages, and how it is organized either at one period in time (Givón on serial verbs, Mithun, Thompson and Mulac) or panchronically (Frajzyngier, Nichols and Timberlake).

The answers to the question whether certain categories must be obligatorily grammaticalized challenge some of the fundamental assumptions some linguists bring to linguistic theory, for example, that there are universal "primitives" such as Subject, Object, Tense (cf. also DuBois, 1985).

5. THE RELATION OF DIACHRONIC GRAMMATICALIZATION TO LANGUAGE CHANGE

For those who see grammaticalization as a diachronic process, the question naturally arises: How can we distinguish grammaticalization from language change? The answer is that grammaticalization is a kind of language change, subject to certain general processes and mechanisms of change (see section 8.), and characterized by certain consequences such as changes in grammar. These are increased syntacticization in its early stages, and increased loss of morphosyntactic independence in its later stages, ultimately leading to zero, i.e. increased morphologization, and phonologization. Like other changes, grammaticalization spreads gradually across linguistic contexts on the one hand (Lichtenberk, Nichols and Timberlake), and across social contexts on the other (cf. Labov, 1972, and much of the sociolinguistic literature on variation and language change in progress). But that does not mean that all change is grammaticalization. To take an obvious example, the semantic change from Middle English *bede* 'prayer' to its modern meaning of a small spherical object often used in necklaces ('bead'), is an example of change by metonymy, but not of grammaticalization. Papers in this volume that particularly address this issue are those by Hopper and Lehmann.

6. THE UNIDIRECTIONALITY OF GRAMMATICALIZATION

Firmly entrenched in diachronic perspectives on grammaticalization is the assumption of a cline of unidirectionality; or more specifically of a pathway that channels change through a limited number of structures that are minimally different from one another. This does not mean that all unidirectionality involves grammaticalization; for example, the well-known tendency for [sy] to become [š] but not vice versa is in itself not an instance of grammaticalization. However, if it results from morpheme boundary loss, then it is an instance of a stage in grammaticalization. The question is precisely what kinds of unidirectionality are necessary or at least typical of grammaticalization, and whether any kinds of reversals of grammaticalization are usefully considered as examples, albeit rare, of grammaticalization (see 7. below).

One kind of unidirectionality often associated with grammaticalization is increase in abstractness. This notion is appealed to in discussions of metaphorical change (Heine et al. on PERSON>OBJECT>SPACE> TIME>PROCESS>QUALITY, Traugott and König on temporal> causal>concessive). However intuitively attractive and widely agreed upon such a cline of abstractness may be, it is essentially a pre-theoretical notion. Certainly, increased abstractness does not in itself require grammaticalization. For example, the shift in meaning from *grasp* in the sense 'seize' to 'understand' is not a case of grammaticalization, although it is an example of what many linguists would consider increased abstractness in meaning.

Much of the literature on unidirectionality characterizes the development of grammatical from lexical meaning in terms of desemanticization, bleaching, and emptying or loss of semantic or pragmatic meaning (see the definitions of grammaticalization in 2. above). Traugott and König challenge this concept and argue that in its early stages grammaticalization actually often involves an increase in pragmatic meaning (though semantic content, strictly speaking, may be reduced as pragmatic meaning increases). For example, a shift from temporal to concessive *while* does not involve primarily bleaching of semantic meaning, but rather increase of pragmatic significance pertaining to the speaker's attitude to what is being said. If this is correct, then we need to modify the standard view of semantic unidirectionality in the process of grammaticalization. It is not always a simple case of more > less semantic, but more often of an implicational hierarchy of the type semantic > pragmatic > less semantic-pragmatic. Note that although this is not a characterization of bleaching it is nevertheless unidirectional, since the claim is that one would not expect to find pragmatic > semantic > less semantic-pragmatic, e.g. concessive *while* > temporal. As Traugott and König indicate, the meaning changes outlined here for grammaticalization are characteristic of meaning change in general, and are therefore not diagnostic for grammaticalization (any more than bleaching is, for that matter).

Sometimes it has been proposed that the lexical item > morpheme and the discourse > morphosyntax perspectives come into conflict with respect to unidirectionality in the earliest stages of grammaticalization (Herring). However, there is actually no inconsistency when we consider that discourse presupposes lexicon; discourse uses lexical items in ways that endow them with pragmatic meaning, and if they have the properties salient to grammaticalization outlined above, and are used more frequently, they may well come to be syntacticized in the kinds of way Givón illustrates. The two formulae "lexical item > morpheme", "discourse > morphosyntax " can therefore be combined as: lexical item used in discourse > morphosyntax.

Another kind of unidirectionality often considered characteristic of grammaticalization is increase in bondedness. Typically, at the clause level independent clauses are combined, and a cline may develop from independent clauses through some kind of loose juxtaposition and coordination to subordination (cf. Wiegand, 1987). At the phrasal level, forms may become less free and more bound via grammaticalization; for example, postpositions become affixes (Craig, Greenberg). Although not confined to grammaticalization, one of its effects is that morphemes undergoing this process move away from cardinal categoriality, and in their later stages lose the ability to refer and to associate with the inflectional and derivational trappings of their morphosyntactic category (cf. Hopper and Thompson, 1984). This leads to the emergence of "linguistic hybrids" which show the properties of several morpheme classes.

Nouns which develop into adpositions, for example, lose nominal characteristics such as the ability to be marked for definiteness or number (Genetti), or verbs which are grammaticalized to case markers tend to lose the ability to be inflected for person, tense, aspect, and mood. Loss of categoriality may also lead to the kind of development of multiple grammaticalization chains in different functional domains that Craig discusses in connection with Rama.

Unidirectionality may suggest a single path of evolution. However, approaches referring to multiple functional domains (cf. Kemmer 1988) or to correlated processes seem closer to reality (cf. Heine and Reh, 1984; Lehmann, 1985; Croft, Forthcoming: Ch. 8). Heine and Reh suggest a tripartite classification of correlations of change: Semantic-pragmatic status, grammatical behavior, and phonological substance. Lehmann uses a bipartite classification according to paradigmatic and syntagmatic processes, i.e. according to the alternatives available on the one hand and the effect of linguistic context on the other. Lehmann's characterization is somewhat theory-bound and leads to the incorrect claim that grammaticalization involves reduction in scope (1985:309), despite the fact that the development of subordinators from pronouns or verbs of saying, for example, clearly involves expansion of the scope of these forms. However, its focus on correlations is of crucial importance. In these volumes, most of the papers alert us to correlations.

It is the phenomenon of correlatable parameters that allows us to project diachronic grammaticalization onto synchronic data. Consider for example, the grammaticalization of body part nouns. If arrayed simply as a case of OBJECT > SPACE > TIME > QUALITY the examples of *megbé* in Heine et al. would not qualify as a case of grammaticalization. They do so precisely because the semantic changes are correlated with a shift from nominal to prepositional structure, and with different syntactic privileges of occurrence.

7. COUNTEREXAMPLES TO UNIDIRECTIONALITY

The discussion so far has focused on unidirectionality, and what kinds of unidirectionality are characteristic of grammaticalization. Virtually nothing is exceptionless, and there are of course instances of change in languages that are counterexamples of tendencies that can be characterized as "less > more grammatical", "main clause > subordinate clause", etc. In these volumes the papers by Campbell and Greenberg explicitly raise counterexamples to unidirectionality (cf. also Matsumoto, 1988). The well-known phenomenon of "lexicalization" is also a counterexample, for example when phonological changes result in morphological loss and the development of idiosyncratic lexical items, such as the English pairs *lie–lay*, *sit–set*, *stink–stench*, all of which have their origins in *i*-umlaut.

It is likely that all these examples are strictly speaking actually not cases of grammaticalization (although once they have occurred they may be subject to the generalization, reduction, loss, and other changes typical of grammaticalization). Rather, the examples Campbell and Greenberg cite can be regarded as instances of reanalysis (Greenberg actually refers to "reinterpretation which...goes beyond what is usually called reanalysis in discussions of grammaticalization"). Nevertheless, since they test the boundaries of what may be considered bona fide cases of grammaticalization, they provide an important perspective on the other papers in these volumes.

8. MECHANISMS OF LANGUAGE CHANGE RELEVANT TO GRAMMATICALIZATION

A number of mechanisms of language change have already been alluded to as being relevant to grammaticalization. This is hardly surprising if indeed grammaticalization is a subset of phenomena occurring in change. Of particular importance for these volumes are: Metaphorical transfer (Heine et al.), metonymic transfer (Traugott and König), reanalysis (Heine et al., Lehmann, cf. also Langacker, 1977), and analogy (Greenberg, Lehmann, Matisoff). Another mechanism is the incorporation of grammatical material from the substrate languages, as illustrated by evidence from Melanesian Pidgin (Keesing). All these are mechanisms that make change possible, but none are restricted to grammaticalization and *all* are independent of the unidirectionality associated with grammaticalization.

9. CONDITIONS LICENSING GRAMMATICALIZATION

A further set of questions for the diachronic perspective on grammaticalization pertains to what conditions have to apply for grammaticalization to take place, in other words, given that a form A exists, what is its potential for becoming grammaticalized, and how do we know when this is happening?

Experience with cross-linguistic studies of typology and of change have revealed extensive and robust evidence that only certain lexical classes are likely to become grammaticalized. For example, it seems unlikely that *wall-paper* would become grammaticalized. This is not to say that such a change is impossible, but rather that it is extremely unlikely. What we find in language after language is that for any given grammatical domain, there is only a restrictive set of lexical fields, and within them only a restricted set of lexical items, that are likely to be sources. For example, case markers, including prepositions and postpositions, typically derive from terms for body parts or verbs of motion; tense and aspect markers typically derive from specific spatial configurations; modals from terms for possession, or desire; middles from reflexives, etc. Furthermore, the paths of change are themselves highly restricted, and suggest step-by-step developments, not discrete leaps across semantic or pragmatic domains. Accounts of why these restrictions apply appeal to cognitive constraints. Whereas some have regarded these cognitive constraints as hard-wired (i.e. essentially arbitrary, cf. Bickerton, 1981), authors represented in these volumes regard them as functionally constrained by salience, communicative strategies, etc. For example, if one is attempting to express something abstract using the resources already available, or attempting to express communicative intent, also using resources already available, then the purposes to which one puts language in part determine the choices one makes. Therefore, one answer to the question concerning what potential a form A has for becoming grammaticalized is: This depends on whether its semantic content or the inferences one can draw from it serve the purposes of creating text, that is, of producing discourse. Ultimately, the question is, can the form be used to serve the metalinguistic purposes of text-construction in a natural and therefore easily understood way? It is hard to imagine a context in which *wall paper* could be used to serve such a purpose.

The fact that a lexical item A has potential for solving the problem of expression does not in itself predict that it is a candidate for grammaticalization. We need to look for additional factors. An example is *corner*, a term which is used metaphorically in temporal expressions (cf. *go round a corner in time*). However, *corner* does not appear to be grammaticalized into tense or aspect. Why might this be? It has been suggested that the operative constraint is perceptual salience: Topological spaces only are grammaticalized (Talmy, 1983; Sweetser, 1988). Although the expected end of a process of grammaticalization is usually zero, in fact there are "graveyards", such as *be*-clefts (Givón) and frozen idioms or lexicalizations (Hopper) that appear to block or at least delay the process of total loss (see especially Greenberg).

It would seem that the point at which grammaticalization stops may be determined by the typological characteristics of the language concerned. There is, for example, a well established channel of grammaticalization leading from postpositions to nominal case inflections. To our knowledge, however, such a development has not been documented for languages of the analytic-isolating type, where grammaticalization is unlikely to lead to the development of inflectional morphology. Observations like these suggest that there may be typological language-internal constraints that block grammaticalization from proceeding beyond a certain point. Mithun suggests that some very specific factors such as the internal shape of the grammar of a particular language may make certain grammatical markers such as subject redundant and may therefore serve to block their development.

Given that a form A is a candidate for grammaticalization both because of its semantic context and its salience, a further condition has to apply for grammaticalization to take place: The form has to be used frequently. The more grammaticalized a form, the more frequent it is (Bybee et al., Givón on serial verbs, Hook). The seeds of grammaticalization are therefore in a correlated set of phenomena: Semantic suitability, salience, and frequency. Only the third actually leads to grammaticalization and hence to fixing, freezing, idiomatization, etc.

10. SOME QUESTIONS FOR THE FURTHER STUDY OF GRAMMATICALIZATION

Among a number of questions still to be answered is what the language-external motivation for grammaticalization may be. If semantic suitability, salience and frequency are among the prerequisites for grammaticalization to start, then the question still remains as to what motivates the beginning of the process. Is it discourse-pragmatic pressure, that is, the need to be informative and processable and expressive all at the same time (cf. Langacker, 1977), the phenomenon of gaps in grammatical paradigms or in the universe of abstract concepts, a "natural propensity" for signaling metalinguistic relations in non-lexical ways (cf. Bybee and Pagliuca, 1985), or some other factor or factors? These questions all point to linguistic problem-solving as a clue to motivations for grammaticalization. Any claim about problem-solving and functional purpose raises issues of teleology. Because grammaticalization does not necessarily happen in any given instance of potential grammaticalization, considerable caution needs to be taken in proposing teleological explanations. Clearly we do not know enough yet about communication to argue that "communicative necessity" motivates the development of grammatical categories. It is primarily through the study of what prevents grammaticalization, or simply fails to trigger it, that we can begin to hope to answer the question of motivation.

Also, what are the social and psychological dynamics that are present in the initial and final stages of grammaticalization? How far is it induced by individuals, and to what extent does it form an act of human creativity, rather than being the result of language-internal drifts or forces? Hardly any answers are available thus far to this type of question, despite extensive sociolinguistic research on the development of morphology. The question in most of this literature has been posed primarily in terms of variation and continua (e.g. Bickerton, 1975; Sankoff, 1980: Part II, Rickford, 1987), or of contact (e.g. Romaine, 1988), but for the most part not in terms of psychological or cognitive motivation (see, however, Slobin's (1985) suggestions regarding cross-linguistic operating principles in child language acquisition).

Yet another unsolved puzzle is what motivates the differential speed with which grammaticalization takes place in different functional domains. Observations on African languages suggest that some kinds of developments proceed faster than others. For example, new categories of tense and aspect have emerged within a relatively short period, and in some cases a new morphology evolving along the same grammaticalization pattern is already emerging, competing with the old one. The development of noun class systems or of verbal derivation, on the other hand, has been much more conservative: morphological paradigms found today can be reconstructed as having already existed in a similar form and function several millennia ago.

Another important question for any theory of language that grammaticalization poses is whether lexical morphemes are by nature different from grammatical ones. If it is true that diachronically grammatical forms ultimately arise out of lexical items (although their immediate sources are often other grammatical items), does this lead to the logical conclusion that they cannot be innovated, whereas lexical items can? Among the highly stable grammatical forms with no certain lexical origin are such forms as the Indo-European *to-* of the demonstrative pronoun (later further grammaticalized to a third person agreement marker). Are we justified in hypothesizing that this form was once derived from a lexical item, as the diachronic perspective on grammaticalization would suggest, or does it provide evidence that grammatical items can arise full-fledged, and if so, under what conditions? These and other questions remain for future empirical study.

11. ORGANIZATION OF THE VOLUMES

Arranging the many papers in a meaningful way turned out to be a difficult task, and the result is to some extent arbitrary. In view of the number and size of the contributions available we decided to divide the work up into two volumes. This division, too, is to some extent arbitrary.

Volume I focuses on theoretical and methodological issues, and is mainly concerned with developing the major themes for the study of grammaticalization outlined above.

Section A deals with some new perspectives on the development and structure of grammatical categories. Hopper discusses five principles which are relevant for describing grammaticalization. Lichtenberk draws attention to the role played by diachrony in explaining synchronic facts, and to gradualness in grammaticalization. By looking at the relationships between temporal packaging and information processing in serial verb constructions, Givón concludes that grammaticalization is not a gradual process, but rather an instantaneous one. Nichols and Timberlake develop a panchronic analysis of morphological realignments resulting from the tension between innovation and conventionalization.

In Section B, various perspectives on directionality are discussed. The first two argue for unidirectionality. The papers by Heine, Claudi and Hünnemeyer and by Traugott and König deal, among other things, with cognitive factors in directionality, especially the role of inference in metaphor and metonymy. Frajzyngier studies directionality of fit in grammar between the domain of the real world and that of speech. Unidirectional views on grammaticalization are challenged in a number of different ways. Herring argues for the independence of the development of grammatical elements out of lexical items and out of discourse-contexts, and the bi-directionality of some changes. Contributions by Greenberg and Campbell suggest that typically unidirectional processes may be reversed under certain conditions. And Keesing shows how areal influence may lead to the elaboration of grammatical structures through borrowing that is socially directional (from substrate to superstrate), but not linguistically so.

The papers in Volume II are for the most part detailed studies of distinct areas of language structure in particular languages or language families.

Section A focuses on the genesis of verbal categories such as tense and aspect. Bybee, Pagliuca, and Perkins summarize their cross-linguistic findings on future marking, and Hook discusses the notion of aspectogenesis in some Indo-Aryan languages.

Section B is concerned with various aspects of the development of argument structure. Shibatani resumes earlier discussion on the development of topic into subject, using evidence from Japanese and Philippine languages. And Haiman explores further the relationship between word order and the development of subject clitics. In a rather different vein, Mithun demonstrates why in some languages, specifically Cayuga (Iroquoian) and Selayarese (Austronesian), there was no need for the development of a subject category at all. In the final part of this section, Rude and Carlson show how non-subject marking arises out of verbal structures in Sahaptian and Klamath and in Senufo respectively.

Two different patterns in the development of subordinate structures are discussed in Section C. Genetti describes the transition from case postpositions to clausal subordinators in Newari (Tibeto-Burman). Givón reconstructs the transfer from relative clause structure to verbal complement subordination in Biblical Hebrew.

Section D is devoted to expressions of modality. Thompson and Mulac present the case of certain English "main clauses" (*I think (that)*) which are reinterpreted as epistemic phrases, and Abraham deals with the development of a set of modal particles in German.

Papers in Section E demonstrate a spectrum of cases of grammaticalization and a diverse array of factors at play. Matisoff investigates the development of a number of verbal and nominal particles, as well as of verbal concatenations in the Southeast Asian linguistic area. Craig shows how in Rama (Chibchan) one verb in different contexts develops multiple grammatical functions, one relating to argument structure, the other relating to tense, aspect and mood; she proposes the term "polygrammaticalization" for this kind of process. Lehmann discusses a number of emergent grammatical patterns in modern German which may or may not be instances of incipient grammaticalization, thereby pushing on the question of how one recognizes an instance of grammaticalization.

ACKNOWLEDGMENTS

This introduction is clearly inspired by all the participants in the symposium on grammaticalization. Particular thanks are due to Dan Slobin whose concluding remarks made the coordination of issues easier, and to Paul Hopper, Frank Lichtenberk, and Suzanne Romaine for comments on an earlier version.

REFERENCES

Bickerton, Derek. 1975. *Dynamics of a Creole System*. Cambridge: Cambridge University Press.

Bickerton, Derek. 1981. *Roots of Language*. Ann Arbor, MI: Karoma Publishers.

Bopp, Franz. 1816. *Über das Conjugationssystem der Sanskritsprache in Vergleichung mit jenem der griechischen, lateinischen, persischen und germanischen Sprachen*. Frankfurt: Andreäische Buchhandlung.

Bybee, Joan. 1985. *Morphology. A Study of the Relation between Meaning and Form*. Amsterdam: John Benjamins.

Bybee, Joan and William Pagliuca. 1985. "Cross-linguistic comparison and the development of grammatical meaning." In *Historical Semantics and Historical Word Formation*, Jacek Fisiak (ed.), 59–83. Berlin: de Gruyter.

Croft, William. Forthcoming. *Typology and Universals*. Cambridge: Cambridge University Press.

DuBois, John W. 1985. "Competing motivations." In *Iconicity in Syntax*, John Haiman (ed.), 343–65. Amsterdam: John Benjamins.

Gabelentz, Georg von der. 1891. *Die Sprachwissenschaft. Ihre Aufgaben, Methoden und bisherigen Ergebnisse*. Leipzig: Weigel Nachfolger.

Givón, Talmy. 1979. *On Understanding Grammar*. New York: Academic Press.

Heine, Bernd and Mechthild Reh. 1984. *Grammaticalization and Reanalysis in African Languages*. Hamburg: Helmut Buske.

Heine, Bernd, Ulrike Claudi and Friederike Hünnemeyer. 1991. *Grammaticalization: a Conceptual Framework*. Chicago: University of Chicago Press.

Hopper, Paul J. 1988. "Emergent grammar and the *a priori* grammar postulate." In *Linguistics in Context: Connecting, Observations, and Understanding*, Deborah Tannen (ed.), 117–34. Norwood: Ablex.

Hopper, Paul J. and Sandra Thompson. 1984. "The discourse basis for lexical categories in universal grammar." *Language* 60:703–52.

Hopper, Paul J. and Elizabeth C. Traugott. In progress. *Grammaticalization*. Cambridge: Cambridge University Press.

Humboldt, Wilhelm von. 1825. "Über das Entstehen der grammatischen Formen und ihren Einfluss auf die Ideenentwicklung." *Abhandlungen der Königlichen Akademie der Wissenschaften zu Berlin*:401–30.

Kemmer, Suzanne. 1988. The Middle Voice: A Typological and Diachronic Study. Unpublished Ph.D. dissertation, Stanford University.

Kuryłowicz, Jerzy. 1965. "The evolution of grammatical categories." *Esquisses Linguistiques* (2):38–54.

Labov, William. 1972. *Sociolinguistic Patterns*. Philadelphia: University of Pennsylvania Press.

Langacker, Ronald W. 1977. "Syntactic reanalysis." In *Mechanisms of Syntactic Change*, Charles N. Li (ed.), 57–139. Austin: University of Texas Press.

Lehmann, Christian. 1985. "Grammaticalization: Synchronic variation and diachronic change." *Lingua e Stile* 20:303–18.

Li, Charles N. and Sandra A. Thompson. 1974. "Historical change and word order: A case study in Chinese and its implications." In *Historical Linguistics I: Syntax, Morphology, Internal and Comparative Reconstruction*, John M. Anderson and Charles Jones (ed.), 199–218. Amsterdam: North-Holland.

Matsumoto, Yo. 1988. "From bound grammatical markers to free discourse markers: History of some Japanese connectives." In *Berkeley Linguistics Society, Proceedings of the Fourteenth Annual Meeting*, 340–51.

Meillet, Antoine. 1948 [1912]. "L'évolution des formes grammaticales." In *Linguistique générale et linguistique historique*, 130–48. Paris: Champion.

Rickford, John. 1987. *Dimensions of a Creole Continuum: History, Texts, and Linguistic Analysis of Guyanese Creole*. Stanford: Stanford University Press.

Romaine, Suzanne. 1988. "Pidgins, creoles, immigrant, and dying languages." In *Investigating Obsolescence. Studies in Language Contraction and Death*, Nancy Dorian (ed.), 369–83. Cambridge: Cambridge University Press.

Sankoff, Gillian. 1980. *The Social Life of Language*. Philadelphia: University of Pennsylvania Press.

Slobin, Dan I. 1985. "Cross-linguistic evidence for the language-making capacity." In *The Cross-Linguistic Study of Language Acquisition. Volume II. Theoretical Issues*, Dan I. Slobin (ed.), 1157–1256. Hillsdale, N.J.: Erlbaum Associates.

Sweetser, Eve. 1988. "Grammaticalization and semantic bleaching." In *Berkeley Linguistics Society, Proceedings of the Fourteenth Annual Meeting*, 389–405.

Talmy, Leonard. 1983. "How language structures space." In *Spatial Orientation: Theory, Research and Application*, Herbert Pick and Linda Acredolo (ed.), 225–82. New York: Plenum Press.

Wiegand, Nancy. 1987. Causal Connectives in the Early History of English: A Study in Diachronic Syntax. Unpublished Ph.D. Dissertation, Stanford University.

SECTION A: GENERAL METHOD

On Some Principles of Grammaticization

Paul J. Hopper
Carnegie Mellon University

1. INTRODUCTION[1]

The earliest known use of the word *grammaticalization*[2] was apparently by Meillet, who defined it as "the attribution of a grammatical character to a previously autonomous word" (1912:131), and noted that in every case where the ultimate historical source of a grammatical form was known, this source could be shown to be an ordinary lexical word. While the search for the origins of grammar was not new (see Lehmann, 1982:1–8), in retrospect we are tempted to see in Meillet's formulations and in his use of the term grammaticalization a sense that a specific kind of historical change was at work which went beyond the neo-grammarian preoccupation with sound change, *Wortgeschichte*, and analogy, and that he was concerned to explicate in broad terms "the history" of "grammar", i.e. the historical antecedents to structure, in a language. Such an interpretation is certainly sympathetic to those who view grammatical structure as a self-contained component; and presumably Meillet, who refers frequently to "le système grammatical [d'une langue]", would in theory have agreed. Yet there are also indications in his writings that what is distinctively grammatical in a language is not its broader structures but the individual grammatical forms which comprise this structure. He notes (Meillet, 1925:25) that the specific identity of a language is not its grammar in the broad sense; French and English are not distinct from one another in showing a relationship between two nouns by means of a particle, but by the form and position of the particle (preposed *de* in French, postposed *-s* in English). Meillet's own philological investigations always emphasized the history of individual grammatical forms, which are referred to unmistakably as 'singular facts' (*faits singuliers*), 'particular facts' (*faits particuliers*), 'specific features' (*traits spécifiques*), and 'particular processes of expression of morphology' (*procédés particuliers d'expression de la morphologie*) (Meillet,

1925:22–25). Moreover, these comparative grammatical studies were interspersed with etymological works on Indo-European cultural vocabulary without any sense that the one or the other aspect of reconstruction and history was more important. Meillet's work, in other words, stressed the *particular* over the general in practically all aspects of change.

It is not that Meillet did not hold a Saussurean view of structure. There are plenty of references in his work to the *grammatical system*, and to *the system of [the] language*. Yet this system consists almost exclusively of morphology, and Meillet's diachronic bias rarely allows him to dwell on its stability and systematicity; almost always when he uses the word 'grammar' (*la grammaire*), it is in a phrase which stresses comparison and historical relationships (*grammaire comparée*, *grammaire historique*) rather than a synchronic system. It is a phenomenon of a later time that linguists came to accord grammar (i.e. morphology and syntax) a privileged status in the study of language, and that as a consequence grammaticization came to be seen as the study of the origins of *grammar* (rather than of the origins of the array of *grammatical forms* constituting its morphology, which is how Meillet usually presents it). Indeed, in his presentation of grammaticization Meillet includes such clearly lexical examples as German *heute* 'today' from a presumed **hiu tagu* 'this day (instr.)' alongside such evidently grammatical examples as Modern Greek *tha* (future tense formative) from *thelō hina* 'I want that', showing that what was at issue was not whether this or that form was "in" the grammar, but the more important question of the processes it had undergone to attain grammaticization. That these processes were the same for lexical forms as for forms which were unambiguously (i.e. by general agreement) 'in' the grammar suggests that for Meillet the notion of *grammaticalisation* did not rest ultimately on a clear definition of a grammatical system as such.

The broadened scope of the study of grammaticization as exemplified, for example, in the work of Givón (1971,1979), Heine and Reh (1984), and others, has shown that the range of phenomena to be studied is not restricted to morphology, but includes what Givón has called *syntacticization*, the fixing of pragmatically motivated word orders into syntactic constructions and agreement patterns. (Meillet had in fact presented the change from free word order in Latin to fixed word order in French (1912:147–8) as an example of grammaticization, and by implication, in saying that in early Indo-European "l'ordre des mots avait une valeur expressive, et non syntaxique; il relevait de la rhétorique, non de la grammaire" (1937:365), made it clear that at least in some languages word order was to be seen as part of grammar.) The more extensive definition of grammaticization implicit in this work raised the question of whether, when grammaticization had done its work, there would in the end be any room left at all for the notion of grammar in the sense of static structural relationships (Hopper, 1987; 1988a; 1988b). If grammar is not a discrete, modular set of relationships, it would seem to follow that no set of changes can be identified which distinctively characterize grammaticization as opposed to, say, lexical change or phonological change in general. The only way to identify instances of grammaticization would be in relation to a prior definition of grammar; but there appear to be no clear ways in which the borders which separate grammatical from lexical and other phenomena can be meaningfully and consistently drawn. Consequently, there seems to be no possibility of constructing a typology of grammaticization, or of constructing principles which will discriminate between grammaticization and other types of change.

Support for such a conclusion comes from research into semantic change. Traugott (1989) examines the kinds of semantic changes which accompany grammaticization as well as semantic change in general, and shows that grammaticization is not distinct from other kinds of semantic change, but that several tendencies, perhaps to be subsumed under an even smaller number of much broader tendencies, seem to govern most semantic change whether thought of as lexical or as grammatical. Later in this paper, I return to the question of the ultimate validity of the principles which I present here.

2. GRAMMAR: SOME WORKING ASSUMPTIONS

While a definition of grammar, and hence of grammaticization, is problematical for an individual language taken in isolation, some working assumptions about grammar are possible from a cross-linguistic perspective. These assumptions may provide an entry-point for an investigation of emergent regularities that have the potential for being instances of grammaticization:

a. Categories which are *morphologized* might safely be said to be part of grammar. Bybee (1985) has shown that aspect, number, tense, and case, among others, occur frequently across languages as affixal morphology. But some of these may also occur in looser collocations in the form of adverbials and other free elements. Therefore categories which are commonly morphologized in one language may be candidates for emergent grammatical constructions in another; an example is Thompson and Mulac's suggestion (these volumes) that the vernacular English 'I think' has assumed near-grammatical status as an evidential.

b. Certain types of lexical items are known typically to evolve into grammaticalized clitics and affixes. Such changes are now so richly documented that only a few examples need be mentioned: Demonstrative pronouns become articles and class markers; copular verbs and verbs of motion become aspectual morphemes; nouns denoting a location become adpositions and eventually case affixes of various kinds. The detailed list of such changes given by Heine and Reh (1984:269–81) for African languages is of universal relevance. The occurrence of certain lexical items in frequent collocations (for example, when the word 'foot' repeatedly occurs in phrases like 'at the foot of the hill', etc.) may be *prima facie* evidence of incipient grammaticization.

The application of such cross-linguistic generalizations about grammaticization is a standard, if usually tacit, technique to guide an investigation of grammaticization in a particular language. Such generalizations are especially necessary if direct historical data are not available, a situation which may occur not only for languages which have no historical records, but even for languages with ample documented histories. Again, the English evidential 'I think' analyzed by Thompson and Mulac provides a good example: Historical data on this construction were sparse because it has presumably always been restricted to the spoken language. Yet many languages possessed morphologized evidentials, and it seemed natural both to look for its pragmatic beginnings in vernacular English and to focus on an epistemic verb like 'think' as a possible candidate. But are there any "intra-language" principles by which we can identify instances of constructions that might be said to be caught up in grammaticization? Can we discriminate in a single-language (i.e. non-comparative, non-historical) context between accidental collocations and ones which are moving toward some kind of grammatical status, however defined?

One approach to this question has been suggested by Lehmann in his 1985 paper, in which several concomitants of grammaticization are described. These are:

— Paradigmatization (the tendency for grammaticized forms to be arranged into paradigms);

— Obligatorification (the tendency for optional forms to become obligatory);
— Condensation (the shortening of forms);
— Coalescence (collapsing together of adjacent forms);
— Fixation (free linear orders becoming fixed ones).

Such principles are useful, indeed indispensable, as guides to historical change, and have repeatedly proven their value in the study of grammaticization. They are, however, characteristic of grammaticization which has already attained a fairly advanced stage and is unambiguously recognizable as such. They work best, in fact, when the stage of morphologization has been reached. It is then usually possible to see that the kinds of changes typified by these labels have indeed occurred. By the time forms and constructions reach the stage of grammaticization implicit in being able to apply this typology, the question whether grammaticization has occurred is usually already answered. The problem of identifying grammaticization when it is not already obvious is precisely that the form or construction in question has not yet reached a stage of being "obligatory", "fixed", and so on. When Lehmann's principles are applied to the more labile sorts of phenomena that typically confront the linguist, they are either not applicable (e.g. Paradigmatization), or else are not distinctively examples of grammaticization (e.g. Coalescence.)

In this paper I will suggest some further principles, ones which (let it be said at the outset) share some of the same defects as Lehmann's, in that they also characterize aspects of change in general, and are not distinctive for grammaticization. In fact, the earlier discussion has made it clear that we should expect that distinctive "principles of grammaticization" can be formulated only to the extent that regularities in language can in principle be isolated which are unambiguously grammatical. Nevertheless I hope that these principles will supplement those suggested by Lehmann in being characteristic of grammaticization not only at the later, more easily identifiable stages, but also at the incipient stages where *variable* phenomena occur, and where the question more cogently arises as to whether we might speak of grammaticization. Like Lehmann's principles, too, they are not intended as novel insights into the nature and course of linguistic change; on the contrary, they are to a large extent part of the general lore about language change as it has been elaborated by linguists since the Neogrammarians, or simple extrapolations from that lore. But they assume a special relevance in the context of grammaticization as being potentially diagnostic of the emergence of grammatical forms and constructions out of already available material, and also of different degrees of grammaticization where grammaticization has already recognizably proceeded.

3. THE PRINCIPLES

The five principles of grammaticization which I am proposing are as follows:

(1) *Layering.* "Within a broad functional domain, new layers are continually emerging. As this happens, the older layers are not necessarily discarded, but may remain to coexist with and interact with the newer layers."

(2) *Divergence.* "When a lexical form undergoes grammaticization to a clitic or affix, the original lexical form may remain as an autonomous element and undergo the same changes as ordinary lexical items."

(3) *Specialization.* "Within a functional domain, at one stage a variety of forms with different semantic nuances may be possible; as grammaticization takes place, this variety of formal choices narrows and the smaller number of forms selected assume more general grammatical meanings."

(4) *Persistence.* "When a form undergoes grammaticization from a lexical to a grammatical function, so long as it is grammatically viable some traces of its original lexical meanings tend to adhere to it, and details of its lexical history may be reflected in constraints on its grammatical distribution."

(5) *De-categorialization.* "Forms undergoing grammaticization tend to lose or neutralize the morphological markers and syntactic privileges characteristic of the full categories Noun and Verb, and to assume attributes characteristic of secondary categories such as Adjective, Participle, Preposition, etc."

These five principles will now be discussed in turn.

3.1. Layering

Within a functional domain, new layers are continually emerging. As this happens, the older layers are not necessarily discarded, but may remain to coexist with and interact with the newer layers.

By a "functional domain", I mean some general functional area such as tense/aspect/modality, case, reference, etc., of the kind which frequently becomes grammaticized. The term is taken from Givón (1984:32–5). The Principle of Layering refers to the prominent fact that very often more than one technique is available in a language to serve similar or even identical functions. This formal diversity comes about because when a form or set of forms emerges in a functional domain, it does not immediately (and may never) replace an already existing set of functionally equivalent forms, but rather the two sets of forms co-exist. They may be specialized for particular lexical items, particular classes of constructions, or sociolinguistic registers; they may have slightly different meanings, or simply be recognized as "stylistic" alternatives. Sometimes layering merely represents a transition from one technique to another, but it may also be quite stable. The different techniques — e.g. (for tense/aspect), phonological alternation, affixation, periphrasis with auxiliary verbs — may exemplify quite vividly the different degrees of grammaticization attained by the different layers.

The tenses and aspects of English provide some good examples. In the past tense it is possible to distinguish an archaic layer of vowel alternations in strong verbs like *drive/drove*, *take/took*. These formations co-exist with a more recent layer making use of an apical suffix [t] or [d], as in *notice/noticed*, *walk/walked*; this suffix was itself almost certainly derived from an auxiliary verb cognate with English *do* (Lühr, 1984). In addition to the tense formations with phonological alternation and suffixation, a periphrastic construction involving *do/did* appears in questions, negatives, and emphatics. Of particular interest in English are the many types of *aktionsarten* represented by constructions like:

(1) *keep (on) + -ing: He keeps (on) signaling to me (iterative)*
(2) *go on + -ing: He went on asking silly questions (iterative)*
(3) *be about + to: We were about to get on the plane (prospective)*
(4) *start + to: They started to laugh (inceptive)*
(5) *take + to: She took to criticizing his work habits (inceptive)*

and others. Nuances of the "future tense" are especially richly represented; in addition to *be about + to* already mentioned, there are (Quirk et al., 1972:87–90):

(6) *will: He will be here in half an hour*
(7) *be going + to: She's going to have a baby*
(8) *be + -ing: The plane is taking off at 5:20*
(9) *be + to: An investigation is to take place*

All the members of these last two groups of forms make use of periphrasis, which is typical of the most recent layer of grammaticized forms. Ablaut and affixation, on the other hand, generally represent earlier layers. For example, English is rich in examples of all three:

a. *Periphrasis*: *We have used it* (newest layer)
b. *Affixation*: *I admired it* (older layer)
c. *Ablaut*: *They sang* (oldest layer)

While different chronological stages may often be identified through such structural clues as ablaut, affixation, and periphrasis, it is not necessary that all layers be differentiated historically from one another; often, in fact, the relative history of different layers cannot be easily inferred and is not documented; *to be + to* and *will* both existed in Old English, for example. This "cluttering" of grammar with functionally similar constructions, possibly inherited from different times over a vast history, and ever being re-created, is not easy to reconcile with any picture of a language as a homogeneous, architectured, and delimited object.

The next principle, Divergence, is conceptually quite close to the principle of Layering, and might easily be regarded as simply a special case of it.

3.2. Divergence

The Principle of Divergence, or Split, as Heine and Reh call it (1984:57–9 et pass.), refers to the fact that when a lexical form undergoes grammaticization, for example to an auxiliary, clitic or affix, the original form may remain as an autonomous lexical element and undergo the same changes as any other lexical items. The Principle of Divergence results in pairs or multiples of forms having a common etymology, but diverging functionally. The grammaticized form may be phonologically identical with the autonomous lexical form, as has happened with the French word *pas* 'not; negative particle' and its cognate *pas* 'pace, step', or the two may be so distinct that the relationship is completely opaque, as has happened with the English indefinite article *a(n)* and the word *one*.

Divergence is perhaps to be understood as a special case of Layering. Layering is somewhat different in that it involves different *degrees* of grammaticization in similar functional domains, usually of quite different lexical forms, while Divergence is applicable to cases where one and the same autonomous lexical item becomes grammaticized in one context and does not become grammaticized in another. It is, however, not always possible to make this distinction, since multiple divergences may result in several layers. For example, by a well described sequence of events, the Latin verb *habere* became a future tense suffix in Modern French, yielding *je chanterai* 'I shall sing' out of *(ego) cantare habeo* 'I have to sing'; it also became the Modern French lexical verb *avoir* 'to have'. But *avoir* itself came to be an auxiliary verb of the perfect in *j'ai chanté* 'I sang, have sung'. Thus *j'ai* is grammaticized as a tense-aspect auxiliary beside the ungrammaticized lexical verb *j'ai* 'I have' (divergence), but it also constitutes a secondary layer of grammaticization, being a periphrastic perfect tense-aspect marker beside the older, suffixal future *-erai*; schematically:

```
              habere
             /      \
           MV        Aux
          /  \          \
        MV    Aux       Affix
        |      |          |
      j'ai   j'ai        -ai
```

When the original form survives as a lexical item, we may still think of divergence as having occurred more than once. We cannot distinguish in principle between grammaticization and other types of change, nor can we tell in principle when a change has resulted in grammaticization and when it has not; consequently there may be no real difference between "divergence" whose outcome is two different layers of grammaticization and "divergence" which results in an autonomous lexical form and a cognate grammatical form.

3.3. Specialization

Specialization refers to the narrowing of choices that characterizes an emergent grammatical construction. It corresponds quite closely to Lehmann's "obligatorification", the loss of choice which occurs when a form is fully grammaticized. "Specialization", however, more closely matches the process involved, in that it is only in the final stages of grammaticization that the use of a form becomes obligatory, and it does not seem appropriate to think of this evolution as being one in which forms become "increasingly obligatory". Indeed, to regard the development as being toward the obligatory use of a form in a construction is perhaps undesirable in that it tends to set apart grammaticization from other kinds of changes, whereas "specialization" is just one possible kind of change which may or may not lead to grammaticization.

A well-known example of specialization is that of negation in Modern French, exemplified in:

(10) *Il ne boit pas de vin* 'He doesn't drink wine'

In the ordinary negative clause, the verb is straddled by two negators, *ne* preceding the verb and *pas* following it. *Pas* is also the general negative particle, for example in *pas beaucoup* 'not much', and so on. Historically the original negator was *ne*, and nouns like *pas* 'step, pace' could reinforce the negation. It can be assumed that the reinforcing noun was once tailored to the nature of the verb; thus verbs of motion could be reinforced with *pas* ('he doesn't go a step'), verbs of giving and eating with *mie* 'crumb' ('he didn't eat a crumb; he didn't give me a crumb'), and so on. Gamillscheg (1957:753) lists several such nouns denoting a 'least quantity' of something which could be used in Old French to reinforce negation:

pas 'step, pace'
point 'dot, point'
mie 'crumb'
gote 'drop'
amende 'almond'
areste 'fish-bone'
beloce 'sloe'
eschalope 'pea-pod'

and others. By the 16th century, the only ones still used with negative force were:

pas 'step, pace'
point 'dot, point'
mie 'crumb'
goutte 'drop'

Even in the 16th century, *pas* and *point* predominated, and by the modern period these were the only two which were still in use. Of them, it is really only *pas* which is a true negator, in that it has overwhelmingly higher discourse frequency, and is the unmarked negator in the sense of being semantically neutral (non-emphatic), and participating in a greater variety of constructions (*pas beaucoup* but not **point beaucoup*, etc.) This means that out of all the competing forms in Old French which might have won out, only *pas* has become a general negator. In the spoken language the *ne* of ordinary verbal negation is usually dropped (*je sais pas* 'I don't know'), leaving *pas* as the only mark of negation (the stage which might be characterized as "obligatorification").

In his contribution to the present volumes, Hook (Volume II) has described in detail the process of specialization as it is manifested in the evolution of compound verbs in Indo-Aryan languages. Compound verbs are double verbs which are found throughout the language family and might be seen as evolving toward Main Verb + Auxiliary status. Hook shows in statistical terms a trajectory which fits precisely with general linguistic expectations:

(1) The textual frequency of compound verbs vs. simple verbs varies in the different languages of the family. In comparable texts there are about six times as many compound verbs in Hindi as in Kashmiri, and twice as many in Gujerati as in Marathi. In other words, grammaticization has proceeded further in Hindi than in Kashmiri, further in Gujerati than in Marathi, and so on.

(2) Concomitant with increased textual frequency, there is a tendency to *narrow* the possible quasi-auxiliary verbs (known as *vector verbs*) that can be used with a "main verb". In the Hindi text sample, with a higher frequency of compound verbs, only 10 different verbs were used as vector verbs; in the Marathi sample, 14 different verbs were used as vector verbs.

(3) The five most frequent vector verbs in the Hindi text sample accounted for 92% of the total number of vector verbs; while in Marathi the five most frequent vector verbs accounted for only 81% of the total number. Moreover, in both the Hindi and Marathi text samples, the most frequently occurring vector verb was the one meaning 'go'. But in Hindi 'go' accounted for 41% of all vector verbs, while in Marathi 'go' accounted for only 32% of all vector verbs.

A final observation that can be made about both the Indo-Aryan compound verbs and the French negation is that at the same time as one part of an emergent construction is specialized, another part is, so to speak, "released". Hook shows that the specialization of the vector verbs in Indo-Aryan is accompanied by a loosening of the constraints on the "main verb", which from being restricted to concrete actions increasingly can refer to mental actions and states. An equivalent loosening presumably also occurred in the French negators, when *pas* 'step, pace' ceased to be restricted to verbs of motion, so that the class of verbs which could be negated with *ne...pas* widened. At an advanced stage of this process combinations of forms settle into paradigms (Lehmann's "paradigmatization") in which one single auxiliary form can combine with any stem whatsoever.

3.4. Persistence

The Principle of Persistence relates the meaning and function of a grammatical form to its history as a lexical morpheme. This relationship is often completely opaque by the stage of morphologization, but during intermediate stages it may be expected that a form will be polysemous, and that one or more of its meanings will reflect a dominant earlier meaning. A good illustration of Persistence is the development in West African languages of object markers ("accusative cases") out of former serialized verbs like *take*, described in Lord 1982. Thus in Gã (Benue-Kwa) (Lord, 286–288), from which the following examples are taken, the form *kɛ̀* in sentences like:

(11) *È kɛ̀ wòlò ŋmè-sī́*
she OBJ book lay-down
'She laid the book down.'

functions as an "accusative case" marker. But *kɛ̀* is originally a verb meaning 'take', which is moving toward grammaticization as a casemarker. Sentences like these are historically of the type 'He took the book [and] laid [it] down,' and reflect a previous stage of polysemy of *kɛ̀*, which could function either as a full verb 'take' or as an accusative case marker. In Gã (but not in all languages of this group), a functional vestige of this polysemy remains: The accusative marker cannot be used if the verb is (1) an effective verb (i.e. a verb whose object is *produced* by the action):

(12) *È ŋmè wɔ̀lɔ̀* 'She laid an egg.'
BUT NOT: **È kɛ̀ wɔ̀lɔ̀ ŋmè* 'She *kɛ̀* egg lay'

or (2) a verb whose object is experienced rather than affected:

(13) *Tɛ̀tɛ̀ nà Kɔ̀kɔ̀* 'Tete saw Koko.'
BUT NOT: **Tɛ̀tɛ̀ kɛ̀ Kɔ̀kɔ̀ nà* 'Tete *kɛ̀* Koko saw'

Thus Gã retains the restriction on the marking of direct objects which derives from the historical antecedent of this morpheme in the lexical verb 'to take': Only objects which can be 'taken' are marked morphologically as grammatical objects of the verb.

The importance of making explicit the assumption of Persistence is discussed by Bybee and Pagliuca (1986) in their study of the "future tense" in English. When we try to identify ways of expressing the "future tense" in English, or conversely to characterize the meaning of its most typical morpheme, the auxiliary verb "will", we find it necessary to make a variety of semantic distinctions. Bybee and Pagliuca show that "the differences in the uses of these future markers (i.e. *will, shall, be going to*) can be understood as continuations of their original lexical meanings (117)". While prediction (the "pure" future) is one of the senses of *will* in Present-Day English, as in Bybee and Pagliuca's example:

(14) *I think the bulk of this year's students will go into industry*

other meanings (called "modal" meanings) also exist, for example:

(15) Willingness: *Give them the name of someone who will sign for it and take it in if you are not at home*

(16) Intention: *I'll put them in the post today*

But these modal meanings were already found in Old English:

(17) Willingness: ... *gif he us geunnan wile þæt we hine swa*
if he us grant will that we him so
godne gretan moton
generous greet should
'... if he will grant that we should greet him who is so generous'
(Beowulf:346–7)

(18) Intention: *Wen ic þæt he wille, gif he wealdon mot, In*
think I that he will if he prevail should in
þæm guþ-sele Geata leode etan unforhte
the battle-hall Geat folk eat fearlessly
'I believe that he will, if he should prevail, devour the people of the Geats without fear' (Beowulf:442–4)

Bybee and Pagliuca suggest that the "predictive" future develops out of the intention/promise use of *will*, and that the future meaning is established in the Middle English period when inanimates incapable of volition begin to appear as the subjects of *will*. When this happened, it did not result in an across-the-board re-semanticization of *will*; the predictive future remains only one of several distinct meanings of *will* in Present-Day English. All that happened was that a new meaning was added to an already polysemous form, and new distributional possibilities were opened for it.

3.5. De-categorialization

One way of characterizing the functional-semantic shift which forms undergo as they move toward grammaticization is to say that they become *de-categorialized.*[3] In Hopper and Thompson 1984 a Categoriality Principle was suggested, according to which the traditional categories of Noun and Verb were to be viewed as proto-typical instantiations of the basic discourse functions of *identifying participants*, especially participants new in the discourse, and *reporting events*. It was claimed that the cross-linguistic morpho-syntactic peculiarities of nouns and verbs were directly attributable to these functions. Thus forms were decked out with characteristically noun-like attributes, such as articles, case markers, classifiers, and so on, to the degree that they functioned to identify actual participants, but would lose these attributes when no identification was involved, e.g. 'drove in *the* bus' vs. 'went there by (0) bus'. The theoretical consequence of seeing categories in this way is to relativize the notion of "category" to discourse, and hence to see membership in a category as being, not determined in advance for a form, but secondary to the deployment of the form in discourse; in other words, to replace the idea of "a category" with one of "degree of categoriality".

The process of grammaticization can usually be seen to involve a loss of the optional markers of categoriality. The functional counterpart of this "de-categorialization" is a *loss of discourse autonomy* for the form: "noun"-like forms no longer identify participants in a discourse, "verb"-like forms no longer report new events. Instead, nouns may appear in secondary roles, such as adverbial and prepositional ones:

(19) *Our thanks were accepted by the mayor — thanks to his generosity*
(20) *His face was pale — in (the) face of these new demands*

And verbs, too, usually in a participial form, may assume less central functions:

(21) *They saw the Northern Lights — Seeing that you have declared bankruptcy, you can hardly make any new investments*

In these new roles, there is a freezing or loss of optionality in morphological trappings. *Thanks* in the expression *thanks to* cannot appear as *our thanks to*;

in (the) face of cannot appear as *in that face of*; *seeing that* cannot appear as *to see that*, *having seen that*, and so on. Similarly with French *pas*:

(22) *Ils se sont éloignés de trente pas*
'they went thirty paces away'
(23) *Ils ne fument pas*
'they don't smoke'
(24) **ils ne fument un pas*
'they don't smoke one step'

And syntactic constraints on the use of a form, for example in co-reference, no longer hold:

(25)(?) *Sitting by the roadside to eat our sandwiches, a heavy shower drenched us to the skin*

(where at least the written language requires that the subject of the main clause and the understood subject of the participial clause be identical), but

(26) *Considering its narrow beam, the boat is remarkably sea-worthy*

(where no variety of English requires such identity).

As can be noted from these examples, the loss of prime categoriality goes hand-in-hand with the tendency for the ex-nouns and ex-verbs to assume discourse functions. Thus *considering* in (26), which is perhaps to be described as a preposition (see Quirk et al., 1972:328–9 for comparable examples), functions very much like a concessive conjunction, but has no properties of the verb *to consider*. This loss of discourse autonomy is precisely what Traugott 1982 has described as a central feature of grammaticization: In her terms, forms as they become grammaticized change their meanings from "propositional" to "textual", that is, from having a meaning independent of the text they change to having a meaning or function that is relative to the text or to some local construction.

Seen in terms of the Categoriality Principle, grammaticization always entails a loss of noun/verb categoriality. Indeed, categories other than noun and verb almost always result from a "down-change" of these two primary categories. Possible exceptions are a small group of adjectives denoting basic properties like 'big' and 'small' (see Dixon, 1982), and deictics like 'this' and 'there', whose non-deictic sources are often obscure.

4. CONCLUSIONS

My first attempts to isolate and describe "principles" of grammaticization were undertaken with a somewhat utilitarian impulse, that of identifying potential instances of grammaticization, possibly before a stage had been reached at which forms were unambiguously part of the grammar of the language. For this reason I tended to think of them as "heuristic" principles, in the sense that with them the linguist would not necessarily begin with already grammaticized forms and ask about their previous history, but would be able to select from among the rhetorical resources of texts those recurrent collocations that were candidates for being, at least marginally, "in" the grammar of the language. They were, in other words, to be an entrée into the study of grâmmaticization in a particular language.

But if grammaticization is not already a given, the principles do not in fact identify it unambiguously. They speak only to the question of "more" or "less" grammaticized, not to the question of "in" or "out" of grammar. Worse still, they do not discriminate between processes of change which result in grammaticization and processes of change which do not result in grammaticization. Layering, Divergence, Specialization, Persistence, and De-categorialization are not the exclusive domain of grammaticization, but are common to change in general. If we consider, for example, the difference between the noun *mistress* and the titles *miss* and *mrs* (misiz), which few would consider to be an example of grammaticization, we find that it neatly exemplifies all of the five principles of grammaticization discussed above:

(1) Layering. *Mistress*, *mrs*, and *miss* represent different degrees of reduction of what was originally the same word. They are different "layers" of terms of address (to which some would now add a further layer, *ms* [miz], intended to be neutral between *miss* and *mrs*).

(2) Divergence. The titular forms *mrs*, *miss*, and *ms* have split off from the original noun *mistress*, but the noun form remains with (allowing for well-understood semantic changes) something like its original meaning.

(3) Specialization. Although data on the antecedents to *mistress* as a term of address are hard to come by, it seems probable that at one time *mistress* was only one of a number of possible titles for women; others probably included kin terms like *mother*, status terms like *widow*, and familiar terms like *gossip* ('god-sib').

(4) Persistence. Clearly the restriction of the title *mrs* to adult women reflects the history of the noun *mistress*, as a feminine form of the middle-class title *master*. The splitting-off of the title *miss* to distinguish young or unmarried women from married ones dates only from the 18th century (Jespersen, 1938:186–7); it too, of course, continues the historical restriction to females.

(5) De-categorialization. The titles *miss*, *mrs*, and *ms* are de-categorialized in the double sense described above: They usually lack the ability to take optional morphosyntactic trappings of nouns such as articles, demonstratives, and possessive pronouns (an exception must be made when *mrs* is re-instated as a full noun in the expressions 'my/your/his missus' and 'the missus'), and (with the same exception) they may not alone refer to a discourse participant.

Are such titles to be regarded as part of grammar? Perhaps, but to do so incurs the danger of defining grammar precisely in terms of principles of grammaticization such as the ones presented here. The point is that since grammaticization is always a question of degree, not an absolute, the criteria which control this gradation are not restricted to grammaticization, but are simply general criteria of change. The implication of this observation is that there are no parts (modules, strata, etc.) to a language which are distinct targets for change, subject to special kinds of changes, and so on; and this in turn must be seen as an argument against stable holistic structures of grammar.

We are thereby brought back to Meillet, who, we noted, backgrounded the project of accounting for "the grammar" of a language, and insisted instead on the study of the history of particular grammatical forms, in effect treating grammar as all and only a collection of such forms. His notion of grammaticalization ("the attribution of a grammatical character to a previously autonomous word") says nothing about forms "entering the grammar" of the language, but suggests only that one and the same word is now lexical, now grammatical in nature. In this core definition, in the same article in which Meillet creates a new verb *grammaticize*, it is significant that he also eschews the noun *grammar* in favor of the adjective *grammatical*.

NOTES

1. I would like to thank the many people who commented on the first version of this paper, and especially Elizabeth Traugott, Sandra Thompson, Bernd Heine, and Friederike Hün-

nemeyer. For the imperfections which have survived their suggestions and criticisms I am wholly responsible.

2. Concerning "grammaticization" vs. "grammaticalization" I have no strong feelings. Some have seen in the -al- form the hint of a suggestion that the resultant forms are "grammatical", i.e. part of "the grammar", and they avoid the -al- form for this reason. Allowing for the slight possibility that such a distinction exists, I here use the form without -al-. However, the -al- form is used when translating Meillet's term *grammaticalisation*.

3. I am indebted to Friederike Hünnemeyer for pointing out the relevance of the work of Sandra Thompson and myself on Categoriality to grammaticization.

REFERENCES

Bybee, Joan L. 1985. *Morphology. A Study of the Relation between Meaning and Form.* Amsterdam: John Benjamins.

Bybee, Joan, and William Pagliuca. 1986. "The evolution of future meaning." In *Papers from the Seventh International Conference on Historical Linguistics*, A. Giacalone Ramat et al. (eds), 108–122. Amsterdam: John Benjamins.

Dixon, R.M.W. 1982. "Where have all the adjectives gone?" In *Where have all the Adjectives gone? and Other Essays in Semantics and Syntax*, R.M.W. Dixon (ed.), 1–62. Berlin: Mouton.

Gamillscheg, Ernst. 1957. *Historische französische Syntax*. Tübingen: Max Niemeyer.

Givón, Talmy. 1971. "Historical syntax and synchronic morphology: An archaeologist's field trip." In *Papers from the Chicago Linguistic Society* 7:394–415.

Givón, Talmy. 1979. *On Understanding Grammar*. New York: Academic Press.

Givón, Talmy. 1984. *Syntax I*. Amsterdam: John Benjamins.

Heine, Bernd and Mechthild Reh. 1984. *Grammatical Categories in African Languages*. Hamburg: Helmut Buske.

Hook, Peter. 1974. *The Compound Verb in Hindi*. Ann Arbor, MI.: Center for South Asian Studies.

Hook, Peter. Volume II. "The emergence of perfective aspect in Indo-Aryan languages".

Hopper, Paul J. 1987. "Emergent grammar". In *Berkeley Linguistic Society, Papers of the Thirteenth Annual Meeting*, 139–157.

Hopper, Paul J. 1988a. "Emergent grammar and the *a priori* grammar postulate." In *Linguistics in Context: Connecting, Observation, and Understanding*, Deborah Tannen (ed.), 117–34. Norwood: Ablex.

Hopper, Paul J. 1988b. "Discourse analysis: Grammar and critical theory in the 1980's." In *Profession 88*, Phyllis Franklin (ed.), 18–24. New York: Modern Language Association.

Hopper, Paul J., and Sandra Thompson. 1980. "Transitivity in grammar and discourse." *Language* 56:251–299.

Hopper, Paul J., and Sandra Thompson. 1984. "The discourse basis for lexical categories in universal grammar." *Language* 60(4):703–52.

Jespersen, Otto. 1955 (1938). *Growth and Structure of the English Language*. Garden City, New York: Doubleday.

Lehmann, Christian. 1982. *Thoughts on Grammaticalization: A Programmatic Sketch.*

Köln: Institut für Sprachwissenschaft, Universität zu Köln. [*Arbeiten des Kölner Universalienprojekts* 48].

Lehmann, Christian. 1985. "Grammaticalization: Synchronic variation and diachronic change." *Lingua e Stile* 20(3):303–318.

Lord, Carol. 1982. "The development of object markers in serial verb languages." In *Studies in Transitivity*, Paul Hopper and Sandra Thompson (eds.), 277–300. London: Academic Press [Syntax and Semantics 15].

Lühr, Rosemarie. 1984. "Reste der athematischen Konjugation in den germanischen Sprachen." In *Das Germanische und die Rekonstruktion der indogermanischen Grundsprache*, Jürgen Untermann and Bela Brogyani (eds.), 29–90. Amsterdam: John Benjamins.

Meillet, Antoine. 1912 (1948). "L'évolution des formes grammaticales." In *Linguistique historique et linguistique générale*, A. Meillet, 130–148. Paris: Champion.

Meillet, Antoine. 1925 (1954). *La méthode comparative en linguistique historique*. Paris: Champion.

Meillet, Antoine. 1937 (1964). *Introduction à l'étude comparative des langues indo-européennes*. University of Alabama Press.

Quirk, Randolph, S. Greenbaum, G. Leech and J. Svartvik. 1972. *A Grammar of Contemporary English*. London: Longman.

Thompson, Sandra A., and Anthony Mulac. Volume II. "A quantitative perspective on the grammaticization of epistemic parentheticals in English."

Traugott, Elizabeth. 1982. "From propositional to textual and expressive meanings: Some semantic-pragmatic aspects of grammaticalization." In *Perspectives on Historical Linguistics*, Winfred P. Lehmann and Yakov Malkiel (eds.), 245–271. Amsterdam: John Benjamins.

Traugott, Elizabeth. 1989. "From less to more situated in language: The unidirectionality of semantic change." In *Papers from the Fifth International Conference on English Historical Linguistics*, Sylvia Adamson, Vivian Law, Nigel Vincent, Susan M. Wright (eds.). Amsterdam: John Benjamins.

On the Gradualness of Grammaticalization

Frantisek Lichtenberk
University of Auckland

1. INTRODUCTION

In recent years, a large number of studies of syntactic change have emphasized the gradual nature of the developments in question, such as changes in basic word order, the rise of new sentence structures, and the development of grammatical markers of various kinds; see, for example, Lord (1973), Li (1975), Chung (1977), Givón (1977), Timberlake (1977), Saltarelli (1980), Gerritsen (1982), Romaine (1983), Silva-Corvalán (1984), Wiegand (1984), and Hopper and Martin (1987), among many others, for different perspectives on the gradualness of syntactic change. Characteristically, such works are interested in the processes whereby one form and/or function is transformed into another.

Although it is true that, given enough time, one structure may completely replace another, it is also true that one commonly finds the old and the new structure coexisting, often for a considerable period of time. Sometimes the two are in free variation everywhere; sometimes they are in free variation in some environments but not in others. Hardly anybody will deny that in every language there are structures whose use is governed by rigid rules ("rigid" at least at a given time). At the same time, there are, in every language, structures whose functions are not easily describable by neat, compact rules. It is the relation between structures and their functions that may be difficult to capture by rules, not so much the structures themselves. The latter are relatively amenable to being characterized by rules. A major virtue of the various approaches to syntactic change that see syntactic change as gradual is not just that they show the pervasiveness of variation (this can be demonstrated by purely synchronic studies), but that they demonstrate the naturalness of variation. Variation is a necessary consequence of the gradualness of language change.

The present study falls squarely in the process-oriented, gradualist view of syntactic change. It is concerned with a number of grammaticalization processes in To'aba'ita, an Austronesian language spoken on the island of Malaita in the southeast Solomon Islands.[1] As the papers in the present collection amply demonstrate, the term 'grammaticalization' is given different interpretations by different linguists. The view of grammaticalization that I take is this: Grammaticalization is a historical process, a kind of change that has certain consequences for the morphosyntactic categories of a language and thus for the grammar of that language. The prototypical consequences of grammaticalization are:

(i) Emergence of a new grammatical category; (ii) Loss of an existing grammatical category; (iii) Change in the membership of a grammatical category.

All three kinds of change may be historically linked. As I discuss in detail in Section 2, To'aba'ita has a category of 'verb-like' prepositions, prepositions that derive from earlier verbs. These prepositions have developed new variants that belong in a different category. There is evidence that the prepositions did not develop the innovative forms all at the same time. When the first innovative form developed, a new formal category came into existence. As other prepositions developed the innovative forms, the membership of the new category changed. And if the innovative forms ever completely replace the old forms, the category of verb-like prepositions will have disappeared from the language.

The three types of change mentioned above may involve either a lexical morpheme becoming a grammatical morpheme, for example a verb becoming a case marker, or an already grammatical element acquiring new properties, for example a case marker becoming a conjunction or a complementizer. Many definitions of grammaticalization characterize grammaticalization in terms of the processes, as the development of lexical morphemes into grammatical ones. I prefer to view grammaticalization in terms of its consequences, as a process that leads to certain changes in the grammar of a language. This emphasis on the effects of grammaticalization processes rather than on the processes themselves better reflects what I take to be an important characteristic of the grammars of natural languages. The grammars of natural languages are ultimately historical phenomena, products of historical developments, grammaticalization among them. I will return to this point in the concluding section.

As linguistic elements acquire new properties, they become members of other categories. Categorial reanalysis is, of necessity, abrupt. One and the same element cannot be simultaneously a member of two distinct categories (cases of inclusion apart). This, of course, does not preclude the possibility of different tokens of a morpheme exhibiting properties characteristic of different categories. This is because a form may be in the process of being reassigned to a different category; some of its tokens exhibit the old properties, others exhibit the new properties.

While categorial reanalysis is abrupt, its entry into the language and its actualization are gradual. There are a number of respects in which a change in morphosyntactic category may be actualized gradually. Thus a form that exhibits properties characteristic of a certain, perhaps lexical, category may begin to lose those properties not simultaneously but one after another. And the innovative form does not displace the old form overnight. Instead, innovative forms typically start out as infrequently used variants, their frequency increases over time, and ultimately they may completely replace the old forms. An innovative form does not normally emerge all of a sudden throughout the language community. It may be more common in some areas than in others, more common with some speakers than with others. Typically, there are generational differences. Frequently, there are differences among the registers. An innovative form may enter a language through one register, and its spread may not be equally rapid in all the registers. It may also happen that more than one member of a category is in the process of undergoing the same change but the individual items have not traveled equally far along the course of the development.

Finally, we can also speak of gradualness of the acquisition of new functions by an element provided we make clear what we mean by this kind of gradualness. What I mean is this: If an element that has a function A acquires a new function B and if subsequently the element that has function B (and possibly still function A) acquires a function C, the change from A to B will be smaller than the change from A to C would have been. I will refer to this generalization as the *Principle of Gradual Change in Function*. This principle can be represented schematically as follows:

$$A \rightarrow B \rightarrow C, \text{ not } A \rightarrow C \rightarrow B$$

where A, B and C stand for functions, the arrows signify changes in functions, and B is in some sense less different from A than C is.

The principle does not say that changes necessarily take place in some crosslinguistically definable minimal steps. All it says is that the change from A to B is smaller than the change from A to C would have been. The size of the steps may be language specific. To'aba'ita, like many other Oceanic languages, makes a formal distinction between positive purpose ('in order to') and negative purpose/precaution ('in order not to'). As will be discussed in Section 4, in the history of To'aba'ita there was a change from an ablative case marker to a negative-purpose/precaution complementizer followed by another change whereby the negative-purpose/precaution complementizer became a positive-purpose complementizer. One would not expect a similar sequence of changes in a language that does not formally distinguish between positive and negative purpose. Of course, one can speak of gradual change in function only where a sequence of at least two changes has taken place. If there is only one change, there is no gradualness. The principle does not predict that sequences of changes will occur, but it does predict that if they do, the changes will occur in certain orders and not in others. Needless to say, in order for the Principle of Gradual Change in Function to be meaningful, one must be able to demonstrate for each instance of relevant change that function B is indeed less different from function A than C is. Two examples of gradual change in function will be given later in this paper.

Most of the aspects of gradualness of change in syntactic category mentioned above are manifested in the To'aba'ita data to be discussed. Due to the limited nature of the data nothing will be said about geographic and register-based variation and only little will be said about generational variation.

The paper is organized as follows: In Section 2, I discuss a set of prepositions that derive from earlier verbs. Most of the prepositions have variant forms, but the relative frequencies of use of the variants are not the same for all the prepositions. The innovative forms, the result of phonological reduction, are members of a subcategory different from that of the old forms. In Section 3, I discuss a coordinating conjunction historically related to one of the prepositions. We will see one manifestation of the Principle of Gradual Change in Function there. In Section 4, I discuss a set of complementizers that are historically related to some of the prepositions, and another manifestation of the Principle of Gradual Change in Function. In Section 5, I draw some conclusions about the To'aba'ita data, about grammaticalization in general and about the value of studies of grammaticalization for our understanding of the nature of grammars of natural languages.

2. VERB-LIKE PREPOSITIONS

In this section, I will discuss in detail one type of To'aba'ita prepositions. These prepositions derive historically from verbs. They have retained some of the formal properties of verbs but have lost others. The prepositions have been undergoing a new change resulting in the loss of another verbal property. This innovation — a phonological reduction with a morphological consequence — has been spreading gradually through the category.

2.1. Indexing of direct objects

Before discussing the prepositions, it is necessary first to discuss the indexing of direct objects of transitive verbs. To'aba'ita is an SVO language, but direct objects can be fronted to the left of the subject. Common-noun direct objects that occur in their 'normal', postverbal position are indexed in the verb by means of the object suffix *-a* unless the object is backgrounded (see below). The suffix *-a* is used regardless of the animacy status of the object and regardless of its grammatical number:[2]

(1) *Wane baa ka ngali-a kaufa baa ...*
man that he:SEQ take -it cover that
'The man took the cover, ...'

(2) *...ka riki-a wane 'eri*
he:SEQ see -him man that
'... (and) he saw the man.'

(3) *...ka na'are-a alo baa ki*
she:SEQ roast -them taro that PL
'... (and) she roasted the taros.'

(4) *Kera thaungi-a ulu wela 'e -ki*
they:PFV kill -them three child that-PL
'They killed the three children.'

Proper-noun objects may but need not be indexed in the verb:

(5) *'O {riki-a /riki} ni Fiona?*
you(SG):PFV {see -her/see} ART Fiona
'Did you see Fiona?'

Objects that are backgrounded are usually not indexed in the verb although under some conditions they may be. The factors governing the backgrounding of objects are rather complex, but basically an object may be backgrounded for one of two reasons: (i) because it is nonreferential, as in

(6) below; or (ii) because its referent is not judged to be important in the given context, as in (7):

(6) *Kamili'a mili lio ka a'i mi -si*
we(EXCL) we(EXCL):PFV look it:SEQ NEG.VB we(EXCL) -NEG
{*riki-a* /*riki*} *ta* wane
{see -him /see} any person
'We looked but didn't see anybody.'

(7) *Nau kwai sa'u kuki 'a -ku'a*
I I:IMPFV wash pot MID.VCE-my
'I am washing pots.' (as a reply to 'What are you doing?', not to 'What are you washing?')

In order to keep the discussion simple, backgrounded objects (of transitive verbs and prepositions) will be disregarded in what follows. (More detail about the relation between the importance of the referents of objects in situations and their indexing may be found in Lichtenberk, 1988a.)

If a verb is not followed by a direct object, because the object has been fronted, in relativization on the object, or in ellipsis, the suffix *-a* is used to index singular objects regardless of their animacy status and also nonhuman plural objects:

(8) *'Ai ne'e na koki kasi-a*
tree this FOC we(DU,INCL):IMPFV fell -it
'It's this tree that you and I will cut down.'

(9) *roo basi na thaina -karo'a 'e thaathaungani-a*
two bow REL mother-their(DU) she:PFV make -them
'the two bows that their mother had made'

(10) *Nia ka ngali-a, ka alu-a laa te'e kaufa*
she she:SEQ take -them she:SEQ put-them inside one cover
'She took them [taros mentioned previously] and put them in a cover.'

If the missing object is plural and human, the suffix *-da* is used:

(11) *To'a na ku riki-da ki mai 'i fafo asi nena*
people REL I:PFV see -them PL hither at top sea that
'Those are the people I saw by the sea.'

(With fronted plural human objects, the suffix *-a* is also possible, but it is not common.)

(12) *wela na kuki thaungi-da*
child REL we(INCL):IMPFV kill -them
'the children that we will kill'

(13) *Ku riki-da*
I:PFV see -them
'I saw them [people].'

There is also a dual object suffix *-daro'a* 'them (two)', but it is rare; the plural suffix is normally used instead.

When the object is an independent personal pronoun, it is not indexed in the verb:

(14) *...kini 'eri ka 'adomi nau*
woman that she:SEQ help me
'... the woman will help me.'

In the third person, there are two options: One is to use an independent personal pronoun, in which case there is no object suffix on the verb; the other is to use an object suffix and no independent pronoun; compare (15) and (16):

(15) *Ku rongo nia*
I:PFV hear him
'I heard him.'

(16) *Ku rongo-a*
I:PFV hear -him
'I heard him.'

The precise difference between the two constructions need not concern us here. Suffice it to say that the independent-pronoun option is used if the object is to be foregrounded (for example, in contrast). Second, the independent pronouns are rarely used with nonhuman reference.

2.2. Verb-like prepositions: Similarities to transitive verbs

To'aba'ita has several prepositions that, for reasons to become apparent below, can be referred to as 'verb-like prepositions'. As will be seen in

Section 2.3, not all of To'aba'ita prepositions are verb-like. The following are the verb-like prepositions:

'ani	instrumental; also used as a 'general' preposition with the oblique objects of many intransitive verbs
fasi	(archaic *fa'isi*) ablative: 'away from'
uri	allative: 'to, toward'; purpose (as in 'come for (to get) something')
suli	prolative: 'along', 'during', 'about' (as in 'speak about something')
bii	comitative: 'with' (as in 'John came with Mary.'); cf. *faafi* below
faafi	confective, corresponding to 'with' in 'He came back with a large parcel.'

With some exceptions, objects of the verb-like prepositions are indexed in the same ways as are objects of transitive verbs. With the exception of the comitative and the instrumental/general prepositions, adjacent nonbackgrounded lexical (as opposed to pronominal) objects are indexed by means of the suffix *-a*, regardless of their animacy status and their grammatical number. (As with transitive verbs, proper-noun objects may but need not be indexed.) The forms of the comitative and the instrumental/general prepositions used in these environments will be discussed in detail in Section 2.4. As will be seen there, the other four verb-like prepositions have parallel optional variants. Following are a few examples of the indexing of adjacent nonbackgrounded lexical objects with prepositions other than comitative and instrumental/general:

(17) *Si fanga 'e -ki ka thada fasi -a foko -na*
PARTV food that -PL they:SEQ fall from-it mouth -her
'The pieces of food fell from her mouth.'

(18) *Thaari baa ka thamo uri -a tai si fanga, ...*
girl that she:SEQ reach toward -it some PARTV food
'The girl reached for some of the food, ...'

(19) *Wane 'e ngata suli -a wela nia ki*
man he:PFV speak about-them child his PL
'The man spoke about his children.'

(20) *Keka oli na'a faafi-a roo subi baa ki*
they:SEQ return PERF with-them two k.o. war club that PL
'They went back with the two *subi* clubs.'

When there is no object adjacent to the preposition, that is, when the object has been fronted, in relativization on the object, or in ellipsis, the suffix

-a is used with all six prepositions to index singular objects regardless of their animacy status and nonhuman plural objects. When an oblique object is fronted, the preposition is stranded behind:

(21) *Tei na 'oki lae bii -a?*
who? FOC you(SG):IMPFV go with-him
'Who will you go with?'

(22) *doo na to'a ne'e ki keki fiifiru ki 'ani -a*
thing REL people this PL they:IMPFV fight PL with-them
'the things [weapons] the people used to fight with'

(23) *Nia ne nguu suli -a ka 'una 'eri: ...*
she FOC:she:PFV sing about-it it:SEQ manner this
'It was her who sang about it like this: ...'

Nonadjacent plural human objects are indexed by means of the suffix *-da*. (As with verbs, the dual object suffix *-daro'a* is used only rarely.)

(24) *Kini lakoo ki ku dora 'ani -da*
woman that PL I:PFV not know GEN.OBL -them
'Those women I don't know.'

(Again as with verbs, the suffix *-a* is occasionally used with fronted plural human objects.)

If the object is an independent personal pronoun, it is not indexed in the preposition:

(25) *Nia 'e ngali-a naifa fasi nau*
he he:PFV take -it knife from me
'He took the knife away from me.'

In the third person, there are two options: One is to use an independent personal pronoun, in which case the preposition carries no object suffix; the other is to use an object suffix and no independent pronoun:

(26) *Nau kwai lae {bii kera/bii -da}*
I I:IMPFV go {with them/with-them}
'I will go with them.'

There is another property that, historically at least, most likely relates the prepositions to transitive verbs: The stems of all of them end in *i*. Pawley (1973) has reconstructed **-i* as a transitive suffix for Proto-Oceanic, a stage remotely ancestral to To'aba'ita (see Figure 1 below). The Proto-Oceanic suffix is not functional in To'aba'ita, but the fact that all six verb-like prepositions end in *i* is unlikely to be due purely to chance. At least some of the forms among the To'aba'ita verb-like prepositions are reconstructible (whether with a verbal or a prepositional function) for Proto-Oceanic (see Pawley, 1973).

Figure 1 gives the position of To'aba'ita in the Austronesian family. At a low level, To'aba'ita is a member of the Cristobal-Malaitan subgroup. Evidence from other Cristobal-Malaitan languages will be relevant in later

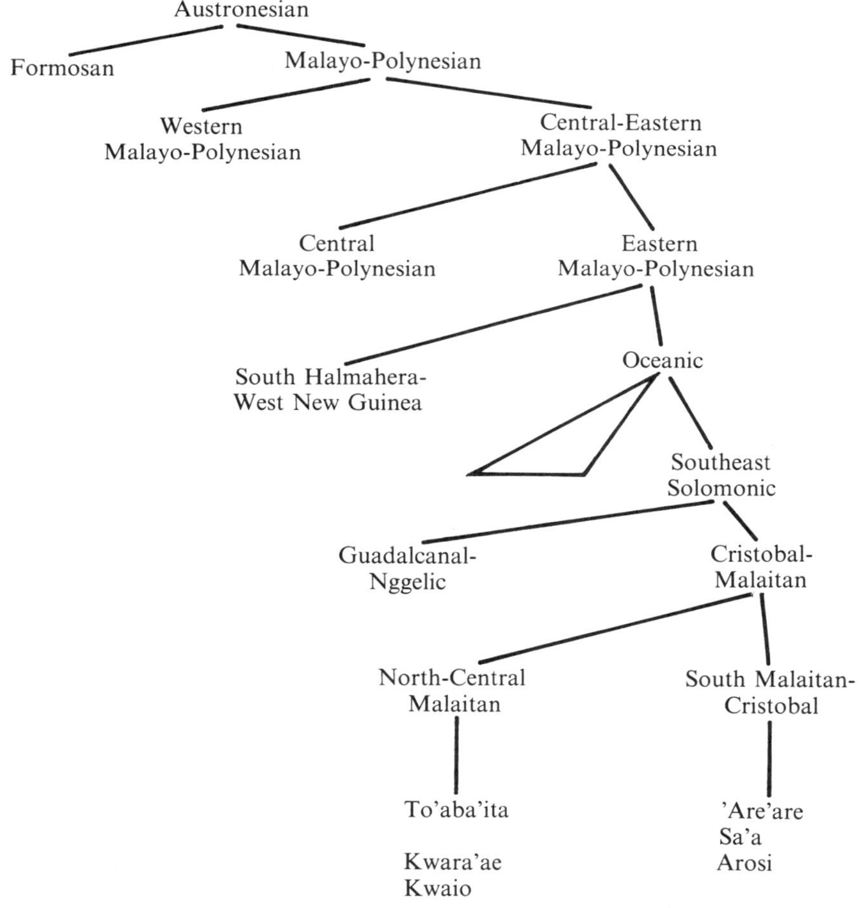

Figure 1. *Position of To'aba'ita in the Austronesian family (after Blust (1980), Grace (1955), Pawley (1972), Lichtenberk (1988b))*

discussion. Only those Cristobal-Malaitan languages are included in the tree diagram from which data will be cited.[3]

None of the six forms, *'ani*, *fasi*, *uri*, *suli*, *bii*, and *faafi*, function as verbs in To'aba'ita. They cannot form predicates, and apart from the object suffixes they do not take any elements associated with verbs: The subject-aspect and subject-sequential markers, directionals, nominalizers, and so on. All six prepositions have prepositional cognates elsewhere in Cristobal-Malaitan (see Table 2 in Section 2.5), and most of them have verbal cognates in addition.

Fasi (with an archaic variant *fa'isi*), the ablative preposition, has verbal cognates in at least two Cristobal-Malaitan languages: Kwara'ae *fa'asi* 'leave, forsake, depart from' and Lau *fasi* 'lose'.

Suli, the prolative preposition, has verbal cognates in at least two Cristobal-Malaitan languages: Arosi *suri* 'follow' and Sa'a *sulu* 'follow'. Verbal cognates with the same meaning are also found outside the Cristobal-Malaitan group.

Bii, the comitative preposition, has verbal cognates in at least two Cristobal-Malaitan languages: Arosi *bei* 'be one with, be an ally/partner' and Sa'a *pe'i* 'be in the company of, be along with'.

Faafi, the confective preposition, also has verbal cognates in at least two Cristobal-Malaitan languages: 'Are'are *haahi* 'load, burden, weigh down' and Kwara'ae *faafi* 'accuse, impute'.

I have found no verbal cognates of the instrumental/general preposition *'ani* or the allative/purpose preposition *uri* whether in Cristobal-Malaitan or elsewhere.

Given the parallelism between the To'aba'ita verb-like prepositions and transitive verbs in terms of the indexing of their objects, the stem-final *i* on the prepositions (see also Section 2.4 below), and the existence of verbal cognates of most of the prepositions, one can assume that the prepositions derive from earlier verbs. I ought to mention though that the main points of this paper would not be materially affected if it should turn out that it was the prepositions and not the verbs that were historically primary.

2.3. Other prepositions

Besides the verb-like prepositions, To'aba'ita has two other types of preposition, which I will call 'noun-like prepositions' and 'bare prepositions'. The noun-like prepositions index their objects by possessive suffixes, used in possessive constructions to index the possessor NP. The noun-like prepositions are normally preceded by the bare preposition *'i* (for which see below).

(27) *Fale-a tai fa 'ota 'i fa-na wane 'ena*
give-them some CLASS betel nut to to-his man that
'Give some betel nuts to the man.'

Compare:

(28) *rake -na wane*
belly-his man
'the man's belly'

The recipient/benefactive preposition *fa* will be of interest later (Section 2.6).

(29) *Te'e kini 'e 'ono 'i buria -ku*
one woman she:PFV sit at behind-my
'A woman sat (down) behind me.'

Compare:

(30) *alinga-ku*
ear -my
'my ear(s)'

The bare prepositions do not index their objects:

(31) *Kwai lae 'i 'Aoke 'i 'usungadi*
I:IMPFV go to A. in tomorrow
'I will go to Auki tomorrow.'

(32) *'E fanga mala botho*
he:PFV eat like pig
'He ate like a pig.'

2.4. Reduced variants of the verb-like prepositions

All six verb-like prepositions exhibit two variant forms: *'ani/'ana* instrumental/general, *fasi/fasa* ablative, *uri/ura* allative/purpose, *suli/sula* prolative, *bii/bia* comitative and *faafi/faafa* confective. For convenience, I will refer to the first member of each pair as the '*i*-form' and to the second member as the '*a*-form'. The *i*-forms were exemplified in Section 2.2, examples (17)–(26). They index their complements in the same ways that transitive verbs index their direct objects. The *a*-forms, on the other hand, do not take any object suffixes. In fact, as I will argue below, the *a*-forms derive historically from the *i*-forms with the object suffix *-a*; that is, *'ana* derives from *'ani-a*, *fasa* from *fasi-a*, and so on.

The *a*-forms cannot be used in all the environments in which the *i*-forms are found. Importantly, they can be used only with adjacent objects and under the same general conditions that govern the use of the *i*-forms with the suffix *-a* before adjacent objects. With most of the prepositions, both the *i*-form with the suffix *-a* and the *a*-form are found in these environments:

(33) *Nau ku rake'iri {uri -a /ura} wane*
I I:PFV be angry {toward-him/toward} man
'I am angry at the man.'

(34) *Wela 'e thaka {fasi-a /fasa} luma*
child he:PFV run {from-it/from} house
'The child ran away from the house.'

(35) *u'unu {suli -a /sula} saiklon Namu*
story {about -it/about} cyclone Namu
'story about Cyclone Namu'

(36) *Wela nau ki keki 'adomi nau {faafi-a /faafa} raa*
child my PL they:IMPFV help me {with-it/with} work
nau ki
my PL
'My children will help me with my work.'

With the comitative preposition, only the *a*-form is possible in these environments; the *i*-form is ungrammatical:

(37) *Nau ku thathami-a kwai ngata {bia /**bii -a}*
I I:PFV want -it I:IMPFV speak {with/ with-her}
thaari na'i
girl this
'I want to speak with this girl.'

With the instrumental/general preposition, apart from one minor exception, only the *a*-form is possible in these environments; the *i*-form is ungrammatical:

(38) *Nau ku dora {'ana /**'ani -a} kini na'i*
I I:PFV not know {GEN.OBL/ GEN.OBL-her} woman this
'I don't know this woman.'

The form *'ani-a* is possible in one restricted environment. It is optionally used after the prolative preposition *suli-a/sula* to express 'about', as in 'speak about something'. *'Ani-a* is redundant in this context; *suli-a* or *sula* alone is sufficient:

(39) *Kwai u'unu {sula 'ani -a /suli -a /sula}*
I:IMPFV tell story {about GEN.OBL-them/about-them/about}
roo wela
two child
'I will tell a story about two children.'

This redundant use of *'ani-a* appears to be archaic, not found in the speech of the young people.

Although there is no direct historical evidence to appeal to, the conclusion is inescapable that the *a*-forms are a later development from the *i*-forms with the suffix *-a* through the loss of the stem-final *i*; that is *'ana* comes from *'ani-a*, *fasa* from *fasi-a*, and so on. If one were to assume that it was the *a*-forms that were historically primary, one would be confronted with an unmotivated appearance of the stem-final *i* and with unmotivated use of the object-marking suffixes on what would earlier have been bare prepositions. Furthermore, there would be no explanation for the present-day restricted distribution of the *a*-forms. The converse hypothesis that the *a*-forms developed from the *i*-forms with the suffix *-a* does not face any of these problems.

The *a*-forms can be used only with adjacent lexical objects under the same conditions that govern the use of the suffix *-a* on the *i*-forms. They are ungrammatical with independent personal pronouns as objects, which are not indexed on the *i*-forms:

(40) *Wane 'e ngata {suli /**sula} 'oe*
man he:PFV speak {about/ about} you(SG)
'The man spoke about you.'

Second, the *a*-forms are not used when there is no adjacent object, that is when the object has been fronted, in relativization, and in ellipsis. An explanation for this will be given in Section 2.6. Suffice it to say here that the reason has to do with the contrast between the object suffixes *-a* and *-da* in those environments.

There are two additional pieces of evidence, each having to do with individual prepositions, that the *i*-forms are historically primary and the *a*-forms later innovations. The first piece of evidence concerns the ablative preposition. The ablative preposition *fasi* has an archaic, rarely used variant *fa'isi*. Now, while the form *fasi* has an *a*-variant (*fasa*), the archaic form *fa'isi* does not:

(41) *Nau ku ngali-a naifa {fasi-a /fasa /fa'isi-a*
I I:PFV take -it knife {from-him /from /from-him
*/**fa'isa} wela*
/ from} child
'I took the knife away from the child.'

This suggests that by the time the ablative preposition began to develop an *a*-form, *fa'isi* was no longer common and consequently failed to develop an *a*-form.

The other additional piece of evidence has to do with the diametrically different frequencies of use of the *a*-forms of the comitative and the confective prepositions. This will be discussed in detail in Section 2.5.

All of the peculiarities of the use of the *a*-forms can be readily accounted for if we assume that the *a*-forms derive historically from the *i*-forms with the suffix *-a* through phonological reduction, a process that commonly befalls grammatical elements. As we will see in Section 2.6, this reduction, the loss of the stem-final *i*, has a structural consequence.

2.5. Frequencies of use of the innovative variants

With the comitative preposition and for all practical purposes with the instrumental/general preposition also only the innovative *a*-forms can be used with adjacent nonbackgrounded lexical objects; the *a*-suffixed *i*-forms cannot. With the remaining prepositions, both variants are grammatical there. However, there are considerable differences among the prepositions with respect to the relative frequencies of use of the two variants.

To determine the relative frequencies of use of the two variants for each of the prepositions, I have made a study of a corpus of oral texts. The corpus consists of 15 texts totaling over 2,800 clauses. Most of the texts are traditional stories, three are personal reminiscences, and one is an evening prayer. All but one text come from a male speaker who is probably in his late fifties. One text, the longest one (over 300 clauses), comes from the man's son, who is in his early twenties.

Table 1 gives the relative frequencies of use of the *a*-forms and the *a*-suffixed *i*-forms with adjacent nonbackgrounded lexical objects for all six prepositions in the corpus. Note that the frequencies of 100% and 0% can reflect either a rule of grammar (only one of the two forms is grammatical) or a statistical property of the corpus (both forms are grammatical, but only one occurs in the corpus). The former is indicated by C (for 'categorial'), and the latter by S (for 'statistical').

The figures in Table 1 demonstrate that the replacement of the *a*-suffixed *i*-forms by the *a*-forms has not progressed equally far for all the prepositions. The process is complete with the comitative preposition and, for all practical purposes, also complete with the instrumental/general preposition. The process is well under way with the allative/purpose preposition, less so with the prolative preposition, and it has barely begun with the ablative and the confective prepositions.

Table 1. *Frequencies of use of the* a-*forms and the* a-*suffixed* i-*forms before nonbackgrounded lexical objects*

	tokens	%		tokens	%
comitative			instrumental/general		
bia	8	100 (C)	*'ana*	159	98.8
bii-a	*0*	0 (C)	*'ani-a**	*2*	1.2
total	8		total	161	
allative/purpose			prolative		
ura	24	34.8	*sula*	9	20
ụri-a	*45*	65.2	*suli-a*	*36*	80
total	69		total	45	
ablative			confective		
fasa	1	3.3	*faafa*	0	0 (S)
fasi-a	*29*	96.7	*faafi-a*	*22*	100 (S)
total	30		total	22	

Grand total of tokens: 335
C — categorial; S — statistical
* *'ani-a* is found only in an archaic construction following *sula*; elsewhere, only *'ana* is possible (100% (C))

If we are indeed dealing with a change in progress, we would not be surprised to find some differences in the relative frequencies of the two variants between the older and the younger speaker for those prepositions where both variants are possible and both are relatively frequent (see Table 1). Since the figures are derived from data that come from only two speakers, and since the numbers of tokens for some of the prepositions are small (especially for the younger speaker), one cannot draw any conclusions from them; nevertheless there are differences between the two speakers, and they are in the expected direction. With the allative/purpose preposition, the younger speaker uses the innovative *a*-form in 46% of all cases, compared to 30% for the older speaker; and with the prolative preposition, the figures are 33% for the younger speaker compared to 18% for the older speaker.

Together, the variation between the innovative *a*-forms and the old *a*-suffixed *i*-forms with most of the prepositions and the differences among the prepositions in the rates of use of their innovative forms are evidence of a change in progress and of gradualness of the actualization of the change. The change has been diffusing through the category; it has affected some members of the category more than others.

There appear to be three factors responsible for the uneven spread of the innovative forms. One has to do with the age of the innovative form. All other things being equal, one would predict that the longer an innovative form has been around, the more frequent it is relative to the old form. There are case-marking cognates of all six prepositions elsewhere in the Cristobal-Malaitan group; see Table 2. Only the forms of the prepositions are given in the table. The functions of the cognates in each set are pretty much the same

Table 2. *Case-marking cognates of the To'aba'ita verb-like prepositions*

To'aba'ita	*'ani/'ana*	*suli/sula*	*bii/bia*
Lau	*'ani/'ana*	*suli*	*fai(ni)*[5]
Kwara'ae	*'ani*	*suli,*	*fa'ini,*
		suil[4]	*fani, hain*[5,6]
Kwaio	*'ani*	*suri*	*fe'eni*[5]
'Are'are	*'ani/'ana*	*suri*	*bei*
Sa'a	*ani/ana*	*suli*	*pe'i*
Arosi		*suri*	*be'i*
To'aba'ita	*faafi/faafa*	*fasi/fasa*	*uri/ura*
Lau	*fafi*	*fasi*	*uri*
Kwara'ae	*faafi,*	*fa'asi,*	
	fafi[7]	*fasi, hais*[6]	
Kwaio	*faafi*	*fa'asi*	
'Are'are			
Sa'a	*haahi*		
Arosi			

across the languages, and the minor differences that there may be are irrelevant to the discussion.

Judging from the available descriptions of the Cristobal-Malaitan languages, only one preposition exhibits an alternation between an *i*-form and an *a*-form outside of To'aba'ita; none of the others do. (For Kwaio and Kwara'ae, the absence of any such alternation has been confirmed to me in personal communications by R. Keesing and K. Watson-Gegeo, respectively.) The alternation is found only with the cognates of the To'aba'ita instrumental/general preposition *'ani*/*'ana*. Beside To'aba'ita, the alternation is found in Lau, 'Are'are and Sa'a. Lau, a very close relative of To'aba'ita, belongs in the same primary subgroup with To'aba'ita; 'Are'are and Sa'a belong in the other primary subgroup (Figure 1 in Section 2.2). Since the alternation is found in both subgroups of Cristobal-Malaitan but not in all the member languages, its existence in To'aba'ita and Lau on the one hand and in 'Are'are and Sa'a on the other is most likely the result of independent parallel developments. It is true that one cannot disregard the possibility of independent parallel developments in To'aba'ita and in Lau, but in the absence of any such evidence one can assume that the *'ana* form is older than the *a*-forms of the other To'aba'ita prepositions. And as Table 1 shows, *'ana* has all but replaced the *a*-suffixed *i*-form. The factor of the age of an innovative form is obviously irrelevant to the comitative preposition, even though there the *a*-form has completely displaced the *a*-suffixed *i*-form.

Another factor that, *a priori*, might be relevant to the rate of replacement of the old form of a preposition by the innovative form is the frequency of use of that preposition. Since the innovative forms are reductions of the old forms, one would predict that, all other things being equal, the more frequent a preposition is relative to the other prepositions, the higher will be the use of its innovative form, again relative to the other prepositions. The relative frequencies of use of the six prepositions vis-à-vis each other in the corpus are given in Table 3. The numbers of tokens, taken from Table 1, are aggregates of the numbers of occurrences of the *a*-forms and the *a*-suffixed *i*-forms before nonbackgrounded lexical objects.

The instrumental/general preposition *'ani-a*/*'ana* is by far most frequent, accounting for nearly one half of all the verb-like prepositional tokens. It is the general, not the instrumental function of the preposition that is responsible for the high frequency of its use. The preposition is used with a large number of intransitive verbs to introduce their oblique objects; for example, *dora 'ana* 'not know X', *lalakwa 'ana* 'not like X', *ma'u 'ana* 'be afraid of X', *kwaithathai 'ana* 'have X ready', 'be ready with X'.

Table 3. *Relative frequencies of use of the verb-like prepositions before nonbackgrounded lexical objects*

	tokens	%
'ani-a/'ana	161	48.1
uri-a/ura	69	20.6
suli-a/sula	45	13.4
fasi-a/fasa	30	9.0
faafi-a	22	6.6
bia	8	2.4
total:	335	100.1

That frequency of use of a preposition is a factor in the rate of use of its innovative form can be seen from a comparison of the frequencies of use of the individual prepositions (from Table 3) with the frequencies of use of their innovative forms (from Table 1). The comparison is given in Table 4.

Table 4. *Comparison of the relative frequencies of use of the verb-like prepositions and the frequencies of use of their* a-*forms*

	relative frequency of use (%)	frequency of use of *a*-form (%)
'ani-a/'ana	48.1	98.8
uri-a/ura	20.6	34.8
suli-a/sula	13.4	20.0
fasi-a/fasa	9.0	3.3
faafia	6.6	0
bia	2.4	100
total:	100.1	

With one glaring exception, the figures in Table 4 show a direct correlation between the frequency of use of a preposition and the frequency of use of its *a*-form. The higher the frequency of use of a preposition, the more common the use of its innovative *a*-form relative to the old *a*-suffixed *i*-form. The comitative preposition is again an exception. Even though it is least common of all six prepositions (but see Section 3 below), its innovative form has completely replaced the old form in the relevant environments.

The last factor relevant to the spread of the innovative *a*-forms has to do with the phonological shape of two of the prepositions. The comitative preposition is the only one without a medial consonant; moreover, in the *i*-form the two vowels adjacent to each other are identical: *bii-a*. Given the stress rules of To'aba'ita (see the next paragraph), the first *i* is stressed; the second *i* is not. The adjacency of the stem-final unstressed *i* to the preceding stressed *i* must have been conducive to the speedy loss of the stem-final *i* before another vowel (the suffix *-a*). Note that the reduction does involve loss of one of two vowels rather than shortening of a long vowel: *bii* is phonetically [*ᵐbíi*], not [*ᵐbí:*]. The reason why the stem-final *i* was not lost when there was no object adjacent to the preposition even though the same phonological conditions obtained will be given in Section 2.6.

The stress factor also helps to account for the slow spread of the *a*-form of the confective preposition *faafi*. Although *faafa* is grammatical, it is rare in speech, and it does not occur at all in the corpus. The confective preposition is the only one with a stem of three syllables; the stems of all the others are disyllabic. When the preposition carries the object suffix *-a* (or *-da*), stress is assigned not only to the first syllable, but also to the stem-final syllable: [ɸáəβíə]. (In To'aba'ita, the first syllable of a word is always stressed, the last syllable of a polysyllabic word is never stressed, and there cannot be more than two unstressed syllables in a row.) It is the presence of stress on the stem-final *i* that inhibits the loss of the vowel.

The diametrically opposed frequencies of use of the *a*-forms of the comitative and the confective prepositions are attributable to differences in the phonological properties of the prepositions, but only on the assumption that it is the *i*-forms, not the *a*-forms, that are historically primary. If one assumed that it was the *a*-forms that were historically primary (*bia*, *faafa*), no such phonologically-based explanation would be available.

There are thus three factors responsible for the uneven spread of the innovating *a*-forms of the verb-like prepositions in present-day To'aba'ita: The length of time the innovating form has been in existence, the frequency of use of the prepositions, and, with two of the prepositions, their phonological form; but none of the factors is relevant to all six prepositions.

2.6. Emergence of a new syntactic subcategory

The rise of the *a*-forms of the prepositions is the result of phonological reduction: The stem-final *i* is lost before the suffix *-a* (when the object follows the preposition). This straightforward phonological process has, however, a structural repercussion. Whereas the old forms are bimorphemic, *'ani-a*, *uri-a*, etc., the new forms are monomorphemic, *'ana*, *ura*, etc. The monomorphemic status of the *a*-forms is a consequence of To'aba'ita phonotactics. At the phonological level, there are no closed syllables in To'aba'ita. (At the phonetic level, closed syllables may arise through vowel deletion under certain conditions, but none of these are relevant to the prepositions.) If the final *a* of the *a*-forms were a separate morpheme, this phonotactic condition would be violated: ***'an-a*, ***ur-a*, etc. Although the condition would not be violated in the case of the comitative preposition (*bi-a*), there is further evidence that the *a*-forms of all the prepositions, including the comitative one, are monomorphemic.

As mentioned repeatedly, the *a*-forms cannot be used if there is no object adjacent to the preposition (when the object has been fronted, in relativization, and in ellipsis). It is here and only here that the two object suffixes *-a* and *-da* contrast. *-da* is used when the fronted or missing object is human and plural; *-a* is used elsewhere:

(42) *Tei no ngali-a naifa {fasi-a /**fasa}?*
who? FOC:you(SG):PFV take -it knife {from-him/ from}
'Who did you take the knife from?'

(43) *doo na to'a ki keki fiifiru ki {'ani-a /** 'ana}*
thing REL people PL they:IMPFV fight PL {with-them/ with}
'the things [weapons] the people used to fight with'

(44) *Nau kwai lae {bii -da /*bia}*
I I:IMPFV go {with-them/ with}
'I'll go with them.'

The exclusion of the *a*-forms from these environments is readily understood if we assume that the innovative *a*-forms are monomorphemic. If the *a*-forms were used without an adjacent object, the functional contrast between the object suffixes *-a* and *-da* would be lost. It is true that there would still be a contrast between no suffix and *-da*, but it is well known that languages prefer relatively heavy and explicit coding of objects in such environments (see e.g. Givón, 1979). With an adjacent lexical object, on the other hand, only the suffix *-a* is possible on the *i*-forms (regardless of the animacy status and the grammatical number of the object). Since in this environment *-a* never contrasts with *-da*, the loss of the morphemic status of the final *a* does not lead to a decrease in coding efficiency.

The factor of coding efficiency can be seen as blocking the use of the *a*-forms without an adjacent object only if we assume, once again, that it is the *i*-forms, not the *a*-forms that are historically primary. This functional factor has blocked the spread of the reduced form of the comitative preposition *bia* into the environments where the two object suffixes do contrast even though the phonological conditions (lack of a medial consonant, and stress placement) favors loss of the stem-final *i* there (Section 2.5).

In two respects, the innovative forms of the verb-like prepositions are like the bare prepositions *'i* and *mala* (Section 2.3). Both types require an adjacent object, and neither indexes the object. However, they are unlike each other with fronted objects. With fronted objects, the *a*-variants of the verb-like prepositions cannot be used; instead, the *i*-variants must be used, the preposition is stranded behind, and the object is indexed:

(45) *Tei na 'oki lae bii-a?*
who? FOC you(SG):IMPFV go with-him
'Who will you go with?'

On the other hand, when the object of a bare preposition is fronted, the preposition must be fronted as well:

(46) *Miki gwee niu 'i 'usungadi*
we(EXCL):IMPFV collect coconut in tomorrow
'We will collect coconuts tomorrow.'

(47a) *'I 'usungadi miki gwee niu*
in tomorrow we(EXCL):IMPFV collect coconut
'Tomorrow we will collect coconuts.'

(47b) ***'Usungadi miki gwee niu 'i*
tomorrow we(EXCL):IMPFV collect coconut in

The *a*-variants of the verb-like prepositions form a separate prepositional subcategory. Although they have verb-like variants, they themselves are not verb-like. And although they are like the bare prepositions in some respects, they are unlike them in others.

The reassignment of the verb-like prepositions into another subcategory is not without precedent in the history of To'aba'ita. There is an earlier case of categorial reanalysis of a verb-like preposition that involves a change more radical than the developments discussed above. As mentioned in Section 2.3, beside the verb-like and the bare prepositions To'aba'ita also has noun-like prepositions. These prepositions index their objects by means of possessive suffixes. One of the noun-like prepositions is the recipient/benefactive preposition *fa* (*fe* before a high vowel). Like all the other noun-like prepositions, *fa* is normally preceded by the bare preposition *'i*:

(48) *Nau ku fale-a fanga 'i fa-na wela ki*
I I:PFV give-it food to to-their child PL
'I gave food to the children.'

Compare:

(49) *thaina-na wela ki*
mother-their child PL
'the children's mother'

(50) *Nia kuki-a raisi 'i fe -ku*
she cook-it rice for for-me
'She cooked rice for me.'

Compare:

(51) *thaina- ku*
mother-my
'my mother'

Although today the recipient/benefactive preposition is noun-like, it ultimately derives from a verb, Proto-Oceanic **pa(nñ)i*[8] 'give'. In a large number of Oceanic languages, **pa(nñ)i* has developed into a verb-like recipient and/or benefactive case marker. A detailed discussion of the reflexes of **pa(nñ)i* can be found in Lichtenberk (1985); here I will give only a brief summary of its development in To'aba'ita and a few other Cristobal-Malaitan languages.

**pa(nñ)i* was reflected in Proto-Cristobal-Malaitan as **fani*. Most likely, **fani* functioned only as a verb-like preposition, not as a verb. It took the suffix **-a* with adjacent nonbackgrounded lexical objects. (This use of the suffix is common throughout Cristobal-Malaitan and must be posited for the protolanguage.) Later, some time after the breakup of Proto-Cristobal-Malaitan, **fani-a* underwent phonological reduction to **fana*. The new form **fana* was structurally ambiguous: It was interpretable as monomorphemic for the same phonotactic reasons that the *a*-forms of the present-day To'aba'ita prepositions are monomorphemic.[9] Alternatively, it was interpretable as bimorphemic, consisting of a stem **fa* and the third person possessive suffix **-na*. **-na* (or possibly **-ña*) as a third-person possessive suffix is of great antiquity; it can be reconstructed back far beyond the Proto-Cristobal-

Malaitan stage. (In To'aba'ita, *-na* can index singular or plural adjacent object or possessor NP's; when there is no adjacent object or possessor NP, *-na* has only a singular-indexing function; compare examples (48) and (49) above and (27) and (28) in Section 2.3. The suffix was used in the same way in the protolanguage.) For example:

(52a) **fana* *wane*
to/for man
'to/for the man'

Or:

(52b) **fa* *-na* *wane*
to/for-his man
'to/for the man'

It was the latter analysis that eventually prevailed. Starting out as a verb, passing through a verb-like prepositional stage and a phonologically and morphologically reduced stage (it did not index its objects), the etymon ended up as a noun-like preposition.

3. A VERB-LIKE PREPOSITION AND A CONJUNCTION

Present-day To'aba'ita has six verb-like prepositions. Beside the verb-to-preposition developments discussed above, some of the etyma have undergone other functional changes. One has developed into a coordinating conjunction; three others have developed into complementizers. It is the former development that I will discuss now; the latter will be discussed in Section 4.

To'aba'ita has a coordinating conjunction *ma* 'and', which has a variety of uses. It can conjoin noun phrases, verb phrases and clauses, and in the latter two functions it can be used both in symmetric and asymmetric coordination.

Noun-phrase coordination:

(53) *Koro* *koki* *kwaithathai* *'ana* *alo*
we(DL,INCL) we(DU,INCL):IMPFV be ready GEN.OBL taro
ma *'ota* *ma* *'ova*
and betel nut and pepper leaf
'Let's get ready (some) taro, betel nuts and pepper leaves.'

Symmetric clausal coordination:

(54) *Thaari 'eri ka thathami-a wela 'eri, ma wela 'eri*
girl that she:SEQ like -him child that and child that
ka thathami-a la'u bo'o thaari 'eri.
he:SEQ like -her also INT girl that
'The girl liked the boy [lit.: 'child'], and the boy too liked the girl.'

Asymmetric clausal coordination:

(55) *Kera laungi 'ana foa -na raaraga 'eri, ma*
they:PFV decorate oneself with fruit-its tree sp. that and
ka le'a 'asia na'a.
it:SEQ be nice very
'They decorated themselves with the fruit of the *raaraga* tree, and it looked very nice.'

Ma is not the only 'and' conjunction of To'aba'ita. 'And' coordination can also be expressed by two forms that also function as the comitative preposition: *bia* and *bii.* (Historical connections between comitative case markers and 'and' conjunctions are, of course, not uncommon crosslinguistically; see, for example, Givón, 1979 and references therein.) The form *bia* is used when the conjunct to the right is a lexical NP; *bii* is used when the conjunct to the right is an independent personal pronoun. The distribution of the two forms in their coordinating function parallels their distribution in the comitative-marking function (Section 2.4):

(56) *Thaina-na bia maka nia kero lae 'ana uusia, ...*
mother-his and father his they(DU):PFV go GEN.OBL market
'His mother and father went to the market, ...'

(57) *Tha Maeli bii nau mera lae 'i ro'o ura*
ART Maeli and I we(DU,EXCL):PFV go in yesterday for
dee-laa
fish-NOM
'Maeli and I went fishing yesterday.'

Note the dual subject-aspect markers in (56) and (57); the subject NP's clearly involve coordination.

Bia/bii and *ma* are interchangeable in some contexts:

(58) *Wane 'oro ki {ma /bia} kini 'oro ki ke -si*
man many PL {and/and} woman many PL they-NEG
thathami-a ara'i kwao na'i.
like -him big man white this
'Many men and many women don't like this European.'

In the next excerpt from a text, first *ma* is used to conjoin two NP's, but in the next clause it is *bia* that is used to conjoin two NP's coreferential with the first pair:

(59) *Maka nia ma thaina -na kero keko lae na'a.*
father his and mother-his they(DU) they(DU):SEQ go PERF
Maka nia bia thaina -na keko sore-a wela 'eri, ...
father his and mother-his they(DU):SEQ tell-him child that
'His father and mother were about to go. The father and mother said to their child, ...'

Although *ma* and *bia/bii* are interchangeable in certain contexts, there are major differences between the two conjunctions. First of all, unlike *ma*, *bia/bii* can conjoin only noun phrases; it cannot conjoin verb phrases or clauses. This prohibition on the use of *bia/bii* in VP and clausal coordination is well reflected in the corpus; see Table 5.

Table 5. *Distribution of* ma *and* bia *in NP coordination and VP/clausal coordination*

	NP coordination		VP/clausal coordination	
	tokens	%	tokens	%
ma	53	63.9	352	100 (C)
*bia**	30	36.1	0	0 (C)
	—		—	
total:	83		352	
Grand total of tokens: 435				

*There are no instances of *bii* in the corpus.

There are no instances of the form *bii* used in coordination in the corpus. (As mentioned above, *bii* is used only if the conjunct to the right is an independent personal pronoun.) As Table 5 demonstrates, approximately 80%

of all cases of 'and' coordination (352 out of 435) in the corpus involve VP or clausal coordination, but not once is *bia* used there. In fact, this absence of *bia* from VP and clausal coordination reflects a rule of To'aba'ita grammar, not merely a statistical property of the corpus. On the other hand, *bia* is well represented in NP coordination.

Second, even though *ma* and *bia/bii* are often interchangeable in NP coordination, there is another difference between the two conjunctions. The difference has to do with the animacy status of the conjoined NP's. *Ma* is freely used to conjoin NP's regardless of their animacy status, be they human, animate (other than human) or inanimate. On the other hand, *bia/bii* is used almost exclusively to conjoin human NP's. (Since *bii* requires the conjunct to its right to be an independent personal pronoun, and since pronouns are rarely used with nonhuman reference, one would not expect to find many instances of *bii* conjoining nonhuman NP's in any case.)

The distribution of the two conjunctions according to the animacy status of the conjoined NP's in the corpus is given in Table 6. Since there are no cases of coordination of nonhuman animate NP's in the corpus, the animacy opposition in Table 6 is human vs. inanimate.

Table 6. *Use of* ma *and* bia *depending on the animacy status of the conjoined NP's*

	human NP's		inanimate NP's	
	tokens	%	tokens	%
ma	29	51.8	24	88.9
bia	27	48.2	3	11.1
	—		—	
total:	56		27	

The figures in Table 6 demonstrate convincingly that while *bia* is as common as *ma* in conjoining human NP's, it is used only infrequently to conjoin inanimate NP's, where *ma* is the norm. The numbers of tokens for the younger speaker are too small to be of significance, but it is interesting that in his six uses of 'and' he always used *bia*, never *ma*, and that two out of the three uses of *bia* to conjoin inanimate NP's in the corpus are his.

Bia/bii is used commonly to conjoin human NP's, infrequently to conjoin inanimate NP's, and not at all to conjoin VP's or clauses. This pattern of distribution can be readily understood if we take into account the origin of the conjunction. The conjunction derives historically from the comitative preposition *bia/bii*. When one considers the animacy status of the objects of the comitative preposition, one finds that the preposition is used almost exclusively with human objects. Table 7 is a comparison of the comitative preposition and the related coordinating conjunction according to the animacy status of the objects and the conjoined NP's respectively. In both functions, the forms are used predominantly with human NP's. (For reasons to become apparent in the next paragraph, with the coordinating conjunction it is the animacy status of the NP to the right of the conjunction that is relevant, but there are no instances in the corpus of NP coordination where the conjuncts do not have the same animacy status.)

Table 7. *Comparison of the uses of the comitative preposition and the related conjunction according to the animacy status of the objects and the conjoined NP's respectively*

	comitative		coordinating	
	tokens	%	tokens	%
human	31	93.9	27	90
inanimate	2	6.1	3	10
total:	33		30	

Of the two coordinating conjunctions, *ma* is historically prior. In fact, *ma* can be reconstructed with this function at least as far back as Proto-Oceanic. *Bia/bii* is a relatively recent innovation that is beginning to make inroads into the territory of *ma*. It is not by accident that it is in strongest competition with *ma* where it is, in conjoining human NP's. When the comitative preposition began to acquire a coordinating function, it was first so used in an environment that was less different from the typical environment of its prepositional function than the other potential environments were, that is with human NP's to its right. Whether *bia/bii* will ever become common in conjoining nonhuman NP's and whether it will ever be used in VP and clausal coordination only future can tell. *A priori*, there is no reason why it could not. In the Sa'a language, the cognate of *bia/bii* is used in VP/clausal coordination:

(60) *E i'o pe'i suke*
he sit and beg
'He sat and begged.' (Ivens, 1918)

What is important is that *bia/bii* first became established in human-NP coordination and not with any other type of conjunct. This is precisely what the Principle of Gradual Change in Function (Section 1) says. The principle also predicts that if ever the conjunction comes to be used commonly in VP and clausal coordination this will happen only after it has been well established in inanimate-NP coordination; this is because VP and clausal conjuncts are more different from human-NP conjuncts than inanimate-NP conjuncts are. (From Ivens' brief account of Sa'a *pe'i* one cannot tell whether the form is common both in inanimate-NP and in VP/clausal coordination.) The first (and so far the only) common coordinating use of *bia/bii* closely reflects the use of its source.

The acquisition of a coordinating function by what used to be only a comitative preposition has given rise to a new subcategory of coordinating conjunctions in To'aba'ita. *Bia/bii* is different from *ma* both functionally and formally. Unlike *ma*, it is used to conjoin only NP's and predominantly human NP's, and unlike *ma* it exhibits two forms, used according to the category status of the conjunct to its right, lexical or pronominal.

Thus far I have assumed that the coordinating function of *bia/bii* is an extension from the comitative prepositional function. It is, of course, conceivable, although for reasons to be specified below unlikely, that the coordinating function developed directly from the original verbal function. Given the meaning to be reconstructed for the original verb, **ba'i* 'be with/in the company of', one can assume that the typical objects of the verb were human. Whatever was said above about the development of the coordinating function from the comitative prepositional function would apply, *mutatis mutandis*, to the development of the coordinating function from the verbal function.

Verbal reflexes of the original verb **ba'i* have been found only in 'Are'are and Arosi, neither of which is a member of the same primary subgroup of Cristobal-Malaitan with To'aba'ita. None of the sister languages of To'aba'ita in the North-Central subgroup of Cristobal-Malaitan for which data are available has a verbal reflex of **ba'i* although they all have prepositional reflexes. Although the possibility of independent losses of the verbal reflex cannot be disregarded, it is more likely that in the history of these languages the etymon ceased to be used as a verb quite some time ago, before the development of its coordinating function in To'aba'ita.

The development of *bia/bii* both in its prepositional and coordinating functions illustrates a characteristic of grammaticalization called 'persistence' by Hopper (This Volume). By 'persistence' Hopper means the reflection by a grammatical element of its own history in terms of its functional and/or formal properties. The comitative preposition and the coordinating conjunction derive from an earlier verb. Given the meaning of the verb 'be with/in the company of', it is a safe assumption that its direct objects were typically human. And as we have seen, both the preposition and the conjunction typically have human NP's in the relevant positions. Second, the original verb most likely indexed its objects in ways not significantly different from the ways in which objects of transitive verbs are indexed in present-day To'aba'ita. This is still reflected in the existence of its reflexes *bia* and *bii* and in their distribution.

There is one more comment that needs to be made concerning *bia*. In Section 2.5 I said that one of the factors affecting the rate of use of the innovative *a*-forms of the verb-like prepositions was the frequency of use of the prepositions: All other things being equal, the higher the frequency of use of a given preposition, the more frequent its *a*-form. The comitative preposition did not fit this pattern at all. Although, judging by the corpus, the comitative preposition is least frequent of the six prepositions, *bia* has completely replaced *bii-a* in the relevant context. However, since the form *bia* functions also as a conjunction, one needs to combine the number of occurrences of *bia* in the two functions. *Bia* occurs in the corpus eight times as a preposition and 30 times as a conjunction. The total of 38 moves *bia* up to the fourth place in Table 3, but this still leaves it behind the allative/purpose and the prolative prepositions, with which the process of replacement is considerably less than half complete (Table 4). This means that it is indeed the phonological shape of the preposition and the conjunction that is the decisive factor underlying the rapid spread of the *bia* form.

4. VERB-LIKE COMPLEMENTIZERS

4.1. Pairings of prepositional and complementizer functions

Beside the comitative preposition-coordinating conjunction functional pairing just discussed, there is another kind of functional pairing that one finds in To'aba'ita. Three of the deverbal etyma originally discussed in Section 2 function not only as prepositions but also as complementizers. The prepositions in question are: *uri* allative/purpose, *fasi* ablative, and *suli* prolative. The forms of the complementizers are *uri*, *fasi* and *suli*, respectively, with or without the object suffix *-a* (see Section 4.2 below). (To'aba'ita also has a few non-verblike complementizers, one of which is exemplified in example (69) in Section 4.3.) Historical connections between case markers and complementizers are common crosslinguistically, and their presence, as such, in To'aba'ita occasions no surprise. What is unusual about the To'aba'ita case is one of the pairings of the prepositional and the complementizer functions. The functional pairings are given in Table 8.

Table 8. *Pairings of prepositional and complementizer functions*

	prepositional functions	complementizer functions
uri	allative, purpose	reason, positive purpose
suli	prolative	reason, 'until'
fasi	ablative	positive purpose

The pairing of allative and purpose prepositional functions with reason and (positive) purpose complementizer functions (in *uri*) is common crosslinguistically. (See further below for positive purpose.) The use of one complementizer to signal both reason and purpose is not unusual. As Thompson and Longacre (1985) point out, reason and purpose clauses have similar functions: They both specify explanations for situations. The difference is that purpose clauses encode as yet unrealized explanatory situations, while reason clauses encode explanatory situations that may already have been realized. The pairing of a prolative prepositional function with reason and temporal-extent complementizer functions (in *suli*) is not unusual either. What *is* surprising is the pairing of an ablative prepositional function with a (positive) purpose complementizer function (in *fasi*). Both *uri* and *suli* have multiple functions as complementizers, but *fasi* is used exclusively as a purpose complementizer, more specifically a positive-purpose complementizer. Positive pur-

Table 9. *Frequencies of use of the complementizers in the positive-purpose, reason and temporal-extent functions*

	positive purpose			reason			'until'	
	tokens	%		tokens	%		tokens	%
fasi	43	68.3	*uri*	31	91.2	*suli*	1	100
uri	20	31.7	*suli*	3	8.8			
total:	63			34			1	

pose can also be signaled by *uri*, but *fasi* is more common. *Uri* is used more commonly to signal reason. Besides *uri*, reason can also be signaled by means of *suli*, but *suli* is so used only rarely. The frequencies of use of the three complementizers in the various functions in the corpus are given in Table 9.

Even though the pairing of an ablative prepositional function and a (positive) purpose complementizer function is unusual, I will argue further below (Section 4.3) that it is not an unnatural result of a sequence of changes. Before addressing that problem, there are some other matters to be dealt with.

4.2. Variant forms of the complementizers

At least two of the complementizers have two variants, one with the object suffix *-a* and one without: *uri-a*/*uri* reason, positive purpose, and *fasi-a*/*fasi* positive purpose. With the third, reason and temporal-extent complementizer *suli*, the situation is unclear. In the corpus, the complementizer always has the form *suli-a*. When the form *suli* is suggested to speakers, it is usually though not always rejected. Following are a few examples of the complementizers:

(61) *Fale-a ta si fanga 'a-na wela na'i {fasi-a /*
give-it some PARTV food to-his child this {POS.PURP-it/
fasi} ka bona
POS.PURP} he:SEQ be quiet
'Give some food to the child so that he is quiet.'

(62) *Wela na'i 'e angi {uri -a /suli -a} 'e thaofa*
child this he:PFV cry {REAS-it/REAS-it} he:PFV be hungry
'The child cried because he was hungry.'

(63) *'E a'i 'o -si lae bii nau uri 'oe*
it:PFV NEG.VB you(SG)-NEG go with me REAS you(SG)
kwai-na wane ramo
wife-his professional killer
'Don't come with me because you are the wife of a professional killer [a man who kills in order to collect bounty put up for someone's death].'

(64) *Wela baa 'e to'o suli -a to'a 'e -ki kera lae na'a.*
child that he:PFV wait until-it people that-PL they:PFV go PERF
'The child waited until the people had left.'

When expressing purpose, *uri* and *fasi* may cooccur, in that order:

(65) *Nia ka sifo uri ta i'a 'i Fafolifua uri -a*
he he:SEQ descend for some fish to Fafolifua POS.PURP-it
fasi nia kai ngali-a mai, kai na'are
POS.PURP he he:IMPFV take -them hither he:IMPFV roast
-a 'a -na
-them MID.VCE-his
'He went down to Fafolifua for some fish to take back and roast.'

The frequencies of use of the suffixful and the suffixless variants of the complementizers in the corpus are given in Table 10. There are three instances of the complex purpose complementizer *uri-a fasi*. Both forms are counted in their respective categories.

Table 10. *Frequencies of use of the suffixful and the suffixless variants of the complementizers*

	tokens	%		tokens	%		tokens	%
fasi-a	3	7	*uri-a*	48	94.1	*suli-a*	4	100 (C?, S?)
fasi	*40*	93	*uri*	*3*	5.9	*suli*	*0*	0 (C?, S?)
total:	43		total	51		total	4	
Grand total of tokens: 98								

The relative frequencies of use of the two variants are not the same for all the complementizers. There are no cases of the suffixless form *suli* in the corpus. As mentioned above, the grammatical status of this form is unclear. The figures for *fasi* and *uri* are virtually mirror images of each other. Once again, the numbers of tokens for the younger speaker are too small to be of significance (4 for *fasi* and 9 for *uri*), and at any rate there are no marked differences between the two speakers.

We are dealing here with another change in progress, this time from an earlier form with the object suffix *-a* to an innovative form without the suffix. The innovation has not affected the three complementizers to the same degree. The change is nearing completion with *fasi*, whereas it has only begun to affect *uri*. And if the occasional, albeit usually hesitant acceptance of the sufixless form *suli* is any indication, the change may be about to begin affecting this complementizer as well.

There are no significant differences in the forms of the three complementizers, and consequently the differences in the spread of the innovative forms are not attributable to differences in phonological shape. The frequency of use of the complementizers may be partly relevant. The reason/temporal-extent complementizer *suli* is by far the least common of the three complementizers (Table 10), and it does not normally occur without the suffix. On the other hand, the frequencies of use of the other two complementizers are pretty much the same; nevertheless the frequencies of use of their suffixless forms are diametrically different.

The factor that does appear to be relevant is the age of the innovation. Complementizer cognates of the To'aba'ita verb-like complementizers are found in several Cristobal-Malaitan languages; see Table 11.

Table 11. *Complementizer cognates of the To'aba'ita verb-like complementizers in Cristobal-Malaitan languages*

To'aba'ita	*fasi-a/fasi* positive purpose	*uri-a/uri* reason; positive purpose	*suli-a(/suli?)* reason; 'until'
Lau	*fasi* positive purpose	*uri* positive purpose; quotative	
Kwara'ae	*fasi* purpose (positive, negative)		*suli-a* reason
Kwaio	*fa'asi-a* negative purpose, precaution		*suri-a* reason
Arosi			*suri-a* reason

Fasi has suffixless cognates in Lau and Kwara'ae, while *uri* has suffixless cognates only in Lau, a very close relative of To'aba'ita. The suffixless form *fasi* thus appears to be older than the suffixless form *uri*, and it is much more common. *Suli*, which does not normally occur without the suffix, has no suffixless cognates.

Even though the innovation consists in removal of the object suffix, there is no loss in coding efficiency. Since on the complementizers the suffix *-a* never contrasts with the plural suffix *-da* or with its own absence, it is redundant, and its removal does not result in any loss of information. The object suffix is also lost in the innovative *a*-forms of the verb-like prepositions, but in a different way. There the phoneme *a* is retained, but it no longer realizes a morpheme. Although they ultimately derive from the same historical sources, the innovative prepositional and complementizer forms have diverged: From *fasi-a* we now have *fasa* and *fasi* respectively, and from *uri-a* we now have *ura* and *uri* respectively. One could hypothesize that this divergence in form reflects a movement towards iconicity (one meaning, one form). This, however, is doubtful because the prepositions too have suffixless forms *fasi* and *uri* (used with independent personal pronouns as objects).

4.3. Pairing of the ablative and the purpose functions

Both *fasi* and *uri* are used to signal positive purpose, 'S1 in order S2', not negative purpose or precaution, 'S1 in order not S2'. The pairing of an ablative prepositional function and a positive-purpose complementizer function in *fasi* is crosslinguistically unusual. When one looks elsewhere in the Cristobal-Malaitan group, one finds the same pairing in Lau, a very close relative of To'aba'ita, which has *fasi* ablative and *fasi* positive purpose.

In other languages one finds different pairings: Kwaio has *fa'asi* as an ablative preposition and *fa'asi* as a complementizer with a function that Keesing (1985) terms 'precautionary'. In this function, *fa'asi* often corresponds to English 'lest'. In Kwara'ae one finds *fa'asi*/*fasi* ablative and *fasi* (with *'iri*) purpose. According to Deck (1934), Kwara'ae *fasi* can be used to signal both positive and negative purpose.

Finally, in at least two languages the etymon also functions as a verb: Kwara'ae *fa'asi* 'leave, forsake, depart from' and Lau *fasi* 'lose'. These verbal meanings (especially those of the Kwara'ae form) are highly compatible with the ablative prepositional function. Both contain the notions of separation, distancing, removal, and thus absence.

It is the ablative-precaution/negative purpose pairings in Kwaio and Kwara'ae that are the key to understanding the ablative-positive purpose pairing in To'aba'ita (as well as in Lau and Kwara'ae). Keesing (1985) says that Kwaio *fa'asi* conveys the meanings 'S1 lest S2', 'S1 to avoid S2' and is also used to signal warnings:

(66) *Nau ku aru-a 'ubu -na nga kesi fa'asi-a wane ta beri -a*
I I:SUBJ put-it inside-its ART case lest -it man DUB steal-it
'I put it in the case lest someone steals it.'

(67) *Rugasi-a masari-la -i fa'asi-a ta kee-'o*
let go -it play -GER-its lest -it DUB bite-you(SG)
'Stop playing with it, or it might bite you.'

(68) *'Oo sia aru-a mone a -i fa'asi-a ta'a ta beri -a*
you(SG) NEG put-it NEG there-its lest -it people DUB steal-it
'Don't put it there, or people might steal it.'

Fa'asi signals negative purpose, precaution or warning: The event of the first clause serves to avert the potential event of the second clause. Note that even though the purpose may be negative, the purpose clause is grammatically positive.

As far as Kwara'ae is concerned, Deck (1934) says that there are several ways to mark negative purpose. It can be marked by means of *sasi* ... (*kata*) or, more recently, by means of *asu* ... *kata*. Deck glosses all of these forms as 'lest'. The purpose clause is grammatically positive. Negative purpose can also be marked by *fasi 'iri* or by *'iri* alone. With either of these two forms, the purpose clause is grammatically negative. As mentioned earlier, *fasi* (in combination with other particles, *'iri* being one of them) is also used to signal positive purpose. Although Deck provides examples of negative purpose being marked by *sasi* ... *kata*, by *asu* ... *kata*, and by *'iri*, and although he gives examples of *fasi* marking positive purpose, he gives no examples of *fasi* marking negative purpose. It may be that at the time when Deck wrote the grammar of the language, the negative-purpose marking function of *fasi* was relatively uncommon.

In To'aba'ita, *fasi* signals only positive purpose. To signal negative purpose or precaution, *ada*, a non-verblike complementizer, is required:

(69) *Riki -a ada 'oko dekwe-a kuki 'ena*
look at-it PREC you(SG):SEQ break-it pot that
'Look out so you don't break the pot.'

Precaution/negative-purpose complementizers are widespread in the Oceanic languages. Positive-purpose and negative-purpose clauses typically receive different marking.[10] Although the precaution/negative-purpose complementizers of the Oceanic languages often correspond to English 'lest', they have none of its archaic flavor. They are used commonly, sometimes even without a preceding clause. In such independent constructions, the complementizers typically signal warning. There is often an implication of precaution, as in the next example from To'aba'ita:

(70) *Ada dani ka 'arungi kulu 'i laa masu'u*
PREC rain it:SEQ fall on us(INCL) in inside bush
[E.g. 'Let's stay at home'] 'We might get caught in the rain in the bush.'

The notions of negative purpose and precaution are related to the notions of separation, distancing and absence inherent in the meanings 'leave, forsake' of the ultimate verbal source of the complementizers and in the meaning 'away from' of the related ablative prepositions. One does X in order for Y not to happen, in order to avert Y.

Most likely, the development of the purpose complementizers took the following course: In the language ancestral to To'aba'ita, Lau, Kwara'ae and Kwaio, there was a verb **fa'asi* 'leave, forsake' and an ablative preposition of the same form. Later, the preposition acquired a new function, that of a negative-purpose/precaution complementizer. This was followed by another change in function whereby the complementizer lost its negative force and so could be used to signal both negative and positive purpose. This stage was still reflected in the Kwara'ae of over 50 years ago, as described by Deck (1934). Later, a further change took place in the language ancestral to To'aba'ita and Lau whereby the complementizer acquired an exclusively positive-purpose marking function. The negative-to-positive purpose shift may have been facilitated by the fact that even though the purpose originally signaled by the complementizer was negative, the purpose clause was grammatically positive. The function of the complementizer was adapted to the grammatical structure of its complement.

If the development of an erstwhile verb into a positive-purpose marker in To'aba'ita (and in Lau) postulated here is indeed the historical one, it is another instance of gradual change in function. First, there was a change from an ablative function, which contains the notions of separateness, distancing and absence, into a negative-purpose/precaution marking function, which too contains these notions. This was followed — in the ancestor of To'aba'ita and Lau — by a change whereby those semantic components were removed. Theoretically at least, the development could have been first from the ablative function into a positive-purpose marking function, which would have involved loss of the notions of separateness, distancing and absence, followed — in Kwaio — by a change into a negative-purpose/precaution marking function, which would have involved reintroduction of those semantic components. The Principle of Gradual Change in Function predicts that such a sequence of shifts in function will not occur.

4.4. Functional shifts among the complementizers

Before leaving the complementizers, one more matter merits discussion. The complementizer *suli* serves to signal reason and also temporal extent ('until'). However, it is used only infrequently to signal reason, the complementizer *uri* being much more common in this function (Table 9, Section 4.1). At the same time, complementizer cognates of *suli* coding reason are found both within (Table 11) and without Cristobal-Malaitan, and this function of *suli* is clearly of some antiquity. Why then is *suli* used so infrequently in To'aba'ita to signal reason?

The most likely explanation is that *suli* is being replaced in this function by *uri*. Now, *uri* too has two functions: It signals reason and positive purpose. In the latter function, it is in competition with *fasi*. In the absence of direct evidence bearing on this issue, what will be said below is of necessity speculative but not implausible. Originally, positive purpose was marked by *uri*. When the reflex of **fa'asi* changed from a negative-purpose/precaution complementizer into a positive-purpose complementizer, it invaded the territory occupied by **uri*. Gradually, *uri* has been ceding its purpose-marking function to *fasi*, while at the same time assuming the function of a reason complementizer. In doing so, it came into competition with the original reason marker *suli*, which has virtually ceded this function to *uri*.

If this scenario does indeed correspond to historical reality, we have here a series of shifts in function in a push chain, some of which lead to a decrease in iconicity (one form, one function), while others are in the direction of restoring iconicity. When an element develops an additional function, there is normally a decrease in iconicity because formal changes typically lag behind changes in function. Thus the acquisition by **fa'asi* of the function of a negative-purpose/precaution complementizer led to a decrease in iconicity (one form, more than one function). The change of the negative-purpose/precaution complementizer into a positive-purpose complementizer also led to a decrease in iconicity (one function, two forms). This latter stage has been followed by a gradual withdrawal of the original positive-purpose complementizer *uri* from this function, which is a change in the direction of restoring iconicity. At the same time, this element has assumed a new function, already signaled by *suli*. The result is a decrease in iconicity. However, *suli*, the original reason complementizer, has by now almost ceased to serve this function, which is a development in the direction of restoring iconicity.

5. SUMMARY AND DISCUSSION

The thread that runs through the discussion of the grammaticalization processes in To'aba'ita is the gradualness of the implementation of the changes. One aspect of the gradualness is manifested by the synchronic alternation between the innovative and the old forms of most of the verb-like prepositions and the verb-like complementizers. Judging by historical evidence, at least some of the alternations have been in existence for generations.

The innovations have affected the individual members of the two categories to various degrees. In fact, the differences are extreme, ranging from no or virtually no replacement to complete or virtually complete replacement. The innovations have been diffusing through the categories lexically. They have not affected the categories as wholes; rather, they affected certain members before others, and they have affected the members unevenly. Categorial reanalyses proceeding by lexical diffusion have been noted by other investigators; see, for example, Li (1975) and Romaine (1983). Here I have attempted to identify the factors underlying the uneven spread of the innovative forms. One factor is the frequency of use; another is the phonological properties of two of the verb-like prepositions. The third factor, the age of the innovative forms, although relevant to their spread is, of course, irrelevant to the inception of the innovations.

In the case of the verb-like prepositions, the innovation — a phonological reduction — has given rise to a new subcategory of prepositions. Similarly, the acquisition of a coordinating function by the comitative preposition has given rise to a new subcategory of coordinating conjunctions. The new prepositional and conjunction subcategories, while exhibiting new formal properties have, thus far at least, retained some of the properties — functional and/or formal — of their sources. As pointed out by Hopper (This volume), such functional and formal persistence is characteristic of grammaticalization. The gradualness of the grammaticalization processes in To'aba'ita, and the pervasiveness of persistence in grammaticalization in general call into question those theories that view categorial reanalysis in terms of radical and rapid restructuring (see, for example, Lightfoot, 1979). It is evident that languages, or rather their speakers, are able to tolerate a great amount of variation between new and old forms even when the new forms exhibit properties that are quite unlike those of the preexisting forms.

The grammars of natural languages are never static; in every language there are always areas that are in flux. Languages may strive toward greater regularity and iconicity by eliminating anomalies and variation; at the same time, however, new patterns emerge elsewhere in the grammar, introducing new anomalies and new variation. Grammars are always *noncomplete*. In the grammar of every language there are, at a given time, many rigid regularities; at the same time, there are also many aspects in every grammar that are not fully determinate and that are malleable to various degrees. Grammars do provide patterns for the construction of discourse, but they do not determine its grammatical form fully. Being noncomplete, they allow speakers a certain degree of freedom in constructing discourse. For whatever reason, certain novel patterns become established, which results in a reshaping of the grammar.

Generative approaches to language typically posit, under various guises, a dichotomy between grammatical systems or *langue* on the one hand and language use or *parole* on the other, and it is the former that is taken as the primary or the only object of study. Grammars are taken to be fully self-contained and determinate systems. However, the relation between grammatical systems and language use is not one of strict opposition; rather it is a symbiotic relation. Grammars shape discourse, and discourse, in turn, shapes grammars. The merits of studies of grammaticalization lie not only in elucidating specific aspects of the grammars of individual languages but also — and more importantly — in revealing an important characteristic of natural languages: *The noncompleteness of grammars.*[11] *Langue* and *parole* are not neatly separable: in order to better understand one, it is necessary to consider the other as well. (On this point see also DuBois, 1988).

The gradual nature of grammaticalization is also manifested in sequential changes in function. Here 'gradualness' has to do with the steps by which new functions develop from earlier functions one after another. I have formulated a Principle of Gradual Change in Function which says that in a sequence of changes in function, a function that is less different from the original function will be acquired before a function that is more different from the original function. The principle has obvious implications for comparative syntax and syntactic reconstruction. If cognate elements in two or more languages have different — but 'related' — functions, it can be used to determine the most likely order of the developments of the functions and to decide which of the functions, if any, the protolanguage is most likely to have had (keeping the possibility of independent developments in mind).[12] Certain sequences of changes are more natural than others.

It is hardly an accident that the innovative forms of the verb-like prepositions, without the object suffix *-a*, have, thus far at least, been introduced only into those environments where the suffix is not functional, where its removal does not result in any loss of coding efficiency. Functional factors *can* play a role in grammaticalization. If the innovative forms do ever spread into the environments where the suffix is functional, this will be another instance of gradual change in function: The forms will have been first introduced into that environment where their presence has minimal structural and functional repercussions.

Finally, the present study has underscored the importance of a historical perspective for understanding grammars. Unless one considers the origin of the To'aba'ita conjunction *bia/bii* 'and', its exclusion from VP and clausal coordination, its rare use in conjoining inanimate NP's, and the distribution of the two forms according to the categorial status of the conjunct to the right will appear to be unmotivated, arbitrary syntactic and semantic restrictions. And unless one considers the origin of the positive-purpose complementizer *fasi*, the crosslinguistically unusual fact that the same etymon is also used as an ablative case marker will remain an oddity.

Grammars are products of their own histories. If one's goal is strictly language description, limiting oneself to synchronic facts is understandable. If, however, one seeks to understand why certain aspects of a language system are the way they are, considerations of diachrony may be crucial. Obviously, diachronic explanations of synchronic facts are not the only valid kind of explanation, but if we are serious about trying to understand the properties of language systems, diachronic considerations have an important role to play.

NOTES

1. My research on the To'aba'ita language has been supported by grants from the University of Auckland Research Fund. I am grateful to a number of participants at the Symposium on Grammaticalization, especially E. Traugott, for valuable comments on an earlier version of this paper.

2. Unless specified otherwise, plural pronominal glosses, such as 'we' and 'them', have plural, not dual, reference. * identifies reconstructions; ** signifies ungrammaticality.

3. The sources of the data are as follows: Capell (1971) (Arosi), Deck (1934), Watson-Gegeo, pers. comm. (Kwara'ae), Fox (1974), Ivens (1921) (Lau), Geerts (1970) ('Are'are), Ivens (1918), (1929) (Sa'a), Keesing (1985) (Kwaio). The To'aba'ita data come from my own field notes.
4. Kwara'ae has a pervasive process of metathesis, hence the variant *suil* (K. Watson-Gegeo, pers. comm.). See also note 6.
5. The Lau, Kwara'ae and Kwaio forms exhibit an irregular reflex of the initial consonant, *f* instead of the expected *b*. Irregularities in the reflexes of labial obstruents are not uncommon in Oceanic languages.
6. K. Watson-Gegeo has informed me that *fa'ini* is often reduced to *fani* and *fa'asi* to *fasi*. Kwara'ae is undergoing a change of *f* to *h*, hence the variants *hain* and *hais* respectively (with metathesis; see note 4).
7. The form *faafi* is from Deck (1934). According to K. Watson-Gegeo (pers. comm.), the form of the preposition is *fafi*.
8. Because of a disagreement among the witnesses concerning the nasal, a doublet has to be reconstructed.
9. In Lichtenberk (1985) I say that **fana* was interpretable as **fan-a*, where **-a* was the object suffix. However, for reasons of phonotactics this could not have been the case.
10. The prevalence of negative-purpose/precaution complementizers in the Oceanic languages is no doubt responsible for the presence of a negative-purpose/precaution complementizer in Melanesian Pidgin (*nogut*, from English *no good*).
11. The notion of the noncompleteness of grammars is related to what Hopper (1987) calls 'emergent grammar'. The notion of emergent grammar is more radical than that of grammars being noncomplete; it denies any independent existence to grammars. On my view, at any time certain aspects of grammars are quite fixed whereas others are fluid to various degrees, but there is never a time where a grammar as a whole is fully determinate.
12. The principle will be irrelevant to cases where the functions of cognate grammatical elements belong in distinct domains, such as an andative directional marker ('thither') in one language and a future tense marker in another language, both arising independently of each other from an erstwhile verb 'go'.

REFERENCES

Ahlqvist, Anders. 1982. *Papers from the 5th International Conference on Historical Linguistics*. Amsterdam/Philadelphia: John Benjamins.

Blust, Robert. 1980. "Austronesian etymologies." *Oceanic Linguistics* 19:1–181.

Capell, A. 1971. *Arosi Grammar*. Canberra: Australian National University [*Pacific Linguistics*, B-20].

Chung, Sandra. 1977. "On the gradual nature of syntactic change." In Li 1977:3–55.

Davenport, Michael, Erik Hansen and Hans F. Nielsen (eds). 1983. *Current Topics in English Historical Linguistics*. Odense: Odense University Press.

Deck, N.C. 1934. *Grammar of the Language Spoken by the Kwara'ae People of Mala, British Solomon Islands*. Wellington. [*Polynesian Society Reprint 5*].

DuBois, John W. 1988. "Discourse as pattern model for grammar: The possessor= ergator affiliation." Paper presented at the Symposium on Grammaticalization, University of Oregon, Eugene, May 1988.

Fisiak, Jacek (ed.). 1984. *Historical Syntax*. Berlin: Mouton.

Fox, C.E. 1974. *Lau Dictionary*. Canberra: Australian National University. [*Pacific Linguistics*, C-25].

Geerts, P. 1970. *'Āre'āre Dictionary*. Canberra: Australian National University [*Pacific Linguistics*, C-14].

Gerritsen, Marinel. 1982. "Word order change in Dutch imperative clauses: The interaction between contextual and syntactic factors." In Ahlqvist 1982:62–73.

Givón, Talmy. 1977. "The drift from VSO to SVO in Biblical Hebrew." In Li 1977:181–254.

Givón, Talmy. 1979. *On Understanding Grammar*. New York: Academic Press.

Grace, George W. 1955. "Subgrouping of Malayo-Polynesian: A report of tentative findings." *American Anthropologist* 57:337–339.

Green, R.C. and M. Kelly (eds). 1972. *Studies in Oceanic Culture History*, Vol. 3. Honolulu: Bernice P. Bishop Museum [*Pacific Anthropological Records*, 13].

Hopper, Paul. 1987. "Emergent grammar." *Berkeley Linguistics Society* 13:139–157.

Hopper, Paul. Volume I. "On some principles of grammaticization."

Hopper, Paul and Janice Martin. 1987. "Structuralism and diachrony: The development of the indefinite article in English." In Ramat et al. 1987:295–304.

Ivens, Walter G. 1918. *Dictionary and Grammar of the Language of Sa'a and Ulawa, Solomon Islands*. Washington: Carnegie Institution of Washington.

Ivens, Walter G. 1921. *Grammar and Vocabulary of the Lau Language, Solomon Islands*. Washington: Carnegie Institution of Washington.

Ivens, Walter G. 1929. *A Dictionary of the Language of Sa'a (Mala) and Ulawa, South-East Solomon Islands*. London: Oxford University Press.

Keesing, Roger M. 1985. *Kwaio Grammar*. Canberra: Australian National University [*Pacific Linguistics*, B-88].

Li, Charles N. 1975. "Synchrony vs. diachrony in language structure." *Language* 51:873–886.

Li, Charles N. (ed.). 1977. *Mechanisms of Syntactic Change*. Austin: University of Texas Press.

Lichtenberk, Frantisek. 1985. "Syntactic-category change in Oceanic languages." *Oceanic Linguistics* 24:1–84.

Lichtenberk, Frantisek. 1988a. "The pragmatic nature of nominal anaphora in To'aba'ita." *Studies in Language* 12:299–344.

Lichtenberk, Frantisek. 1988b. "The Cristobal-Malaitan subgroup of Southeast Solomonic." *Oceanic Linguistics* 28:24–62.

Lightfoot, David W. 1979. *Principles of Diachronic Syntax*. Cambridge: Cambridge University Press.

Lord, Carol. 1973. "Serial verbs in transition." *Studies in African Linguistics* 4:269–296.

Pawley, Andrew K. 1972. "On the internal relationships of Eastern Oceanic languages." In Green and Kelly 1972:1–142.

Pawley, Andrew K. 1973. "Some problems in Proto-Oceanic grammar." *Oceanic Linguistics* 12:103–188.

Ramat, Anna G., Onofriu Carruba and Giuliano Bernini (eds). 1987. *Papers from the*

7th International Conference on Historical Lingustics. Amsterdam/Philadelphia: John Benjamins.

Romaine, Suzanne. 1983. "Syntactic change as category change by re-analysis and diffusion: Some evidence from the history of English." In Davenport et al. 1983:9–27.

Saltarelli, Mario. 1980. "Syntactic diffusion." In Traugott et al. 1980:183–191.

Shopen, Timothy. 1985. *Language Typology and Syntactic Description*, Vol. II: *Complex Constructions*. Cambridge: Cambridge University Press.

Silva-Corvalán, Carmen. 1984. "Semantic and pragmatic factors in syntactic change." In Fisiak 1984:555–573.

Thompson, Sandra A. and Robert E. Longacre. 1985. "Adverbial clauses." In Shopen 1985:171–234.

Timberlake, Alan. 1977. "Reanalysis and actualization in syntactic change." In Li 1977:141–177.

Traugott, Elizabeth C., Rebecca Labrum and Susan Shepherd (eds). 1980. *Papers from the 4th International Conference on Historical Linguistics*. Amsterdam/Philadelphia: John Benjamins.

Wiegand, Nancy. 1984. "Creating complex sentence structure." *Berkeley Linguistics Society* 10:674–687.

Serial Verbs and the Mental Reality of 'Event': Grammatical vs. Cognitive Packaging

T. Givón
Linguistics Department
University of Oregon, Eugene

1. THE PHENOMENON*

Verb serialization may be defined ostensively, and somewhat simple-mindedly, in the following cross-linguistic terms:

(1) An event/state that one language codes as a simple clause with a single verb, is coded in another language as a complex clause with two or more verbs.

Such a definition systematically excludes from the scope of phenomenon structures that are coded in *all* languages by (at least) two verbs, such as:

(2) *Modality-verbs with complements (including purpose clauses)*:
John *wants* to *eat* an apple
Mary *ran* to *reach* the house

(3) *Manipulative-verb with complements (including causatives)*:
Mary *told* John to *eat* an apple
Mary *made* John *eat* an apple

(4) *Cognition-utterance verb with complements*:
John *knew* that Mary *lied* to him
Mary *said* that she *was* sick
She *saw* him *running* out of the house

(5) *Main clauses with tightly-bound adverbial clauses*:
Having *worked*, he *retired*
Fearing for her life, she *went* back
He *came running*

Serial-verb constructions have been described most often in non-European languages, and have been considered somewhat exotic, given their perceived paucity in European languages. They can be divided into a number of more or less distinct types. We will illustrate the most common ones below, by giving only their English morphemic glosses.

a. *Case-role marking*:
In this type, most conspicuous in West-African (Stahlke, 1970; Hyman, 1971; Lord, 1973; Givón, 1975a), South East Asian (Matisoff, 1969; Goral, 1980) and Oceanic (Durie, 1982; Crowley, 1987) languages, different serial verbs are used as grammaticalized markers of nominal case-roles, as in:

(6) a. she *take*-stick *break* (patient)
'She broke the stick'
b. she *walk go*-market (locative)
'She walked *to* the market'
c. he *work give*-her (benefactive)
'He worked *for* her'
d. She *take*-knife *cut* meat (instrumental)
'She cut the meat *with* the knife'

b. *Verb co-lexicalization*:
In this type, common in Mandarin (Thompson, 1973), Papua-New Guinea (Pawley, 1966; 1980; 1987; Bradshaw, 1982;) and Oceanic (Crowley, 1987), two or more verb-stems are co-lexicalized to create a more complex verbal concept. Such complex concepts — or collocations — are just as stable, stereotyped and contextually predictable — in characterizing conventionalized situations —as single words. Thus consider:

(7) a. She *hit-break* the glass
'She broke the glass'

b. She *frighten-die* him
'She frightened him to death'

c. He *sleep-perceive*
'He dreamed'

d. She *eat-perceive* the meat
'She tasted the food'

e. He *cut-split* wood
'He chopped wood'

c. *Deictic-directional marking*:
In this type, common in Tok Pisin (Givón, 1988) and Oceanic (Crowley, 1987), Amerindian (Talmy, 1970), and Tibeto-Burman languages (DeLancey, 1980), verbs with deictic values, such as 'come' and 'go', are grammaticalized to impart those deictic values to other motion or transfer verbs, as in:

(8) a. He walked he-*go*
'He walked *away* (from a reference point)'

b. She took the book she-*come*
'She took the book *toward* (a reference point)'

d. *Tense-aspect marking*:
This type, sometime indistinguishable from verb complementation (as in (2) above), is found in Tok-Pisin, West African, South East Asian, Austronesian and Creoles, *inter alia.* Aspectual or modal functions are marked by serial verbs, as in:

(9) a. He *stay* work
He *is* work*ing*' (durative)
b. He *go* work
'He *will* work' (future)
b. He work *finish*
'He *has already* worked' (perfective)

e. *Evidentiality and epistemic marking*:
The last general type, sometime indistinguishable from complementation (as in (4) above), is found in Iroquois (Mithun, 1986) or spoken English (Thompson and Mulac, Volume II), *inter alia.* Here verbs such as 'think', 'say', 'hear' or 'know' become evidential markers, as in:

(10) a. *They say* she's coming (hearsay)
b. *I understand* he's leaving (hedge)
c. *I think* she's home (inference)
d. She's left, *y' know* (co-option)

2. THEORETICAL ISSUES: GRAMMAR VS. COGNITION

The issues raised by the existence of serial-verb constructions, and their unequal genetic and areal distribution, goes to the very heart of the relationship between grammar and cognition. Note, first, that one may give an alternative, and seemingly non-ostensive, definition of verb serialization as:

(11) The use of more than one verb in a *single clause* that codes what seems to be, at least *prima facie*, a simple *single event*.

Definition (11) remains a problematic straw man. On the structural side, 'single clause' is a notion that retains a high potential for circularity. One can easily define 'clause' as *a construction with a single verb at its core*. On the cognitive side, 'single event' is just as susceptible to the very same circular definition, and linguists are notoriously prone to letting grammatical structure define what is a 'single event' (cf. Bradshaw, 1982, p. 28; *inter alia*). Even when one believes in the ultimate — if rough — isomorphism between grammatical and cognitive organization, these circular definitions remain uncomfortable.

The substantive issue alluded to here has, of course, a well known antecedent in the earlier discussion concerning the *formal status* of serial-verb constructions (cf. Stahlke, 1970; Hyman, 1971; Awobuluyi, 1972; 1973; Lord, 1973; Bamgbose, 1974; Li and Thompson, 1973; 1974; Schachter, 1974): Are they independent or embedded? Conjoined or subordinate? Are the serial verbs themselves lexical or grammatical morphemes? Verbs or prepositions? These questions are the formal isomorphs of the substantive issues concerning the relation between grammar and cognition.

In approaching the relation between grammar and cognition, one may adopt either one of two extreme positions. These positions may be given as the two alternative approaches to *cross-cultural translation*. Consider the standard 3-line linguistic transcription of an event clause:

Line 1: event clause in the source language
Line 2: morph-by-morph linguistic gloss
Line 3: free meaning translation

Position A, which I will call the *extreme universalist* position (cf. Katz, 1978), holds that line-3 is the proper translation of line-1, thus an adequate representation of the cognized event in the source language.

Position B, which I will call the *extreme relativist* position,[1] holds that line-2 is the proper translation of line-1, thus an adequate representation of the cognized event in the source language. Extreme universalists thus argue from translation to cognition. Extreme relativists argue — after Whorf (1956) — from grammar to cognition.

In arguing from grammar to cognition, Pawley (1980, 1987) has staked out what can be interpreted, at least under one reading, as an extreme culture-relative position.[2] Languages that use serial verb constructions, Pawley seems to be suggesting, differ fundamentally from those (like English) that don't, in the way their speakers cognize or package unitaıy 'events'. Speakers of serial-verb languages view some of *our* unitary 'events' as a concatenation of fragmented sub-events. To support his theoretical position, Pawley quotes from Grace (1983):

> ...The syntactic function which more than any other seems to hold the key to human language is that which permits the specification of what I call "conceptual situation" ... The conceptual situation is a model of *clause-sized chunk of reality or imagined reality*. The syntactic mechanisms involved are primarily those which mark the case-relations of the verb ... (1983, pp. 7–8; emphases are mine; TG)

In summarizing his own specific observations, Pawley notes:

> ... We may conclude from the foregoing that there is no universal set of episodic conceptual events. Indeed, it seems that languages may vary enormously in the kind of resources they have for the characterization of episodes and other complex events ... (1987, p. 351)

And further:

> ...Kalam and English do share a body of more or less isomorphic conceptual events and situations, namely *those which both languages may express by a single clause*. This common core presumably reflects certain characteristics of external world and human experience that are salient for people everywhere. But it is *a fairly small core*, in relation to the total set of conceptual situations which English can reduce to a single clause expression... (1987, p. 356)

The intellectual force of Pawley's argument is firmly anchored in a belief in the iconic relation between grammar and thought. The specific iconism that concerns us here harken all the way back to Aristotle's conception of the verb ('predicate') as the code-element at the core of the proposition, and of the proposition as the code-unit for states and events.[3]
Multi-verb sequences thus code multi-propositional sequences, which in turn code multi-states or multi-events.

Note, in passing, that the opposite view — that a cluster of serial verbs code a *single* 'event' — can be argued on, essentially, the same iconicity grounds, by invoking other grammatical criteria to determine what is an 'event'. Such an argument may be also found in works by Bradshaw (1982), Crowley (1987) or Foley and Olson (1985), *inter alia*.

3. EMPIRICAL ISSUES: GRAMMAR VS. BEHAVIOR

The empirical bind inherent in the general program of inferring cognition from grammar, even after one detaches it from Aristotle's empiricism, may be summed up as follows: One takes for granted the *complete* isomorphism between the *cognitive package* called 'event', and the *grammatical package* called 'proposition' (or 'sentence', or 'clause'). Grammatical packaging is of course relatively easy for the linguist to define. Cognitive packaging is then left undefined. One winds up then with an inevitable circularity: Grammar is first used to *define* cognition, and then is said to *correlate* with it.

The study whose early results are reported here has been designed to investigate the correlation between the grammatical and cognitive packaging of 'events', by relying on some well-known phenomena in the *temporal packaging* of linguistic information: The use of *delivery rhythm* (Just & Carpenter, 1980; Aronson & Ferres, 1983), *intonation contours* (Kumpf, 1987), and most particularly, the placement of *pauses* (Eisler-Goldman, 1958a; 1958b; 1961; 1968; Chafe, 1979; 1987; Tomlin, 1987a). It is widely recognized (see discussion in Haiman (ed.), 1985a; 1985b; Givón, 1985a; *inter alia*) that:

(12) The temporal-physical distance between chunks of linguistically-coded information correlates directly to the conceptual distance between them.

Observation (12) is indeed one of the major *iconicity principles* underlying syntactic structure. It may thus be reasoned that if serial-verb constructions indeed reflect a unique strategy of cognitive segmentation of 'events', then pauses of the type that characteristically appear — in non-serializing languages such as English — at the boundaries of finite ('main') verbal clauses, will also appear in serial-verb languages at serial-verb clause boundaries.

4. METHODOLOGY

4.1. Languages

In attempting to resolve these issues empirically, a comparative, text-based distributional study was conducted on a sample of both serializing and non-serializing languages, involving a number of speakers from each language. For the initial study, 4 Papuan languages in Papua-New Guinea were chosen. Two — Kalam, Alamblak — have been reported to have a high and a fair degree of verb serialization, respectively. For two others — Tairora and Chuave — no verb serialization had been previously reported. These four are all strict SOV languages in which serial-verb constructions *precede* the main/finite verb. The fifth language, Tok Pisin (Neo-Melanesian Pidgin), has been shown to have only few — albeit conspicuous — serial-verb constructions. In a sense Tok Pisin thus constitutes a base-line for the phenomenon, but within the same cultural basin. In addition, Tok Pisin is an SVO language in which serial-verb constructions *follow* the main/finite verb.

4.2. Text elicitation

4.2.1. The 'chicken story' movie

A 6.25 minute long video movie was prepared, telling the story of a man and a woman in a rural non-Western setting. The actors were black Africans speaking Swahili. Clothing, demeanor and activities were designed in consultation with two experienced New Guinea anthropologists.[4] The following is a short synopsis of the story:

A man walks toward a tree, leans his farming implements on it and goes on to chop wood with an axe. A woman appears and walks to him. After some conversation she takes the wood, moves aside and collects some more wood, then carries it all away. The man quits his chopping, collects his tools and walks off toward a grove. The scene shifts to the woman coming around a small shed. She unloads her wood, lights a fire, fetches water from a barrel and sets a pot of water to boil. She disappears behind the shed and comes back carrying a chicken. She tries to slaughter it with a knife but clumsily bungles the job and the chicken escapes. After some perfunctory chasing, the woman goes back to the house, brings out some bread and cheese, makes a sandwich, wraps it up and leaves with it. The scene shifts to the man working the field. The woman arrives and offers him the package. They sit down, the man unwraps the food, rejects it, throws it back at the woman, then chases her around the tree with his hoe.

The movie was designed to present many simple transitive activities, with characteristic agents using conventional instruments, manipulating prototypical patients, and moving to and from natural locations. The choice was designed to maximize the opportunity for using the most common serial-verb constructions.

4.2.2. Elicitation procedures and speakers

Following loosely the methodology of Chafe (1980), the movie was shown, using portable battery-run video equipment, to 4–8 speakers of each of the five languages. They were instructed, in their native language, to watch the movie once, then during the second presentation to describe orally exactly what they were seeing. From each speaker we obtained two types of description of what they saw: (i) During the presentation ('on-line'); and (ii) after the presentation ('post-viewing'). The somewhat artificial nature of the 'on-line' text is of course acknowledged. However, it tends to maximize the amount of pauses in running text, given the relatively slow pace of the action. We reasoned that if any elicitation condition would force pauses upon serial-verb constructions, this condition would. Both descriptions were tape-recorded. The texts elicited from the four most fluent speakers of each language were subjected to further analysis. Whenever possible, a gender-balanced sample was chosen.[5]

4.3. Transcription of texts

The collected texts (two texts per four speakers per language) were transcribed, translated and double-glossed, by a cooperative effort of literate native speakers and linguists fluent in the respective languages.[6] In one case (Tok Pisin) the transcription and translation was done partly by a non-native.[7] The output transcripts for each language give the verbatim text, the morph-by-morph gloss, and a free English translation.

4.4. Phonetic processing of tapes

The recorded tapes of all the analyzed texts were subjected to sound-wave extraction, performed at the Phonology Laboratory, Linguistics Dept., UC Berkeley.[8] The continuous sound-wave record of the various texts was plotted on paper (at 10 mm per second). The paper-plotted record discriminates well between periods of phonation and silence.

4.5. Pause measurement

All pauses exceeding 100 milliseconds were measured and marked on the paper-record of the sound-wave. By simultaneously comparing the transcripts, the running tapes and the paper-record of the sound-wave, the pauses were marked in the appropriate place in the transcribed texts. These pause-marked texts constituted the input to the quantitative analysis.

5. RESULTS OF QUANTITATIVE ANALYSIS

5.1. Preamble

In this section the results of our quantitative analysis are presented language by language. Before presenting the tabulated results for each language, a grammatical analysis of verb serialization in the language is given. In this paper we present in detail the results from Tok Pisin, Kalam and Tairora.

5.2. Tok Pisin

5.2.1. Verb serialization in Tok Pisin

Tok Pisin is a strict SVO language in which serial-verb constructions invariably *follow* the main/finite verb. There are only two sub-types verb serialization in Tok Pisin, both involving grammaticalization. The first subtype utilizes the two verbs 'come' and 'go' in *deictic-directional* functions, as in:

(13) *Deictic-directional serial clauses*:

a. ...i-wokabaut *i-go...* (INTRANSITIVE)
PRED-move PRED-go
'...he went *away (from a reference point)...*'

b. ...tromwe *i-go...* (TRANSITIVE)
throw PRED-go
'...(he) threw (it) *away...*'

c. ...i-wokabaut *i-kam...* (INTRANSITIVE)
PRED-move PRED-come
'...she moved *toward (a reference point)...*'

d. ...em karim *i-kam...* (TRANSITIVE)
she carry PRED-come
'...she brings (it) *over (toward a reference point)...*'

The second sub-type involves the use of *stap* ('be') as a *durative* aspect and *pinis* ('finish', without the predicate-marker *i-*) as the *completive* aspect, as in:

(14) *Aspectual verb serialization*:

a. ...em brukim *i-stap*... (DURATIVE)
he break PRED-be
'...he *keeps* break*ing* (it)...'

b. ...em wokim paya *pinis*... (COMPLETIVE)
she make fire *finish*
'...she gets the fire start*ed*...'

Main/finite clauses in Tok Pisin were divided into two types: (i) Those with *zero* conjunction, and (ii) those with an overt conjunction, most commonly *na*, *tasol* or *nau*. To illustrate, respectively:

(15) a. *Zero conjunction*:
...em kisim sospan, wokabaut i-go...
she get saucepan move PRED-go
'...she takes a saucepan, she goes away...'

b. *Overt conjunction*:
...em putim pinis, *na* em kisim tamiok...
he put finish, *and* he get axe
'...he drops it down, *and* he picks up a/the axe...'

The majority of finite/main clauses in our Tok Pisin texts do not differ morphologically from the serial-verb clauses, since they are by-and-large unmarked for tense-aspect (except for the occasional post-posed aspectual-serial constructions, as in (14), above). The presence vs. absence of the predicate-marker *i-* is no structural clue either, since neither in main/finite clauses nor in serial-verb clauses is its presence fully predictable. For the purpose of text measurements, we further divided serial-verb constructions tentatively into three types:

(a) *Simple* ones, either deictic-directional or aspectual, as in (13) and (14) above.

(b) Causative serial-verb constructions, as in:

(16) ...em *lait* nau paya *i-kamap*...
she light now fire PRED-come-up
'...she *gets* the fire *going*...'

(c) Relative-clause constructions, as in:

(17) ... na i-go long hap [we] man blong-en *i-stap*...
and PRED-go to place [where] man GEN-her PRED-be
'...and she goes to where her man is...'

Category (b) above, infrequent in our Tok Pisin texts, is also found in some of the Papuan languages studied. Category (c) is rather infrequent in our texts, and probably should not have been counted as 'serial'.

5.2.2. Quantitative results: Tok Pisin

5.2.2.1. On-line text

a. *Serial verb density*

In the combined on-line text (over all 4 speakers) we counted 98 serial-verb clauses of all sub-types, distributed over 534 main/finite clauses. The ratio of serial verbs over main clauses in these combined texts is thus 98/534 = 0.183. We shall refer to this ratio as the SV-density index. (For the combined post-view texts index was 62/371 = 0.167) This is clearly a low value, less than one serial construction per five main/finite clauses. It corroborates our decision to use Tok Pisin as the base-line of the verb serialization scale.

b. *Pause distribution*

In Table 1, below, we present the overall distribution of pauses associated with the three *non-serial* categories:

(i) Mid-clause pauses following lexical items;
(ii) Pauses following main/finite clauses with zero conjunction;
(iii) Pauses following main/finite clauses with overt conjunction.

In Table 2, below, we present the overall distribution of pauses associated with serial-verb constructions in the on-line text:

For comparing the frequency of pauses associated with (i.e 'following') serial-verb construction with some expected base-line, the ratio of the mid-

Table 1 *Overall distribution of pauses associated with non-serial categories; Tok Pisin, on-line*

Pause size	Mid-clause		Inter clause			
			Ø-conjunction		overt conjunction	
	N	%	N	%	N	%
0.1>	NA	NA	32	12.5	90	32.3
0.1–0.4	98	60.4	53	20.7	52	18.7
0.5–0.7	40	24.6	67	26.1	47	16.9
0.8–1.0	16	9.8	38	14.8	33	11.8
1.1–1.5	5	3.0	30	11.7	24	8.6
1.6–<	3	1.8	83	32.4	33	11.8
total:	162	100.0	256	100.0	278	100.0

Table 2 *Distribution of pauses preceding serial-verb constructions; Tok Pisin, on-line*

Speaker	Simple	Causative	Relative	Total	preceded by pause
I	23	3	/	26	0
II	13	4	7	24	0
III	18	1	1	20	0
IV	28	/	/	28	2 (.3 , .4)
total:	82	8	8	98	2

clause lexical pauses (following nouns, adjectives or adverbs) was computed as a fraction of the total number of the main/finite clauses. There are some problems associated with this choice, and possible correction factors that may bring it into range are discussed further below. Nonetheless, this ratio serves as some base-line for comparison. For our on-line Tok Pisin text, this ratio is 162/534 = 30.3%. That is, there is a 30.0% probability that a main/finite clause will display a mid-clause lexical pause.

In Table 3, below, we plot the probability of a pause occurring with all categories:

Table 3 *Probability of pauses in all the categories; Tok Pisin, on-line*

serial-verb clause	mid-clause post-lexical	finite/main clause overt conjunction	finite/main clause zero conjunction
2/98 = 2.0%	162/534 = 30.0%	188/278 = 67.6%	224/256 = 87.5%

Given that the duration of the conjunctions *na*, *tasol* and *nau* is 0.2, 0.3 and 0.3 seconds on the average, respectively, one should consider that category as actually displaying 100% pause probability. The results display vividly the order-of-magnitude difference between serial and main/finite clauses in Tok Pisin. Further, the probability of a serial construction being separated by a pause from its main clause is much lower than the probability of a normal lexical pause occurring at mid-clause positions.

If pause probabilities are any indication of cognitive packaging, serial-verb constructions in the on-line Tok Pisin texts behave as if they are either *co-lexicalized* or *co-grammaticalized* with the main verbal clause. One way or another, they are *tightly-packaged* into the main/finite clause.

c. *Adjacency and the potential for co-lexicalization or co-grammaticalization*

To assess the potential for co-lexicalization or co-grammaticalization of serial-verb clauses, we counted the frequency of serial verbs directly following the main/finite verb in the clause. The results, for our on-line text, are given in Table 4, below.

Table 4 *Probability of a serial verb directly following a main verb; Tok Pisin, on-line*

Speaker I:	19/24 = 79.1%
Speaker II:	13/24 = 54.5%
Speaker III:	14/20 = 70.0%
Speaker IV:	23/28 = 82.1%
total:	69/96 = 71.8%

The significance of the absolute values here is to some extent tainted by the following consideration: The bulk of the serial-verbs in transitive clauses (see (13b,d), above) have the direct object intervening between them and the main verb. And just about 100% of serial-verbs in intransitive clauses (see (13a,c), above) directly follow the main verb. Thus:

(18) a. ...i-*wokabaut i-go*... (INTRANSITIVE, ADJACENT)
PRED-move PRED-go
'...she goes away...'

b. ...em *layt* nau paya *i-kamap*... (TRANSITIVE,)
she light now fire PRED-come-up NON-ADJACENT)
'...she lights the fire up...'

As we shall see further below, in Kalam, an SOV language, serial-verbs display a much higher frequency of adjacency to another verb stem — thus a higher potential for co-lexicalization or co-grammaticalization.

5.2.2.2. Post-view text

a. *Serial verb density*

For the combined post-view texts (over 4 speakers), the ratio of serial-verbs per main/finite clauses was: 62/371 = 0.167. This falls closely within the range of the on-line text.

b. *Pause distribution*

In Table 5, below, the pause distributions for non-serial categories in the post-view Tok Pisin texts are given.

Table 5 *Overall distribution of pauses associated with non-serial categories; Tok Pisin, post-view*

Pause size	Mid-clause		Inter-clause			
			∅-conjunction		overt conjunction	
	N	%	N	%	N	%
0.1 >	NA	NA	49	29.0	83	41.1
0.1–0.4	70	62.5	44	26.0	36	17.8
0.5–0.7	16	14.3	39	23.0	49	24.2
0.8–1.0	11	9.8	20	11.8	13	6.4
1.1–1.5	11	9.8	14	8.3	14	6.9
1.6-<	4	3.5	3	1.8	2	0.9
total:	112	100.0	169	100.0	202	100.0

In Table 6, below, the distribution of pauses associated with serial-verb constructions in the post-view text is given.

Table 6 *Distribution of pauses preceding serial-verb constructions; Tok Pisin, post-view*

Speaker	Simple	Causative	Relative	Total	preceded by pause
I	14	1	/	15	1 (.2)
II	11	/	1	12	0
III	22	/	1	23	0
IV	12	/	/	12	3 (.1,.2,.4)
total:	59	1	2	62	4

In Table 7, below, we give the probability of pauses being associated with the various categories in the post-view text.

Table 7 *Probability of a pause associated with all categories; Tok Pisin, post-view*

serial-verb clause	mid-clause post-lexical	finite/main clause overt conjunction	finite/main clause zero conjunction
4/62=6.4%	112/371=30.1%	119/202=58.9%	120/169=71.0%

With minor variation in the absolute values, the results closely follow those seen for the on-line text of Tok Pisin.

c. *Adjacency and potential for co-lexicalization or co-grammaticalization*

In Table 8, below, we give the probabilities of a serial verb being adjacent to (i.e. directly following) a main verb.

Table 8 *Probability of a serial-verb directly following a main verb; Tok Pisin, post-view*

Speaker I:	9/14=64.3%
Speaker II:	4/12=33.3%
Speaker III:	9/23=39.1%
Speaker IV:	10/12=83.3%
total:	32/61=52.4%

Again, the wide variation in ratios across speakers is attributable to the percentage of transitive constructions involved (see discussion above).

5.3. Kalam

5.3.1. Verb serialization in Kalam

Kalam is a rigid OV, clause-chaining language, typical of the bulk of Papuan Highlands languages. Serial-verb clauses always *precede* the main verb within the main/finite clause. The clause-chaining system further divides Kalam main clauses into three major types, according to various morpho-syntactic criteria:

a. 'Fully finite' chain-final clauses, with tense-aspect, mood and subject agreement marking and no switch-reference morphology
b. 'Medium-finite' different-subject (DS or 'switch reference') medial clauses, with tense-aspect, subject agreement and switch-reference marking
c. 'Least finite' same subject (SS or 'non-switching') medial clauses, with no tense-aspect or subject agreement morphology, but with one marked mode (irrealis), and two cataphoric temporal categories (see below).

Both types of medial clauses are further marked for their cataphoric ('anticipatory') temporal relation vis-a-vis the following clause: Either *simultaneous* or *sequential*. Further, the different subject (DS) sequential verb form also marks the anticipated person/number agreement of the subject of the *following* clause. A full description of Kalam morphology may be found in Pawley (1966). The most common categories of main clauses occurring in our texts are:[9]

(19) a. *Final clauses in perfective aspect*:
...bi-nak ak spet ominal dand sand-ip...
man-your DEF spade two carry leave-PERF/3S
'...The man carries away two spades...'

b. *Final clause in durative aspect*:
...mon kamb ak yupiri-sap...
wood heap DEF gather-DUR/3S
'...she's gathering the wood-pile...'

c. *Medial simultaneous-DS (immediate-past), (followed by medial-sequential-SS)*:
...kikaruk am-nak-nin, nuk kimb-iy...
chicken go-IPAST/3S-SIM/DS she leave-SEQ/SS
'...the chicken having gone away, she leaves...'

d. *Medial sequential-DS (remote-past),*
(followed by medial-simultaneous-immediate-past DS):
...ny-ek, nuk dand korip ow-ak-nin...
give-RPAST-SE/DS she carry house come-IPAST/3S-SIM/DS
'...(he) having given it to her, she brings it over to the house...'

e. *Medial sequential-SS:*
...nyaip nyilung ak d-iy, konam tik-iy...
knife small DEF take-SE/SS throat cut-SE/SS
'...she picks a knife and cuts its throat...'

f. *Medial simultaneous-SS:*
...kikaruk gok tangiy-ying a-sp-ay akan...
chicken some walk-SI/SS say-PRES-3PL Q
'...(I wonder if it's) chicken walking and making noise...'

A small fraction of medial-SS clauses in our recorded narratives are *irrealis* clauses, as in:

(20) *...nying mal-ning gi-sap...*
water fill-IRR/SS do-PRES
'...she intends to fill (it with) water...'

Technically speaking, such irrealis-SS clauses should not have been counted as main clauses, since they are embedded complements of a main verb, a category we have excluded across the board (see section 1, above). However, in quite a few cases, only a single verb appears, so that no complementation exists, as in:

(21) ...mindak kind nuk pik-juw-ning...
later back her hit-dislocate-IRR/SS
'...later he aims to dislocate her back...'

For the sake of uniformity, all irrealis-SS clauses were therefore counted as medial-SS clauses.

Two non-serial clause-type was *not* considered main/finite independent clauses. Both are embedded constructions, so that one does not expect them to display the same pause probability as main clauses. The first is *relative clauses*, as in:

(22) *...ki-yon g-ak ak d-iy...*
there-up do-IPAST/3S DEF take-SE/SS
'...he took those that he had already done...'

The second is *complements* of the verb 'say'. They are, characteristically, inflected for first-person-subject agreement, technically thus marked as *direct quote*, as in:

(23) ...'*korip bi-ndon am-jak-sip-yin' ang-ak...*
house there-over go-COMPL-PRES-I say-IPAST/3S
'...(she) wanted to return to the house...'
(lit.: '...(she) said: "I'm returning to the house"...')

Serial verbs in Kalam have been described extensively by Pawley (1966, 1976, 1987). Structurally, we define them here (with one exception, see further below), as verb stems that appear with neither medial nor final verbal morphology. They are thus most typically *bare stems*. One can further sub-divide them into three types:

(a) Lexical
(b) Tense-aspect
(3) Causative-lexical

Type (a) is numerically predominant in our texts. Kalam has only 95 or so lexical verb stems. Many conventional states, processes, events or actions, whose number far outstrip 95, thus require lexical coding by — often long — verb combinations, often with no intervening elements. To illustrate this from our texts, consider:

(24) a. ...***d-am d-am*** *mon kinyin bi-yan ay-sap...*
take-go take-go tree base there-down put-PRES/3S
'...he is carrying and putting (them) at the base of the tree...'

b. ...*tuw band* ***dand*** *sand-ip...*
axe piece carry leave-PERF/3S
'...he carries the axe away...'

c. ...*mon kamb ak* ***d***-ap *ay-ip...*
wood heap DEF take-come put-PERF/3S
'...he brings and puts it (in) the wood-pile...'

d. ...*gok ak tapin* ***timb***-*rik-sap...*
those DEF too chop-cut-PRES/3S
'...he's cutting those (pieces) too...'

e. ...*konay nep* ***timb***-*rik* ***tip***-*pang yok-sap...*
much very chop-cut chop-break throw-PRES/3S
'...he's chopping and cutting and throwing much more...'

f. ...mon ***tip**-pang* ***kom moch*** g-ip...
wood chop-break roll crush do-PERF/3s
'...he cuts, chops rolls and crushes the wood...'

Type (b), found only sparsely in our texts, involves the grammaticalization of verbs as the completive aspect. In our texts, this involves primarily the verb *jak* 'rise', 'arrive', as well as, more infrequently, the verb *d* 'take'. Thus consider:

(25) *...bi-nen ap-jak-sap...*
there-up come-COMPL-PRES/3s
'...he's arriving up there...'

Jak can be still used as a lexical verb, as in:

(26) *...kun ak kosond gunap jak-ip...*
that DEF kunai-grass some rise-PERF/3s
'...some kunai-grass seems to be growing there...'

Type (c) is somewhat aberrant in that it involves the use of more finite medial-verb morphology. Nonetheless, it represents a clear case of stable lexical compounding, quite parallel to the Mandarin Chinese resultative verb compounds (Thompson, 1973). In our Kalam texts, this type occurs with all speakers in exactly the same context: Describing the lighting of a fire or the heating/boiling of water, in both instances using the combination of the transitive verb *(d)-angiy* 'light' in the first clause, and the intransitive *yin* 'burn', 'boil', 'heat up' in the second. Thus consider:

(27) *...mon* ***d**-angiy*-ek *yin-imb*
wood take-light-RPAST/SE/DS/3s burn-PERF/3s
'...she lights the wood...'
(Lit.: '...she lights the wood and it burns...')

Other fixed collocations of this kind are found in our text only sporadically, as in:

(28) *...wong ak* ***yim***-ek *ar-an-jap...*
garden DEF plant-RPAST/3s/DS/3s up-grow-PRES/3s
'...he is planting (his) garden...'
(Lit.: '...he's planting the garden and it grows...')

One must note, finally, that on purely semantic/functional grounds at least some medial-sequential-SS verbs (i.e. with the suffix *-iy*) can be considered 'serial'. Typically, the verb *d* 'take' is involved, probably the most common serial verb in our texts. Thus, the first medial verb clause in the two expressions below may be considered 'serial':

(29) a. ...*tiy-tawel bap* ***d-iy*** *kom-kom g-iy...*
tea-towel piece take-SE/SS wrap-wrap do-SE/SS
'...she takes a tea-towel and wraps it in it...'
'...she wraps it in a tea-towel...'

b. ...*timb-**rik-iy*** *man-man g-iya-k...*
chop-cut-SE/SS like-like do-3PL-RPAST
'...(where) they had cut and chopped wood...'
'...(where) they had chopped the wood...'

Since sometimes it is hard to make decisions about what verbal clauses should be included in this type, and since this type is relatively infrequent in our Kalam transcripts, it was decided to go by structural criteria here, and not count such instances as serial (but rather as medial-SS clauses).

5.3.2. Quantitative results: Kalam

5.3.2.1. On-line text

a. *Serial verb density*

The ratio of serial verbs per main clause in the combined on-line Kalam texts was: 656/711 = 0.911. This is over 5-times the density of serial verbs observed in Tok Pisin, thus clearly marking Kalam as a highly-serializing language.

b. *Pause distribution*

The pause distribution for the non-serial categories in Kalam, for the combined on-line texts, is given in Table 9, below.

The distribution of pauses associated with serial-verb constructions are given in Table 10, below. Only two sub-types were observed: Bare-stem (collapsing the 'lexical' and 'aspectual' types) and causative-lexical. Pauses appeared only with the 'lexical' category. Of the total serial-verb sample of 656, 614 (93.6%) were bare-stem, overwhelmingly 'lexical', and 16 (4.4%) 'causative'.

Table 9 *Overall distribution of pauses associated with non-serial categories; Kalam, on-line*

Pause size	Mid-clause		Inter-clause					
			Medial-SS		Medial-DS		Final	
	N	%	N	%	N	%	N	%
0.1>	NA	NA	121	76.6	19	67.8	98	18.6
0.1–0.4	38	48.7	18	11.4	5	17.8	93	17.7
0.5–0.7	15	19.2	7	4.4	/	/	40	7.6
0.8–1.0	6	7.7	4	2.5	1	3.6	51	9.7
1.1–1.5	8	10.2	4	2.5	1	3.6	77	14.6
1.6–<	11	14.1	4	2.5	2	7.1	168	32.0
total:	78	100.0	158	100.0	28	100.0	525	100.0

The pause distribution in the serial categories in the combined on-line texts in Kalam is given in Table 10, below.

Table 10 *Distribution of pauses following serial-verb constructions; Kalam, on-line*

Pause size	N	%
0.1>	627	95.6
0.1–0.4	18	2.7
0.5–0.7	4	0.6
0.8–1.0	3	0.4
1.1–1.5	3	0.4
1.6–<	1	0.1
total:	656	100.0

In Table 11, below, we give the probability of pauses associated with all categories.

As can be seen, the probability of a pause following a serial-verb clause is the lowest. As in Tok Pisin, it is lower than the probability of mid-clause lexical pauses. The three main-clause type scale according to their degree of 'morphological finiteness': The least-marked medial-SS clauses (predomi-

Table 11 *Probability of pauses in the various categories; Kalam, on-line*

Serial verbs	Mid-clause/ lexical	Medial-SS clauses	Medial-DS clauses	Final clauses
29/656=4.4%	78/711=10.9%	37/158=23.4%	9/28=32.1%	427/525=81.3%

nantly sequential-SS) show the lowest pause probability; the medium-marked medial-DS clauses show a higher pause probability; and the most marked final clauses show a pause probability within the range observed for main clauses in Tok Pisin (87.5% there, 81.3% for Kalam).

c. *Adjacency and potential for co-lexicalization or co-grammaticalization*

The results of this measurement for the Kalam on-line texts are given in Table 12, below. In Kalam we compare in this case serial verbs with the two medial-clause categories. Either of those, given their below-50% pause probability, have a certain potential for directly preceding another verb stem. Further, we considered for this comparison only the tokens of these two categories that were *not* followed by a pause.

Table 12 *Probability of a verb in serial and medial clauses* **not** *being followed by another verb stem; Kalam, on-line*

Serial	No-pause-medial-SS	No-pause-medial-DS
85/656=12.9%	39/132=29.5%	14/26=53.8%

As one can see, only 12.9% of Kalam serial verbs *fail* to be followed by another verb stem. This probability more than doubles for no-pause medial-SS verbs, and exceeds 50% for medial-DS verbs. This gradation, like that of the pause probability, closely follows the scale of 'degree of finiteness'.

d. *Adjacency to a preceding object noun: Another grammaticalization potential*

The 'classical' serial-verb languages of West Africa and S.E. Asia (Matisoff, 1969; Givón, 1975a) show an overwhelming serial-verb type so far not represented in our sample — the *case-marking* type. While not predominant, this type may be in fact present in Kalam, at least potentially. It is limited, at least in our texts, almost exclusively to the use of two verbs *d* 'take' following both accusative and instrumental objects, and *dand* 'carry' following accusative objects.[10] To illustrate these, consider:

(30) a. ...*bin-ak ak spet ominal* ***d**-ap...*
man-DEF DEF spade two take-come
'...the man brings over two spades...'

b. ...*nyaip nyiluk ak* ***di*** *timb-rik-iy...*
knife small DEF take chop-cut-SE/SS
'...she sliced it with the knife...'

c. ...*tuw band ak* ***dand*** *sandi-p...*
axe piece DEF carry leave-PERF/3S
'...he carries the axe away...'

To assess the potential for these two verbs to develop a grammaticalized case-marking usage, we calculated the probability of either direct or instrumental objects being preceded by 'take' or 'carry'. Only non-zero full NPs were considered. The results of this measure are given in Table 13, below.

Table 13 *Probability of an accusative or instrumental object NP being directly followed by the serial verbs 'take' or 'carry'; Kalam, on-line*

Speaker	accusative and instrument NPs directly followed by serial verbs		total accusative and instrument NPs	
	N	%	N	%
I	21	42.0%	50	100.0
II	28	53.8%	52	100.0
III	22	45.9%	48	100.0
IV	18	50.0%	36	100.0
total:	89	47.8%	186	100.0

The probability of the case-role of an accusative or instrumental object being marked by a serial verb ranges around 50%. General considerations suggest that grammaticalization requires a considerably higher frequency.[11]

Another indication that the grammaticalization potential for case-marking is not fully realized in Kalam comes from analyzing the actual cases where accusative or instrumental objects are, or are not, followed by 'take' or 'carry'. Most typically, an object is followed by a serial verb when the concrete meaning of 'take/ carry with the hand' is still quite literal. Examples of this kind are:

(31) a. *...spet ominal* ***dand*** *sand-ip...*
spade two carry leave-PERF/3S
'...he *carries* two spades away...'
'...he *carries* two spades and *leaves...*'

b. *...mon kamb* ***di*** *yok-ip...*
wood bunch *take* throw-PERF/3S...
'...she *throws* the firewood down...'
'...she *takes* the firewood and *throws* it down...'

In contrast, serial verbs typically do *not* follow an object when the sense of 'take/carry with the hand' is not natural, as in:

(32) a. *...nying songi-sap...*
water pour-PRES
'...she's pouring the water
(into the pan, from the bucket)...'

b. *...biyn nuk nup pik-ay-iyn ang-iy...*
woman his her hit-put-EXHORT/I say-SE/SS
'...he aims to hit his wife...'

c. '*...nungumiy hoe ak* ***d-iy*** *wong g-amb...*
husband hoe DEF take-SE/SS garden do-IPAST
'...the husband was working the garden with the hoe...'

Example (32c) is particularly instructive. It appears at the end of a post-view narrative, when the scene had just shifted back to the husband who was in the middle of hoeing. The instrumental 'hoe' is marked by 'take', even though only the consequence of taking — 'hold' — is present. But the accusative 'garden' is unmarked, since it is not under any circumstances hand-held.

Given the much higher potential of both 'take' and 'carry' in Kalam to *co-lexicalize* with the *following* verb, (about 88% adjacency, see table 12, above), their grammaticalization potential as case-role markers is probably — as of yet —unrealized.

5.3.2.2. Post-view text

a. *Serial verb density*

The ratio of serial-verb per main clause in the combined post-view texts in Kalam was 357/321 = 1.112 per clause. This is even higher than in the on-line text (0.911), though the difference is probably not significant.

b. *Pause distribution results*

The pause distribution for non-serial categories in the combined post-view Kalam texts are given in Table 14, below.

Table 14 *Overall distribution of pauses associated with non-serial categories; Kalam, post-view*

Pause size	Mid-clause		Inter-clause					
			Medial-SS		Medial-DS		Final	
	N	%	N	%	N	%	N	%
0.1>	NA	NA	74	51.0	17	39.5	38	28.6
0.1–0.4	15	68.2	38	26.2	15	34.9	44	33.0
0.5–0.7	3	13.6	26	17.9	9	20.9	29	21.0
0.8–1.0	3	13.6	4	2.7	1	2.3	14	10.5
1.1–1.5	1	4.5	2	1.4	1	2.3	4	3.0
1.6–<	/	/	1	0.6	/	/	4	3.0
total:	22	100.0	145	100.0	43	100.0	133	100.0

Of the total of 357 serial-verbs in the post-view text, 11 were of the 'causative' type (3.0%). The rest were overwhelmingly of the 'lexical' type, the only type that allowed any of the 21 observed pauses (5.8%). The pause distribution for the serial-verb constructions (combined) is given in Table 15, below. In Table 16, below, we give the probability of pauses associated with all categories, serial as well as non-serial.

The only discernible change from the on-line results (Table 11, above) is the considerably larger probability of pauses associated with medial clauses, both SS and DS. This again underscores the consistently lower probability of pauses associated with serial-verb clauses.

Table 15 *Distribution of pauses following serial-verb constructions; Kalam, post-view*

Pause size	N	%
0.1>	336	94.1
0.1–0.4	15	4.2
0.5–0.7	3	0.8
0.8–1.0	2	0.5
1.1–1.5	/	/
1.6–<	1	0.2
total:	357	100.0

Table 16 *Probability of pauses in the various categories; Kalam, post-view*

Serial verbs	Mid-clause/ lexical	Medial-SS clauses	Medial-DS clauses	Final clauses
21/357=5.4%	22/321=6.8%	71/145=48.9%	26/43=60.4%	95/133=71.4%

c. *Adjacency and potential for co-lexicalization or co-grammaticalization*

In Table 17, below, we give the results of the adjacency measure for serial, no-pause medial-SS and no-pause medial-DS clauses for the combined post-view Kalam texts. The results virtually duplicate those of the on-line text (Table 12), again marking the serial verbal clause as the most likely candidate for co-lexicalization or co-grammaticalization.

d. *Adjacency to a preceding noun: Another grammaticalization potential*

In Table 18, below, we list the results of this measure for the post-view Kalam texts.

Table 17 *Probability of a verb in a serial or medial clause* **not** *being followed by another verb stem; Kalam, post-view*

Serial	No-pause medial-SS	No-pause medial-DS
52/357=14.5%	23/74=31.0%	13/17=76.4%

Table 18 *Probability of an accusative or instrumental object NP being directly followed by the serial verb 'take' or 'carry'; Kalam, post-view*

Speaker	Accusative and instrument NPs directly followed by serial verb		Total accusative and instrument NPs	
	N	%	N	
I	12	52.1%	23	100.0
II	11	47.8%	23	100.0
III	15	60.0%	25	100.0
IV	20	54.0%	37	100.0
Total	58	53.7%	108	100.0

The results fall closely within the roughly-50% range observed for the on-line text, above.

5.4. Tairora

5.4.1. Verb serialization in Tairora

Tairora is a clause-chaining SOV language of the Gorokan group, Trans-Highlands phylum. The available descriptions are confined to verbal and nominal morphology (Vincent, 1973a, 1973b) and make no mention of verb serialization. Still, serial-verb constructions turn out copiously in our Tairora texts, though not at the same high density observed in Kalam. The clause-chaining system of Tairora involves no rigid morphological separation between chain-medial and chain-final clauses. Rather, main clauses are divided as follows:

(a) *Tense-marked ('finite') clauses*:
with full tense-aspect marking & subject agreement; further sub-divided into:
   (i) *DS-marked*: Cataphoric subject-switching clauses
   (ii) *Non-DS-marked*

(b) *Non tense-marked ('non-finite') clauses*:
with only (3rd person) subject pronominal agreement, tacitly interpreted then as *cataphoric-SS* marking

In the 3rd sg. pronoun/agreement predominant in our text, the same suffix *-ro*, is thus used in a double function. If the clause is non-finite (b), *-ro* simply marks 3rd person subject agreement, and tacitly also cataphoric-SS. This may be seen in the main verbs in (33), (34) and (35) below. However, if the clause is highly-finite, thus marked for tense-aspect and its own subject agreement, *-ro* then marks *switch subject — cataphoric-DS* — to 3rd person singular in the *following* clause (see (35) below). Three marked tense-aspects are found in our texts: The irrealis *-re* appears in mostly embedded complements, as in:

(33) *...vainti vi-va* ***naaho kai'a vara-re-va*** *vi-ro...*
man DEM-SUBJ garden work take-IRR-3s go-3s/ss
'...the man goes *to work his garden...*'

Together with another complement type (following 'say' verbs) these irrealis clauses are counted as neither main nor serial clauses. An example of the second type is:

(34) ...*"**Te iha te'a-ke vata-uro**" ti-ro...*
I wood cut-ASP put-PAST/I say-3s/ss
'..."*I've cut and stacked wood*" he said...'

The second marked tense-aspect found in our Tairora texts is the anterior *-ira*/*-ina*. It is confined obligatorily to embedded background clauses, primarily *relative* clauses, as in:

(35) *...saavori paepae vata-ira vi-vare-ro...*
shovel knife put-ANT/3s go-take-3s/ss
'...he goes back to *where he put the shovel and knife...*'

Again, we count such clauses as neither main nor serial-verb clauses, since they are syntactically embedded. Finally, all finite DS-clauses in our text are marked with the *past-perfective* aspect *-iva* (3rd person singular subject agreement form), as in:

(36) *...v-iva-ro, vainti-vano iha mini ke-ro...*
go-PAST/3S-DS/3s man-SUBJ wood there leave-3s/ss
'...she having left, the man now leaves the wood there...'

We divide the serial-verb constructions in Tairora into three types.

(a) Simple bare-stem
(b) Aspectual
(c) ss-marked serial verbs

Category (a) is the predominant one in our texts, with examples such as:

(37) a. *...ihai* ***utu*** *vare-ro...*
knife pick take-3s/ss
'...she takes the knife...'

b. *...kara vi-ra* ***vara*** *an-ira...*
food DEM-OBJ take come-ANT
'...the food that she had brought (him)...'

c. *...vi-ra* ***vuru*** *ami-ro...*
DEM-OBJ bring give-3s/ss
'...she brought-and-gave it (to him)...'

Category (b) is infrequent, involving the use of the verb *-vai* 'be' as a durative aspect, as in:

(38) *...vi-ra-ma* *iha* vara-***vai***-*ro...*
there-OBJ-EMPH wood take-be-3s/ss
'...there he's taking some wood...'

Category (c), again numerically infrequent, reflects an attempt to assess a phenomenon already observed in the study of Kalam: That some serial-looking verbs are nonetheless marked as 'semi-finite' SS-clauses. We thus recognize a potential gradation between bare-stem and SS-marked serial constructions, and have chosen to assess the behavior of this 'semi-finite' category in Tairora. Bruce (1985) made somewhat similar observation concerning gradation of serial-verb constructions in Alamblak. An example of this category is:

(39) a. *...iha* ***vare-ro*** *maa'a-ini ani-ro...*
wood take-3s/ss home-LOC come-3s/ss
'...she carried the wood home...'

b. *...vi-ra-ma* ***an-ira-nte-ro*** *vara ani-ro...*
DEM-OBJ-EMPH come-ANT-return-3s/ss take come-3s/ss
'...there she's bringing it back...'

In (39a), the combination 'take...come' (='carry to') is used with an SS-marked semi-finite *vare-* 'take'. In (39b) the frozen combination 'come-ANT-return-' is used with that semi-finite morphology, while 'take' is used as bare-stem, in serial combination with 'come'.

5.4.2. Quantitative results: Tairora

5.4.2.1. On-line text

a. *Serial-verb density*

The ratio of serial verbs per main clause for the combined on-line texts in Tairora was 408/596=0.684 per clause. This falls between the Tok Pisin and Kalam values.

b. *Pause distribution results*

In Table 19, below, we present the distribution of pauses associated with the various non-serial categories.

Table 19 *Overall distribution of pauses associated with non-serial categories; Tairora, on-line*

Pause size	Mid-clause		Inter-clause			
			Finite-DS		Finite-SS	
	N	%	N	%	N	%
0.1>	NA	NA	50	64.1	131	25.3
0.1–0.4	28	34.5	11	14.1	46	8.9
0.5–0.7	22	27.1	5	6.4	37	7.1
0.8–1.0	6	7.4	4	5.1	47	9.1
1.1–1.5	14	17.3	2	2.5	85	16.4
1.6<	11	13.6	6	7.7	172	33.2
Total	81	100.0	78	100.0	518	100.0

The pause distribution for the three serial categories is given in Table 20, below.

Table 20 *Distribution of pauses following serial-verb constructions; Tairora, on-line*

Pause size	Serial-verb type					
	Aspectual		Semi-finite-SV		Bare-stem-SV	
	N	%	N	%	N	%
0.1>	51	100.0	73	100.0	279	98.2
0.1–0.4	/	/	/	/	3	1.0
0.5–0.7	/	/	/	/	/	/
0.8–1.0	/	/	/	/	1	0.3
1.1–1.5	/	/	/	/	/	/
1.6–<	/	/	/	/	1	0.3
total:	51	100.0	73	100.0	284	100.0

As can be seen, the 'semi-finite' category, with SS-clause morphology, is just as devoid of pauses as the others. In Table 21, below, we give the pause probabilities computed for all categories in the on-line text.

Table 21 *Probability of pauses in all categories; Tairora, on-line*

Serial clauses	Mid-clause/lexical	Finite-DS clauses	Finite-SS clauses
5/408 = 1.2%	81/596 = 13.6%	28/78 = 35.9%	387/518 = 74.7%

Much as in Tok Pisin and Kalam, the serial-verb category displays the lowest pause probability, followed by mid-clause lexical pauses. The fact that finite-DS clauses show a lower probability of pauses than finite-SS clauses in Tairora at first seems to reverse the trend seen in Kalam. However, in Tairora the finite-SS clauses combine chain-medial and chain-final positions. Thus, the higher pause-probability for this category probably reflects the expected higher pause-probability of chain-final clauses, and thus may be in fact compatible with the Kalam results.

c. *Adjacency and potential for co-lexicalization or co-grammaticalization*

The results of the measure of adjacency to a following verb-stem, for the combined Tairora on-line texts, are given in Table 22, below. The finite-SS and finite-DS main-clause categories include only the tokens that were *not* followed by a pause.

Table 22 *Probability of a verb* **not** *being followed by another verb-stem; Tairora, on-line*

Serial-verb clauses			No-pause finite-SS	No-pause finite-DS
Aspectual	SV-bare	SV-finite		
0/51 = 0.0%	73/284 = 25.7%	11/73 = 5.0%	101/131 = 77.1%	42/50 = 84.0%

The results clearly separate the behavior of serial-verb clauses from that of finite clauses. Further, they also show that the 'semi-finite' serial-verb category, with SS-marking morphology, if anything shows a higher potential for co-lexicalization with another verb than the main ('bare-stem') serial category.

5.4.2.2. Post-view text

a. *Serial-verb density*

The ratio of serial verbs per main clauses in the combined post-view Tairora texts was 264/317 = 0.832.

b. *Pause distribution results*

The results of this measure, for the combined post-view text in Tairora, are given in Table 23, below. The pause-distribution for the three serial-verb categories is given in Table 24, below. The probability of pauses in all categories in the post-view texts in Tairora is given in Table 25, below. The results closely follow the trend seen in the on-line text.

c. *Adjacency and potential for co-lexicalization or co-grammaticalization*

The results of the measure of adjacency to a following verb-stem, for the various categories in the combined post-view text of Tairora, are given in Table 26, below. The results are again rather consistent with those given above for the on-line text in Tairora, again separating the behavior of serial-verb constructions from that of main-finite clauses.

Table 23 *Overall distribution of pauses associated with non-serial categories; Tairora, post-view*

Pause size	Mid-clause		Inter-clause			
			Finite-DS		Finite-SS	
	N	%	N	%	N	%
0.1 >	NA	NA	55	59.8	109	48.4
0.1–0.4	29	65.9	15	16.3	41	18.2
0.5–0.7	5	11.3	13	14.1	35	15.5
0.8–1.0	7	15.9	6	6.5	25	11.1
1.1–1.5	3	6.8	2	2.2	11	4.9
1.6 <	/	/	1	1.1	4	1.8
total:	44	100.0	92	100.0	225	100.0

Table 24 *Overall distribution of pauses associated with serial categories; Tairora, post-view*

Pause size	Serial-verb type					
	Aspectual		Finite		Bare-stem	
	N	%	N	%	N	%
0.1 >	17	100.0	39	92.8	194	86.2
0.1–0.4	/	/	1	2.4	7	3.4
0.5–0.7	/	/	1	2.4	2	0.9
0.8–1.0	/	/	1	2.4	1	0.4
1.1–1.5	/	/	/	/	/	/
1.6 <	/	/	/	/	1	0.4
total:	17	100.0	42	100.0	205	100.0

Table 25 *Probability of pauses in all the categories; Tairora, post-view*

Serial clauses	Mid-clause/lexical	Finite-DS clauses	Finite-SS clauses
14/264 = 5.3%	44/317 = 13.9%	37/92 = 40.2%	116/225 = 51.5%

Table 26 *Probability of a verb in a serial or medial clause* **not** *being followed by another verb stem; Tairora, post-view*

Serial-verb clauses			No-pause finite-SS	No-pause finite-DS
Aspectual	SV-bare	SV-finite		
0/17=0.0%	49/205=23.9%	8/42=19.0%	71/120=59.1%	45/57=78.9%

6. OVERALL COMPARISON

In this section we compare the quantitative results for Tok Pisin, Kalam and Tairora.

6.1. Serial-verb density

Tok Pisin and Kalam represent the two extremes of our 5-language study, with Tok Pisin presenting the lowest density of serial verbs per verbal clause, and Kalam the highest. Tairora represents a mid-point between the two. The results of this comparison are summarized in Table 27, below.

Table 27 *Average number of serial verbs per verbal clause: Three-language comparison*

	Text type	
	on-line	post-view
Tok Pisin	0.183	0.167
Tairora	0.684	0.832
Kalam	0.911	1.112

6.2. Pause distribution

The three languages compared here, with serial-verb 'density' varying from around 0.1 per main clause (Tok Pisin) to around 1.0 per main clause (Kalam), are amazingly consistent in showing the same sharp order-of-magnitude differences between pause probabilities associated with main/finite clauses and those associated with serial-verb constructions. The 3-language comparison, for both on-line and post-view texts, is given in Table 28, below.

Table 28 *Pause probability in various clause-types: Cross-language comparison*

Language/ text	Pause probability		
	Serial verb clauses	Mid-clause lexical	Range for various main-clause types
Tok Pisin			
on-line	2.0%	30.0%	67.6–87.5%
post-view	6.4%	30.1%	58.9–71.0%
Tairora			
on-line	1.2%	13.6%	35.9–74.7%
post-view	5.3%	13.9%	40.2–51.5%
Kalam			
on-line	4.4%	10.9%	23.4–32.1–81.3%
post-view	5.4%	6.8%	48.9–60.4–71.4%

While the absolute values vary from language to language, the scalar relation remains amazingly consistent. Serial-verb constructions have pause probabilities in the range of 1-6%, while finite clauses have pause probabilities in the range of 20–80%. Further, the most frequent main-finite clause-type in all three languages is the one displaying the *highest* values, at the range of 50–90% pause probability. The main-clause types with lower pause probability in Tairora and Kalam in fact represent an *intermediate* point on the scale of 'finiteness' or 'independence' of clauses. In Tok Pisin, the main-clause type with the lower pause-probability is the one displaying an overt conjunction — which itself counts as a *temporal gap*. This clause-type thus displays 100% pause-probability.

Why are the pause-probabilities of serial-verb constructions consistently lower than random mid-clause lexical pauses? One can think of two alternative explanations. First, the difference may be due to the different base-levels chosen for the computation. For serial-verbs, we computed the percent of pauses out of the total sample of *serial-verbs*. For mid-clause lexical pauses, we computed the percent of pauses out of the total sample of *finite clauses*. If one assumes that on the average a main clause in connected discourse has 2–4 non-verbal lexical words (nouns, adjectives, adverbs), a correction factor of 2–4 may be applied to the average values of the mid-clause lexical pause category. Such a correction will bring the pause probability of this category — newly expressed now as *mid-clause pauses per non-verbal lexical words* — roughly into line with serial-verb pause probability.

An alternative explanation may be that serial verb stems, in Kalam as elsewhere, tend to be either co-lexicalized or grammaticalized. As such, they have presumably become *part of a larger word.* Pauses associated with serial verb stems would thus be mid-word pauses, whose probability is bound to be much lower than that of between-word pauses.

In sum then:

(i) The probability of serial-verb constructions showing a pause is much lower, by a clear order of magnitude, from the pause probability associated with typical main clauses; and
(ii) The pause probability of serial-verb constructions falls within the probability range of mid-clause pauses associated with lexical words, or is even lower, i.e. falling within the range of the probability of mid-word pauses between grammatical morphemes.

6.3. The effect of the on-line text-elicitation technique on pause distribution

One may recall that we proposed to employ the on-line elicitation technique in order to maximize the potential for pauses. If one examines again Table 28, above, our expectations in this regard seem to have been borne out — but only for one conspicuous category: main/finite clauses. In order to foreground this aspect of the results, we re-cast the data of the pause-probabilities (Table 28, above) in Table 29, below, using as the most representative category of finite/main clauses, the most frequent — and morphologically most finite — clause type.

The trends evident in these results may be summarized as follows:

(a) The probability of pauses associated with main/finite clauses indeed *increases* when the less-than-natural text-elicitation technique of on-line narration is used.
(b) This contrasts sharply with the virtual insensitivity of mid-clause lexical pauses to the effect of on-line elicitation.
(c) It contrasts even more sharply with the apparent (though probably not significant) *decrease* in pause probability for serial-verb constructions under the on-line condition.

Table 29 *The effect of the on-line text elicitation on percent of pauses in the three main categories*

Language	Pause probability					
	Serial-verb clause		Mid-clause/ lexical		Most common main clause	
Language	post-view	on-line	post-view	on-line	post-view	on-line
Tok Pisin	6.4%	2.0%	30.0%	30.1%	71.0%	87.5%
Tairora	5.3%	1.2%	13.9%	13.0%	51.5%	74.7%
Kalam	5.4%	4.4%	6.8%	10.9%	71.4%	81.3%

Once again, sharp difference are observed between the temporal packaging behavior of serial-verb constructions as compared with that of main/finite verbal clauses.

6.4. Adjacency to another verb-stem and the potential for co-lexicalization or co-grammaticalization

In Table 30, below, we present the cross-language comparison of this measure, in terms of the probability of a serial or medial-clause verb being adjacent to another verb stem.

Table 30 *Probability of adjacency of verbs to other verb stem: Cross-language comparison*

Language/ text	Serial verb clauses	Mid-clause lexical	No-pause main-clause type
Tok Pisin			
on-line	71.8%	/	/
post-view	52.4%	/	/
Tairora			
on-line	79.5%	32.9%	16.0%
post-view	77.6%	40.9%	17.1%
Kalam			
on-line	87.1%	71.5%	46.2%
post-view	85.5%	69.0%	24.6%

The results suggest that in both Kalam and Tairora, both of which have a much higher serial-verb density than Tok Pisin, the potential is very high for serial verb stems to either co-lexicalize with other verb stems and yield complex lexical verbs (the most frequent option), or to co-grammaticalize (as tense-aspect markers; a much less frequent option). The adjacency probabilities, and thus the potential for co-lexicalization or co-grammaticalization, are lower for non-serial chain-medial verbs with SS (same subject) morphology, and lowest for medial verbs with DS (different subject) morphology.

One emphasizes, as Pawley (in personal communication) does, that high adjacency probability is only one — necessary but not sufficient — factor contributing to the potential for co-lexicalization or co-grammaticalization. The other, equally necessary, factor is the frequency of *specific recurrent combinations* (‘*collocations*’). Quantitative data on this are not yet available for our sample. What is more, the texts elicited in this research depict such a restricted domain of experience, that one would hesitate to consider the frequency distribution of specific collocations in them as indicative of their overall frequency in the speakers’ verbal-cognitive behavior.

6.5. Adjacency to object or instrument nouns: Potential for grammaticalization as case-markers

In the one language we took this measure, Kalam, we found that accusative and/or instrumental objects have the probability of *47.8%* (in the on-line text) and *53.7%* (in the post-view text) of being followed by either ‘take’ or ‘carry’.

This probability, while quite high, in our view falls considerably below the frequency range where a potential for grammaticalizing serial verbs as the accusative or instrumental case-markers may be viable. This contrasts sharply with *85–87%* adjacency to another verb in Kalam, or even the *77–79%* adjacency to another verb in Tairora. Both of the latter probabilities approach the range of near-categoriality that makes co-lexicalization (or co-grammaticalization) a viable potential.

Finally, since only a small portion of our serial-verb samples in either Tairora (durative) or Kalam (completive) involve grammaticalization as tense-aspect, one may tentatively conclude that the bulk of serial-verbs in those two languages are either co-lexicalized with other verb-stems, or at the very least exhibit a strong potential for such co-lexicalization. This potential is apparent from two factors measured in our study:

(a) The systematic lack of clause-final pause that tends to characterize finite lexical verbs in text; and
(b) The very high frequency of serial verbs being adjacent, in text, to other verb stems.

To the extent that such adjacent verb stems are indeed co-lexicalized, they jointly code *stereotyped chunks of experience* for which the verbal lexicon does not contain the appropriate single verbal stem.

7. SOME TENTATIVE CONCLUSIONS

7.1. Empirical methodology

The languages we report on here differ widely in the density of verb-serialization: From the 0.1–0.2 ratio of serial-verbs per main clause in Tok Pisin, to the 0.9–1.2 ratio in Kalam. Serialization type is also rather different. In Tok Pisin it is predominantly grammaticalized. In Kalam and Tairora it is primarily lexical. These languages also represent a considerable typological cleavage: Tok Pisin is an SVO language, with no clause-chaining, and post-verbal serial constructions. Kalam and Tairora are OV languages, with clause-chaining, and pre-verbal serial clauses. Given such diversity, our results are rather consistent. One may conclude, tentatively, that our methodology at the very least produces consistent results. The temporal packaging of serial-verb constructions in the languages studied here contrasts sharply with the packaging accorded main/finite verbal clauses.

Another important feature of our methodology is that it is non-circular, relying on neither grammar nor intuitive free translation to infer cognition. The iconic correlation between temporal packaging and cognitive packaging is widely documented in both experimental psychology and linguistics.

To the extent that one accepts this, our results constitute grounds for rejecting tentatively at least an extreme, perhaps straw-man, version of Pawley's (1980; 1987) implicit hypothesis. Serial-verb constructions in Kalam (as in Tok Pisin and Tairora) display pause probabilities that fall within or below the range characteristic of pauses associated with lexical words *within the clause*. These pause probabilities diverge dramatically from those characteristic of inter-clausal transition. The fact that events coded in English by single-verb clauses are coded in a language like Kalam by multi-verb clauses, *by itself*, reflects no deep differences in event cognition.

7.2. Grammar and culture: Typological vs. cognitive variability

Our results suggest, tentatively, that serial verb constructions do not represent a different *cognitive* way of *segmenting reality*. The significance of this grammatical phenomenon is thus *not* primarily *cross-cultural* or *cognitive*, but rather *typological*. It represents the kind of typological variability one finds in most areas of the grammar, where different languages perform roughly-similar speech-processing tasks by slightly different — though often related — structural means. The range of cross-language typological variability in grammar is far from unconstrained. But whatever the range is, it does not necessarily imply a corresponding range of cross-culture cognitive variability.

Does grammar mirror cognition? Paradoxically, yes and no, depending on which feature of grammar one considers. The feature selected by Pawley, that of *lexical verbhood*, turns out to be less cognitively significant as well as less universal. One must note, however, that our study points out to a strong correlation between pause-distribution and another grammatical feature — the *degree of finiteness of verbal clauses*, or *grammatical verbhood*. Consistently, the more finite — or morphologically prototypical —a verb is, the higher is the probability of a pause being associated with its clause. Serial verbs thus reveal themselves, with great cross-language consistency, to be rather non-prototypical verbs. They lack most grammatical trimmings of verbhood; they are not coded as typical verbs, but rather as stripped-down stems. It is thus not lexical verbhood per se, but rather *grammatical verbhood*, that turns out to reflect cognition. And at least in this case, the reflection tends toward the universal rather than the language/culture-specific.

Whether primarily a device for enriching the grammar (as in Tok Pisin), or for enriching a limited verbal lexicon (as in Kalam), verb serialization should be viewed within the context of the typology cross-language *coding variability*, rather than the typology of cross-culture *cognitive diversity*. This does not close the door on the possibility that some grammatical features may turn out to reflect the latter type of diversity. But verb serialization is probably not one of those.

Thus, for example, Slobin (1987) and his associates have recently reported a series of empirical studies that pursued a similar issue.[12] They focused on the converse clause of the Sapir-Whorf hypothesis — not language as a *reflection* of thought, but rather language as a *constraint* on thought:

> ...users of markedly different grammars are pointed by their grammars towards different types of observations and different evaluations of exter-

> nally similar acts of observation, and hence are not equivalent as observers but must arrive at somewhat different views of the world... (Whorf, 1940/1956, p. 221)

Slobin's experimental results suggest that some facets of grammatical organization indeed constrain the way members of different speech communities — i.e. cultures — organize their *thinking for speaking*. What these studies suggest is that cognitive organization *for the purpose of* verbal communication is more language-specific, thus distinct from human-universal cognitive organization. It is more rigidly constrained by the available grammatical categories of the language. Within such a framework, Pawley's original intuitions may indeed find a more natural context.

8. POSSIBLE EXTENSIONS

8.1. Other types of verb serialization

One major type of verb serialization, the *case-marking* type, is almost entirely absent in our sample of Papua-New Guinea languages. This is the type that provoked the original controversy about the status of serial-verb constructions in the early 1970s. The areal distribution of this type is both wide and significant: A vast expanse of the Niger-Congo family in West Africa (Stahlke, 1970; Hyman, 1971; Awobuluyi, 1971; 1973; Lord, 1973; Bambose, 1974; Schachter, 1974; Givón, 1975a); a vast area of South-East Asia, including Chinese (Li and Thompson, 1973; 1974), Mon Khmer, Austro-Tai and Tibeto-Burman (Matisoff, 1973; Goral, 1980) languages; a wide area of Austronesian (Schütz, 1969; Bradshaw, 1982; Durie, 1982; Crowley, 1987; Foley and Olson, 1985); sporadic reports in the Caribbean Creoles (Huttar, 1981). It would be useful to be able to extend our methodology to representative languages of this major serial-verb type.

8.2. The clause-type continuum

As noted above, there exists in Papuan languages, a clear continuum of clause-types, graded by *degree of finiteness*. In terms of temporal packaging, serial-verb clauses, on the one hand, and prototypical main/finite clauses, on the other, behave as two extreme points on this scale: The former as *co-lexical stems* (or grammatical morphemes) within a clause; the latter as full-fledged *independent clauses*. However, chain-medial verbs exhibit pause probabilities and adjacency probability somewhere between the two extreme poles. This scalarity resurrects, in a better empirical context, the early suggestions made by Ross (1972, 1973; see also Givón, 1980) concerning the continuum of finiteness (or 'noununiness') of verbal clauses. The methodology developed in this study has turned out to be rather sensitive to such gradations. It may be easily extended to probe the temporal packaging behavior of other dependent clauses:

(a) various types of adverbial clauses
(b) verb complements
(c) various types of conjunction
(d) restrictive vs. non-restrictive REL-clauses

Continuum phenomena of one type or another have been noted in most of these clause-types (Givón, 1980a for verb complements; Givón, 1980b for conjoined clauses). The extension of our methodology to these new areas will yield better understanding of the nature of inter-clausal relations and the grammatical sub-systems that code it cross-linguistically.

8.3. Gradual vs. instantaneous grammaticalization

Our pause-distribution and stem-adjacency measurements lend themselves also to the study of another well-known continuum, that of *grammaticalization*. Several earlier studies of verb serialization (Hyman, 1971; Lord, 1973; Givón, 1975a) suggested that grammaticalization was a *gradual* process. That is, for example, that serial-verb constructions developed gradually from independent, finite verbal clauses, through various stages of reduced finiteness toward eventual full grammaticalization.

But there are reasons to suggesting the exact opposite perspective: That *cognitively*, grammaticalization is not a gradual process, but rather an *instantaneous* one. It involves the mental act of the mind *recognizing a similarity relation* and thereby exploiting it, putting an erstwhile lexical item into grammatical use in a novel context. The minute a lexical item is used in a frame that *intends it as grammatical marker*, it is thereby grammaticalized.

Taking this second perspective, one must distinguish rigorously between the two aspects of grammaticalization:

(a) functional analogical extension (semantics, pragmatics)
(b) structural code adjustment (phonology, morpho-syntax)

In diachronic change, as has been widely suggested, structural adjustment tends to lag behind creative-elaborative functional reanalysis (Givón, 1971; 1975a; 1979; ch. 6; Lord, 1973; Heine and Reh, 1984; Heine and Claudi, 1986). The studies purporting to show the gradual nature of grammaticalization have, in all likelihood, reported on the protracted structural adjustment at the code level, adjustments that follow — sometime long after — the original developments at the *functional level.*

This view, of instantaneous grammaticalization at the functional level and gradual adjustment at the structural level, is somewhat divergent from that presented in Bybee et al. (Volume II), where it is suggested that '...formal and semantic reduction proceed in parallel...' If 'in parallel' means 'at the same gradual pace', the two positions are indeed rather different.

Until very recently, this type of argument could have only proceeded in an empirical vacuum. The methodology employed in this study can be easily adapted to pursue this issue in a more meaningful way. Temporal-intonational packaging is the oldest, most subtle, most iconic and most ubiquitous element in syntactic structure. It takes place almost automatically and is extremely sensitive to the cognitive dimensions of information processing and chunking. Our quantified methodology can probably detect the early, functional, onset of grammaticalization long before its more conventionalized structural correlates come on line.

ACKNOWLEDGEMENTS

* The research reported here was supported in part by a grant from the National Endowment for the Humanities (1985–87; 1988–1990; 'Serial verbs and the mental reality of "event"'); in part by a grant from the John Simon Guggenheim Foundation (1986; 'The Pragmatics of Human Language'); in part by a Fullbright lectureship (1986; 'The American Indian: Past and present'); and in part by a grant from the Deutsche Forschungsgemeinschaft (1987; 'Lectures on Pragmatics'). The National Science Foundation has rather consistently declined to support this research. I am also indebted to the SIL organization in Ukarumpa, Papua-New Guinea for much help and encouragement during my stay in Papua-New Guinea.

For the original inspiration for this project, for much continuous help and many helpful comments, I am indebted to my good friend Andy Pawley. Helpful comments on earlier presentations were also made by the faculty and students of the Anthropology Department, Auckland University; the Linguistics Department, Australian National University; the Institut für Afrikanistik, Universität zu Köln; the Linguistics Colloquium, University of Oregon; participants in the

Third Pacific Linguistics Conference, University of Oregon, 1987; and participants in the Symposium on Grammaticalization, Eugene, Oregon, May 1988.

NOTES

1. While it is easy to document the position of extreme universalists, such as Chomsky or Katz, extreme relativists of the Whorfian mold are harder to pin down. The only one I am aware of who makes no apology for his bold convictions is my friend Pete Becker. The extreme relativist position I describe here may thus be somewhat of a straw-man.
2. Pawley (in personal communication) has objected to my interpretation of his position. The reader may wish to judge for her/himself.
3. See *The Categories* and *De Interpretatione*, in Ackrill (tr. and ed., 1963). For Aristotle, thoughts ('affectations of the soul') coded real-world states or events, and propositions ('words') in turn coded thoughts. Most of us nowadays, certainly including Grace and Pawley, feel safer in allowing that propositions code *mental representations* of states or events, whose exact isomorphic matching with some presumed 'reality' remains to be determined.
4. With special thanks to Edward and Bambi Schieffelin.
5. Speakers that produced steadier verbal descriptions and spoke louder were preferred. Women under those settings tended sometimes to speak too softly or produce less verbal description. Only in one case (Alamblak) did this necessitate using 3 men and only 1 woman in the sample.
6. Acknowledging here the generous help and hospitality of Lyle and Helen Scholz (Kalam), Alex and Lois Vincent (Tairora), Pat and Melenda Edmiston (Alamblak) and Robin and Ruth Thurman (Chuave). The Kalam transcripts were also inspected and corrected by Andy Pawley, to whom special thanks are due for comments, suggestions and encouragement.
7. Acknowledging here the generous help of Linda Cruz Givón. By definition, the Pidgin speakers were not native. Three of them spoke Tok Pisin since childhood (Two women from the Sepik region; one man from Morobe province). One man (from an off-shore island in Milne Bay province) learned the Pidgin as adult in the Highlands. All four speakers were recorded at Ukarumpa, Eastern Highlands province. All were tri-lingual (English, Pidgin and their respective native language).
8. Acknowledging here the generous technical help of John Ohala and Maricela Amador.
9. Lyle Scholz's Kalam writing system (slightly adjusted) is followed here. In this system, the predictable ('epenthetic') vowel [ɨ] is written as /i/, and the high-front vowel [i] as /iy/. The rest of the system is transparent.
10. *dand* may itself be, historically, a composite of *d* 'take' plus **and*, with the latter possibly a verb at some earlier time. This is obviously a speculation. Pawley (in personal communication) suggests that *dand* is not a verb at all, but rather an adverbial meaning 'in the hand, carrying'. This may be synchronically the case. My own feeling is that diachronically it is of verbal origin.
11. Generative grammarians will of course insist on 100%. The study of curves of diachronic

change, i.e. grammaticalization, suggests that somewhere between 75–80% speakers begin to treat the lopsided frequency as a categorial phenomenon. For discussion, see Givón (1985b).

12. See also Berman and Slobin (1987).

REFERENCES

Ackrill, J.L. (ed.). 1963. *Aristotle's Categories and De Interpretatione*. Oxford: Clarendon Press.

Aronson, Doris and Steven Ferres. 1983. "A model for coding lexical categories during reading." *Journal of Experimental Psychology: Human Perception and Performance* 9:700–25.

Awobuluyi, Oladele. 1971. "'Splitting verbs' in Yoruba." *Annales de l'Université d'Abidjan, Série H, Fascicule Hors Série* 1:151–64.

Awobuluyi, Oladele. 1973. "The modifying serial construction: A critique." *Studies in African Linguistics* 4:87–111.

Bamgbose, Ayo. 1974. "On serial verbs and verbal status." *Journal of West African Languages* 9:17–48.

Berman, R. and D. I. Slobin. 1987. "Five ways of learning how to talk about events: Crosslinguistic studies in children narratives." *Berkeley Cognitive Science Report* 46.

Bradshaw, J. 1982. Word Order Change in Papua-New Guinea Austronesian Languages. University of Hawaii at Manoa, Ph.D. dissertation.

Bruce, L. 1985. Serialization: The Interface of Syntax and Lexicon. MS.

Chafe, Wallace L. (ed.). 1980. *The Pear Stories: Cognitive, Cultural, and Linguistic Aspects of Narrative Production*. Norwood, N.J.: Ablex [*Advances in Discourse Processes 3*.].

Chafe, Wallace L. 1987. "Cognitive constraints on information flow." In Tomlin 1987b. 21–51.

Chafe, Wallace L. and Johanna Nichols (eds). 1986. *Evidentiality: The Linguistic Coding of Epistemology*. Norwood, N.J.: Ablex.

Crowley, Terry. 1987. "Serial Verbs in Paamese." *Studies in Language* 11:35–84.

DeLancey, Scott. 1980. Deictic Categories in the Tibeto-Burman Verb. Indiana University, Ph.D. dissertation.

DuBois, John W. 1987. Constraint and Strategy: Transitivity in the Management of Information Flow. University of California, Los Angeles, MS.

Durie, Mark. 1982. Clause Crunching in Oceanic. MS.

Foley, William A. and Mike Olson. 1985. "Clausehood and verb serialization." In Nichols and Woodbury 1985. 17–60.

Fujimura, Osamu (ed.). 1973. *Three Dimensions of Linguistic Theory*. Tokyo: TEC Company.

Givón, T. 1971. "Historical syntax and synchronic morphology: An archaeologist's field trip." In *Papers from the Seventh Regional Meeting of the Chicago Linguistic Society*, 394–415.

Givón, T. 1975a. "Serial verbs and syntactic change: Niger-Congo." In Li 1975. 47–112.

Givón, T. 1975b. "Focus and scope of assertion: Some Bantu evidence." *Studies in African Linguistics* 6:185–205.
Givón, T. 1979. *On Understanding Grammar*. New York/San Francisco/London: Academic Press.
Givón, T. 1980a. "The binding hierarchy and the typology of complements." *Studies in Language* 4:333–77.
Givón, T. 1980b. *Ute Reference Grammar*. Ignacio, Colorado: Ute Press.
Givón, T. 1985a. "Iconicity, isomorphism and non-arbitrary coding in syntax." In Haiman 1985a:187–219.
Givón, T. 1985b. "Function, structure and language acquisition." In Slobin 1985:1005–27.
Goral, D. 1980. Verb Concatenation in South East Asian Languages: A Crosslinguistic Study. University of California, Berkeley, PhD dissertation.
Grace, George. 1983. "The linguistic construction of reality." *Ethnolinguistic Notes* (Honolulu) 3(4).
Haiman, John (ed.). 1985a. *Iconicity in Syntax*. Amsterdam/Philadelphia: John Benjamins [Typological Studies in Language 6].
Haiman, John. 1985b. *Natural Syntax: Iconicity and Erosion*. Cambridge: Cambridge University Press.
Heine, Bernd and Mechthild Reh. 1984. *Grammaticalization and Reanalysis in African Languages*. Hamburg: Helmut Buske.
Heine, Bernd and Ulrike Claudi. 1986. *On the Rise of Grammatical Categories: Some Examples from Maa*. Berlin: Dietrich Reimer.
Huttar, George L. 1981. "Some Kwa-like features of Djuka syntax." *Studies in African Linguistics* 12:291–323.
Hyman, Larry M. 1971. "Consecutivization in Feʔ Feʔ." *Journal of African Languages* 10:29–43.
Just, Marcel A. and Patricia A. Carpenter. 1980. "A Theory of reading: From eye fixation to comprehension." *Psychological Review* 87(4).
Kumpf, Lorraine E. 1987. "The use of pitch phenomena in the structuring of stories." In Tomlin 1987b:189–216.
Leben, William R. (ed.). 1974. *Papers from the Fifth Annual Conference on African Linguistics* [Studies in African Linguistics, Suppl. 5].
Li, Charles N. and Sandra A. Thompson. 1973. "Serial verb constructions in Mandarin Chinese: Subordination or coordination?" In *You Take the High Node and I'll Take the Low Node: Papers from the Comparative Syntax Festival* 96–103. Chicago: Chicago Linguistic Society.
Li, Charles N. and Sandra A. Thompson. 1974. "Co-verbs in Mandarin Chinese: Verbs or prepositions?" *Journal of Chinese Linguistics* 2:257–78.
Li, Charles N. (ed.). 1975. *Word Order and Word Order Change*. Austin/London: University of Texas Press.
Lord, Carol. 1973. "Serial verbs in transition." *Studies in African Linguistics* 4:269–96.
McKaughan, N. (ed). 1973. *The Languages of the Eastern Family of the East New Guinea Highlands Stock* Vol. 1. Seattle: University of Washington Press.
Matisoff, James A. 1969. "Verb concatenation in Lahu: The syntax and semantics of 'simple' juxtaposition." *Acta Linguistica Hafniensia* 12.2: 171–206.
Matisoff, James A. 1973. *A Grammar of Lahu*. University of California, Berkeley: UC Press.

Mithun, Marianne. 1986. "Evidential diachrony in Northern Iroquoian." In Chafe and Nichols 1986.
Nichols, Johanna and Anthony C. Woodbury (eds.). 1985. *Grammar Inside and Outside the Clause*. Cambridge: Cambridge University Press.
Pawley, Andrew. 1966. The Structure of Kalam: A Grammar of A New Guinea Highlands Language. University of Auckland, MS.
Pawley, Andrew. 1976. On Meeting a Language That Defies Description by Ordinary Means. University of Auckland, MS.
Pawley, Andrew. 1987. "Encoding events in Kalam and English: Different logics for reporting experience." In Tomlin 1987b:329–60.
Ross, John Robert. 1972. "The category squish: Endstation hauptwort." In *Papers from the Eighth Regional Meeting of the Chicago Linguistic Society* 316–28. Chicago: Chicago Linguistic Society.
Ross, John Robert. 1973. "Nouniness." In Fujimura 1973:137–257.
Schachter, Paul. 1974. "A non-transformational account of serial verbs." In Leben 1974:253–70.
Schütz, Albert J. 1969. *Nguna Grammar*. Honolulu: University of Hawaii Press [*Oceanic Linguistic Publications 5*].
Slobin, Dan I. (ed.). 1985. *The Crosslinguistic Study of Language Acquisition* Vol. 2: *Theoretical Issues*. Hillsdale/New Jersey/London: Lawrence Erlbaum.
Slobin, D. I. 1987. "Thinking for speaking." In *Berkeley Linguistics Society, Proceedings of the Thirteenth Annual Meeting*, J. Aske, N. Beery and H. Filip (eds), 435–44.
Stahlke, Herbert F.W. 1970. "Serial verbs." *Studies in African Linguistics* 1:60–99.
Talmy, Leonard. 1970. The Semantic Structure of English and Atsugewi. University of California, Berkeley, Ph.D. dissertation.
Thompson, Sandra A. 1973. "Resultative verb compounds in mandarin Chinese: A case for lexical rules." *Language* 49:361–79.
Thompson, Sandra A. and Anthony Mulac. "A quantitative perspective on the grammaticization of epistemic parentheticals in English." Volume II.
Tomlin, Russell S. 1987a. "Linguistic reflections of cognitive events." In Tomlin 1987b:455–79.
Tomlin, Russell S. (ed.). 1987b. *Coherence and Grounding in Discourse: Outcome of a Symposium, Eugene, Oregon, June 1984*. Amsterdam/Philadelphia: John Benjamins [*Typological Studies in Language* 11].
Vincent, A. 1973a. "Tairora verb structure." In McKaughan 1973.
Vincent, A. 1973b. "Notes on the Tairora Noun Morphology." In McKaughan 1973.
Whorf, Benjamin Lee. 1956. Language, thought, and Reality. John B. Carroll, (ed.) Cambridge, Mass.: M.I.T. Press.

Grammaticalization as Retextualization

Johanna Nichols and Alan Timberlake
University of California, Berkeley

1. INTRODUCTION

The study below describes an instance of change in grammar which is *not* grammaticalization in the extensional sense in which the term is commonly used. As we read the recent literature, the term is apparently, by a wide margin of preference, understood to refer to changes in morphemes — a lexical word becomes a grammatical morpheme, or a partially grammatical morpheme becomes more grammatical. While we would not wish to dispute the fact that this occurs, the character of this scenario, both synchronically and diachronically, may be less straightforward and obvious than is usually assumed. Synchronically, the putative end point of this change — the state of grammaticalization — probably cannot be defined. Diachronically, the received notion of grammaticalization appears to make an implicit claim that the natural direction of change is towards ossification, towards idiomatization, towards a kind of semiotic entropy. But this is only half of the story. Change in grammar is a constant trade-off between, on the one hand, the innovation of novel tokens of text that did not exist before and, on the other hand, a constant pressure to regularize, to idiomatize, to conventionalize such innovations.

The change described below is the gradual extension of the use of instrumental case (at the expense of the nominative) in Old Russian with *predicative* nouns, these being nouns that predicate a property of a major argument of the host predicate.[1] The instrumental case is otherwise used for a variety of functions, including to express the instrument or means of an action. Except for trivial sound changes, the morphemes involved have remained stable. The change, then, is not so much a change in morphemes as in syntactic patterns. Further, it is change whose source was quite likely a syntactic idiom which was fully grammaticalized at the outset. Examination of this change leads us to suggest a view of grammatical networks that is not synchronic or diachronic in orientation, which we accordingly term *panchronic*.

On a panchronic view, any grammatical network will have areas that are relatively rigid (in which case usage is syntagmatically predictable) and areas that are less rigid (in which case usage is not syntagmatically predictable, and hence is associated with covert textual values). The relatively fixed areas of a grammatical network are then *exemplars* with characteristic properties; exemplars are pieces, perhaps minimal units, of text. Because a grammar based on exemplars necessarily underspecifies usage, new tokens of text may arise by extrapolating from given examplars. These new tokens of usage can be conventionalized as exemplars (grammaticalized, if you will), setting the stage for more innovations. This dual process of innovation and conventionalization we term *retextualization*.

2. DESCRIPTIVE NOTIONS

To analyze predicatives, we distinguish three semantic levels. The lowest is the *predicative syntagm*, consisting of three parts: the *predicative* itself (we consider only nouns, among other reasons because they develop the predicative instrumental much earlier than adjectives); the *host predicate*, various past-referring forms of the verb 'be' in the following; and the *controller*, the referent of the argument of the host predicate of which the predicative noun is predicated. At the next level, the syntagm is oriented according to the temporal-modal coordinates of the text, a level we call *aspectuality*. The highest level we will call *textuality*, the relationship between the current sentence and the adjacent text.

At each level, one can distinguish three semantic values. The predicative construction itself can *identify* a unique individual, *describe* an individual, or report its *functioning* in a certain capacity. Aspectually, the predicative state can be *continuative* (no end point specified), *inceptive* (initial end point specified), or *durative* (both inception and cancellation specified). Textually, we distinguish between *digressive* (explication or expansion of the current information of the text), *transitional* (sequential narrative of developments), and *culminative* textuality (stating resolutions of sequential developments); other typologies are possible. The levels are not always clearly distinguishable, precisely because there are relations of similarity that hold across the different levels; for example, as we will illustrate shortly, a function predicative (one which states that an individual acts in a certain capacity for a certain interval of time, under certain conditions) is most naturally used with durative aspectuality (which states that in fact the predicative relation began, persisted for an interval of time, and then was cancelled); in turn a durative predicative is naturally used with transitional or culminative textuality (Timberlake, 1989).

3. OLD RUSSIAN PREDICATIVE INSTRUMENTAL

Before describing the earliest attested stage, we should acknowledge the problems that arise in tracing the diachronic development of usage, problems which have not been mitigated by sufficient nose-to-the-grindstone philology. Given that much of the impetus for case selection is covert, textual, and pragmatic, one can never be sure, in attempting to compare usage across time, that the respective speakers were trying to communicate the same message. Additionally, there is the problem that written Russian from earlier periods was inevitably some compromise between the sacral Slavonic language (in its East Slavic variant) and a secular, more indigenous East Slavic (eventually specifically Russian) register, closer to the spoken language. One can never be sure *a priori* whether a given snippet of text is more Slavonic than Russian (or vice versa), or whether it is consistently one or the other in all respects.[2] Hence one can never be sure, in comparing texts across time, that the texts are Russian (or Slavonic) to the same degree. Having conceded that the task of investigating historical semantics of grammatical morphemes is in principle impossible, we proceed to sketch what seems a plausible path of development.

In Old Russian (=OR) chronicles, the earliest stage of attestation, we distinguish three contexts of usage.[3] At this (rather broad) stage, the instrumental is attested rarely: The instrumental appears only with *function* nouns — nouns that report functions, roles, occupations (e.g. *cěsarь* 'tsar; secular leader', *vladyka* '(church)leader', *voevoda* 'commander', *černьсь* 'monk', *černica* 'nun').[4] The instrumental never appears with either *descriptive* nouns — those that describe an individual by a set of properties — or *identificatory* nouns — those that identify a unique individual. (1) illustrates a descriptive (national) noun, and (2) a purely descriptive noun; (3) illustrates both descriptive and identificatory types, and (4) an identificatory predicative.*

(1) *U Jaropъlka že žena grekini* NOM *bě* IF
'The wife of Jaropolk was IMPERF a Greek NOM'

(2) *I bě nesytъ bluda, privodja kъ sobě mužьsky ženy, i děvicě rastьljaja. Bě* IMPERF *bo ženoljubьсь* NOM, *jakože i Solomanъ.*
'And he never tired of sin, inasmuch as he took other men's wives for himself and defiled virgins. For he was IMPERF a philanderer NOM, like Solomon.'

(3) ... *otьcь že bě* IMPERF *ima Malъko* NOM *Ljubьčaninъ, i bě* IMPERF *Dobrynja ui* NOM *Volodimeru*
'... the father of the two was IMPERF Malko Ljubchanin NOM, thus was IMPERF Dobrynja uncle NOM to Volodimer.'

(4) *Bě bo tъgda voda tekušči vъzdъlě gory Kyevьskyja, i na podolii ne sědjaxu ljudie, nъ na gorě; gradъ že bě* IMPERF *Kyevъ* NOM
'For there was water flowing along the Kiev Mountain, and people did not settle in the valley, but on the mountain; that city was IMPERF Kiev NOM.'

Descriptive and identificatory nouns occur exclusively with the imperfect of 'be' with continuative aspectuality, which reports a state that extends in both directions from the temporal-modal reference. Further, this context usually is textually digressive, since it explicates or expands on the current state of information in the text. Examples (1–4) are all of this type.

Function nouns are likewise nominative in this context. Continuative aspectuality is forced by punctual time adverbials that localize the temporal-modal reference. Thus *pereže* 'formerly' in (5) imparts the reading 'there was a certain time, earlier than now, around which the predicative state held'.

(5) *V lěto 6864 prestavisja Ivanъ episkopъ Rostovьskii, čto bylъ* IMPERF *pereže arximandritъ* NOM *u svjatogo Spasa na Moskvě*
'In the year 6864 Bishop Ivan of Rostov died, he who was IMPERF formerly the archimandrite NOM at the Church of the Savior in Moscow.'

The continuative sense of imperfect 'be' can be implicit:

(6) *I rodi Adamъ Kaina i Avelja; i bě* IMPERF *Kainъ ratai* NOM, *a Avelь pastuxъ* NOM
'And Adam sired Cain and Abel. Cain was IMPERF a tiller NOM of the soil and Abel a shepherd NOM.'

Thus, in the first context — imperfect of 'be' with continuative aspectuality — the predicative noun may be either function or non-function, but the nominative is used exclusively.

The next context, maximally distinct from the context just discussed, has two characteristics: the noun must be a function noun, and aspectuality is durative. Accordingly, the predicative state has different values over each of three time intervals: the state begins, persists, and then is cancelled. Examples are (7), (8), and (9).

(7) *A bylъ* PERF *arxiepiskopomъ* INS *Feofilъ do vzjatia Novagrada 6 lět*
'And Feofil was PERF [=had been?] archbishop INSTR six years until Novgorod was seized.'

(8) *A Davidъ bě* IMPERF *vladykoju* INSTR *17 lětъ i prestavisja fevralja 5, i položiša i vъ pritvorě svjatyja Sofěi podlě Klimenta*
'David was IMPERF the leader INSTR for seventeen years and he died on February 5, and they laid him in the portico of Saint Sofia alongside Clement.'

(9) *Prestavisja arxiepiskopъ Novgorodčkij Semeonъ. Bystъ* AOR *vladykoju* INSTR *5 lětъ i 3 měsjaca*
'Archbishop Simon of Novgorod died. He was AOR (church)leader INSTR for five years and three months.'

To compare, in (5) above (continuative context), what is reported is that there was an earlier time at which an individual held a certain function, while in (7–9) (durative contexts) the total span of time over which the individual held an office is specified.

Durative adverbs (and the instrumental of predicative nouns) occur with all three past-tense forms of 'be', probably with somewhat different textuality: (7), with the perfect form, reports one event as transitional to another ('up to the taking of Novgorod'); (8), with imperfect, is transitional; (9), with aorist, summarizes the total experience of the predicative state, and may well be textually digressive. The durative context requires instrumental, independent of the textuality of the predicative sentence. The periphrastic pluperfect can be considered a subcontext of the durative, in which the instrumental is likewise required:

(10) *U Jaropъlka že žena grekini bě, i bjaše* IMPERF *byla* PERF *černiceju* INSTR, *juže bě* IMPERF *privelъ otьcь ego Svjatoslavъ, i vъda ju za Jaropъlka, krasy radi lica eja*
'Jaropolk had a Greek wife, who had been IMPERF(PERF) a nun INTR, whom his father Svjatoslav had brought and he married her to Jaropolk, on account of the beauty of her face.'

A third context, aorist of 'be' in its inceptive sense, is the most interesting because it allows variation. In this context, the nominative is usual, as illustrated in (11), (12), and (13):

(11) *Pri semь bo starьci Feodosii prestavisja, i bystь* AOR *Stefanъ igumenъ* NOM, *i po Stefaně Nikonъ, semu starьcju i ešče suščju. Edinoju emu stojaščju na utrьni, i vidě osьla, stojašča na igumeni městě*
'With this the elder Theodosius died, and it happened that Stefan was AOR [=became?] abbot NOM, and after Stefan, Nikon, which elder is still alive. Once when he was at matins, he saw an ass standing in the place of the abbot.'

(12) *Umьrъšju že Iisusu, bystь* AOR *sudia* NOM *v nego město Ijuda*
'Once Jesus died, in his place Judas was AOR [=became?] the judge NOM.'

(13) *Po Aleksandrě carstvova Maksimijanъ, lět 6; se preže pastyrь* NOM *bě* IMPERF, *i potomъ voinъ* NOM *bystь* AOR, *i potomъ carь* NOM *bě* IMPERF
'After Aleksander reigned Maksim, for six years; he was IMPERF formerly pastor NOM and then was AOR [=became?] a warrior NOM and then he was IMPERF tsar NOM.'

The instrumental, however, is possible, as in (14):

(14) *V lěto 6567. Izjaslavъ i Svjatoslavъ i Vьsevolodъ vysadiša stryja svoego Sudislava knjazja is poruba, sěděvъša lět 20 i 4, zavodivъše i krьstu, i bystь* AOR *čьrnсьmь* INSTR
'In the year 6567, Izjaslav, Svjatoslav, and Vsevolod liberated their uncle Prince Sudislav, who had sat for 4 and 20 years, from prison, converting him to Christianity, and he was AOR [=became] a monk INSTR.'

In this context the selection of case is not syntagmatically conditioned. With either case, the aorist means that the state came into existence at some specific time in the past, so the aspectuality is *inceptive* in all the examples above. The selection of case is correlated with different textualities. In (14) the inception of the predicative state is presented as the culmination of the temporally prior events. In the other examples modal sequencing (causality, resultativity) is absent or downplayed. In (11), the inception of abbot-hood for Stefan is an accidental fact reported as a transition between the stories of Theodosius and Nikon, who (as monks who saw visions) are central to the narrative of this passage. The sense of (11), then, is something like 'what happened next is that Stefan became abbot' rather than 'what Stefan did next was to become abbot'. (12), though it reports a change of state, is identificatory; it reports who became the judge rather than what happened to Judas. (13) is perhaps the most subtle. In (13) there is a single hero, Maksim, who has had various functions in his life. But the middle fact — that at some point he became a warrior — is not a narrative fact; it is not reported as a result of the preceding state nor as a condition for the following state. The three states reported are merely various properties characterizing this individual at different phases of his life. Note in (13) that the inceptive aorist is coordinated with two imperfect forms of 'be' in their continuative sense. Thus, the instrumental in this third context signals only the most virulent form of sequentialized narrative, which we termed culminative.[5]

In a panchronic model of grammatical networks, we need perhaps two exemplars representing the two contexts in which case usage is syntagmatically predictable. In (15), the notation '*x*/*y*' means both *x* and *y* occur freely, and '*x* *y*' is to be read as '*x* motivates *y*'. Exemplar (15)⟨a⟩ is the context of continuative aspectuality with nominative (function or non-function nouns); continuative aspectuality motivates digressive textuality. Exemplar (15)⟨b⟩ is the durative context with instrumental of function nouns; durativity motivates transitional or culminative textuality.

(15) Grammatical Network (Old Russian)

⟨a⟩ ... *bě* IMPERF *Kyevъ* NOM/*grekini* NOM/*episkopъ* NOM
'...was IMPERF Kiev NOM/a Greek woman NOM/bishop NOM
i. identificatory/descriptive/function predicative
ii. continuative aspectuality
⋑iii. digressive textuality

⟨b⟩ ... *bě* IMPERF/*bystь* AOR/*bylъ* PF *voevodoju* INSTR *6 lětъ*
'...was IMPERF/was AOR/was PERF commander INSTR six years'
i. function predicative
ii. durative aspectuality
⋑iii. transitional/culminative textuality

⋑⟨b′⟩ ... *bystь* AOR *voevodoju* INSTR
'...was AOR [=became] a commander INSTR'
i. function predicative noun
ii. inceptive aspectuality
⋑iii. culminative textuality

As noted above, the syntagm with an aorist of 'be' in its inceptive sense shows variation in case. For this context, it may well have been that there was no clear examplar. Instead, the values associated with case choice were derived, as it were, on the hoof, by comparing this context to the fixed exemplars (15)⟨a–b⟩. In particular, use of instrumental in (15)⟨b′⟩, *bystь* AOR *voevodoju* INSTR 'he became a commander INSTR', is apparently an innovative extrapolation on the basis of the conventionalized exemplar of (15)⟨b⟩. Speakers might have reasoned as follows. Under durativity ((15)⟨b⟩), both the inception and the cancellation of the state are mentioned, or at least understood; it is bounded at two places on a single axis. Inceptive aspectuality reports only one of those boundaries, the initial one, and is therefore a weaker form of aspectuality. But if inceptive aspectuality is combined with culminative textuality, then the resulting semantic constellation is analogous to durativity: Whereas durativity is double bounding on a single axis, inception plus culminative textuality is bounding on two axes. This derivation is encoded in (15) in the statement that (15)⟨b⟩ ⋑ (15)⟨b′⟩.

This reconstruction of the grammar and usage of OR relies on two principles governing the organization of synchronic grammatical networks and indirectly also diachrony. On the one hand, it must evidently be possible to compare semantic operations across different levels. In the example above, a certain value for textuality (the role of the sentence in the surrounding text) is taken to be comparable to a certain value for the more local notion of aspectuality. On the other hand, there is evidently a kind of conservation of semantic operations involved here in the highly variable use of the instrumental with the aorist, the context of (15)⟨b′⟩. The instrumental is justified only if a threshhold of limitation has been reached (durative or inceptive aspectuality plus culminative textuality).

In our exposition of OR, we have assumed that the variable usage in context (15)⟨b′⟩ was derived actively by comparison with other, more stable patterns. That point is difficult to prove. Prevailing analytic methods prejudice one to the view that any distribution of morphemes (such as nominative and instrumental here) should be completely determined; and given the rather finite evidence, it would be possible to write a deterministic grammar of case choice for predicatives in OR. We suspect, however, that the corpus of texts can never be completely determined by a grammar. No grammar could ever specify completely all the possible contextual variations that could, and do, arise in text; if a grammar did, it would be unlimited. But even if one were to construct a completely deterministic grammar for OR, it must be recognized that the context with the aorist of 'be' is the only context with variation, and that the variation attested in this context is dependent on the properties of other, more fixed patterns (those of (15)⟨a–b⟩). Thus, even a deterministic grammar will have to distinguish between primary contexts, in which usage is relatively fixed, stable and syntagmatically predictable, and secondary contexts, in which usage is variable, paradigmatic and, crucially, derivative of usage in primary contexts.

To summarize at this interim point, we have suggested that grammar be viewed as an active process that manipulates a relatively limited network of exemplar constructions. To determine the meaning of a token of case selection in context, a given syntactic construction is compared to available patterns. If the match is not complete, as it is not in context of the aorist of 'be', a meaning is assigned to the construction analogous to the meanings of fixed exemplars.

4. PREHISTORY OF THE PREDICATIVE INSTRUMENTAL

Let us now work backwards and forward from the OR situation. Looking backwards in time, we note that in Old Church Slavic (=OCS), the most archaic attested form of Slavic,[6] the predicative instrumental with 'be' is not attested in the more archaic codices. It appears to be attested only in the syntactically most innovative document (the Codex Suprasliensis), and then not in the past tense, but only in the future or with participles.[7] This indicates that the predicate instrumental with 'be' was just in the process of being innovated at the time when the earliest attestations arose and that it is of recent (not Indo-European) origin. The most appealing of the various hypotheses that have been made about the origin of the predicate instrumental is that it derives from a predicative-like structure (often called *appositive*) with a semantically autonomous verb of motion, position, or location; the sense is 'go/sit/arrive in the capacity of; *qua*'. This construction, illustrated in (16) and (17), is attested in OR; it occurs only with the instrumental of nouns, never with the nominative (a related construction with adjective, coincidentally also illustrated in (17), does take the nominative):

(16) *...glagoljušče: kto vzydetъ* PRES *s nami voevodoju* INSTR *na Xananeja sěščisja s nimi?*
'...saying: who will go PRES with us as commander INSTR against the Canaanites to fight with them?'

(17) *Vъ to že lěto ide* AOR *Nězdylo Pěxtinyčь voevodoju* INSTR *na Luky; [...] ubiša ixъ 40 mužъ, a ženy ixъ i děti poimaša, a sami priidoša* AOR *na Luky vsě zdorovy* NOM
'In that year Nezdylo Pextinych went AOR to Luky as commander INSTR [...] they killed forty men, and took their wives and children, while they themselves all arrived AOR at Luky healthy NOM.'

Although the construction type *ide* AOR *voevodoj* INS 'he went AOR as commander INSTR' is not attested in OCS — probably because the relevant idiom is never demanded by the limited content of the canonical texts — it is most likely a Common Slavic construction which antedated the predicative instrumental with 'be' and provided the source for it.[8] Reconstructing backwards from OCS and OR, then, we can assume a relatively late stage of prehistoric Slavic in which the instrumental was used (not in paradigmatic opposition to the nominative) with a restricted set of autosemantic verbs, a usage which provided the source for the subsequent development of the instrumental with 'be'.[9]

How could the extension from the construction with autosemantic verbs to the copular construction have taken place? There are two, or perhaps three, points of interest. First, the host predicate. The host predicate describes an activity and imposes an activity sense on its predicative, the sense of 'functioning in a certain capacity'. When the instrumental is extended to 'be', the host predicate is imputed an activity sense ('be, acting as').

Second, the original construction of 'go, acting as' implies the constant possibility that the state could have the opposite polarity. The state is imputed to hold only over the time at which the activity reported by the host predicate holds; the state may well not have held before that and may not hold after that time. In OR, the predicative instrumental with 'be' is entrenched in durative contexts. Whereas with the original idiom *ide* AOR *voevodoju* INSTR inception and cancellation of the state are merely presumptions, with *bě* IMPERF *voevodoju* INSTR *6 lětъ* the state is necessarily cancelled. As the instrumental is extended from 'go' to 'be', durativity becomes obligatory.

Third, if we assume a general pattern of incremental development, it would be natural to hypothesize that the predicate instrumental appeared first as an 'optional' variant associated with some covert textual value. The instrumental may have implied that the predicative state culminated the episode, (8) above being an example. The relationship between instrumental with autosemantic verbs and extrapolated instrumental with 'be' is sketched in (18).

(18) Grammatical Network (Prehistoric Slavic)

⟨a⟩ ... *bě* IMPERF *Kyevъ* NOM/*grekini* NOM/*episkopъ* NOM
'...was IMPERF Kiev NOM/a Greek woman NOM/bishop NOM'
i. identificatory/descriptive/function predicative
$\Supset$ii. continuative aspectuality
$\Supset$iii. digressive textuality

⟨b⟩ ... *ide* AOR *voevodoju* INSTR
'...went AOR as commander INS'
i. 'go functioning as'
$\Supset$ii. durative aspectuality
$\Supset$iii. digressive/transitional/culminative textuality

$\Supset$⟨b′⟩ ... *bě* IMPERF/*bystъ* AOR/*bylъ* PERF *voevodoju* INSTR *6 lětъ*
'...was IMPERF/was AOR/was PERF commander INSTR six years'
$\Supset$i. 'be' = 'function as'
ii. durative aspectuality
$\Supset$iii. culminative textuality

Thus, the first extension of the predicative instrumental to 'be' in *bě* IMPERF *voevodoju* INSTR *6 lětъ* 'he was IMPERF [= acted as] commander INSTR for six years' can be motivated on the basis of the existing pattern of *ide* AOR *voevodoju* INS 'he went AOR as commander INSTR'. All that is required is the imposition of an activity sense on 'be' and a tightening of the belt with respect to aspectuality (the scenario of inception, state holding, and cancellation becomes actual in the narrative, not merely a typical associated scenario) and perhaps also textuality as well.

Once this textual token *bě* IMPER *voevodoju* INSTR *6 lětъ* is itself adopted as an exemplar of the grammatical network, it can serve as the model for further deviations. If (hypothetically) *bě* IMPERF *voevodoju* INSTR *6 lětъ* was first used only in sequential narrative (recall (8) above), that condition can be subsequently eliminated (as it is in (9) above). And while in the hypothesized *bě* IMPERF *voevodoju* INSTR *6 lětъ* both temporal boundaries are overtly specified — both the inception and the cancellation — the condition on temporal boundaries can subsequently be weakened and the instrumental could then come to be used in contexts where only one of the boundaries is in focus, namely the inception (with the aorist of 'be'). As we observed above, however, in this (presumably relatively new) context for the predicative instrumental, the choice of case is correlated with further textual values, digression vs. sequential narrative.

5. MIDDLE RUSSIAN PREDICATIVE INSTRUMENTAL

Projecting forward from Old Russian, we can sketch the further development of the predicative instrumental in later Russian.[10] A stage we might term *Middle Russian* can be described as minimal extensions of the OR situation.

To judge by the infrequent examples in the late seventeenth century descriptive prose of Kotošixin,[11] usage has changed somewhat from OR. Descriptive nouns still occur in the nominative (only one example):

(19) *I kotorye vory byli* PT *ljudi* NOM *bogatye i oni ot svoix běd otkupalis*
'And whatever thieves were PT rich people NOM, they could buy their way out of their troubles.'

Function nouns now require the instrumental in the past tense, instead of merely allowing it as an option (6xx instrumental/6xx total). Thus, in (20), the instrumental of a function noun is used digressively, where in Old Russian one would have expected nominative:

(20) *Posle crja Ivana Vasileviča ostalisja dva syna i edinъ byl* PT *crem* INSTR, *a drugoi sъ materiju otdelenъ bylъ*
'After Tsar Ivan Vasil'evich there remained two sons. One was PT tsar INSTR, the other was isolated with his mother.'

(20) is not durative. It may be inchoative ('he was the one who would become the tsar'), though that interpretation is not necessary – the sense may be simply 'he is the one who was the tsar'. Even if (20) is taken as inchoative, it is still textually digressive. The instrumental in (20) can be contrasted with an identical context a little earlier (end of the fifteenth century):

(21) *Korol že sestru svoju vzjat, i so dvema synmi, v Ugorskuju zemlju na Budin. Edin pri kraleve syne živet, a drugij byl* PT *u Varadinskogo biskopa* NOM
'The king took his sister, along with her two sons, back to the Hungarian land, to Buda. One lives with the son of the king, while the other was PT a bishop NOM with Varadin.'

The comparison of (20) with (21) shows that, by the seventeenth century, the instrumental had become nearly obligatory for function nouns, regardless of aspectuality or textuality.

In Middle Russian, one begins to see a new distinction emerge in predicative nouns. *Quasi-function* predicative nouns — nouns that vaguely hint at activities, even if they are not culturally sanctioned roles — begin to allow the instrumental. (22) vs. (23) is close to a minimal pair:

(22) *i eželi postroitsja domom kakoi prikaznoi člvkъ, obolgut crju i mnogie carskie krivdy učinjat, čto butto onъ byl* PT *posulnikъ* NOM *i zloimatel* NOM
'and if an some official should build a house, people will lie to the tsar and will cause many lies, that, supposedly, he was PT a bribe-giver NOM or a bribe-taker NOM.'

(23) *i těxъ vorov pytajut nakrěpko, vprjam li tě ljudi na kotoryx oni govorjat s nimi v tom vorovstvě tovaryščami* INSTR *ili stanovščikami* INSTR *i oberegalščikami* INSTR *byli* PT *i ne naprasno l na nixъ govorjat po nasertke*
'and these thieves are questioned thoroughly as to whether exactly the people they are accusing in this crime were PT comrades INSTR or accessories INSTR or lookouts INSTR, or whether they are not accusing them without justification, out of malice.'

(22), which reports a generalized property, has continuative aspectuality. In contrast, (23) reports a property restricted to a particular occasion (cf. *v tom vorovstvě* 'in that act of thievery').

The exemplars of the grammatical network of the seventeenth century, based on the data available, can be summarized as in (24). Here only a single form of 'be', labelled preterite, is given, since by this time the etymological perfect form was the universal past tense. Descriptive and identificatory nouns still occur only in the nominative ((24)⟨a⟩); pure function nouns now occur only in the instrumental (so that now the aspectuality and textuality are irrelevant). A quasi-function noun allows variation in case; instrumental motivates durativity, as stated in (24)⟨b′⟩.

(24) Grammatical Network (Seventeenth Century)
⟨a⟩ … *byli* PT *ljudi* NOM *bogatye*
'…were PT rich people NOM'
i. non-function predicative
⋑ii. continuative aspectuality
⋑iii. digressive textuality

⟨b⟩ … *bylъ* PT *caremъ* INSTR
'…was PT the tsar INS'
i. function predicative
⊇ ii. continuative/inceptive/durative aspectuality
⊇ iii. digressive/transitional/culminative textuality

⊇⟨b′⟩ … *byli* PT *oberegalščikami* INSTR
'…were PT lookouts INSTR'
i. quasi-function predicative
⊇ ii. durative aspectuality
⊇ iii. digressive/transitional/culminative textuality

Usage in the seventeenth century differs somewhat from that of OR: Pure function nouns, which previously allowed variation (in contexts of inceptive aspectuality), now virtually require the instrumental, regardless of aspectuality or textuality. At the same time, quasi-function nouns now allow the instrumental in the specfic context of durative aspectuality. The overall effect has been to fix usage in one domain and develop variation in another. We suspect that this is characteristic of change in grammatical networks: Contexts in which usage is optional become contexts in which usage is obligatory, and contexts in which only one alternative had been possible become contexts of optional usage. The process of extending the instrumental is a cyclical process of generating new tokens of text that are analogous but not identical to preexisting exemplars followed by conventionalization of these new tokens as exemplars themselves. In each instance, the new tokens of text differ minimally, by the adjustment of one or two parameters, from the preexisting patterns. In this way change is (as has long been noted) highly incremental and close to imperceptible to the users of the language.

6. CONCLUSIONS

Against the background of this description, let us return to general issues. What the example of OR shows, at the very minimum, is that all changes in grammar do not follow the scenario whereby lexical words become grammatical morphemes. The changes here involve morphemes that, both phonologically and in their other syntactic uses, are remarkably stable over time. The scenario of grammaticalization in its usual extensional sense appears to involve two things: It presupposes that the distinction between grammatical and non-grammatical phenomena is clear; and it suggests that the basic direction of development will be towards ossification, towards idiomatization, towards entropy. Both of these assumptions we have disputed. The synchronic situation in OR (and again in the seventeenth century, and now in the twentieth century) is a complex blend of syntagmatic predictability and textual value; usage at every stage is simultaneously 'grammaticalized' and fluid. The transition from one stage to another involves fixing usage in certain contexts and opening up variation in others.

One may also discern in the panchronic model sketched above an alternative to the model for change proposed some years ago by Andersen (1973). In Andersen's model of change, change is set in motion by (speaking metaphorically) a cataclysmic reanalysis of surface data (*abduction*, in Andersen's terms); the actual, day-to-day, incremental mapping out of the change takes place by gradually removing restrictions on the usage in order to make usage accord with the underlying change in grammar (*deduction*, in Andersen's terms).

This model embodies four claims we find dubious. First, the initial abductive leap must contain the final goal of the change.[12] In the problem at hand, that would be tantamount to the assumption that the first usage of *bě* IMPERF *voevodoju* INSTR was in effect a decision to implement a complete usage of predicative instrumental in the language. This claim is difficult to argue with, but we see no reason to assume that the complete history of the predicate instrumental was ordained in 863 AD. Second, this model requires that there be well-defined universal principles, accessible to every language learner, that define what concrete rules of usage are consistent with the underlying grammatical decision. This implication is likewise hard to evaluate; it would be hard to state what the most ideal implementation of a distinction in predicative case should be. We have pointed out that there are analogies across different levels of the grammatical network. Specifically, the fact that case may signal a distinction of narrative vs. digressive textuality (in some subcontext) is analogous to the distinction of continuative as opposed to durative or inceptive aspectuality. But these analogies can be derived without recourse to a universal notion of the ideal predicative construction. Third, Andersen's model also assumes, like all generative models, that usage can be determined by grammar. This is likewise an assumption that makes us nervous. Short of specifying all sentences and contexts, a grammar can never fully determine output. A fourth issue, likewise elusive but of considerable interest, is whether innovations arise only through the abductive reanalysis of previous data on the part of the addressee, as Andersen's model claims,[13] or whether it is not possible that innovations arise, by extrapolation, directly in speaker's production. We suggested above, for example, that the original idiom *ide* AOR *voevodoju* INSTR '[he] went as commander' might have given rise directly to *bě* IMPERF *voevodoju* INSTR *6 lětъ* '[he] acted as commander six years' without a prior abduction that reinterpreted the conditions of usage for the instrumental.

What we have done here is attempt to illustrate a dynamic, panchronic model of grammar oriented around exemplars. Text tokens that do match any exemplar are always possible, and even likely; if these are conventionalized, they themselves become exemplars. In this model, the forces of innovation and conventionalization (idiomatization) are simultaneously always present, at every diachronic stage. They imply each other. Rather than focusing attention exclusively on grammaticalization (as it seems to us the grammaticalization literature does), we have emphasized the interactive nature of the innovative and idiomatizing forces.

ABBREVIATIONS

PT = preterite
PRES = present (including perfective 'non-past')
NOM = nominative
INSTR = instrumental

Notes

* Uncharacteristically, the verb 'be' distinguished three simple past tenses, at least in certain persons and numbers: e.g. 3d sg. *bjaše*, *bě*, and *bystь*. The first was clearly imperfect, the third aorist, and the intermediate form functionally probably an imperfect (though see van Schooneveld 1959). The identification of the fourth past-referring tense form *bylъ* (originally a participle that demanded another form of the verb 'be' as an auxiliary) as perfect holds only for the oldest period. This form eventually takes on the general function of past tense in Russian. We have glossed it in OR as perfect; by the seventeenth century, when this historical perfect has almost completely displaced the aorist in written Russian, it seems appropriate to label the form simply preterite.

OR examples OR are cited from *Polnoe sobranie russkix letopisej* [= *PSRL*] (directly or with an indication of the secondary source) or Šaxmatov, A.A. (ed.) 1916 [1969]. *Provest 'vremennyx let, 1: Vvodnaja Čast'. Tekst. Primečanija.* The Hague/Paris: Mouton [Slavic Printings and Reprintings 98] [Pov. vr. 1]. Examples from Kotošixin are cited from the edition of Pennington 1980, with certain simplifications (no distinction between multiple graphemes for single phonemes, and no notation of superscripted letters).

Citations:

(1): *Pov. vr. l.*, 90
(2): *Pov. vr. l.*, 96

(3): *Pov. vr. l.*, 81
(4) *Pov. vr. l.*, 63
(5) *Letopisec Rogožskij*, *PSRL* 15:64; Schaller, 1975:180
(6) *Pov. vr. l.*, 109
(7) *Novg. vt. letopis'*, *PSRL* 30:200; Schaller, 1975:178
(8) *Erm. letopis'*, *PSRL* 23 (pril. 1):165; Schaller, 1975:178
(9) Patokova 1929:5
(10) *Pov. vr. let.*, 90
(11) *Pov. vr. l.*, 243
(12) *Pov. vr. l.*, 120
(13) *Letopis' Avraamki*, *PSRL* 16:18; Schaller, 1975:181
(14) *Pov. vr. l.*, 206
(16) *Xronograf 1512*, *PSRL* 22:92; Schaller 1975:175
(17) *Tverskaja letopis'*, *PSRL* 15:290
(19) Kotošixin, f. 147^{r-v}
(20) Kotošixin, f. 27
(21) Ja. S. Lur'e, *Povest' o drakule. Issledovanie i podgotovka tekstov.*
(22) Kotošixin, f. 226^{V}
(23) Kotošixin, f. 169^{r-v}

1. The general framework and modern usage are described in Nichols 1981.

2. This reduces the value of the standard strategic move of assuming that if a given passage is Slavonic (respectively, Russian) in some respects, it will be so in all respects, including case selection.

3. Our discussion relies on the investigations of Patokova (1929), Busch (1960:177–191), and Schaller (1975:171–186), as well as our own partial examination of primary sources. With considerable philological queasiness, we lump together chronicles that are by no means comparable in terms of age of composition and/or age of compilation. The most archaic portions of the chronicles were compiled by the eleventh century, but these portions were presumably revised as additions were made; copies date from considerably later.

4. Busch (1960:182, fn. 36) suggests that the instrumental is restricted to newly borrowed terms, as if their stylistic coloring were relevant. The instrumental was used with *voevoda* 'secular (war)lord' and *vladyka* '(church)leader', which are etymologically Slavic, though their senses may nevertheless be cultural borrowings.

5. As this description should show, it would not be possible to say unambiguously whether the instrumental is syntagmatically conditioned or syntagmatically free; it is both, in a complicated mix. This remark is addressed to an implicit or putative definition of 'grammaticalized' as syntagmatically conditioned. Though this is only one possible way of defining grammaticalized, we suspect that the complexity documented here would cause discomfort for any other definition of 'grammaticalized'.

6. To repeat, the relationship of OCS to OR written language is complex. Genetically, OCS is some manner of early written South Slavic (perhaps with a pan-dialectal character), and in this sense did not directly antecede Russian, which developed out of the East Slavic dialect zone of Slavic. Yet at the same time, because of the cultural and historical priority of OCS, the norms of this language constituted the basis for 'Old Russian' texts from which we are obliged to take evidence about older stages of East Slavic.

7. Bauerová, 1963; Vaillant, 1964:190.
8. One could go back further and derive this use from the 'instrumental of comparison', but we are not interested in pursuing the origin further back than this construction.
9. As suggested by various scholars: Potebnja, 1888/1958; Fraenkel, 1925; Patokova, 1929; Nichols, 1973(143, 209).
10. There is a general assumption that the situation described above was relatively stable for an extended period of time, perhaps up to the sixteenth century, but that observation may be artefactual — it may result from the preponderance of conservative, ecclesiastical texts until the sixteenth and seventeenth centuries, when (rather suddenly) texts written in a more vernacular style appear.
11. In this text written in 1666–67, a largely non-historical description of court mores, predicative nouns with the past tense of 'be' (a total of ten examples) come up accidentally in the occasional historical passages.
12. Cf.: "this means that, before a change begins to be manifested little by little, its end result is already given in the underlying representations" (p. 788).
13. Cf.: "the source of abductive innovations is to be found in distributional ambiguities in the verbal output from which the new grammar is inferred" (p. 789).

REFERENCES

Andersen, H. 1973. "Abductive and deductive change." *Language* 49:765–793.

Bauerová, M. 1963. "Bespredložnyj tvoritel'nyj padež v staroslavjanskom jazyke." In Josef Kurz (ed.), 1963:287–311.

Busch, U. 1960. *Die Seinsätze in der russischen Sprache*. [=Slavisch-Baltisches Seminar der Westfälischen Wilhelms-Meisenheim am Glan Universität Münster 4.].

Fraenkel, E. 1925. "Der prädikative Instrumental im Slavischen und Baltischen und seine syntaksischen Grundlagen." *Archiv für slavische Philologie* 40:77–117.

Kurz, Jozef (ed.), *Issledovanija po Sintaksisu Staroslavjanskogo Jazyka*. Prague.

Nichols, J. 1973. The Balto-Slavic Predicate Instrumental: A Problem in Diachronic Syntax. Ph.D. dissertation, University of California, Berkeley.

Nichols, J. 1981. *Predicate Nominals: A Partial Surface Syntax of Russian*. Berkeley, CA. [UCPL 97].

Pennington, A. E. (ed.). 1980. *Grigorij Kotošixin. O Rossii v carstvovanie Alekseja Mixajloviča. Text and Commentary*. Oxford: Clarendon.

Patokova, O. V. 1929. "K istorii razvitija tvoritel'nogo predikativnogo v russkom literaturnom jazyke." *Slavia* 8:1–37.

Potebnja, A. A. 1888/1958. *Iz zapisok po russkoj grammatike*, 1–2. Kharkov.

Schaller, H. 1975. *Das Prädikatsnomen im Russischen. Eine bescreibend-historische Untersuchung*. Köln/Wien: Böhlau [Slavistische Forschungen, 18].

Thelin, Nils B. (ed.). 1990. *Aspect in Discourse*. Amsterdam/Philadelphia: John Benjamins [PXB NS5].

Timberlake, A. 1989. "The aspectual case of predicative nouns in Lithuanian texts." In Nils B. Thelin (ed.) 1990.

Vaillant, A. 1964. *Manuel du vieux slave* 1: *Grammaire*. Paris.

van Schooneveld, C. H. 1959. *A Semantic Analysis of the Old Russian Finite Preterite System*. The Hague: Mouton [Slavistic Printings and Reprintings, 7].

SECTION B: DIRECTIONALITY

From Cognition to Grammar — Evidence from African Languages

Bernd Heine, Ulrike Claudi and Friederike Hünnemeyer
University of Cologne

1. INTRODUCTION[1]

Grammaticalization problems have been a topic in linguistics almost since its beginnings. Scholars like Bopp (1816), Wilhelm von Humboldt (1825), von der Gabelentz (1891) and Meillet (1912) have laid the foundation for a research field which has attracted a remarkable amount of scholarly attention during the last two decades. Kuryłowicz (1965:52) has provided the by now classical definition of the term: "Grammaticalization consists in the increase of the range of a morpheme advancing from a lexical to a grammatical or from a less grammatical to a more grammatical status, e.g. from a derivative formant to an inflectional one." Roughly the same definition has been used by other scholars[2] and will be adopted here as well. A number of alternative terms like reanalysis (see 3.1), syntacticization (Givón, 1979:208ff.), semantic bleaching (see 2.3.1), semantic weakening (Guimier, 1985:158), condensation (Lehmann, 1982:10/11), reduction (Langacker, 1977:103–107), subduction (Guillaume, 1964:73–86), etc. are occasionally used as synonyms or near-synonyms, but in most cases they refer to specific aspects, like the semantic or syntactic characteristics of grammaticalization. Grammaticalization has also been referred to as "grammaticization" (Givón, 1975:49; Bolinger, 1978:489; Bybee and Pagliuca, 1985).[3]

What is common to all definitions of grammaticalization is, first, that it is conceived as a *process*. Although this process can be interpreted synchronically as well (cf. Li, 1975a; Lehmann, 1982:2; Heine and Claudi, 1986) there is wide agreement that it forms essentially a diachronic phenomenon. Second, most scholars treat grammaticalization as a *morphological* process, as one which concerns the development of a given word or morpheme. A third characteristic which is implicit in these definitions and has frequently been mentioned as an intrinsic property of the process is that grammaticalization is *unidirectional*, i.e. that it leads from a "less" to a "more grammatical" unit but not vice versa. A few counterexamples have been cited (e.g. Kahr, 1976; Jeffers and Zwicky, 1980) but have been refuted by Lehmann (1982:16–20). Although some examples can be adduced to show that the process may be reversed, that is, that "degrammaticalization" may in fact take place, such examples are less usual and will be ignored in the remainder of this paper.[4]

While abundant data on grammaticalization processes have become available during the last 15 years there are a number of problems that remain unsolved. In the present paper we wish to look at two of these problems in more detail, one that concerns the causes of grammaticalization and another one that relates to its implications for language structure. It will be argued that grammaticalization is the product of a specific type of conceptual manipulation and can immediately be accounted for with reference to this manipulation (see 2.3, 2.4).

Grammaticalization may be influenced by various factors, like contact between languages, interference between the written and the spoken form of a given language, the socio-cultural context, or overall typological developments.[5] All these factors will remain out of consideration here since we will be confined to the most basic structure of grammaticalization.

2. THE COGNITIVE SETTING

2.1. An underlying principle

One of the main claims made here is that underlying grammaticalization there is a specific cognitive principle called the "principle of the exploitation of old means for novel functions" by Werner and Kaplan (1963:403). By means of this principle, concrete concepts are employed to understand, explain or describe less concrete phenomena. In this way, clearly delineated and/or clearly structured entities are recruited to conceptualize less clearly delineated or structured entities, non-physical experiences are understood in terms of physical experiences, time in terms of space, cause in terms of time, or abstract relations in terms of kinetic processes or spatial relations, etc.[6]

According to this view, grammaticalization can be interpreted as the result of a process which has *problem-solving* as its main goal, its primary function being conceptualization by expressing one thing in terms of another.

This function is not confined to grammaticalization, it is the main characteristic of metaphor in general (cf. Lakoff and Johnson, 1980).

This view might suggest that the development of grammatical structures is motivated, e.g. by unfulfilled communicative needs, or by the presence of cognitive contents for which there do not exist adequate linguistic designations. While this may be the case, we will not deal with this point here but rather reserve it for a separate discussion. It may suffice to note that various students of grammaticalization have pointed out that new grammatical devices have developed despite the existence of old, functionally equivalent structures (cf. Bybee, 1985), and König (1985:280) for instance has drawn attention to the principle of creative language use according to which there is a constant attempt to express the same (grammatical) meaning in other words.

2.2. Source structures

It would seem that there is a limited number of basic cognitive structures forming the input or source of grammaticalization. We will now try to characterize this input. In the following sections (2.3 and 2.4) we will discuss the relation between input and output, which, as we claim, is metaphorical in nature, and section 3 will be concerned with the output or target of grammaticalization.

2.2.1. Concepts

Concepts which enter into grammaticalization processes in the vast majority of cases refer to concrete objects, processes or locations, although there are a few deictic and interrogative concepts in addition (cf. Traugott, 1982:246).

The term "source concept" is to be understood as a relative notion. Some entity is a source concept only with reference to some other, more "abstract", concept which may itself be the source of another, even more "abstract", concept. For instance, a concrete object like a body part (*back*) may serve as a source concept for space (*three miles back*) which again may be the source for time (*three years back*) (see 2.3.3).

Source concepts have been described as "fundamental elements (symbolic and deictic in function) in a typical speech situation".[7] They are of frequent and general use (cf. Bybee and Pagliuca, 1985:72), although it is likely that their frequent use is due to their being "fundamental elements".

Linguistically, source concepts are coded ultimately as lexemes. These have much in common with what in lexicostatistics is called the basic vocabulary, i.e. lexemes which are less subject to replacement than others. Both include for instance body part items like 'head', 'breast', 'back', 'belly', 'hand', 'foot', natural phenomena like 'earth' and 'sky', some human items like 'person', 'father', 'mother' and 'child', process verbs like 'come', 'give', 'take/hold', posture verbs like 'stand', 'sit', a mental process verb like 'say', or quantifiers like 'one' or 'many', or basic demonstratives (cf. Swadesh, 1951; Gudschinsky, 1956). Both have in common as well that they include items which are largely culture-independent, that is, they tend to be conceived in a similar way across linguistic and ethnic boundaries. There are however some remarkable differences, as we shall see below.

Source concepts may be said to refer to some of the most elementary human experiences; they are typically derived from the physical state, behavior or immediate environment of man. What appears to make them eligible as such is the fact that they provide "concrete" reference points for human orientation which evoke associations and are therefore exploited to understand "less concrete" concepts (see 2.3). The human body for instance offers a convenient pool of reference points for spatial orientation. Parts of the body are recruited for instance as source concepts for the expression of grammatical concepts because of their relative location: 'back' or 'buttock' for the space behind, 'breast', 'chest', 'face', 'eye', or even 'head' for the front, 'belly', 'stomach' or 'heart' for inside, 'head' for above, and 'anus' or 'foot' for below.[8] Body parts like 'liver' all belong to the basic vocabulary of lexicostatistics but do not seem to form reference points for spatial orientation and, hence, do not evoke associations relevant for the expression of spatial concepts, or any other grammatical concepts for that matter.[9]

But location is not the only characteristic of body parts which is exploited; there are some alternative associations as well. For instance, the association between holding an object in one's hand and owning that object has led to the development of the body part 'hand' as a marker of possession in some West African languages (cf. Claudi and Heine, 1986; see 2.2.2 below), and the observation that the head as the center of intellectual activity is responsible for human behaviour might have induced the choice of 'head' as a reference point for some more abstract concept, CAUSE/PURPOSE, which again has triggered the grammaticalization of 'head' as an adposition and/or complementizer of cause/finality. One should also mention that various body parts as well as the term 'body' itself have provided the source for the development of reflexive pronouns in many African languages (Keith Allan, Derek Nurse, p.c.; Essien, 1982, Awolaye, 1986).

With regard to processes, source concepts refer to some of the most basic human activities, like 'do/make', 'take/hold', 'finish' or 'say', or movements like 'go', 'come', 'leave' or 'arrive'. Furthermore, a number of items specifying a position or state are among the most common source concepts, typically coded linguistically as state verbs, such as 'be/exist', 'be at', 'sit', 'stand', 'lie (down)', 'stay/live'. Some concepts expressing desire ('want/like') or obligation ('shall', 'ought to') provide source items as well in a number of languages. On the other hand, there are some verbs figuring in the basic vocabulary list of lexicostatisticians which one might consider as candidates for source concepts but which nevertheless are not. These include 'eat', 'drink', 'hear', 'sing', 'hit', 'die' and many others.

2.2.2. Propositions

In addition to the source concepts there are some more complex structures which we tentatively refer to as source propositions. These propositions express states or processes which appear — like source concepts — to be basic to human experience and can be rendered by means of linguistic predications typically involving two participants. Perhaps the most common of these predications are:

(1)	"X is at Y"	(locational proposition)
(2)	"X moves to/from/along Y"	(motion proposition)
(3)	"X is part of Y"	(part-whole proposition)
(4)	"X does Y"	(action proposition).

Source propositions describe in an elementary way where an object is, where it moves from or to, how one object is related to others, and what one does. It may be useful to distinguish between propositions that are static or time-stable (see Givón, 1979:320–321), like (1) and (3), and those that are dynamic, like (2) and (4), or between propositions having a spatial dimension, like (1) and (2), and those that do not, like (3) and (4).

Each of these propositions may give rise to differing grammatical structures. The locational proposition (1) is employed for instance to develop verbal aspects or moods like progressive or intentional when the constituent represented by Y is filled with a nominalized process verb.[10] Thus in many languages a construction "X is at/in/on Y" has been reinterpreted as meaning "X is doing Y". Constructions of this type, labelled PP-periphrasis in Heine and Reh (1984:115), have developed into progressive and similar aspects in over one hundred African languages.[11] That such constructions may also give rise to grammatical categories expressing intention may be surprising, but has been recorded for Ewe:[12] In this language, a structure "X is at Y's place" has acquired the meaning "X is about/intends to do Y" and has been grammaticalized to a verbal aspect referred to in grammars of this language as "ingressive" or "intentional".[13] But the locational model has also given rise, e.g. to expressions of verbal possession (see below). In this case, X is understood as the possessed and Y as the possessor participant of the locational relationship. Underlying this type of conceptualization there appears to be an implication of the kind "what is at Y's place[14] belongs to Y".

While one source proposition may give rise to differing grammatical categories, one and the same grammatical category may as well be derived from entirely different propositions. Verbal possession ('to have, own') for instance may not only be derived from the locational model, but also from the action model, the latter being based on a metaphorical transfer from "Y takes/seizes X" to "Y owns X". The former is the case for instance in Ewe, where verbal possession ("Y has/owns X") goes back to a construction "X is in Y's hand"), as can be seen in the following sentence:

(5) *xɔ le así-nye*
house be at hand-POSS:1SG
'I have a house.'

Examples for the action proposition as the source for verbal possession can be found in a number of Eastern Cushitic languages, where a clause like "Y has/owns X" is rendered linguistically as "X seizes Y", as can be seen in the following sentence from Waata, an Oromo dialect spoken at the Kenyan coast:

(6) *ani mín k'awa*
1SG house seize
'I have a house.'

More research is needed on the exact role source propositions of this kind play in the process of grammaticalization. This applies in particular to their interrelationship with the source concepts discussed in the previous section. What is important to note is that such propositions may, but need not, be present in the process of grammaticalization. They are never present for instance when a concept turns up as the dependent constituent, rather than the head, of a construction undergoing grammaticalization (see 3.1).

2.2.3. Source structures and target structures

One of the most urgent problems in the analysis of grammaticalization concerns the relationship between input and output, i.e. between the source and the target within this process. This problem entails in particular the following questions:

(1) What source concepts and/or propositions give rise to which grammatical concepts?
(2) Given some grammatical category, is it possible to unambiguously define its non-grammatical source?
(3) To what extent are the source and target structures, as well as the relationship holding between them, universally determined?

A number of data relevant to these questions have been presented during the past decade and valuable generalizations attempted. But we are still far from being able to answer these questions with a degree of certainty approaching prediction. It is by now well established that one source concept can give rise to more than one grammatical category and, conversely, a given grammatical category may be historically derived from more than one source concept or structure. An example from So, a Kuliak language of northeastern Uganda, may illustrate this. The verb *ac* 'come' of this language has developed on the one hand into a verbal derivative suffix *-ac* ("venitive") denoting movement towards the speaker or deictic centre. On the other hand, it has become an auxiliary and eventually a verbal proclitic denoting future tense. There is however a second verbal proclitic denoting future, *gá*, derived from another motion verb, *gá* 'go'.[15] Thus, we find in this example instances of both one source giving rise to two grammatical categories and of one grammatical category having two different lexical concepts as its source. An additional question that arises therefore is:

(4) Is it possible to define the factors determining the choice between *alternative* sources available and, conversely, under what condition does a source concept develop, respectively, into grammatical category A rather than B, or into B rather than A, or into both?

2.3. Transfer

2.3.1. Some prerequisite notions: "Bleaching" and "abstraction"

In a number of works, grammaticalization has been described under labels like "semantic bleaching" (Givón, 1975; Lord, 1976:183/189) , "semantic depletion" (Lehmann, 1982:127), "semantic weakening" (Guillaume, 1964:73–86; Guimier, 1985:158), "desemanticization" (Heine and Reh, 1984)[16] or "generalization or weakening of semantic content" (Bybee and Pagliuca, 1985:59/63). In these works grammaticalization is viewed from the perspective of the source concept which carries the "full meaning" whereas the output of the process is interpreted as an impoverished form, one that is emptied of, or has bleached out, the semantic specificities of its source. Usually, this view implies that the process concerned acts like a filtering device which sifts out anything except the semantic core. In this way, complex meanings are reduced to less complex, but more grammatical, contents.

While the "bleaching" view, as we will call it, captures one important aspect of grammaticalization, it would seem that it ignores certain other characteristics of this process, and of the nature of the resulting structures.

In the process of grammaticalization, the source meaning may disappear completely (cf. Traugott, 1980:48), or it may be replaced by what appear — from a synchronic point of view — to be totally unrelated meanings or functions, like the French negative markers *pas, personne, point* and *rien* which go back to nouns denoting, respectively, 'step', 'person', 'point' and 'thing'. Given the right context, grammaticalization may take directions which are difficult to reconcile with the "bleaching view".

That the output of grammaticalization is "more abstract" than its input has been pointed out in a number of discussions (see Zirmunskij, 1966:83; Traugott, 1980:46–47; Lehmann, 1982:128),[17] and we will also use the term "abstraction" to describe the nature of grammatical concepts with reference to their respective source.

Among the many types of uses to which the term "abstraction" has been put there are three which are of particular interest to our discussion. One, called *generalizing abstraction*, consists in reducing the number of distinguishing features of a concept to its most "central characteristics", or "nucleus". This type of abstraction evokes taxonomic reasoning, and it appears to be present for instance in biosystematic folk taxonomies of the kind described by Berlin, Breedlove and Raven (1973; 1974) where taxa are classified into a specific (e.g. *cork-oak*), generic (*oak*), life form (*tree*) and unique beginner rank (*plant*), thereby being increasingly emptied of their distinguishing features. A second type, *isolating abstraction*, separates one particular property or feature which is not necessarily the "core" or "nucleus characteristic" of that concept.[18]

Both generalizing and isolating abstraction appear to be present as well when grammaticalization is analyzed in terms of bleaching: Lexemes become more "abstract" by losing their semantic specificities and being increasingly reduced to their respective core meaning (generalizing abstraction) or to one particular part of their meaning (isolating abstraction). Abstraction of both types implies that its output is necessarily part of its input, i.e. that what happens in the course of grammaticalization is that concepts are merely reduced in their intensional, and expanded in their extensional, content.

Another type is called *metaphorical abstraction* (cf. Schneider, 1979). This type appears to be more complex and, hence, is more difficult to describe. It serves to relate "more abstract" contents with more concrete contents *across conceptual domains*, where the latter form the metaphorical vehicles for the former. Some of the typical distinctions characterizing this relation are summarized in Table 1.[19]

It is abstraction of the metaphorical, rather than any other, type which underlies grammaticalization. Abstraction of this kind concerns the way we understand and conceptualize the world around us. Objects which are close to us, are clearly structured and clearly delineated, are less "abstract" than objects which are more distant, less clearly structured and/or delineated. And abstraction also relates to referentiality or manipulability in discourse. Objects which refer, which are autonomous speech participants, are less "abstract" than those that show a low degree of referentiality or manipulability (cf. Givón, 1982; Hopper and Thompson, 1984).[20]

2.3.2. Metaphor

We have argued elsewhere that the process underlying grammaticalization is metaphorically structured (Claudi and Heine, 1986; cf. Sweetser, 1982, 1987; Fleischman, 1989),[21] leading from source structures as described in section 2.2 to grammatical structures. The relevant process may be described in terms of a few basic categories which can be arranged lineally in the following way:[22]

PERSON > OBJECT > PROCESS > SPACE > TIME > QUALITY

Each of these categories can be viewed as representing a domain of conceptualization which is important for structuring experience. The relationship among them is metaphorical, i.e. any of them may serve to conceptualize any other category to its right. The above arrangement of categories may therefore be interpreted as consisting of a number of what we have proposed to call *categorial metaphors*,[23] like SPACE IS AN OBJECT or TIME IS SPACE, where the first category forms the topic and the second the vehicle within a

Table 1 *Vehicle and topic in metaphorical abstraction*

	VEHICLE	TOPIC
IDEATIONAL	Clearly delineated, compact	fuzzy, diffuse
	physical (visible, tangible, etc.)	non-physical, mental
	thing-like objects	qualities
	sociophysical interactions	mental processes (Sweetser, 1982:503)
	process	state
	space	time, cause, manner
	individual	mass, class, non-countable
	absolute or quantified magnitude	relative magnitude (cf. Talmy 1986:4)
	autonomous	relational
TEXTUAL	"real world"	"world of discourse"
	less discourse-based	more discourse-based, or "speaker-based" (Traugott 1986:540f.)
	referential	non-referential
	central participant	circumstantial participant
	new	old
	presentational	relational
	independent of context	context-dependent
INTERPERSONAL		
	expressive	non-expressive.

metaphorical equation. In many languages for instance the lexeme for the body part 'back' is used as a metaphorical vehicle to express a spatial concept, 'behind' (=SPACE IS AN OBJECT), and the latter again serves as a vehicle for a temporal concept, 'after' (=TIME IS SPACE).[24]

The arrangement of categories is unidirectional, it proceeds from left to right and can be defined in terms of "metaphorical abstractness" (see above), where a given category is "more abstract" than any other category to its left and "less abstract" than anything to its right. This is in agreement with our claim that grammaticalization is the result of a problem-solving strategy according to which concepts that are more immediately accessible to human experience are employed for the expression of less accessible, more abstract concepts (see 2.1).

There are a number of conceptual domains which are difficult to locate along the scale of basic categories presented above. One of them is predicative possession. At the present stage of research we will assume that possessive concepts belong to the domain of QUALITY, in particular because of the following observations:

(1) The first observation is negative: possession does not show any of the salient characteristics of any of the categories to the left. For example, it does not have thing-like, spatial, or process-like contours — it is most appropriately understood as a non-physical, time-stable entity, in the same way as qualities and states are.

(2) A survey of possessive constructions in African languages (see 2.2.2) suggests that among the most prominent domains for the expression of possession are SPACE ("Y is at X's place" > "X owns Y") and PROCESS ("X seizes/holds Y" > "X owns Y"). In view of the unidirectionality principle underlying grammaticalization we must assume that possession is located to the right of these two categories, which serve as a source for possessive concepts. And since, apart from TIME, there is only one major category to the right of SPACE and PROCESS, possession most likely is a member of that category, QUALITY.

The distinction of cognitive categories like the ones figuring in the metaphorical chain presented above is reflected in various aspects of language structure. Interrogative pronouns for instance tend to be structured lexically in a way that largely mirrors this distinction. Thus, all African languages known to us have separate pronouns for the categories PERSON ('who?'), OBJECT ('what'), PROCESS ('what?'), SPACE ('where?'), TIME ('when?') and QUALITY ('how?'). Note that OBJECT and PROCESS tend to have identical pronominal expressions — a fact that might be suggestive of a special metaphorical relationship between these two categories,[25] which is also reflected, e.g. in the grammaticalization of complement constructions involving the coding of a verb as the nominal complement of a transitive (auxiliary) verb.

Second, there appears to be some kind of correlation between these metaphorical categories and the division of both word classes, or sub-classes, on the one hand and constituent types on the other. Thus, the following prototypical correlations may be established:

Category	*Word type*	*Constituent type*
PERSON	human noun	noun phrase
OBJECT	non-human noun	noun phrase
PROCESS	verb	verb phrase
SPACE	adverb, adposition	adverbial phrase
TIME	adverb, adposition	adverbial phrase
QUALITY	adjective, adverb	modifier.

Third, it would seem that the various hierarchies which have been identified, e.g. as determinants of word or constituent order, are structured in a way which is suggestive of a similar or even identical underlying cognitive patterning (cf. Allan, 1987). For instance, the case hierarchy proposed by Givón (1984:174) might be correlated with the metaphorical chain distinguished here roughly in the following way:

Case function	*Category*
agent	
benefactive	PERSON
dative	
accusative	OBJECT
locative	SPACE
instrument and others	QUALITY

Similarly, structures such as the personal, social status and role hierarchies (see Allan, 1987:57ff.) appear to imply a basic pattern according to which there is a human category preceding a non-human one, which again is followed by more abstract categories relating to non-physical, quality-like referents.

2.3.3. Chaining

In the preceding section we have interpreted the process underlying grammaticalization as a problem-solving strategy whereby "abstract" concepts are described or understood in terms of less "abstract" concepts. This process is metaphorical in nature and involves a transfer in discrete steps from one cognitive domain to another.

In the present section we will argue however that the process is gradual and continuous rather than discrete. Once again we will use the concept BACK to exemplify this point. Our example concerns the noun *megbé* 'back' from Ewe (see also 3.3).[26]

The development from a body part noun ('back') to a prepositional and/or adverbial entity ('behind, back') has been alluded to above. In accordance with the structure of categorial metaphors discussed in 2.3.2 this development may be reconstructed for the Ewe lexeme *megbé* as involving essentially the following categories:

OBJECT > SPACE > TIME > QUALITY

Thus, in sentence (7) *megbé* denotes a body part, hence a concept of the OBJECT category, while in (8) it expresses a locative content (SPACE), either as an adverb, as in (8a) or a postposition, as in (8b), and in (9) a temporal content (TIME). Finally, in (10) it exhibits yet another meaning, 'mentally retarded', which neither denotes a thing-like nor a spatio-temporal concept but rather one of the QUALITY category:

(7) *é-pé megbé fá* OBJECT
3SG-POSS back be cold
'His back is cold.'

(8) a. *é le xɔ á megbé* SPACE
3SG is house DEF behind
'He is at the back of the house.'

b. *é nɔ megbé* SPACE
3SG stay behind
'He stays back.'

(9) *é kú le é-megbé* TIME
3SG die be 3SG-behind
'He died after him.'

(10) *é tsí megbé* QUALITY
3SG remain behind
'He is backward/mentally retarded.'

While this interpretation in terms of metaphorical transfers accounts for much of the "polysemy" of *megbé*, there remain some problems. One relates to semantic ambiguity. In quite a number of sentences in which this lexeme is used it may refer at the same time to more than one of the categories distinguished above. In sentence (11), for instance, *megbé* may in the same way denote a body part ('back') and the 'back part' of an inanimate item, and in (12) it may mean either the 'back part' of an object or the 'space behind' that object. Sentence (13) again may have either a spatial or a temporal meaning. Finally, sentence (14) (=(10)) has both a temporal and a qualitative significance.

(11) *megbé keke-áɖé le é-sí*
back broad-INDEF be POSS-hand
(a) 'He has a broad back.'
(b) 'Its backside is broad.'

(12) *dzra xɔ-á pé megbé ɖó*
prepare house-DEF POSS back ready
'Prepare the back wall of/the place behind the house!'

(13) *é le megbé ná-m*
3SG be behind PREP-1SG
(a) 'He is behind me (spatially)'
(b) 'He is late (=he could not keep pace with me).'

(14) *é tsí megbé*
3SG remain behind
(a) 'He remained behind/is late.'
(b) 'He is mentally retarded.'

It would seem that these cases of overlapping meaning are not coincidental but rather form an integral part of the development from a lexeme to a grammatical morpheme. Thus, the categories OBJECT, SPACE, TIME and QUALITY are not completely separated from one another. Their relationship should be rendered graphically rather as something like (15).

(15) 

Overlapping of this kind offers nothing extraordinary; it is a common feature of grammaticalization processes and has been described in Heine and Reh (1984:57–59) under the label *split*.[27] The transfer of *megbé* from a "thing-like" (OBJECT) to a spatial entity (SPACE) for instance does not necessarily imply a sudden replacement of the former by the latter but rather a stage where, at least for some time, the former coexists side by side with the latter, the result being overlapping.

What appears superficially as a chain of discrete, though overlapping, categories, can however equally well be interpreted as representing a *continuum* without any clear-cut internal boundaries. We noted that sentences (7) through (10) are suggestive of the presence of distinct categories like OBJECT, SPACE, TIME or QUALITY, yet it is equally possible to isolate conceptual entities intermediate between these categories. The OBJECT–SPACE chain for instance consists of at least four such entities, as the following sentences show. In (16), *megbé* denotes the body part 'back' (OBJECT/PERSON)[28] and in (17) it is transferred from the human (or animal) body to other physical items meaning 'back part' (OBJECT). In (18), *megbé* is further transferred from the 'back part' of X to the 'place behind' X, i.e. it denotes a spatial entity which is still conceived as an object (OBJECT/SPACE). Finally, in (19), it refers to a purely spatial concept (SPACE). Thus, there are two intermediate points between the nominal meaning 'back of body' and the adverbial meaning 'behind'.

(16)=(7) *é-pé megbé fá*
3SG-POSS back be cold
'His back is cold.'

(17) *e kpɔ́ xɔ-á pé megbé nyúié má a?*
2SG see house-DEF POSS back nice DEM Q
'Do you see that nice back wall of the house?'

(18) *xɔ-á megbé le nyúié*
house-DEF back be nice
'The place behind the house is nice.'

(19)=(8a) *é le xɔ-a megbé*
3SG be house-DEF behind
'He is at the back of the house.'

In a similar way, intermediate points can be identified between the SPACE and the TIME categories: As sentence (20) shows, *megbé* is first conceptualized as a temporal object ('the time after'; OBJECT/TIME) before it appears as a purely temporal concept (TIME), as in (21). The range of conceptual distinctions expressed by this lexeme has now increased to seven and can be represented graphically as (22):

(20) *é dzó le núɖuɖu-á pé megbé*
3SG leave be food-DEF POSS behind
'He left after the eating time.'

(21)=(9) *é kú le é-megbé*
3SG die be POSS-behind
'He died after her.'

(22) OBJECT/ >OBJECT >OBJECT/ >SPACE
PERSON SPACE

>OBJECT/ >TIME >QUALITY
TIME

These are but a few examples suggesting that there is no discontinuity between categories like OBJECT and SPACE. Many more intermediate entities could be identified if more contexts were considered. It is hoped that these few examples may suffice to give an impression of the continuum nature of the process from OBJECT to SPACE, or of any other categories. The conclusion to be drawn from such observations is that an analysis in terms of discrete metaphorical jumps captures only one aspect of the process. There is both discontinuity and continuity, or metaphorical transfer and gradual extension, involved in grammaticalization. The presence of such divergent cognitive activities may be the result of an interplay between conceptual-taxonomic behaviour on the one hand and pragmatic-textual strategies on the other.

2.4. Context-induced reinterpretation (CIR)

The observations made in the preceding sections suggest that grammaticalization consists of both a discrete and a continuous component. We shall now argue that the former is metaphoric in nature and largely free from discourse pragmatic constraints, whereas the latter appears to be *metonymic* and depends strongly on the linguistic and extra-linguistic context. Consider the following sentences:

(23) From Cologne to Vienna it is 600 miles
(24) From Cologne to Vienna it is 10 hours by train
(25) He was asleep all the way/all the time from Cologne to Vienna
(26) To get to Vienna, you travel from morning to evening

The prepositions *from* and *to* have a locative meaning in (23) but a temporal one in (26). We are dealing here with another instance of the SPACE-to-TIME metaphor (cf. 2.3.2). In (24) and (25), however, the situation is not all that clear: These prepositions can be understood either spatially or temporally, or else as being neither clearly spatial nor temporal. The prepositional meaning in these two sentences appears to mark an intermediate stage, or one out of many possible intermediate stages, in the transition from SPACE to TIME. If we accept this position then it follows that we are dealing here with a type of conceptual contiguity which is to be described more appropriately in terms of a metonymic relationship than in terms of a metaphoric "jump" (cf. Traugott and König, These volumes).

What appears to be responsible for the rise of metonyms is a discourse pragmatic manipulation of concepts whereby these are subjected to contextual factors in utterance interpretation (Sperber and Wilson, 1986:1). We will refer to this process as *context-induced reinterpretation* (CIR). This means, for instance, that, given the right context, spatial concepts may licence temporal implicatures. The result is, for instance, that the prepositions *from* and *to* in (23) may receive a temporal interpretation like the one underlying (24) or (25). Once this interpretation becomes conventionalized, the ground is prepared for yet another interpretation according to which a concept that may be understood either spatially or temporally is interpreted exclusively as a temporal entity in contexts like the one underlying (26).

This analysis has been inspired by Traugott and König (these volumes) who argue that metonymy in such cases serves the "strengthening of informativeness" (see also Traugott, 1987). According to them, semantic change of this kind contrasts with that involving metaphor in that it is "associated with solving the problem of being informative and relevant in communication", whereas metaphor "is correlated with solving the problem of representation."

It would seem that metaphor and metonymy form different components of one and the same process, i.e. grammaticalization, leading from "concrete" to "abstract", grammatical, concepts. On the one hand, this process is made up of a scale of contiguous entities which are in a metonymic relationship to one another. On the other hand, it contains a smaller number of more salient and discontinuous categories, such as SPACE, TIME, or QUALITY. The relationship between these categories, which we have discussed briefly in 2.3.2, is metaphoric but can also be described as being the result of a number of metonymic extensions. In spite of their differing nature, the metonymic and the metaphoric component both co-exist in the process of grammaticalization and have the following structure in common,

$$A \rightarrow A,B \rightarrow B$$

which suggests that in the transition from a conceptual entity A to B there is an intermediate stage (A,B) where the preceding and the succeeding entity co-exist side by side.[29] The presence of this intermediate stage, which has been described in the literature on grammaticalization under labels such as *split* (Heine and Reh, 1984:57), is responsible in language structure for some kinds of both ambiguity and free variation.

This view differs slightly from that of Traugott and König who argue that metaphor and metonymy correlate with shifts to different types of grammatical function:

> 'Metaphor is largely correlated with shifts from meanings situated in the external described situation to meanings situated in the internal evaluative, perceptual, cognitive situation, and in the textual situation. Metonymy is largely correlated with shifts to meanings situated in the subjective belief-state or attitude toward the situation, including the linguistic one" (Traugott and König, This Volume).

According to the claim made here, both metaphor and metonymy are part and parcel of one and the same process, grammaticalization, although in the case of a particular grammatical function one of them may be more prominent than the other. The development of concessive, causal and reference markers discussed by Traugott and König (This volume) are examples suggesting that conversational inferences lead to metonymy and may provide the main parameter for conceptual shift, e.g. from a temporal to a causal interpretation. It would seem, however, that even in the case of these examples metaphor is involved. This can be demonstrated by looking at the following sentences cited by Traugott and König (This volume) to exemplify a transition of the conjunction *since* from a temporal marker, as in (27), via a temporal marker having a causal implicature (28) to a purely causal marker (29).

(27) I have done quite a bit of writing *since* we last met
(28) *Since* Susan left him, John has been very miserable
(29) *Since* you are not coming with me, I will have to go alone

It would seem that underlying this causal inference from a temporal expression there is a TIME-to-CAUSE metaphor whereby a sequence of events in time is used metaphorically to refer to a sequence of events in a causal relationship. Once the implication "what happens earlier is the cause of what happens thereafter" becomes conventionalized the result is a shift from a metaphorical category of TIME to one which is more "abstract", like that of CAUSE.

Linguistically, the result is that a complement of time turns into a complement of reason.

No attempt is made here to justify that an assumption of the kind: "since X *happens earlier than* Y, X must be *the cause of* Y" may give rise to a metaphor which forms part of a more general parameter of conceptualization. This topic will be reserved for a separate treatment.[30] Furthermore, we will not deal here with the interrelationship between the metaphoric and the metonymic component in the process of grammaticalization. It might turn out that it is the former which is responsible for defining the direction of conceptual change, but this is an issue that requires much further research.

3. GRAMMAR

In the preceding section we were dealing with the cognitive base of grammaticalization, most of all with the metaphorical manipulation of concepts. We will now be concerned with the question as to how this affects language structure.

3.1. Reanalysis

Perhaps one of the most spectacular effects conceptual manipulation of the type discussed here has on language can be seen in the reanalysis of linguistic structures. The term "syntactic reanalysis" has been used for a number of different phenomena. The most elaborate treatment of it is that of Langacker (1977) who defines it as "change in the structure of an expression or class of expressions that does not involve any immediate or intrinsic modification of its surface manifestation" (1977:59). What we consider here as reanalysis essentially falls under what Langacker (1977:79) calls "syntactic/semantic reformulation".[31]

In some other works "reanalysis" has been used as a near-synonym for grammaticalization (cf. Lord, 1976:179), i.e. for the development from lexical to grammatical entities. Heine and Reh (1984:95ff.) propose to separate reanalysis from grammaticalization, essentially because of the unidirectionality principle, which is an inherent property of the latter but not necessarily of the former.[32]

The term reanalysis has also been employed to refer to what Heine and Reh (1984:110) called *constituent-internal reanalysis*, i.e. to one specific form of the more general process of reanalysis which has the effect of re-defining constituent boundaries.[33] This process turns a structure like (i) into a new structure (ii):

(i) (A,B) C
(ii) A (B,C)

In this paper we will confine the discussion of reanalysis to cases where conceptual manipulation of the type considered above causes a linguistic structure to be treated as some alternative structure. In this way, pragmatic constructions may be reanalyzed as syntactic structures and syntactic or morphosyntactic structures as differing morphosyntactic structures.[34] Some of the more common types of syntactic reanalysis have been discussed in Heine and Reh (1984:95–111), where however no attempt was made to look into its causes. On the basis of the observations made above we will now try to account for reanalysis.

There is a remarkable amount of iconicity between cognitive and linguistic patterning. We have drawn attention to the fact that the metaphorical categories distinguished in 2.3.2 are not only reflected in the lexical structure, but that there is also a correspondence between these categories and word classes (cf. Claudi and Heine, 1986:301).

Now, once a transfer from one category to another takes place this is likely to affect the status of the word type used to express that concept as well. For instance, when an entity of the OBJECT category serves to conceptualize an entity of the category SPACE or TIME then this is likely to trigger a linguistic development from a nominal to an adverbial word, either an adverb or an adposition. Thus, the change from a noun 'back' to a postposition 'behind' might be viewed as the result of an activity which aims at restoring a one-to-one relationship between cognitive and linguistic structure. This process is paralleled by reanalysis, whereby a given noun phrase, e.g. 'back of the mountain', is reanalyzed as a prepositional phrase, 'behind the mountain'.

Typically, reanalysis accompanies grammaticalization, i.e. when a given morpheme is grammaticalized not only its own pragmatic or syntactic position is affected, but also that of the constituent it belongs to or, conversely, when reanalysis takes place this is likely to involve the grammaticalization of at least one morpheme within the structure undergoing reanalysis. In such cases, both grammaticalization and reanalysis are the result of one and the same strategy, namely the one which aims at expressing more "abstract" concepts in terms of less "abstract" ones. On the other hand there is reason to assume that while both appear like inseparable twins they have, nevertheless, to be kept strictly apart, especially because of the following considerations:

(1) Whereas grammaticalization is essentially a unidirectional process, reanalysis is not, as is shown in Heine and Reh (1984:95ff).

(2) There exist cases of both grammaticalization without reanalysis and reanalysis without grammaticalization. The former occurs, for instance, frequently when the grammaticalized unit is the dependent unit of the constituent affected by grammaticalization (see 3.2). Thus, when a demonstrative turns into a definite article (*this man* > *the man*), the definite article into a non-generic article, etc. (see Greenberg, 1978), or the numeral 'one' into an indefinite article (*one man* > *a man*; Givón, 1981) then we are dealing with the grammaticalization of a demonstrative or numeral, but no reanalyis is involved: The syntactic status of the determiner — head phrase remains unchanged. The latter is the case, for instance, when two coordinate clauses are reanalyzed as a new structure: Main clause — subordinate clause. This process may imply that the morphology used for linking the two clauses is grammaticalized from a coordinating to a subordinating device. However, when there is no linking morphology involved then we are dealing with a case of reanalysis without grammaticalization. This would be the case for instance in a sentence like *She went to bed, she was tired*, consisting on the surface of a sequence of two main clauses. The interpretation this sentence is likely to receive is that the second clause is reanalyzed as a subordinate clause, a causal complement of the first clause. In cases like these, we are dealing with reanalysis without grammaticalization since there is no morphological material to be grammaticalized (see below).

While one may argue that we are dealing with an instance of grammaticalization when a main clause is reanalyzed as a subordinate clause (Traugott, p.c.), there are also cases of opposite developments where subordinate clauses are reanalyzed as main clauses, and where the possibility that such developments constitute instances of grammaticalization can be ruled out. We may exemplify this from Teso, which[35] has a morphological sex gender system and a VSO syntax. In the following sentence, however, it exhibits an SVO word order:[36]

(30) *mam petero e-koto ekiŋok*
not Peter 3SG-want dog
'Peter does not want a dog.'

This sentence is historically derived from the complex sentence **e-mam petero e-koto ekiŋok* 'It is not Peter (who) wants a dog', consisting of a main clause (*e-mam petero*) and a subordinate clause (*e-koto ekiŋok*). The SVO order of this sentence is due to the fact that the main verb *-mam* 'not to be' was grammaticalized to a negation marker. This single instance of grammaticalization was responsible for a number of instances of reanalysis, like the following:

a. The complex sentence was reanalyzed as a simple sentence.
b. The subordinate clause was reanalyzed as the main clause.
c. The subject of the erstwhile main clause was reanalyzed as the subject of the new sentence.
d. Due to the grammaticalization of the verb *-mam* 'not to be', the main clause was reanalyzed as a grammatical marker.
e. The former VSO structure was reanalyzed as SVO, with the effect that Teso has introduced an SVO word order in negative clauses.

Examples like this, where one instance of grammaticalization triggers a series of reanalysis, are not difficult to come by. The way in which the various manifestations of reanalysis in such examples are interrelated would seem to require a separate treatment.

3.2. Dependency

Throughout this paper a distinction between a cognitive and a linguistic domain is maintained, based on the assumption that certain linguistic structures require an analysis that transcends the limits of linguistic methodology. In doing so, we have ignored the question as to where the boundary between the two domains is to be located. In the present section we wish to look at one issue that has been mentioned repeatedly in previous sections (see 2.2.2, 3.1). This issue concerns dependency relations.

There are some developments that do occur when the unit undergoing grammaticalization forms the governing, but never when it forms the dependent member of the construction in question. The presence of source propositions like the ones presented in 2.2.2 or of reanalyis structures (3.1) is confined to constructions where the grammaticalized unit forms the governing member or head. Thus, when in a given language the noun 'back' is grammaticalized to a preposition or postposition ('behind', 'after') then this involves both a source proposition, in this case a part-whole proposition, and reanalysis. The effect of grammaticalization in this case is that a genitive construction like *back of the mountain* is reanalyzed as an adverbial phrase *behind the mountain*. Nothing of this sort happens when the unit undergoing grammaticalization forms the dependent member, as is the case, e.g. when the demonstrative 'this' is grammaticalized to a definite marker ('the'), turning a phrase: Demonstrative — noun (*this man*) into a phrase: Definite article — noun (*the man*). There is neither a source proposition involved nor is there any discernible reanalysis pattern.

This suggests that dependency forms a parameter which is of immediate relevance to our discussion. Whether a given entity governs or is governed by another entity is likely to determine its fate in the process of metaphorical use and of grammaticalization. Since Tesnière (1959) at the latest, dependency relations have become a central concern of linguistic analysis. Their equivalent in cognitive psychology however is less clear. There is reason enough to assume that they are equally relevant to cognition as to language structure.

3.3. Grammaticalization chains

Both transfer and context-induced reinterpretation are responsible for what turn up in language structure as *grammaticalization chains*, which we interpret as a somehow frozen result of conceptual manipulation. Grammaticalization chains reflect linguistically what has happened on the way from more concrete to abstract contents, and they make it possible to reconstruct that process.

It may be useful to distinguish "grammaticalization chain" from a similar term, "grammaticalization channel", which has found some currency during the past decade (Givón, 1979; Lehmann, 1982; Heine and Reh, 1984). Both refer to the same phenomenon, though highlighting differing aspects of it. The latter term relates mainly to alternative ways or paths of grammaticalization. In Heine and Reh (1984:113) grammaticalization channels are therefore described as alternative options available to languages for introducing a new grammatical category. While in that usage channels are defined with reference to their endpoint, they may equally be viewed from their starting point, or source. This is the case, for instance, when one tries to establish what a given conceptual entity, say a body part, may develop into, like a grammatical marker of time, manner, purpose, cause, etc. In such cases, the term "grammaticalization channel" refers to different development lines of one and the same source concept.

Grammaticalization chains[37] on the other hand concern the *internal structure* of channels, or parts thereof; they relate to the cognitive and linguistic nature of these channels. They can in the same way be interpreted as relationship patterns or processes, as synchronic or diachronic phenomena, or even as dynamic, *panchronic* entities. Lehmann (1982:26) claims that the relationship among elements figuring in a grammaticalization channel is a diachronic one.

Within a diachronic perspective one might characterize grammaticalization as a process turning an item, in most cases a lexical item, from a "less grammatical to a more grammatical status" (Kuryłowicz, 1965:52). With the term "grammaticalization chain" we wish to draw attention to a few characteristics of this process. These characteristics concern in particular *overlapping* and *asymmetry*.

To demonstrate what these terms stand for we will come back to the development of the Ewe lexeme *megbé* 'back' which was discussed briefly in section 2.3.3. As we saw there, this lexeme stands for at least seven differing conceptual entities constituting a chain of increasing "abstractness" extending from a concrete, visible/tangible entity, a body part, to a non-physical entity expressing a quality, 'backward, mentally retarded'. The presence of such a chain has considerable linguistic implications; it is immediately reflected, e.g. in morphosyntactic behavior. This behavior is summarized in (31) and can be described in the following way. As a noun denoting a human body part (OBJECT), *megbé* shows all the properties that concrete nouns in Ewe have. It may form the head of a noun phrase (NP) and take any kind of nominal qualifiers. When used as the head of a genitive construction it is linked with the genitival modifier by means of the "alienable" possessive marker *pé*.[38] At the other end of the chain *megbé* appears as a grammaticalized word which has turned from a nominal into an adverbial entity, may no longer accept any qualifiers, or be associated with the genitive marker *pé*.

Between these two extremes there are a number of intermediate stages showing a similar structure as those of the conceptual chain. The transition from one stage to the next is gradual, first involving the case morphology: Once *megbé* no longer refers to a human body part but is still conceived as an OBJECT concept, the use of the genitive marker becomes optional (stage B). In stages C and D, where *megbé* appears, respectively, as a SPACE and a TIME concept but is still treated as OBJECT, it may optionally form the head of an adverbial phrase (AP) although it behaves like a noun which may take qualifiers like adjectives, demonstratives, etc. Stages E and F, where *megbé* no longer has OBJECT-like features, are marked by two linguistic innovations: It may no longer be associated with the genitive marker *pé* and, although it can still be found occasionally with nominal (possessive) modifiers, it has turned from a noun into either an adverb or a postposition.

Table 2. *The morpho-syntax of* megbé

Category	*Gloss*	*Word class* (N = noun, A = adverb, P = post-position)	*Constituent type* NP = head of a noun phrase, AP = head of an adverbial phrase)	*Morphology* (p = presence of the possessive marker *pé*)
OBJECT/ PERSON	'back of body'	N	NP	p
OBJECT	'back part'	N	NP	p/-
OBJECT/ SPACE	'place behind'	N	NP/AP	p/-
OBJECT/ TIME	'time after'	N	NP/AP	p/-
SPACE	'behind'	N/A/P	AP	-
TIME	'after'	N/A/P	AP	-
QUALITY	'retarded'	A	AP	-

This transition from a full-fledged noun to an adverb or postposition shows some properties which appear to be characteristic of grammaticalization processes. The first is that it is marked by *overlapping*: There is always a stage where the preceding and the following structure co-exist side by side as optional variants, before the former gives way to the latter. In stage B overlapping concerns the case morphology, in stages C and D the constituent type and in E and F the word class involved. Thus, we meet the same type of chaining in morphosyntactic structure that we observed in the case of the conceptual structuring (cf. 2.3.3).

In cases of overlapping the categorial status of the items involved is difficult to describe. In stages E and F of Table 2, for instance, *megbé* is not made up of a combination of the properties of nouns, adverbs and postpositions although it exhibits properties of all three word classes; *megbé* rather is, and has in fact been described in traditional grammars as, a linguistic "hybrid" which is elusive of the established linguistic taxonomy and may best be characterized as an entity which is no longer a noun but not yet quite an adverb or postposition, just somewhere in between.

While in cases like this the linguistic situation appears to be an immediate reflection of conceptual manipulation, there is also a decisive difference: Conceptual chaining precedes morphosyntactic chaining. This difference is somehow predictable since it can be derived from the nature of the process concerned. As we have tried to demonstrate above, grammaticalization is the result of conceptual manipulation, and cognitive re-structuring therefore precedes linguistic change. In Table 2, for instance, we notice that the lexeme *megbé* has a spatial or temporal significance in stages C and D, respectively, but is still encoded as a noun, and even in stages E and F it still has nominal traits although it turns up as a pure spatial or temporal concept, respectively. This means that the iconicity between conceptual and linguistic structure alluded to in 3.1 is consistently interfered with. The result is *asymmetry* between cognitive and linguistic structure, which appears to be another salient characteristic of grammaticalization chains.[39]

As we will see below, these characteristics of grammaticalization chains are immediately relevant to linguistic description.

3.4. Grammaticalization and discourse role

Chains like the one presented above display a predictable correlation with the discourse pragmatic parameter of referentiality/manipulability: The lexeme *megbé* is maximally referential when used as an OBJECT-like entity and minimally referential when associated with the QUALITY category. It would seem, however, that this relationship is complex and that not much is gained by reducing cognitive-ideational phenomena of the kind under consideration to pragmatic-textual interpretation, or vice versa.

We may use another example from Ewe to illustrate this point. Our example involves the lexeme *ŋútsu* 'man, adult male', which can be regarded as a "prototypical noun". Depending on the respective context, this lexeme displays a remarkable range of semantic and morphosyntactic variation. Sentences (31) to (33) are characteristic of some of the uses which are associated with *ŋútsu*. In (31), *ŋútsu* denotes a concrete noun which exhibits all characteristics of a "good noun": It fills the syntactic slot of a noun and may take any of the qualifiers which commonly associate with nouns, like number markers, determiners, etc. In (32) it also behaves syntactically like an object noun but is not animate as in (31) and may not take any qualifiers, and in

(33) it occupies the position of an object noun but is no longer "nominal in meaning" and takes modifiers like *ŋútɔ́* 'very', which are governed by adjectives and adverbs but not by nouns, and hence behaves more like an adjective or adverb than a noun.

(31) *me le ŋútsu nyúíé áɖé dí-ḿ*
1SG COP man nice INDEF want-PROG
'I am looking for a nice man.'

(32) *é de ŋútsu la me ná-m*
3SG put man body POSTP PREP-1SG
'He has given me courage.'

(33) *é wɔ ŋútsu ŋútɔ́*
3SG do man very
'He behaved very bravely.'

The case of *ŋútsu* is in no way peculiar or idiosyncratic; the Ewe dictionary is full of cases of a similar nature. The strategy of lexicographers dealing with them is to list the various uses of the relevant lexeme as "polysemes" or "homonyms" and leave it at that (cf. Westermann, 1905:410/411). One way of accounting for such cases is suggested by Hopper and Thompson (1984) who analyse variations in the use of nouns and verbs in terms of their respective *discourse roles*. In sentence (31), for instance, *ŋútsu* may be said to form an example of a highly salient discourse participant which is *autonomous* and *manipulable* and represents a prototypical noun, hence its capacity to associate with the whole range of nominal morphology. In (32) and, even more so, in (33), on the other hand, *ŋútsu* may be interpreted as a non-manipulable, dependent and non-individuated entity which is low in categorial status and therefore lacks the morphological trappings characteristic of prototypical nouns.

The present approach may be viewed as complementing that of Hopper and Thompson (1984). Rather than looking at the discourse value it focusses on the conceptual manipulation of linguistic units. As we have seen above, concrete, visible/tangible objects are employed to conceptualize less concrete entities. We have proposed a number of cognitive categories like PERSON, OBJECT, SPACE, etc. which stand in a metaphorical relationship governed by *cognitive distance*. This relationship is essentially unidirectional, where less distant categories tend to be employed to understand and/or describe more distant categories. In this way, concepts associated with the category PER-

SON may serve to describe concepts of a higher degree of cognitive distance, like OBJECT or QUALITY. Exactly this appears to have happened in the case of *ŋútsu*. In sentence (31) this lexeme stands for a concrete, human concept. Sentence (32) is an example where *ŋútsu* no longer refers to a human being but rather to a quality associated with that concept, although being expressed like an OBJECT-like entity. In (33) finally *ŋútsu* designates purely a quality, thereby competing with word classes normally employed by Ewe speakers to encode qualities, like adjectives and state verbs. Thus it would seem that the conceptual range of this lexeme includes three cognitive categories, PERSON, OBJECT and QUALITY, and, depending on the relevant category it is associated with in a given context, it shows a differing morphosyntactic behaviour: It takes the full range of nominal morphology when referring to the category PERSON but lacks nominal characteristics when referring to an OBJECT-like entity. Finally, when standing for a QUALITY concept it has more in common with adjectives than with nouns.

The view adopted here differs however at least in one aspect from that proposed by Hopper and Thompson (1984). A lexeme like *ŋútsu* no doubt experiences what they refer to as *decategorialization* when used in certain contexts: It loses the ability to act as an autonomous discourse participant, it loses in manipulability and "cardinal categoriality" and it no longer behaves like a prototypical noun. But these losses are counter-balanced by the fact that there are also gains: In the same way as *ŋútsu* ceases to refer to an OBJECT-like unit, a visible, tangible entity, it acquires the contours of an alternative cognitive domain, that of qualities, and its loss in noun-like properties tends to be compensated by a gain in properties of other word classes like those of adjectives or adverbs.[40] The lexeme *ŋútsu* certainly constitutes a "more important" and a "more salient" discourse participant when used as a referential unit but it might be cognitively more complex and expressive when used non-referentially.

3.5. Problems of grammatical description

We have interpreted grammaticalization as a result of the transfer from concrete to less concrete conceptual domains, a process that is essentially metaphorical in nature. This leads to the emergence of grammaticalized structures as the frozen, linguistic product of that cognitive activity. In the present section we will look into the question how all this affects synchronic grammar.

3.5.1. 'Back' in So

To start with, let us look at another example involving the lexeme 'back', this time from So, a Kuliak language spoken in northeastern Uganda. So is a VSO language distinguishing three cases, absolute (unmarked), dative (-V*k*) and ablative (*-o*, *-ɔ*, *-a*). Our example is confined to the ablative (ABL) case marker, but we could have taken any other case instead. The use of this marker is obligatory with certain verbs. The verb *nɛ́kɛ* 'be somewhere' for instance requires its locative complement to be in the ablative case. There is however some variation as to when and where case has to be marked. In (34) below, three largely synonymous sentences are presented, all being translated as 'He is behind the mountain'.

(34) a. *nɛ́kɛ íca sú-o sóg*
be 3SG back-ABL mountain
b. *nɛ́kɛ íca sú-o sóg-o*
c. *nɛ́kɛ íca sú sóg-o*

These sentences differ only in the fact that the ablative case is marked on 'back' in (34a), on both 'back' and 'mountain' in (34b) and on 'mountain' in (34c).

While (34) offers a case where differing morphophonemic structures express essentially one and the same meaning, the opposite case exists as well, where several meanings correspond to one form only, like in (35), where 'back' may either denote a body part (a) or a spatial concept, a prepositional entity. Whenever (a) obtains then 'back' forms the head of a genitive construction, while in the case of (b) it has the function of a preposition within an adverbial phrase.

(35) *nɛ́kɛ cúc sú-o ím*
be fly back-ABL girl
a. 'There is a fly on the back of the girl.'
b. 'There is a fly behind the girl.'

A grammar of So has to account, *inter alia*, for questions like the following:

a. Why are there three optional variants in (34) expressing much the same meaning?

b. Why can case in (34) be marked either on the head or on the modifier or on both? Are there any linguistic clues to explain this situation?

c. Why is (35) semantically ambiguous?

d. Why does the lexeme *sú* have two rather divergent meanings, denoting on the one hand a body part 'back' and on the other hand a preposition 'behind'?

e. Why is case marking on *sú* obligatory when it denotes a noun but optional when it denotes a preposition?

It would seem that answering such questions is hardly possible using any of the models of language description that are on the market. What we are dealing with here are structures which are the immediate result of conceptual manipulation leading from a lexical to a grammatical entity, and sentences (34) and (35) represent differing stages of this process. As we have demonstrated above, this process does not proceed straight from one category to another but rather involves *overlapping*, i.e. a stage where the former meaning still exists while a new meaning is introduced. The result is semantic ambiguity, as can be observed in (35), where the morphosyntax is still that of the first stage, while semantically the first stage (35a) co-exists side by side with the second stage (35b). (35b) also exhibits another characteristic of grammaticalization chains, asymmetry (see 3.3): Whereas the meaning has shifted from body part noun to preposition, the morphology is still that of a noun, i.e. conceptual transfer has not yet affected the morphosyntax.

Asymmetry is even more pronounced in example (34). This sentence represents a stage where the conceptual transfer from the body part noun 'back' to the preposition 'behind' has been concluded, yet morphosyntax has not quite kept pace with this process. Thus, while *sú* clearly has the function of a preposition it still retains the case morphology of a noun in (34a) and (34b), and only in (34c) the case marker is eliminated.

Sentence (34) exemplifies yet another feature of grammaticalization chains, which has been described by Heine and Reh (1984:98ff.) under the label *adjustment* and which relates to the strategy of restoring a kind of iconicity between semantic and morphosyntactic structure: With the reanalysis of the genitive noun phrase *sú-o sóg* 'back of the mountain' as a prepositional phrase 'behind the mountain' the erstwhile head noun 'back' is reanalyzed as a preposition and the modifying genitive noun 'mountain' as the "semantic head" of the emerging prepositional phrase. (34) exemplifies the three major stages of the adjustment process: (34a) represents the initial stage where the erstwhile head noun still shows the case morphology. (34b) marks the typical overlapping stage, where the case morphology is still on the erstwhile head noun but has also been introduced on the new, "semantic head". Iconicity is restored in (34c), where the preposition exhibits no more case marking, which is now entirely confined to the "new head". Thus, example (34) exhibits a case shift from the preposition to the noun governed by that preposition, whereby the intermediate stage is marked by a kind of case agreement, where the case marker is suffixed to both the preposition and the noun.

An additional problem a descriptive linguist is confronted with when dealing with sentences like (34) and (35) is the following. In (34) we have isolated a "preposition" which has either the shape *sú-o* or *sú*. The morphosyntax of this lexeme is complex. It has both nominal and prepositional characteristics, but there are reasons to suggest that it forms neither of these but rather a word class intermediate between nouns and prepositions. The same lexeme shows two different meanings in (35), both a nominal and a prepositional meaning. It would equally be possible to define the meaning of *sú-o* in (35) as one that contains semantic features of both a body part noun and a spatial preposition but which cannot be reduced to an element that combines the semantics of both, rather constituting a unit intermediate between a noun and a preposition. We have alluded to this problem above (see 3.3); it may suffice to note here that the continuum-like nature of grammaticalization chains makes it difficult to maintain a heuristic approach to linguistic description which takes discrete word classes for granted. A good part of language behavior takes place between, rather than within, linguistic categories.

3.5.2. Some conclusions

The discussion about the lexeme *sú* in So concerns only a small segment of a grammaticalization chain, like the one sketched in more detail in section 3.3. Chains like these are not isolated instances occurring in some exotic languages, rather they may be observed in any language and have to be accounted for in a theory of language description. Such a theory has to take into consideration the following kind of observations which are immediately derived from grammaticalization phenomena, as we have seen in the preceding sections:

a. Grammaticalization can be conceived as a process mapped onto language structure. It is hard to understand the structure without understanding the process that has given rise to it.

b. The dynamics of this process are reflected, e.g. in the form of grammaticalization chains figuring in synchronic language structure. An "adequate" description of that structure has to provide information in particular on:
— the number and types of grammaticalization chains occurring in that language,
— the number of members involved in each of these chains,
— the type of contexts associated with each member,
— the semantic, morphological and syntactic properties of each member.

c. A not insignificant part of what turns up in grammar as polysemy or homophony represents different members of one and the same grammaticalization chain. Members which are close to one another in such a chain tend to be interpreted as polysemes while more distant members are likely to be interpreted as homonyms. For instance, within the grammaticalization chain presented in section 3.3, the meanings 'back of body' and 'back part (e.g. of a house)' are likely to be regarded as polysemes, while any of these meanings and the meaning 'mentally retarded' might be regarded as homonyms.

d. In addition to their discrete characteristics, grammaticalization chains behave like continua without clear-cut boundaries, and they are therefore elusive to a taxonomic approach to language description in terms of discontinuous taxa like constituent types, word categories, or morpheme classes.

e. As we have seen above (3.3) overlapping, where an earlier stage coexists side by side with a subsequent stage, is an intrinsic property of grammaticalization chains. Overlapping has various implications for synchronic grammar. One effect is that it creates ambiguity, whereby either one form shows several meanings or else one meaning is associated with two or more different forms.

f. Since conceptual shift precedes morphosyntactic and phonological shift, the result is asymmetry between meaning and form. All languages we are familiar with show examples of morphemes or constructions which have acquired a new meaning or function although they still retain the old morphosyntax. In this way, grammaticalization may, and in fact frequently does, interfere with the iconicity structure holding between form and meaning.

4. Summary

One main purpose of this paper was to look at one of the major problems of grammaticalization studies, the question of what motivates or causes grammaticalization processes. We concentrated on some cognitive aspects of grammaticalization and argued that the rise of grammatical categories is the result of what we call conceptual manipulation as a problem-solving strategy which serves to understand or describe more "abstract" concepts or conceptual domains in terms of more concrete ones. This process is metaphorical in nature and can most appropriately be described by means of categorial metaphors on the one hand and context-induced reinterpretation on the other.

Transfer and the chaining processes are responsible for what turns up in language structure as grammaticalization chains — one of the most striking characteristics of grammaticalization processes, interpreted as the result and linguistic reflection of that cognitive activity.

Assuming that language as a whole is metaphorically structured (cf. Mauthner, 1901; Lakoff and Johnson, 1980) and that grammaticalization and grammaticalization processes are in no way exceptional, the question arises how "true" metaphors are distinguished from those leading to grammatical structures. We have drawn attention to the "source structures", including source concepts and source propositions, which can be characterized as referring to basic human activities, providing reference points for human orientation and being capable of evoking relevant associations. Moreover, source concepts seem to be of a very general, unspecified content.

Apart from questions such as what motivates grammaticalization and what constrains the input of grammaticalization such as its source concepts, other topics have been addressed, among them the relationship between metaphor and context, the nature of chaining, and the way grammaticalization affects synchronic language structure.

Traugott and König (this volume) argue that grammaticalization involves metonymy. This is supported by our own observations. The main claim made in the present paper is that, rather than forming mutually exclusive cognitive activities, metaphor and metonymy are both present in the development of grammatical categories; they form complementary aspects of this process.

NOTES

1. For valuable comments we are indebted to Keith Allan, Derek Nurse, Talmy Givón, Elizabeth Traugott, Joan Bybee, Fritz Serzisko and Eithne Carlin. Our gratitude is also

due to Kossi Tossou for information on his mother tongue, Ewe and to the *Deutsche Forschungsgemeinschaft* (German Research Society) for having sponsored this research.

2. Cf. Lehmann (1982:v): "From the diachronic point of view, it (i.e. grammaticalization; authors' note) is a process which turns lexemes into grammatical formatives and renders grammatical formatives still more grammatical." In a similar way, grammaticalization is described in Heine and Reh (1984:15) as a process or "evolution" "whereby linguistic units lose in semantic complexity, pragmatic significance, syntactic freedom, and phonetic substance, respectively. This is the case for instance when a lexical item develops into a grammatical marker."
3. For a discussion of this term see Lehmann (1982:9).
4. Cf. Givón's discussion of English "*up*" which appears to experience a kind of degrammaticalization to a process verb (Givón, 1975:96). See also Campell and Greenberg, this volume.
5. Concerning a discussion of such factors, see Traugott (1982:265).
6. For more details see section 2.3.2. From a slightly different perspective, Traugott (1980:54) comments the meaning change to be observed in grammaticalization in the following way: "The speaker needs to specify a new relation, or to strengthen one that already exists but has become eroded ...The exigencies of having to be clear direct the speaker to the most concrete term possible."
7. Cf. Traugott (1982:246). Kuryłowicz (1964:245) notes: "Fundamental categories directly based on the speech-situation (*ego* or *hic*, *nunc*) are the starting-point of the elaboration of higher (grammatical) categories."
8. Svorou (1986:526) has shown that there are three kinds of nouns developing into locative adpositions:
   (1) *Body part nouns*: head, heart, anus, mouth, face, neck, ear, forehead, back, loins, rib, body, breast, chest, blood, foot, waist, belly, and stomach.
   (2) *Object-part nouns*: front, edge, top, back, bottom, side, flank, end, middle, entrance, circumference, outside, interior, exterior, upper space, space in between.
   (3) *Environmental landmarks*: field, ground, canyon, sky, house.
9. One may wonder however why body parts like 'nose', 'hair', etc. are apparently never exploited as a concept for spatial orientation.
10. Nominalization can be achieved by morphological forms like infinitives, gerundials, participles, *nomina agentis* and the like.
11. The English progressive construction might as well owe its origin to the locational proposition.
12. Ewe, also called Gbe, is a West African Niger-Congo language spoken in Togo and eastern Ghana.
13. Thus, the Ewe sentence *me le yi-yi gé* (I be going intentional) 'I am about to go, I intend to go' is historically derived from **me le yi-yí gbé* (I be go-go-nominalization area/place) 'I am at the place/area of going'.
14. The phrase "at Y's place" may be rendered in individual languages as "at Y's home", "in Y's hand", etc.
15. *So* has a third future marker, *ko-* for which there is no etymology. Note that the *ac* future is largely confined to the Tepes dialect whereas the *gá* future occurs in the Kadam dialect

of So. What the So verbs *ac* and *gá* have in common, in spite of their opposite deictic content, is that both imply a goal case.

16. Whereas Heine and Reh (1984) define desemanticization essentially as a shift from a "lexical" to a "grammatical" meaning, Greenberg (these volumes) uses this term for a process whereby a given morpheme loses its grammatical (or lexical) meaning, thereby becoming a "functionally empty" segment.
17. "Since the initial meaning is richer, more specific, it is also more palpable, more accessible to the imagination ("anschaulich") and, in this sense, more concrete; whereas the meanings of strongly grammaticalized signs, such as "of", "will" or "and", do not yield mental images, cannot be illustrated and are, in this sense, more abstract" (Lehmann, 1982:128).
18. This is only one of the ways in which "isolating abstraction" has been used; various other ways have been proposed as well.
19. A number of these distinctions are closely interrelated, some may be viewed as expressing essentially the same thing in different ways. The division into an ideational, a textual and an interpersonal domain is based on Halliday (1970:143).
20. This point will be further taken up in 3.4.
21. As we shall see below, this is but one aspect of the process, though perhaps the most salient one. Furthermore, it is important to note that we are dealing here with only one of various types of metaphor, one that serves to describe or understand conceptually complex phenomena in terms of less complex phenomena. This type has been discussed under the label "conceptual metaphor" by Lakoff and Johnson (1980). Thus, both *expressive metaphors*, which serve to enrich the expressiveness of an utterance, or *taboo metaphors*, which serve to conceal or obscure reality (cf. Claudi and Heine, 1986:299), remain out of consideration here.
22. Note the rearrangement of the categorial metaphors PROCESS and SPACE in comparison to former publications, cf. Claudi & Heine, 1986: 301.
23. Concerning the term "categorial metaphor" and the way it is to be distinguished from the conceptual metaphors proposed by Lakoff and Johnson (1980) see Claudi and Heine (1986). The former represent a more "abstract" level of analysis in that each of them includes a cluster of conceptual metaphors.
24. In a number of languages an additional metaphor, QUALITY IS TIME, has been applied, with the result that the lexeme for 'back' has also acquired the meaning 'mentally back, retarded' (see below).
25. In this context, Keith Allan (p.c. of 28.9.1987) draws attention to the fact that PROCESS implies a proposition and is itself a sort of abstract object.
26. Ewe is a tone language having an analytic-isolating morphosyntax. It has SVO as its basic word order, though SOV order occurs in the progressive and ingressive aspects (see Heine and Reh 1984:188–190), and a possessor–possessed syntax.
27. "A characteristic of virtually all developments is that when a given linguistic unit undergoes a certain process then it does not do so in all its uses; it tends rather to be retained in its former status as well, so that there are two coexisting forms of that unit: One that still represents the old status and another that marks the new status resulting from grammaticalization" (Heine and Reh, 1984:57).
28. The labels "OBJECT/PERSON" stand for an OBJECT concept which is typically associated with human beings, though less typically also with animals.

29. Elizabeth Traugott (p.c.) points out that this structure presents a fundamental principle of all language change.

30. Note that the TIME category may give rise to categories other than CAUSE, like CONDITION or QUALITY, see Heine (1990).

31. In Langacker's terminology, reanalysis is further classified into resegmentation and reformulation.

32. One of the effects of grammaticalization is for instance that it turns governing into governed constituents. This process may trigger an opposite development of the erstwhile governed to a governing constituent (cf. Heine and Reh, 1984:95; 104–105). Both developments involve reanalysis but only the former grammaticalization (see below).

33. Langacker (1977:64) refers to constituent-internal reanalysis, perhaps more appropriately, as boundary shift, which he treats as one form of resegmentation, the other forms being boundary loss and boundary creation. This type of reanalysis has been observed in a number of languages but will not be further considered here since it does not seem to be a property directly relevant to grammaticalization.

34. In Heine and Reh (1984:95), the term was applied only to syntactic and pragmatic, but not to morphological structures; this restriction is not maintained here.

35. Teso is an Eastern Nilotic language of the Nilo-Saharan family spoken in western Kenya and eastern Uganda.

36. The sentence is taken from Hilders and Lawrence (1956:XIX); see also Heine and Reh (1984:104–105).

37. Grammaticalization chains must not be confused with grammaticalization scales, which according to Lehmann (1982:26) are descriptive constructs involving functionally similar signs.

38. Concerning the distinction "alienable"/"inalienable" in Ewe see Claudi and Heine (1986:316), Claudi and Heine 1989.

39. This observation has been made already in earlier works. Givón (1975:86) for instance notes: "It is highly unlikely that a verb would change suddenly into a preposition by all semantic, morphological and syntactic criteria at once. One thus expects to find, for a long time, many different types of intermediate cases in the language, where by some criteria a 'particle' is already a preposition, while by others it is still 'a verb' In particular, morphological and syntactic behavior is likely to lag behind the more progressive semantic re-analysis, and thus quite often represent vacuous relics of the older semantic situation."

40. In accordance with the terminology proposed by Hopper and Thompson (1984) one might talk in this case of "recategorialization" which follows decategorialization.

REFERENCES

Allan, Keith. 1987. "Hierarchies and the choice of left conjuncts (with particular attention to English)." *Journal of Linguistics* 23:51–77.

Awolaye, Yiwola. 1986. "Reflexivization in Kwa languages." In Gerrit J. Dimmendaal (ed.) 1986:1–14.

Berlin, Brent, Dennis E. Breedlove and Peter H. Raven. 1973. "General principles of classification and nomenclature in folk biology." *American Anthropologist* 75:214–242.

Berlin, Brent, Dennis E. Breedlove and Peter H. Raven. 1974. *Principles of Tzeltal Plant Classification: An Introduction to the Botanical Ethnography of a Mayan-Speaking Community in Highland Chiapas*. New York: Academic Press.

Bolinger, Dwight. 1978. "Intonation across languages." In Greenberg et al. (eds). 1978:471–524.

Bopp, Franz. 1816. *Über das Conjugationssystem der Sanskritsprache in Vergleichung mit jenem der griechischen, lateinischen, persischen und germanischen Sprachen*. Frankfurt (M.): Andreäische Buchhandlung.

Bybee, Joan L. 1985. "On the nature of grammatical categories." Paper presented at the Second Eastern States Conference on Linguistics, Buffalo, October 3, 1985.

Bybee, Joan L. and William Pagliuca. 1985. "Cross linguistic comparison and the development of grammatical meaning." In Fisiak (ed.) 1985:59–83.

Claudi, Ulrike and Bernd Heine. 1986. "On the metaphorical base of grammar." *Studies in Language* 10(2):297–335.

Claudi, Ulrike and Bernd Heine. 1989. "On the nominal morphology of 'Alienability' in some African languages." In Paul Newman and Robert D. Botne (eds). Dordrecht: Foris.

Croft, William, Keith Denning, and Suzanne Kemmer (eds). 1990. *Studies in Typology and Diachrony*. Amsterdam and Philadelphia: John Benjamins [*Typological Studies in Language* 20].

Dimmendaal, Gerrit J. (ed.). 1986. *Current Approaches to African Linguistics* Vol. 3. Dordrecht/Cinnaminson: Foris [*Publications in African Languages and Linguistics* 6].

Essien, Okon E. 1982. "The so-called reflexive pronouns and reflexivization in Ibibio." *Studies in African Linguistics* 13(2):93–108.

Fisiak, Jacek (ed.). 1985. *Historical Semantics, Historical Word Formation*. The Hague: Mouton.

Fleischman, Suzanne. 1989. "Temporal distance: A basic linguistic metaphor." *Studies in Language*. 13(1):1–50.

Gabelentz, Georg von der. 1891. *Die Sprachwissenschaft: Ihre Aufgaben, Methoden und bisherigen Ergebnisse*. Leibzig: Weigel Nachfolger.

Givón, Talmy. 1975. "Serial verbs and syntactic change: Niger-Congo." In Li (ed.) 1975:47–112.

Givón, Talmy. 1981. "On the development of the numeral 'One' as an indefinite marker." *Folia Linguistica Historica* 2:35–54.

Givón, Talmy. 1982. "Logic vs. pragmatics, with human language as the referee: Toward an empirically viable epistemology." *Journal of Pragmatics* 6:81–133.

Givón, Talmy. 1984. "Direct object and dative shifting: Semantic and pragmatic case." In Plank 1984:151–82.

Givón, Talmy. 1989. *Mind, Code and Context: Essays in Pragmatics*. Hillsdale, N.Y.: Erlbaum.

Greenberg, Joseph H. 1978. "How does a language acquire gender markers?" In Greenberg et al. (eds). 1978(3):47–82.

Greenberg, Joseph H., Charles A. Ferguson, and Edith Moravcsik (eds). 1978. *Universals of Human Language*, 4 Vols. Stanford: Stanford University Press.

Gudschinsky, Sarah C. 1956. "The ABC's of lexicostatistics (Glottochronology)." *Word* 12:175–210.

Guillaume, Gustave. 1964. *Langage et Science du Langage*. Paris, Nizet and Quebec: Presses de l'Université Laval.

Guimier, Claude. 1985. "On the origin of the suffix -ly." In Fisiak (ed.) 1985:155–170.

Halliday, M.A.K. 1970. "Language structure and language function." In Lyons (ed.) 1970:140–165.

Heine, Bernd. 1990. "The Dative in Ik and Kanuri." In Croft et al. (eds) 1990: 129–149.

Heine, Bernd and Ulrike Claudi. 1986. *On the Rise of Grammatical Categories. Some Examples from Maa*. Berlin: Dietrich Reimer.

Heine, Bernd and Mechthild Reh. 1984. *Grammaticalization and Reanalysis in African Languages*. Hamburg: Helmut Buske.

Hilders, J.H. and J.C.D. Lawrance. 1956. *An Introduction to the Ateso Language*. Kampala: The Eagle Press.

Hopper, Paul J. and Sandra Thompson. 1984. "The discourse basis for lexical categories in universal grammar." *Language* 60:703–752.

Humboldt, Wilhelm von. 1825. "Über das Entstehen der grammatischen Formen und ihren Einfluß auf die Ideenentwicklung." *Abhandlungen der Königlichen Akademie der Wissenschaften zu Berlin* 1825:401–430.

Jeffers, Robert J. and Arnold M. Zwicky. 1980. "The evolution of clitics." In Traugott et al. (eds) 1980:221–231.

Kahr, Joan C. 1976. "The renewal of case morphology: Sources and constraints." *Working Papers on Language Universals* 20:107–151.

König, Ekkehard. 1985. "Where do concessives come from? On the development of concessive connectives." In Fisiak (ed.) 1985:263–282.

Kuryłowicz, Jerzy. 1964. *The Inflectional Categories of Indo-European*. Heidelberg: Carl Winter.

Kuryłowicz, Jerzy. 1965. "The evolution of grammatical categories." In Kuryłowicz 1975:38–54.

Kuryłowicz, Jerzy. 1975. *Esquisses Linguistiques II*. München: Fink

Lakoff, George and Mark Johnson. 1980. *Metaphors We Live by*. Chicago/London: University of Chicago Press.

Langacker, Ronald W. 1977. "Syntactic reanalysis." In Li (ed.) 1977:57–139.

Lehmann, Christian. 1982. *Thoughts on Grammaticalization: A Programmatic Sketch*. Vol.1. Köln: Universität zu Köln, Institut für Sprachwissenschaft [*Arbeiten des Kölner Universalien-Projekts* 48].

Lehmann, Christian. 1985. "Grammaticalization: Synchronic variation and diachronic change." *Lingua e Stile* 20(3):303–318.

Lehmann, Winfred P. and Y. Malkiel (eds). 1982. *Perspectives on Historical Linguistics*. Amsterdam: John Benjamins.

Li, Charles N. 1975a. "Synchrony vs. diachrony in language structure." *Language* 51(4):873–886.

Li, Charles N. (ed.). 1975b. *Word Order and Word Order Change*. Austin/London: University of Texas Press.

Li, Charles N. (ed.). 1977. *Mechanisms of Syntactic Change*. Austin/London: University of Texas Press.

Lord, Carol. 1976. "Evidence for syntactic reanalysis: From verb to complementizer in Kwa." In *Chicago Linguistics Society, Papers from the Parasession on Diachronic Syntax*, 179–191.

Lyons, John (ed.). 1970. *New Horizons in Linguistics*. Harmondsworth: Penguin Books Ltd.
Mauthner, Fritz. 1901. *Beiträge zu einer Kritik der Sprache*. Stuttgart: Cotta.
Meillet, Antoine. 1912. "L'évolution des formes grammaticales." Reprinted in Meillet, A. 1921–36. *Linguistique historique et linguistique générale*, Vol 1, 130–148. Paris: Klincksieck.
Newman, Paul and Robert D. Botne (eds). 1989. *Current Approaches to African Linguistics* Vol. 5. Dordrecht/Providence: Foris [*Publications in African Languages and Linguistics* 8].
Norvig, Peter and George Lakoff. 1987. "Taking: A Study in lexical network theory." In *Berkeley Linguistics Society, Proceedings of the 13th Annual Meeting*, 195–206.
Planck, Frans (ed.). 1984. *Objects: Towards a Theory of Grammatical Relations*. London: Academic Press.
Schneider, Wolf. 1979. *Wörter machen Leute. Magie und Macht der Sprache*. Reinbeck: Rowohlt.
Sperber, Dan and Deirdre Wilson. 1986. *Relevance: Communication and Cognition*. Cambridge, Mass.: Harvard University Press.
Svorou, Soteria. 1986. "On the evolutionary paths of locative expressions." In *Berkeley Linguistic Society, Proceedings of the 12th Annual Meeting*, 515–527.
Swadesh, Morris. 1951. "Diffusional cumulation and archaic residue as historical explanations." *Southwestern Journal of Anthropology* 7:1–21.
Sweetser, Eve E. 1982. "Root and epistemic modals: Causality in two worlds." In *Berkeley Linguistics Society, Proceedings of the 8th Annual Meeting*, 484–507.
Sweetser, Eve E. 1987. "Metaphorical models of thought and speech: A comparison of historical directions and metaphorical mappings in the two domains." In *Berkeley Linguistics Society, Proceedings of the 13th Annual Meeting*, 446–459.
Talmy, Leonard. 1986. "The relation of grammar and cognition." Paper No. 165, Series A, July 1986. Duisburg: L.A.U.T.
Tesnière, Lucien. 1959. *Elements de syntaxe structurale*. Paris: Editions Klincksieck.
Traugott, Elizabeth Closs. 1980. "Meaning-change in the development of grammatical markers." *Language Sciences* 2(1):44–61.
Traugott, Elizabeth Closs. 1982. "From propositional to textual and expressive meanings: Some semantic-pragmatic aspects of grammaticalization." In Lehmann and Malkiel (eds) 1982:245–271.
Traugott, Elizabeth Closs. 1986. "From polysemy to internal semantic reconstruction." In *Berkeley Linguistics Society, Proceedings from the 12th Annual Meeting*, 539–550.
Traugott, Elizabeth Closs. 1987. "On the rise of epistemic meanings in English; an example of subjectification in semantic change." *Language* 65:31–55.
Traugott, Elizabeth Closs, Rebecca LaBrum, and Susan Shepherd (eds.). 1980. *Papers from the Fourth International Conference on Historical Linguistics*. Amsterdam: John Benjamins.
Werner, Heinz and Bernard Kaplan. 1963. *Symbol-Formation. An Organismic-developmental Approach to Language and the Expression of Thought*. New York/London/Sydney: Wiley and Sons.
Westermann, Diedrich. 1905. *Wörterbuch der Ewe-Sprache*. Berlin: Dietrich Reimer.
Zirmunskij, V. M. 1966. "The word and its boundaries." *Linguistics* 27:65–91.

The Semantics-Pragmatics of Grammaticalization Revisited

Elizabeth Closs Traugott and Ekkehard König
Stanford University and Freie Universität Berlin

1. INTRODUCTION

"Grammaticalization", as used in this paper, refers primarily to the dynamic, unidirectional historical process whereby lexical items in the course of time acquire a new status as grammatical, morpho-syntactic forms, and in the process come to code relations that either were not coded before or were coded differently (Givón, 1979; Forthcoming).[1] The study of grammaticalization challenges the concept of a sharp divide between *langue* and *parole*, and focuses on the interaction of the two. It also challenges the concept of categoriality, and takes as central the concept of a continuum of bondedness from independent units occurring in syntactically relatively free constructions at one end of the continuum to less dependent units such as clitics, connectives, particles, or auxiliaries, to fused agglutinative constructions, inflections and finally to zero (cf. Bybee, 1985:11–12; Lehmann, 1985:304).

There has recently been considerable interest in the semantic-pragmatic processes involved in early stages of grammaticalization, specifically the development of lexical items into clitics, particles, auxiliaries, connectives, etc. Traugott (1982) suggested that the main path of change at this early stage of grammaticalization is: Propositional (>textual)>expressive. More recently she has revised this formulation and specified the shift as one from meanings grounded in more or less objectively identifiable extralinguistic situations to meanings grounded in text-making (for example connectives, anaphoric markers, etc.) to meanings grounded in the speaker's attitude to or belief about what is said, and has shown that it is part of the larger mechanism of semantic change in general (Traugott, 1989; 1990). In these papers she refers to principles of inferencing, but with only very general sketches of the kinds of inferencing that are involved. Our purpose here is to show that different kinds of inferencing are at work, depending on the particular kind of grammatical function that is evolving. We will argue that the development of markers of tense, aspect, case and so forth involve primarily metaphoric inferencing (as is widely accepted, cf., among others, Bybee and Pagliuca, 1985; Sweetser, 1988; Heine et al., These volumes). By contrast, the kind of inferencing that is dominant in the development of connectives, specifically causals such as *since*, concessives such as *while*, and preference markers such as *rather (than)*, is strengthening of informativeness as a conversational implicature becomes conventionalized. It is the latter kind of inferencing that will be the major focus of this paper. Of course, metaphor and strengthening of informativeness are not inconsistent with each other, but rather can be regarded as complementary kinds of pragmatic processes, provided we analyse metaphor as involving a kind of inferencing (cf. Levinson, 1983; Sperber and Wilson, 1986).[2]

There has been some difficulty in the past in thinking about the semantics-pragmatics of grammaticalization because there has been an assumption since at least Meillet (1948 [1912]) that grammaticalization involves semantic weakening, also known as bleaching. Heine and Reh, for example, define grammaticalization as: an evolution whereby linguistic units lose in semantic complexity, pragmatic significance, syntactic freedom, and phonetic substance, respectively. (1984:15) (cf. also Givón, 1975; 1979) From this point of view, grammaticalization is a kind of impoverishment, or deficit — as Lehmann puts it, a process whereby signs lose their integrity (1985:307). Certainly, bleaching can occur, but, we would argue, most clearly only in the later stages of grammaticalization, for example in the development of the main verb *do* into a dummy auxiliary in Standard English,[3] in the development of third person pronouns into agreement markers, or more generally in the process of paradigmatic fixation.

Bleaching and grammaticalization must be uncoupled if we are to understand the semantic-pragmatic processes of early stages of diachronic grammaticalization. Sweetser (1988) rightly argues that in cases of grammaticalization where image-schematic metaphoric transfer occurs, there is less elaboration of the source meanings than in lexical change, but the grammatical meaning is added; therefore "bleaching" is an inappropriate concept. With reference to examples such as the development of future *go*, she says:

> ...we lose the sense of physical motion (together with all its likely background inferences). We gain, however, a new meaning of future prediction or intention — together with *its* likely background inferences. We thus cannot be said to have merely "lost" meaning; we have, rather, exchanged

> the embedding of this image-schema in a concrete, spatial domain of meaning for its embedding in a more abstract and possibly more subjective domain. (Sweetser, 1988:392).

She also elaborates on the proposal that grammatical meaning is inherently topological and schematic, but that lexical meaning need not be. For example, grammatical relations may express topological relations on a linear parameter, but not precise distances between points on the scale. Or they may express the relative spatial position of two objects, such as sequence and adjacency, but not precise angles, e.g. *corner in time* does not grammaticalize, although front-back, up-down and other spatial relations do (cf. Talmy, 1983; Traugott, 1985a). Sweetser argues that when a lexical item becomes grammaticalized, only the topological image-schema is transferred in metaphorical mappings: the meaning transfer "... is to a fairly abstract, topological domain...so there is less fleshing-out of meaning. However, the meaning of the new domain itself is added." (Sweetser, 1988:393)

In the present paper we will be focusing on what is added in the process of grammaticalization, most particularly on strengthening of the expression of speaker involvement. Consider, for example, the development of the phrase *þa hwile þe* 'at the time that' into the temporal connective *while*. Here the textual meaning is strengthened and pragmatic functions pertaining to meta-linguistic text-building are added. Later temporal *while* developed into the concessive *while* in the sense 'although', which construes a world that has no reference in the described situation, but only in the speaker's world of belief about coherence, especially about correlations between situations or eventualities. At this stage the pragmatics of the speaker's belief-state is strengthened.

The fundamental process we see at work is a principle of informativeness or relevance, essentially the principle: Be as informative as possible, given the needs of the situation (cf. Atlas and Levinson, 1981). This contextualized view of informativeness recognizes that there is a trade-off between speakers' tendencies to say no more than they must (i.e. the principle of economy), given assumptions about hearers' willingness and ability to be cooperative, and hearers' tendencies to select the most informative among possible competing interpretations. It is a view coherent with Lehmann's claim that "every speaker wants to give the fullest expression to what he means" (1985:315), but puts bounds on it. If Lehmann's principle were unbounded, presumably each meaning would be expressed by a different form. But we know this not to be true. One form may mean several things, as do *while*, *since* and *rather (than)*. The principle of informativeness or relevance adopted here demands only that the contribution is as informative as required, and presupposes that more will be read in, cf. Levinson (1983:146–7) and:

> ...human cognitive processes...are geared to achieving the greatest possible cognitive effect for the smallest amount of processing effect...to communicate is to imply that the information communicated is relevant...the principle of relevance is enough on its own to account for the interaction of linguistic meaning and contextual factors in utterance interpretation. (Sperber and Wilson, 1986:1)[4]

From a historical perspective, the principle of informativeness and relevance presumably drives speakers to attempt to be more and more specific through grammatical coding, and most especially to invite hearers to select the most informative interpretation. It does not, however, require a teleological movement to one-meaning-one-form that an unbounded principle of expressiveness would require.

2. SOME THEORETICAL AND METHODOLOGICAL ASSUMPTIONS

Before proceeding, a few assumptions should be stated. A fundamental assumption of all work on language change is that only linguistic phenomena that can be identified in contemporary languages should be reconstructed (the "uniformitarian principle", cf. Romaine, 1982); therefore only inferences that are attested in a modern language may be reconstructed.

As is also true of all linguistic change, the processes outlined are possible and not necessary. For example, there was no necessity for temporal *while* to develop the concessive sense of 'although'; indeed, in German, the cognate *weil* developed a causal, not a concessive, meaning even though the conversational implicatures relevant for concessiveness must have been present in some contexts.

A further assumption is that all languages as we know them have both semantic and pragmatic meanings. Both are equally present, although pragmatic meanings may be expressed in different ways at different times in different languages (e.g. by intonation, particles, clitics, word order, etc.). The claim in this paper that pragmatic meanings are grammaticalized later than non-pragmatic (or propositional) ones does not mean that a language can at one stage have only propositional meanings; it means simply that, given a form X, the pragmatic polysemies associated with it, if any, will have developed later than the propositional ones, that is, they will have been coded at a later stage. That is, meanings typically shift from what is said to what is meant, not vice versa. To put it another way, concessive meanings will not precede temporal ones (concessive $\not>$/ temporal), although the reverse can be true (temporal $>$ concessive).

In seeking to account for this kind of unidirectionality, we need to ask ourselves what could motivate it. It is this question that leads us to a theory of inference and of informativeness and relevance. As we will show, inferences from temporal to concessive are well-attested and comprehensible, but an inference from concessive to temporal is not (how would we infer a temporal from *Although you like your oysters raw, I prefer them cooked*?) The inferences in question are typically not strictly deductive to the logical form, but rather abductive, that is, they are inferences to the best explanation of why the sentence might be true or relevant in the context (for the theory of abduction, see Peirce, 1955; Givón, 1989; Hobbs et al., 1988; and, within the historical domain, Andersen, 1973).

Essential to the present study is the distinction between those pragmatic meanings that are conventionalized (coded, whether lexically, grammatically, or prosodically) and those that are inferred in context, largely through conversational processes of meaning-specification. Even where absence of coding is concerned, many inferences are largely predictable. For example, conjoined clauses without any connective (i.e. without any coding of coherence) are likely to be interpretively enriched as having some coherence simply because they are uttered in sequence. Typically the relationship inferred, if the clauses are action/event clauses, will be that of temporal sequence, as in 1a), but other relationships can be inferred if the sequence is temporally and logically inconsistent, as in 1b) (examples adapted from Blakemore, 1987:113):

(1) a. The road was icy. She slipped
    b. She slipped. The road was icy

If a grammatical form is present, e.g. *and*, *because*, *you see*, this element will further 'constrain the relevance of the proposition it introduces' (Blakemore, 1987:130). But this constraint is not absolute; being an instruction to hearers how to interpret, the grammatical form may itself be augmented, as was *while*. New inferences may arise from it which may themselves be understood in terms of conversational and conventionalized inference.

The approach taken here is that distinct new polysemies of a form are new conventional meanings. The germ of this idea is to be found in Grice's statement that it is possible 'for what starts life...as a conversational implicature to become conventional' (1975:58). Although analyses may differ concerning when polysemy does or does not occur, it is generally accepted that out of context *after* is not polysemous in English; however, in context it allows various inferences about immediacy of precedence. By contrast, out of context *since* is polysemous between temporality and causality. We argue that the polysemies of *since* have arisen through the conventionalizing of earlier conversational inferences. The inferences in question are presumably stereotypical ones, since only standard inferences can plausibly be assumed to have a lasting impact on the meaning of an expression or to function cross-linguistically.

3. THE CONVENTIONALIZING OF CONVERSATIONAL IMPLICATURES

3.1. Inferred causation

One of the best known instances of an abductive inference involving pragmatic strengthening is the classical fallacy *post hoc ergo propter hoc* (cf. Geis and Zwicky, 1971; Atlas and Levinson, 1981; and Horn, 1984:33). Consider such well-known instances in PDE[5] as:

(2) a. After we heard the lecture we felt greatly inspired (+ >because of the lecture we felt greatly inspired)
b. The minute John joined our team, things started to go wrong (+ >because J joined out team, things started to go wrong)

In (2) the inferences are conversational, i.e. not part of the meaning of any particular element in the utterance. They are relevance-based, or strengthen informativeness because they embellish the relation between *After the lecture* or *The minute John joined our team* and the rest of the utterance, and provide an interpretation of why the speaker thought it was relevant to include these temporal facts.

Consider by way of contrast the temporal and the causal meanings of *since* in 3):

(3) a. I have done quite a bit of writing since we last met (temporal)
b. Since Susan left him, John has been very miserable (temporal, causal)
c. Since you are not coming with me, I will have to go alone (causal)

d. Since you are so angry, there is no point in talking with you (causal)

With *since*, when both clauses refer to events, especially events in the past, the reading is typically temporal, as in (3)a. When one clause refers to a non-past event or to a state, the reading is typically causal, as in (3)c. and (3)d., but the causal reading is not required, as (3)b. indicates. The contrastive readings in (3)b. signal polysemy, i.e. conventionalized meanings, not just conversational ones.

It has often been pointed out that temporal-causal polysemies can arise historically through changes in the status of inferences (cf. Geis & Zwicky, 1971:565; Abraham, 1976; Braunmüller, 1978). The following examples are all instances of grammatical markers that appear to have undergone a change from 'temporal' to 'causal' (the temporal itself may be derived from an original spatial, as in the case of *consequently*):

(4) Eng. *since, consequently*; Gm. *infolgedessen* (therefore); Fr. *puisque* (<Lat. *posteaquam* 'after', 'ever since'); Sp. *pues* (<Lat. *post*); Swed. *eftersom, emedan* (cf. <*medan* 'during); Rum. *din moment ce* 'from the moment on', 'because'; Du. *want* 'because' (<PGmc 'when + then'); Eston. *paräst* 'after, because of' (cf. *parastlouna* 'afternoon'); Finn. *koska* 'when', 'because', 'as'.

A look at some of the data in the history of English can begin to give us some insight into some of the contexts in which the change of *since* (originally *siþþan*) came about. In OE texts between ca.850 and 1050 A.D. *siþþan* as a preposition was used almost exclusively to mean 'after' (Mitchell, 1985:Par.2670) cites a total of three likely examples of a causal reading); the standard causal was the originally deictic *for þæm þe* 'for that that'. As a connective *siþþan* meant 'from the time that', that is, it marked the lower temporal boundary of the event in the main clause, and signalled an overlap with some point in an earlier event.

In certain contexts, however, the modern reader may detect a causal implicature. For example, Mitchell (1985:II, 352) cites as a putative example of causal *siþþan*:[6]

(5) Or. 156.11
þa, siþþan he irre wæs & gewundod,
then, after/since he angry was and wounded,
he ofslog micel þæs folces
he slaughtered much of-that troop

When we read this sentence out of its larger context, the participle *gewundod*, being perfective and involving change of state, seems to favor a temporal reading, but the adjective *irre* favors a causal one, since it appears to express state. Nevertheless, a temporal reading with the adjective is plausible if we assume that *wæs* is inceptive/resultative or perfective, i.e. 'had come to be' rather than 'was'. In other words, the adjective in this context can be interpreted as expressing a contingent rather than a general state (the latter would more probably have been expressed by *bið*[7]). And indeed we find that this sentence occurs in the context of a narrative concerning the legendary Pyrrhic victory. In the battle a Roman soldier wounds an elephant in the navel; this elephant, having become enraged on being wounded, wreaks mayhem on the army. *Siþþan* in (5), then, must be interpreted as a temporal (indeed it partially translates the Latin adverbial *postquam* 'afterward'), and is therefore not a conclusive example of the conventionalizing of causative inference in OE.

One virtually indisputable example is:

(6) Bo. 36 104.26
Ac ic þe wille nu giet getæcan þone weg...
But I thee will now still teach that way...
siððan ðu ongitst þurh mine lare hwæt sio
since thou seest through my teaching what that
soðe gesælð bið, & hwær hie bið
true happiness is, and where it is
'But still I will now teach you the way...since through my teaching you see what true happiness is, and where it is'

Here *siþþan* translates the Latin causative *quoniam*; but even without the Latin original we must assume it is causative since the context is non-narrative: The stative perception/mental verb 'see, undertand' introduces an aspectual generic clause signalled by the verb *bið* instead of the contingency verb *is*.

We may hypothesize that the occurrence of *siþþan* in contexts which did not block a causal interpretation, such as (5), came to be conventionalized by frequent use. By the fifteenth century, i.e. very late ME, the form is attested frequently in stative and other non-completive environments where the temporal reading is blocked, as in (6). In other words, although the causal inference is detectable in OE, enough other examples are undecidable that we cannot establish that the causal inference had truly become conventionalized until the fifteenth century.

The formulation *post hoc ergo propter hoc* suggests that it is strict sequence of events, $event_1$ *followed by* $event_2$, that gives rise to causal implicatures. And indeed it does account for some causal inferences from temporals, as in the case of *After John entered the room, Bill jumped out of the window.* However, as we have seen, states are more likely to give rise to causal interpretations than sequences of events, so a more appropriate formula would be *state*$_1$ *relevant to state*$_2$. Furthermore, the traditional formulation *post hoc ergo propter hoc* taken literally might lead one to wonder why it is that some temporals that seem to be stereotypically non-sequential, or at least can be used both sequentially and non-sequentially, can be interpretively enriched to causal relations. Consider the conversational implicatures in the following PDE sentences:

(7) a. I couldn't work when the television was on.
b. I can't sleep now that I am alone.

Historically, too, we frequently encounter the conventionalizing of causals that were formerly not necessarily sequential:

(8) *weil* (<OHG *dia wila so* 'so long as'); Lat. *dum* 'when, as long as, because'; Fr. *quand* when, because'; Finn. *kun* 'when, while, as, since, because'; Eston. *kuna* 'while, as, since, because'.

It appears then that what is needed for a causal inference to arise is partial temporal overlap, not sequence. More specifically, the meaning 'from the time that' licenses (but does not require) causal implicatures to become conventionalized. A good example is OE *nu*, which was used as an adverb meaning 'now'; as a connective it almost always has a causal meaning. We can postulate that a context such as is found in PDE (7b), where one clause (the matrix) expresses a state, was the entry-point for the shift from temporal > causal. Consider:

(9) AECHom I, 24 350.21
Efne nu þu eart gehæled ne synga þu heononforð
Even now thou art saved not sin thou henceforth
'Now you are saved, don't sin from now on.' (+ > because you are saved, don't sin from now on)

This may be interpreted as 'note that as of the present time you are/have become saved, and treat it as the starting point of future behavior', with an inferential enrichment + > 'because you note this, therefore from this time forth modify your behavior'. In (9) causality may be only a conversational implicature, since temporal relations are clearly distinguished (past participle *gehæled*, future adverb *heononforð*). However, it is presumably conventionalized in the following, where there is no tense change and indeed the context implies that there has been no change of state.

(10) AECHom I. 26.378.6
Untwylice þu lyhst þæt ðu god sy, nu ðu
Unquestionably thou liest that thou god art, because thou
nast manna geþohtas
not-knowest men's thought
'Without question you are lying when you say that you are God, because you do not know the thoughts of men.'

The adverbial *nu* 'from this time forth' is sufficiently informative to convey a relation between the clause it initiates and the main clause, but invites the inference that more was meant; why else would the speaker have mentioned the temporal relation at all? Note that (10) does not code an external causal relationship that can be regarded as true in the world, but rather an epistemic causal augmenting the inference that the speaker has evidence for the proposition (cf. Sweetser, 1990; Blakemore, 1987:139 analyses causals of this type as indicating dependent relevance, i.e. relevance between propositions).

As would be expected in any kind of language change, the temporal meaning that the causal adverbials and connectives discussed here originally had was not lost immediately, but was typically maintained alongside the causal meaning for a long time (for detailed studies of coexistence of polysemies in these volumes, cf. papers by Abraham and by Heine et al.). In the instance of *since*, the meanings have coexisted since the twelfth century. In other instances, either the temporal or the causal meaning has disappeared as a separate polysemy. An example of the latter is causal *now*. An example of the loss of the temporal is provided by *consequently*, formed in the fifteenth century from Latin via Old French in both the temporal and causal senses. The temporal meaning, exemplified in (11a), survived until the seventeenth century, but was eventually replaced by the causal, as in (11b):

(11) a. 1450 (c1405) Purvey Determ. 175/181 (MED)
If it is leueful to preche þe naked text to pe pupel, it is
It it is lawful to preach the straight text to the pupil, it is
also lefful to write it to hem & consequentliche,
also lawful to write it to him and afterwards
by proces of tyme, so al þe Bibil
by process of time, similarly all the Bible

b. 1447 Bokenham Sts. 519 (MED)
Than folwyth it thus ful consequently That thou
Then follows it thus completely with-reason That you
clepyst crist thy god
call Christ your god

What is important here is that an older meaning that has been lost, such as temporal *consequently*, does not seem to be recoverable by inferences; however, if a later meaning such as causal *now* is lost, it will still exist as a conversational inference, as in (7b). This is exactly what we would expect if the hypothesis of the unidirectionality of inferences alluded to in Section 2. is correct.

3.2. From concomitance to concessivity

We turn now to another example: The concessives. Among the major sources in the development of concessive connectives are expressions whose original or at least earlier, meaning was 'concomitance' or 'cooccurrence', and certain negative expressions (cf. König, 1985; 1986; 1988; Forthcoming):

(12) a. connectives originally expressing simultaneity or temporal overlap: *while*, *still*, *yet*; Gm. *zugleich*, *indes(sen)*, *dennoch*; Fr. *cependant*; Turk. *iken* 'while', 'although'; Indonesian *sekali-pun* 'although' (<'at the same time + even'); Hawaiian *oiai* 'while', 'meanhile', 'although'; Jap. *nagara* 'while', 'although'

b. connectives originally expressing simple cooccurrence or concomitance, or even similarity: EME *withal* (<'along with the rest'), *all/just the same*; Gm. *gleichwohl*, *bei all*; Dan. *evenwel*; Rum. *cu toate ca* 'with all (things) that'); Turk. *bununla beraber* 'together with this'); Hopi *naama-hin* 'although' (<'together' + 'thus'); Quileute *-t'e* 'with, although'

c. negation of asymmetry (e.g. negation of opposition, negation of negative correlation): *notwithstanding*, *nevertheless*, *nonetheless*; Fr. *n'empeche que*; Gm. *nichtsdestoweniger*

As in the case of causal connectives, many of the concessive connectives have retained their original meaning alongside the concessive implicature that has become part of the conventional meaning. Sometimes it may still constrain the environments in which a form may occur. The fact that, for instance, *while* is still awkward for some speakers in contexts expressing anteriority of one event to another shows that this conjunction has not entirely lost its original meaning of temporal overlap:

(13) ?While our business was extremely successful last year, this year does not look too promising.

(contrast *although* which is acceptable for all speakers in this context).

PDE examples such as those in (14) illustrate the fact that expressions of simultaneity, concomitance, or correlation can synchronically be amplified and interpreted as expressions of concessivity:

(14) a. He can play the Beethoven sonatas and he is only seven years old
b. It is midnight and Mary is still working
c. It is difficult to find a method that is effective and, at the same time, inexpensive
d. Not having any money, all the same I went into this expensive restaurant

There are so many things going on simultaneously and there are so many things cooccurring that mere cooccurrence or concomitance of two situations (states, in particular), is rarely highly relevant information. Nevertheless, there are some contexts in which concomitance may be highly relevant and worthy of pointing out. One of these contexts is where there is a general incompatibility between the two situations, i.e. where one situation does not normally cooccur with the other. Thus in (14a) the situation of being seven years old is assumed not normally to cooccur with the ability to play the Beethoven sonatas. What may occur 'normally' is of course not always fully agreed on. In the case of (14b), the speaker uses *and* to draw attention to coocurrence and thereby invites the hearer to interpret the speaker as meaning that in the speaker's view it is not normal for Mary (or people in general) to work when it is midnight.

While originated in OE in an adverbial phrase translatable as 'at the time that' consisting of the dative distal demonstrative, the dative noun *hwile* 'time', and the subordinator *þe*, a highly explicit coding of simultaneity, cf.

(15) ChronA(Plummer) 913.3
& wicode þær þa hwile þe man þa burg worhte
and camped there that time that one that fortress worked-on
& getimbrede
and built
'and camped there while the fortress was worked on and built'

This phrasal expression was reduced by late OE to the simple conjunction *wile*:

(16) ChronE(Plummer) 1137.36
ðæt lastede þa [xix] wintre wile Stephne was king
that lasted those 19 winters while Stephen was king

In the process, the precise specification of simultaneity signalled by the demonstrative was lost, allowing for other, less precise, inferences to play a part. Among such inferences is that the conditions specified in the subordinate clause serve not only as the temporal frame of reference for those in the main clause, but also as the grounds of the situation (the disasters lasted nineteen years because Stephen was king). Such an inference to grounds of the situation is dominant over temporality in some examples dating from the later 14th century:

(17) 1375 Barbour's Bruce 1.60 (OED)
Thar mycht succed na female, Quhill foundyn mycht be ony male
'No female was able to succeed while any male could be found.'

(cf. *as long as*, *at the same time as*, which also came to have concessive inferences). In some languages, among them German, this inference to the grounds of the situation, and thence to cause, has become the main extension of 'while'. In English yet another augmentation led to the inference of surprise overlap in time or surprise relations between event and ground, hence to the adversative, concessive meaning. Probable instances of the coding of surprise and hence concessivity appear in the early seventeenth century, cf.:

(18) 1617 Sir W. Mure Misc. Poems xxi.23 (OED)
Whill others aime at greatnes boght with blod, Not to bee great thou stryves, bot to bee good
'While others aim at greatness that is bought with blood, you strive to be not great but good.'

This could be interpreted as a statement about simultaneous behaviors. However, there is a strong inference, reinforced by the inversion in the second line, that it is unusual not to be blood-thirsty.

To sum up, although the formal semantic analysis of the concessive presents many puzzles that have not been solved satisfactorily, it is intuitively plausible to consider concessive relations of the type:

(19) a. although p, q

as presupposing a conditional:

(19) b. if p, then normally ~ q

Thus, for (14b) *If it is midnight, then normally she would not still be working*, for (18) *If others strive to be great, then normally you would not strive to be (just) good, not great.*

The meaning of general incompatibility makes the concessive meaning a favored target for certain types of negative expressions. Before we turn to the grammaticalization of negative terms to express concessivity, consider:

(20) a. He stays home although he is not sick

Here the negative concessive amounts to an assertion of the positive

(20) b. He stays home although he is well

because *sick* is a semantically negative adjective standing in a complementary relationship to the positive *well.* In either case, the logical meaning is actually *If he stays home, then normally he is/should be sick/not well.* (20a) is a more oblique way than (20b) of expressing incompatibility because of the multiple layers of negation it involves: *although he is not sick = then normally he is not (not sick).*

In several Indo-European languages (and possibly other languages, though we have not discovered any to date), we find that negated semantically negative terms have been grammaticalized to concessives. *Notwithstanding*, for example, involves the negative of 'against' + 'stand' (OE *wið* was the term for opposition that retained its old meaning in a few fixed expressions like this concessive and *fight with the enemy* in the sense of 'fight against the enemy'). To say something is 'not opposing' amounts to asserting that it is congruent, correlated, etc. Similarly, *nonetheless/nevertheless* presumably coded relationships of the kind:

(21) p, not the less q (despite the expectation that q is less valued)
(22) p, not the less frequently q (despite the expectation that less frequent is less valued)

What is not less (nor more), and not less frequent (nor more so), is equal in quantity or frequency, therefore correlated. The various negative terms, therefore, logically compute as members of the same semantic field as positive terms like *just/all the same*. Such positive terms assert parity, but imply expected disparity.

(23) p, in exactly the same way q (despite the expectation that q is inversely proportional to p)

Whether the phrases are negative or affirmative, in each case the more literal meaning has been augmented as the phrase has become grammaticalized. In other words, the more literal meaning has been specialized to a limited set of adverbs or conjunctions that can express concessivity (cf. Hopper on specialization, These volumes). In their earlier histories, when they were fully lexical, they were members of relatively open sets where their literal meanings prevailed. For example, in Middle English *never the less* contrasted with phrasal adverbs like *never the wiser/better/worse/more/nearer*, but unlike them became specialized as a clausal connector denying the anticipated presupposition connected with the clause. An early example is:

(24) c1330 R. Brunne Chron. 61 (OED)
Neverþeless to William he ȝeld him wele his bone
'Nevertheless he fittingly granted William his prayer.'

Nonetheless (often spelled *none the less*) contrasted in its literal meaning with *none the more/wiser/worse/better* right up until the nineteenth century, when the concessive use arose (OED); all of these except the first survive in PDE, but are not part of the same paradigm as *nonetheless* either in meaning or in syntactic position. Likewise, *all the same* was a member of a lexical set including *all the more/better/richer*, etc., but, along with *just the same* came to take on a contrastive, concessive function in the nineteenth century. One of the earliest examples cited in the OED is:

(25) 1845 Disraeli Sybil vi.iv (OED)
What you say is well worth attention; but all the same I
feel we are on the edge of a regular crisis.

3.3. From temporals to preference to denial markers

Another instance of a standard interpretive augmentation that has left its imprint on the conventional meaning of related expressions in a variety of languages is provided by the historical development of preference adverbs and connectives like *rather (than)* from temporal adverbs, which may themselves have derived from spatial terms (cf. Dieterich and Napoli, 1982). Some examples are:

(26) Eng. *sooner (than)*, *rather (than)* (<OE *hraþor* 'sooner'); Gm. *ehe*, *eher (als)*, *bevor*; Span. *antes* (<Lat. *ante* 'before'); Fr. *plutôt* (<*plus tôt* 'more soon'); Russ. *skoree* 'more quickly, rather'; Ruman. *mai curînd* 'earlier, rather'; Finn. *pikemmin* (cf. *pika* 'at once'), *ennen* 'before, rather'. In PDE the preferential reading of *soon(er)* coexists with the temporal reading in PDE, cf.

(27) a. Bill died sooner than Mary (temporal)
b. Bill would sooner die than marry Mary (preference)

It is most frequently encountered in contexts of volitional *will/would*, and invites the inference that q is something the subject does not want (to do). Sometimes, however, a term for 'earlier' can be truly ambiguous with a temporal (at least within the bounds of an intonational sentence). Quirk et al. (1985:112 note b.) for example, cite:

(28) He'd sit alone in the dark before he'd watch television

One reading gives the temporal habitual (*every evening he sat in the dark before watching TV*), and another the preference (*he prefers sitting in the dark to watching TV*).

In the case of *sooner*, both the temporal and the preference sense date back to early ME, when the comparative *sooner* came to be attested (there are no examples of the comparative in OE, and only a few of *sona*, all in the temporal sense). We can therefore not gain insight from *sooner* into the development of the preference reading. However, when we turn to *hraþor*, (the comparative of *hræþe* 'quickly, soon'), we can trace how 'sooner, more quickly' came to mean 'preferably', via the inference that 'the sooner the better'. The temporal meaning of *rather* essentially disappeared by the ENE period. *Rather than* in PDE has a preference reading and, in addition, what can be called a metalinguistic denial meaning (Thompson, 1972; Dieterich and Napoli, 1982). Consider:

(29) a. He recites rather than sing
b. He recites rather than sings

(29a), with the non-finite verb *sing* illustrates the preference *rather than*. As pointed out by Thompson (1972:242–3) the preference *rather than* "presupposes that there is a preference on the part of the subject for the situation of the main clause over that of the adverbial clause", thereby excluding such locutions as:

(29) c. *It rains rather than snow

Furthermore, "the action of the first clause will render the second clause unnecessary or impossible to carry out". Therefore (29a) implicates:

(29) d. He recites because he is unable to sing/so that he does not have to sing

By contrast (29b), with the finite verb *sings*, is the metalinguistic *rather than*, and expresses the speaker's preference for the formulation *He recites* and denial of a presupposed or expressed *He sings*. In essence (29b) means

(29) e. I prefer to say/assert that he recites and deny that he sings

In French the contrast between the equivalent two connectives is coded by the distinction not between non-finite and finite verb but between absence or presence of the negative *ne*. The latter codes speaker's denial. Thus (30a) parallels (29a) and (30b) parallels (29b):

(30) a. *Il recite plutôt qu'il chante*
b. *Il recite plutôt qu'il ne chante*

A brief look at the development of *rather than* shows at least one path by which such readings can arise from a temporal. In OE we find *hraþor* meaning 'sooner, earlier':

(31) AECHOM I 25 356–28
iohannes wæs hraðor mannum cuð þurh his mærlican
John was sooner to-men known through his splendid
drohtnunga þonne crist wære: for þan þe he ne
conversations than Christ was: for that that he not
æteowde his godcundan mihte ær þam þe he wæs
manifest his divine might before that that he was
þrittig geara on þære menniscnysse
thirty years in that human incarnation
'John (the Baptist) was known to men sooner than Christ through his splendid preachings, because Christ did not reveal his divine power before he was thirty years old.'

Sometimes *hraþor* is used in a context not of events but of states, and here the adverb has the meaning 'more' (note the inference in (31) that John was known more because he was known sooner). An example is the translation provided by AElfric in his Grammar of the Latin *magis* 'more':

(32) AEGram 241.2
magis swyþor: magis hoc uolo quam illud swyðor oððe
magis more: magis hoc volo quam illud more or
hraðor ic wille þis þonne ðæt
rather I want this than that

In modal contexts of wish, expectation, etc. when the comparand was present *hraþer þonne* was augmented to express preference, cf.

(33) AELS (Agnes) 301
wiste þæt seo dohtor þe drihten hæfde gecoren hraðor
knew that that daughter who Lord had chosen rather
wolde sweltan þonne ceorlian
wanted to-die than to-take-a-husband
'knew that his daughter, who had chosen the Lord, would rather die than get married'

As is typical of preference *rather than*, there is a negative implicature, in this case 'die so that she would not have to get married'. This kind of inference of rejection of one alternative presumably allowed strengthening of the connective to express rejection of a metalinguistic alternative, particularly in declarative contexts. In (34) the intentional force of the subject (*we*) is embedded in a complement to *mater* 'reason', and potential ambiguity between preferred action by the subject and preferred choice of words can be inferred:

(34) c1380 Wyclif Sel. Wrks. I.409. (OED)
We have litil mater for to laughe, but rather for to morne

In essence this is ambiguous between: 'There is little reason for us to laugh; we should prefer to mourn' and 'There is little reason for us to laugh; more correctly speaking we should mourn'. Later we find unambiguous metalinguistic denial of one alternative with non-human subjects as in:

(35) 1611 Shakespeare, Tempest II.i.60
The rarity of it is...That our garments, being...drench'd in the sea, hold notwithstanding their freshness and glosses, being rather new-dy'd than stain'd with water.

The implicature that the clause introduced by *rather than* is unnecessary or impossible to carry out has been augmented to express preference for the formulation *our garments were new-dy'd* and denial that they were stained. The metalinguistic preference reading has been conventionalized and in PDE requires syntactically contrastive contexts such as (29a) and (29b).

4. STRENGTHENING OF INFORMATIVENESS VS. METAPHORIC PROCESSES

We have argued that certain kinds of grammaticalization are instances of strengthening of informativeness, or the conventionalizing of conversational inferences. We turn now to discussion of which kinds of grammaticalization in its early stages involve this kind of change.

So far we have not discussed examples of another kind of inference, metaphor. Metaphor has traditionally been regarded as central to semantic change in general. Although definitions of metaphor vary, most share certain concepts in common, especially understanding and experiencing one kind of thing in terms of another, and directionality of transfer from a basic, usually concrete, meaning to one more abstract, cf. Sapir (1977), Lakoff and Johnson (1980), Claudi and Heine (1986). Although metaphorization has traditionally been recognized primarily in lexical change, recently many arguments have been put forward that the development of grammaticalization is also strongly motivated by metaphoric processes, cf. Sweetser (1988, 1990), Bybee and Pagliuca (1985), Claudi and Heine (1986), Heine and Claudi (1986), Heine et al. (These volumes). For example, Claudi and Heine say of the "vehicle of a metaphor and the lexeme undergoing grammaticalization" that they:

> ...are governed by an arrangement of conceptualization...which is unidirectional and proceeds from concrete to abstract, and from concepts which are close to human experience to those that are more difficult to define in terms of human cognition. (1986:328)

Claudi and Heine discuss the development of body part terms into locatives, of spatials into temporals, etc. in terms of conceptual metaphors such as SPACE IS AN OBJECT, TIME IS SPACE.

Examples of spatio-temporal metaphors in the process of grammaticalization are widely known and will be only touched on here. They include the use of GO for future (*I'm going to go*), COME for perfect (Fr. *je viens de le faire*), BE AT/BE IN for progressive, cf. Traugott (1978), Fleischman (1982), Bybee (1987), and of verbs of motion for case, cf. Givón (1975).

In each case, more concrete concepts come to serve as models for more abstract ones and metaphor is clearly at work. What the changes just cited have in common is one of three tendencies that have been identified for semantic change in general, both lexical and grammatical (Traugott, 1989:34), which can be expressed as follows:

(36) *Semantic-pragmatic Tendency I:*
Meanings based in the external described situation > meanings based in the internal (evaluative/perceptual/cognitive) situation

By "internal" situation is meant the situation as perceived or understood by a sentient being, not necessarily the speaker. For example, temporal relations are "internal" in the sense that they have fewer physical correlates. The extension of the originally spatial preposition *æfter* to the temporal preposition *æfter* in Old English is an instance of Tendency I: A shift from reference to a concrete, physical situation to reference to a cognitive, perceptual situation. When the spatial term is itself derived from a body part, which is often the case (cf. BEHIND), Tendency I may operate twice, once from OBJECT > SPACE, and then again from SPACE > TIME.

Other well-known examples of metaphoric changes in the grammaticalization of spatial terms include the development of adverbs or prepositions into clause connectives, for example of Old English prepositional *æfter* 'following behind, later' to the Middle English subordinating *after*. These are examples of a second tendency in semantic change, identified by Traugott (1989:35) as

(37) *Semantic-pragmatic Tendency II.*
Meanings based in the described external or internal situation > meanings based in the textual situation

where 'textual' means 'cohesive'. When *æfter* became a temporal connective, it underwent Tendency II and shifted to a marker of textual, cohesive relations. The metaphor presumably at work here is that events expressed in clauses are treated as objects with spatio-temporal correlates.

But is metaphor the right or the only process to adduce for all cases of grammaticalization? Recently some nervousness about the universality of metaphor in grammaticalization has been expressed. For example, Heine et al. (These volumes) acknowledge that metaphor is not the only process involved; and although Bybee and Pagliuca (1985) cite metaphor as the process involved in the development of deontic from 'agent-oriented' modalities, e.g. *must, have to*, in Bybee (1987) metaphor is abandoned as an explanation of the development the hypothetical uses of the modals *could* and *would*.[8] It is difficult to see in what sense a causal is an analog of a temporal, or a concessive of a coocurrence relation. We have suggested that strengthening of informativeness and conventionalizing of conversational inferences are the prime processes at work in the development of causals, concessives, and preference/denial connectives.

These three cases of grammaticalization involve not only Tendency II but also the third tendency in semantic change identified in Traugott (1989:35):

(38) *Semantic-pragmatic Tendency III*
Meanings tend to become increasingly situated in the speaker's subjective belief-state/attitude toward the situation

Causals, concessives and particles of denial are all essentially expressions of speaker attitude to the relationship of elements within the proposition or of propositions to each other, as well as of the compatibility of those relations. Temporal *siþþan*, which is a textual marker, comes via Tendency III to express the speaker's view of a causal relation between states of affairs. Similarly, temporal *while*, also a textual marker, comes by Tendency III to express the speaker's surprise at the relation between two propositions.

In the case of *hraþor* a temporal adverb came by Tendency I to have a preference (evaluative) meaning; the textual connective *hraþor þanne*, developed by Tendency II, could express either a temporal (the older) or a preference (the newer) meaning. The shift from the preference to the denial connective occurred through the operation of Tendency III. As a preference marker, *rather than* connects clauses the subjects of which must be human but not necessarily the speaker, cf. Benveniste's (1973) 'sujet d'énoncé'. By contrast, in the denial reading, the connective connects clauses the subjects of which can be any noun, but the subject of the denial is the speaker (Benveniste's 'sujet d'enonciation'). We may note further that the development of the denial meaning is an example of shifts from non-epistemic to epistemic meanings such as have been noted in Shepherd (1982), Bybee and Pagliuca (1985), Hanson (1987), Traugott (1989). To give just one example, *must* in the epistemic sense of 'I conclude that' derived from the obligative sense of 'ought to' by strengthening of conversational inferences and subjectification. If I say *She must be married* in the obligation sense, I invite the inference that she will indeed get married. This inference is of course epistemic, pertaining to a state of affairs that is anticipated to be true at some later time. When this epistemic inference is conventionalized its origin in the speaker's subjective belief-state is strengthened as well (cf. also Abraham, These volumes, on the development of epistemic meanings in German modal particles).

Strengthening of informativeness has no well-established place in the taxonomy of semantic changes, which includes metaphor, metonymy, extension, restriction, among others (Anttila, 1972). One approach would be to add strengthening of informativeness to that taxonomy. However, to treat it as something separate from the other processes is to miss some generalizations. We suggest that strengthening of informativeness is in fact a type of metonymy.

Metonymy is usually paired with metaphor as a type of semantic change. However, it has not been assigned a status equivalent to metaphor. For example, Dirven speaks of metaphor as a "major associative leap" but of metonymy as a "minor process" (1985:98). In the tradition deriving from Jakobson and Halle's (1956) classic distinction between metaphor as choice functioning on the paradigmatic axis versus metonymy as association and sequence functioning primarily on the syntagmatic axis, metaphor is thought to lead to homogeneity and coherence, metonymy to juxtaposition and potential incoherence (Sapir, 1977:4). Another view of the difference between metaphor and metonymy that is more useful to us gives metonymy a more important role. This is Anttila's suggestion that metaphor concerns semantic transfer through a similarity of sense perceptions, and is therefore analogical and iconic, while metonymy is semantic transfer through contiguity and is therefore indexical (1972:142). By "indexical", Anttila means that metonymy points to semantic relations in certain contexts.

Three types of context have been much discussed:

a. Contiguity in socio-physical or socio-cultural experience: e.g. (i) Lat. *coxa* 'hip' > Fr. *cuisse* 'thigh' (the parts of the body are spatially contiguous in the physical world) (Ullmann 1964:218); (ii) *boor* 'farmer' > 'crude person' (association of behavior with a certain person or class of persons); (iii) Lat. *lingua* 'tongue' > 'language' (association of activity with an enabling factor) (Kronasser, 1952:29); (iv) *concern* 'interest, solicitous regard' > 'matter that concerns' (association of a mental state with its object or cause (Stern, 1968:376)),
b. Contiguity in the utterance (that is, collocation), often ending in ellipsis, cf. *painting by Picasso* > *a Picasso* (Anttila, 1972:142); French *ne...pas* > *pas*

c. Synecdoche, or the part-whole relation, e.g. *redbreast*> 'robin' (Ullmann, 1964:219), and most especially body part changes, cf. Wilkins (1980) on FINGERNAIL > FINGER > HAND.

As these examples suggest, the contiguities and associations usually cited with reference to metonymy tend to be concrete. The main exceptions have to do with behavioral-judgmental associations (cf. *boor*). However, some examples of metonymy have also been cited in the literature on semantic change. Most pertinent to our discussion is Brinton's suggestion with regard to the development of English *have* as an auxiliary verb, that "Rather than bleaching, the semantic change involved in the development of the perfect seems to have been metonymic" (1988:102).

We propose extending the notion of metonymy from traditional concrete and overt contexts to cognitive and covert contexts, specifically the pragmatic contexts of conversational and conventional inference. The contiguity involved is based in the discourse world. The 'indexing' involved is the pointing to relevance that conversational inferences about stereotypical situations entail. With regard to the development of the causal meaning of *siþþan*, the following hypothesis can be made: An originally conversational implicature arising in the context of communication of temporal sequence came to be associated with *siþþan* 'from the time that' and then came to be a conventional implicature pointing to or indexing cause, somewhat as assumptions about the behavior of farmers came to be associated with *boor*. Similarly, an originally conversational implicature that a marker of simultaneity would not be used unless there was something remarkable about that simultaneity came to index the surprise factor and thus the concessive. If this is an acceptable analogy between pragmatic strengthening and metonymy, then it should be noted that the development of conventional implicatures is a case of synecdoche (part > whole).

The germ of the idea put forward here is to be found in Stern (1968 [1931]). Stern views permutation (his term for metonymy) as resulting from "a word [being] used in a phrase where a notion in some way connected with its meaning is liable to form an element of the context" (1968:353). Stern rejects a hypothesis he attributes to Leumann that permutations result from "a difference between the meaning intended by the speaker and that comprehended by the hearer" on the grounds that the speaker must be assumed to know his native language (1968:360). In other words, he rejects the view that the change results from speaker's improper processing (or inadequate learning). He suggests instead that permutations result from "striving to fulfill as adequately as possible the symbolic and communicative functions of speech" (1968:359); in other words, speaker's communicative intent and desire to be fully expressive is central. He goes on to list under examples of permutation the development of the logical meanings of *considering*, *supposing*, of Gm. *weil*, and concessive *while*.

5. CONCLUSION

In discussing the principle of exploiting old means for novel functions, and the recruitment of concrete for more abstract terms, Heine et al. (These volumes) suggest that:

> ...grammaticalization can be interpreted as the result of a process which has *problem-solving* as its main goal, its primary function being conceptualization by expressing one thing in terms of another. This function is not confined to grammaticalization, it is the main characteristic of metaphor in general.

In other words, semantic change in general, not just grammaticalization, can be interpreted as problem-solving. The authors identify one principal problem: That of representing members of one semantic domain in terms of another, in other words, metaphor. But in semantic change (including the process of grammaticalization) there is a second problem: The search for ways to regulate communication and negotiate speaker-hearer interaction. We have suggested that this is a kind of metonymic change, indexing or pointing to meanings that might otherwise be only covert. The main direction of both types of problem-solving is toward specification. Metaphorical change involves specifying one, usually more complex, thing in terms of another not present in the context. Metonymic change involves specifying one meaning in terms of another that is present, even if only covertly, in the context. In the changes we have discussed, the metonymic change is from less to more informative, that is, in the direction of explicit coding of relevance and informativeness that earlier was only covertly implied; in other words, like metaphor, it is a case of pragmatic inferencing and strengthening, but along a different axis of relations.

We have argued that semantic change in the early stages of grammaticalization does not necessarily involve bleaching; on the contrary, it usually involves specification achieved through inferencing. Second, the inferencing is of two kinds: Metaphor and metonymy, which, as would be expected, are not totally inseparable, but which correlate with shifts to different types of grammatical function. Metaphor is largely correlated with shifts from meanings situated in the external described situation to meanings situated in the internal evaluative, perceptual, cognitive situation, and in the textual situation. Metonymy is largely correlated with shifts to meanings situated in the subjective belief-state or attitude toward the situation, including the linguistic one. Note this formulation is couched in terms of preference rules (cf. Jackendoff, 1983 with reference to rather different semantic domains). Therefore it is not inconceivable that metonymy might operate in the domain typical of metaphor or vice versa.[9]

An example of the difference can be highlighted by examination of the development of the words *prefer(ence)* and *rather*. *Prefer* is an evaluative verb derived (already in Latin) by Tendency I from the Latin spatial verb *prae-fere* 'to bear before, carry in front' (*prae* 'in front, before', *fere* 'carry'). Here there is a metaphorical transfer from the domain of motion in space to mental evaluation. A fairly concrete image schema (Sweetser, 1988) is involved and the process is fairly obviously metaphorical. In the case of *rather*, an image-schema involving transfer of 'sooner' to 'preferably' is harder to conceive, since the concepts are both somewhat abstract, and conceivably metonymy may have been at work even here. But in the case of the extension of the textual preference *rather* (by Tendency II) to the metalinguistic assertive *rather* (by Tendency III), the notion of image-schema becomes totally problematic. If there is mapping from preference for a situation to preference for an expression, it is very indirect — note the shift from syntactic subject to speaker subject, among other things. Here indexing of speaker's belief-state and spelling out of communicative relevance, rather than mapping, is at work.

In sum, while metaphor is correlated primarily with solving the problem of representation, metonymy and conventionalizing of conversational meanings are associated with solving the problem of expressing speaker attitudes, including metalinguistic overlays of meaning.

NOTES

1. Elizabeth Traugott thanks Suzanne Kemmer and Stephen Levinson for comments on an earlier version of this paper. Bernd Heine and Peter Hook raised issues that helped clarify the arguments presented here. Of course, none of them are responsible in any way for the content of this paper.

   Parts of this paper are based on König and Traugott (1988) and Traugott (1988).

Ekkehard König gratefully acknowledges the financial support received from the Deutsche Forschungsgemeinschaft.

2. Sperber and Wilson (1986) treat metaphor under relevance; the relationship of inferences of metaphorical and conversational relevance to the proposition in question is, however, rather different, see Section 5.

3. Fischer (Forthcoming), based on Denison (1985), suggests a pragmatically motivated development of *do* via narrative completive constructions.

4. Important to discussions of relevance and of strengthening of inferences is the current debate whether there is only one kind of pragmatic inference, characterized as relevance by Sperber and Wilson (1986), or two kinds, characterized as the mutually interactive Q-Principle and R-Principle by Horn (1984; 1989). The Q-Principle is "make your contribution sufficient, say as much as you can" (given R), while the R-Principle is "make your contribution necessary, say no more than you must" (given Q). Horn suggests that the Q-Principle, which puts upper bounds on implicata and invites hearers to infer no more and possibly less than they hear, blocks formations such as *nall* from *not all*, since *nall* would be no more informative than *some* (1989:256). The R-Principle, which puts lower bounds on implicata, and invites hearers to infer more than they hear, accounts, among other things, for the development of modal auxiliaries from main verbs, and the development of speech act inferences (Horn, 1984:30–31). Since all examples of grammaticalization discussed here involve strengthening of relevance, this debate is not pursued here. Its relevance for grammaticalization will be the focus of another paper.

5. Abbreviations and approximate dates for stages of English are: Present Day English (PDE) c. 1700 on; Early Modern English (ENE) c. 1500–1700; Middle English (ME) c. 1100–1500; and Old English (OE) c. 600–1100.

6. All examples from OE are cited in the form in Healey and Venezky (1980). Others are from the Oxford English Dictionary (OED) and the Middle English Dictionary (MED).

7. There is no categorial contrast between *wesan* and *beon* in OE, but in general *beon* is used to express future, generic, and stative 'be' (cf. Spanish *ser*), *wesan* to express contingency, activity, and past (narrative) tense (cf. Spanish *estar*). The two verbs merged in the suppletive paradigm of *be* during the ME period.

8. Cf. also Frajzyngier (1986) on the non-usefulness of metaphorical explanations for the development of switch reference. Frajzyngier suggests that the development of switch reference is 'not a metaphorical extension and not even a syntactic reanalysis. It is rather a logical conclusion about the utilization of certain functional properties of a morpheme in a certain environment.' While switch reference may be a case of non-metaphorical inference, it is problematic to think of the change as a response to new environments, since this approach presupposes use of a word in a new environment where its usual meaning would be inappropriate. We argue here that semantic-pragmatic change can occur only when it is licensed by inferences from extant contexts.

9. Heine et al. (These volumes) suggest that metonymy operates quite widely. The development of switch-reference discussed by Frajzyngier (1986) may be an example of metonymic change in the development of a textual marker, cf. Ft. 8.

REFERENCES

Abraham, Werner. 1976. "Die Rolle von Trugschlüssen in der Diachronie von Satzkonnektoren." In *Opuscula Slavica et Linguistica*, H.P. Pohl and N. Salnikow (eds), 11–72. Festschrift für A. Issatschenko. Klagenfurt.

Abraham, Werner. Volume II. These volumes. "The grammaticization of the German modal particles."

Andersen, Henning. 1973. "Abductive and deductive change." *Language* 49:765–93.

Anttila, Raimo. 1972. *An Introduction to Historical and Comparative Linguistics*. New York: Macmillan.

Atlas, Jay D. and Stephen C. Levinson. 1981. "*It*-clefts, informativeness, and logical form." In *Radical Pragmatics*, Peter Cole (ed.), 1–61. New York: Academic Press.

Benveniste, Emile. 1973. *Indo-European Language and Society* trans. by Elizabeth Palmer. Coral Gables, Florida: University of Miami Press.

Blakemore, Diane. 1987. *Semantic Constraints on Relevance*. Oxford: Blackwell.

Braunmüller, Kurt. 1978. "Remarks on the formation of conjunctions in germanic languages." *Nordic Journal of Linguistics* 1:99–120.

Brinton, Laurel J. 1988. *The Development of English Aspectual Systems*. Cambridge: Cambridge University Press.

Bybee, Joan. 1985. *Morphology: A Study of the Relation Between Meaning and Form*. Amsterdam: John Benjamins.

Bybee, Joan. 1987. "The grammaticization of tense and aspect." Paper presented at the LSA Winter meeting, San Francisco, December.

Bybee, Joan and William Pagliuca. 1985. "Cross-linguistic comparison and the development of grammatical meaning." In *Historical Semantics: Historical Word Formation*, Jacek Fisiak (ed.), 59–83. Berlin: de Gruyter.

Claudi, Ulrike, and Bernd Heine. 1986. "On the metaphorical base of grammar." *Studies in Language* 10:297–335.

Denison, David. 1985. "The origins of periphrastic *do*: Ellegard and Visser reconsidered." In *Papers from the Fourth International Conference on English Historical Linguistics*, Roger Eaton, Olga Fischer, Willem Koopman, and Frederike van der Leek (eds), 45–60. Amsterdam: John Benjamins.

Dieterich, Thomas G. and Donna Jo Napoli. 1982. "Comparative *rather*." *Journal of Linguistics* 18:137–65.

Dirven, René. 1985. "Metaphor as a basic means for extending the lexicon." In *The Ubiquity of Metaphor*, Wolf Paprotté and René Dirven (eds), 85–119. Amsterdam: John Benjamins.

Fischer, Olga. Forthcoming. "Middle English Syntax." In *Cambridge History of English* Vol. II, Norman Blake (ed.). Cambridge: Cambridge University Press.

Fleischman, Suzanne. 1982. *The Future in Thought and Language: Diachronic Evidence from Romance*. Cambridge: Cambridge University Press.

Frajzyngier, Zygmunt. 1986. "Grammaticization through analysis: A case of switch reference." In *Proceedings of the Second Annual Meeting of the Pacific Linguistics Conference*.

Geis, Michael L. and Arnold M. Zwicky. 1971. "On invited inferences." *Linguistic Inquiry* 11:561–6.

Givón, Talmy. 1975. "Serial verbs and syntactic change: Niger-Congo." In *Word*

Order and Word Order Change, Charles N. Li (ed.). Austin: University of Texas Press.

Givón, Talmy. 1979. *On Understanding Grammar*. New York: Academic Press.

Givón, Talmy. 1989. "Modes of knowledge and modes of processing: The routinization of behavior and information." Chap. 7 of *Mind, Code and Context: Essays in Pragmatics*, 237–67.

Grice, H. Paul. 1975. "Logic and conversation." *Syntax and Semantics III: Speech Acts*, Peter Cole and Jerry Morgan (eds), 41–58. New York: Academic Press.

Hanson, Kristin. 1987. "On subjectivity and the history of epistemic expressions." *Chicago Linguistic Society* 23:132–47.

Healey, Antonette and Richard Venezky. 1980. *A Microfiche Concordance to Old English*. The Dictionary of Old English Project, Centre for Medieval Studies, University of Toronto.

Heine, Bernd and Mechthild Reh. 1984. *Grammaticalization and Reanalysis in African Languages*. Hamburg: Helmut Buske.

Heine, Bernd and Ulrike Claudi. 1986. *On the Rise of Grammatical Categories; some Examples from Maa*. Berlin: Dietrich Reimer.

Heine, Bernd, Ulrike Claudi, and Friederike Hünnemeyer. Volume I. "From cognition to grammar — Evidence from African Languages."

Hobbs, Jerry R., Mark Stickel, Paul Martin, and Douglas Edwards. 1988. "Interpretation as Abduction." MS.

Hopper, Paul J. Volume I. "On some principles of grammaticization."

Horn, Laurence R. 1984. "Toward a new taxonomy for pragmatic inference: Q-based and R-based implicature." In *Meaning, Form, and Use in Context: Linguistic Applications*, Deborah Schiffrin (ed.), 11–42. Georgetown University Round Table. Washington: DC: Georgetown UP.

Horn, Lawrence R. 1989. *A Natural History of Negation*. Chicago: University of Chicago Press.

Jackendoff, Ray. 1983. *Semantics and Cognition*. Cambridge, Mass.: MIT Press.

Jakobson, Roman and Morris Halle. 1956. *Fundamentals of Language*. The Hague: Mouton.

König, Ekkehard. 1985. "Where do concessives come from? On the development of concessive connectives." In *Historical Semantics: Historical Word-formation*, Jacek Fisiak (ed.), 263–82. Berlin: De Gruyter.

König, Ekkehard. 1986. "Conditionals, concessive conditionals and concessives: Areas of contrast, overlap and neutralization." In *On Conditionals*, Elizabeth C. Traugott, Alice ter Meulen, Judith S. Reilly, and Charles A. Ferguson (eds), 229–46. Cambridge: Cambridge University Press.

König, Ekkehard. 1988. "Concessive connectives and concessive sentences: Cross-linguistic regularities and pragmatic principles." In *Explaining Language Universals*, John Hawkins (ed.), 145–66. Oxford: Blackwell.

König, Ekkehard. Forthcoming. "Concessive relations as the dual counterpart of causal relations." In *Universal Semantics — Semantic Universals*, Dietmar Zaefferer (ed.). Dordrecht: Foris.

König, Ekkehard and Elizabeth C. Traugott. 1988. "Pragmatic strengthening and semantic change: The conventionalizing of conversational implicature." In *Understanding the Lexicon: Meaning, Sense and World Knowledge in Lexical Semantics*, Werner Hüllen and Rainer Schulze (eds), 110–24. Tübingen: Max Niemeyer Verlag.

Kronasser, Heinz. 1952. *Handbuch der Semiasiologie*. Heidelberg: Carl Winter.

Lakoff, George and Mark Johnson. 1980. *Metaphors we Live by*. Chicago: Chicago University Press.

Lehmann, Christian. 1985. "Grammaticalization: Synchronic variation and diachronic change." *Lingua e Stile* 20:303–18.

Levinson, Stephen C. 1983. *Pragmatics*. Cambridge: Cambridge University Press.

Meillet, Antoine. 1948 [1912]. "L'évolution des formes grammaticales." In *Linguistique générale et linguistique historique*, 130–48. Paris: Champion.

Mitchell, Bruce. 1985. *Old English Syntax*. London: Oxford University Press, 2 Vols.

Peirce, Charles Sanders. 1955. *Philosophical Works of Peirce*, Justus Buchler (ed.). New York: Dover.

Quirk, Randolph, Sidney Greenbaum, Geoffrey Leech, and Jan Svartvik. 1985. *A Comprehensive Grammar of the English Language*. London: Longman.

Romaine, Suzanne. 1982. *Socio-historical Linguistics: Its Status and Methodology*. Cambridge: Cambridge University Press.

Sapir, J. David. 1977. "The anatomy of metaphor." In *The Social Use of Metaphor: Essays on the Anthropology of Rhetoric*, J. David Sapir and J. Christopher Crocker (eds). Philadelphia: University of Pennsylvania Press.

Shepherd, Susan C. 1982. "From deontic to epistemic: An analysis of modals in the history of English, creoles, and language acquisition." In *Papers from the Fifth International Conference on Historical Linguistics*, Anders Ahlqvist (ed.), 316–23. Amsterdam: John Benjamins.

Sperber, Dan and Deirdre Wilson. 1986. *Relevance. Communication and Cognition*. Cambridge, Mass.: Harvard University Press.

Stern, Gustav. 1968 [1931]. *Meaning and Change of Meaning: with Special Reference to the English Language*. Bloomington: Indiana University Press.

Sweetser, Eve. 1988. "Grammaticalization and semantic bleaching." In *Berkeley Linguistics Society, Proceedings of the Fourteenth Annual Meeting*, 389–405.

Sweetser, Eve. 1990. *From Etymology to Pragmatics*. Cambridge: Cambridge University Press.

Talmy, Leonard. 1983. "How language structures space." In *Spatial Orientation: Theory, Research and Application*, Herbert Pick and Linda Acredolo (eds), 225–82. New York: Plenum Press.

Thompson, Sandra A. 1972. "*Instead of* and *rather than* clauses in English." *Journal of Linguistics* 8:237–49.

Traugott, Elizabeth C. 1978. "On the expression of spatio-temporal relations in language." In *Universals of Human Language, Vol. III: Word Formation*, Joseph H. Greenberg, Charles A. Ferguson, and Edith Moravcsik (eds), 369–400. Stanford: Stanford University Press.

Traugott, Elizabeth C. 1982. "From propositional to textual and expressive meanings; some semantic-pragmatic aspects of grammaticalization." In *Perspectives on Historical Linguistics*, Winfred P. Lehmann and Yakov Malkiel (eds), 245–71. Amsterdam: John Benjamins.

Traugott, Elizabeth C. 1985a. "'Conventional' and 'Dead' metaphors revisited." In *The Ubiquity of Metaphor: Metaphor in Language and Thought*, Wolf Paprotté and René Dirven (eds), 17–56. Amsterdam: John Benjamins.

Traugott, Elizabeth C. 1985b. "Conditional markers." In *Iconicity in Syntax*, John Haiman (ed.), 289–307. Amsterdam: John Benjamins.

Traugott, Elizabeth C. 1986. "From polysemy to internal semantic reconstruction." In *Berkeley Linguistics Society, Proceedings of the Twelfth Annual Meeting*, 539–50.

Traugott, Elizabeth C. 1988. "Pragmatic strengthening and grammaticalization." *Berkeley Linguistics Society, Proceedings of the Fourteenth Annual Meeting*, 406–16.

Traugott, Elizabeth C. 1989. "On the rise of epistemic meanings in English: An example of subjectification in semantic change." *Language* 65:31–55.

Traugott, Elizabeth C. 1990. "From less to more situated in language: The unidirectionality of semantic change." In *Papers from the Fifth International Conference on English Historical Linguistics*, Sylvia Adamson, Vivien Law, Nigel Vincent, and Susan Wright (eds). Amsterdam: John Benjamins, 496–517.

Ullmann, Stephen. 1964. *Semantics: An Introduction to the Science of Meaning*. Oxford: Blackwell.

Wilkins, David. 1980. Towards a Theory of Semantic Change. Ph.D. dissertation, Australian National University (Forthcoming at SUNY Press).

The *De Dicto* Domain in Language

Zygmunt Frajzyngier
University of Colorado at Boulder

1. PURPOSE AND SCOPE OF THE PAPER

I take the notion of grammaticalization in both diachronic and synchronic sense. Although I am interested in how grammatical morphemes emerged from individual lexical items, I am more interested in the question of what semantic and pragmatic functions are encoded in the grammatical system of language. The means of grammatical encoding, including the lexical sources of grammaticalization, will emerge as a by-product of such an approach. The purpose of the present paper is to show that languages make a distinction between the domain of reality and the domain of speech and also to show how this distinction is encoded. In the study of language the domain of speech as opposed to the domain of reality has only been implicitly invoked, mainly for the distinction between anaphoras and deictics, in both formal and functional studies. However, certain notions to be discussed in this paper have been raised in one form or another by other scholars, especially in connection with the development of definite articles (Greenberg, 1985). Traugott, 1980 makes a distinction between 'the world being talked about' and 'the speaker's organization of that world in the act of speaking' (Traugott, 1980:47). In various papers one may also find scattered usage of the terms 'linguistic', 'metalinguistic', in reference to some antecedent of the anaphora, but these terms have too wide a scope (cf. Dubois et al., 1973:317) to be of use in the present paper. I propose that the distinction between the domain of reality and the domain of speech is marked in at least two areas of language structure: In the marking of embedded clauses and in the system of reference, where languages differentiate between sets referring to the domain of reality and sets referring to the domain of speech. Usually, the set referring to the domain of reality encodes more distinctions than the set referring to the domain of speech.

Using the notion of the domain of speech, one can explain functional syncretisms and provide an explanation for the similarity of various morphemes considered hitherto as unrelated. The explanation that I will provide will account for several of the phenomena discussed by Anderson and Keenan, 1985 as a 'relativization of deixis'. Although I draw data and examples from a variety of languages, I do not want to claim that the distinction is universal. It is entirely possible that not all languages encode this distinction in their grammatical systems.

For the sake of brevity I will refer to the domain of speech as the domain *de dicto* and to the domain of the real world as the domain *de re*. The domain *de dicto* in the present paper includes the hypothetical mood. Justification for this inclusion will be provided later in the paper. The terms *de dicto* and *de re* are used here with the meaning such expressions have in Latin, and independently of various interpretations they have had since middle ages in philosophical literature (cf. Hughes and Cresswell, 1968:183ff; Parsons, 1971; and also Wright and Givón, 1987). I do not intend in this paper to reconcile the differences between the philosophical and linguistic understanding of the terms that I am going to propose, nor will I consider the points in which philosophical and linguistic interpretations may overlap.

Arguments in support of the proposed distinction between the *de dicto* and *de re* domain in language are discussed in two sections. In the first section I provide an explanation for the development of demonstratives into complementizers. One of the results of this explanation will be an answer to the question why the forms of the definite article and the complementizer after verbs of saying are similar in many unrelated languages. Note that the two morphemes belong to different syntactic categories, one of them, the complementizer, has no independent lexical meaning (at least according to the current literature) and therefore, a metaphorical extension is not a good explanation for the two morphemes having the same form. In this section I will also provide an explanation for the relationship between complementizers and relative clause markers. In the second section I discuss some of the properties of the systems of reference with respect to a hypothetical mood. In particular I will show that in some languages the system of reference with respect to the *de dicto* domain has a reduced number of distinctions when compared with the system of reference to the domain *de re*.

The following problems will be discussed in the paper: 1. An explanation of how demonstratives become complementizers; 2. A connection between the *de dicto* domain and the 'hypothetical' mood; 3. A speculation on the relative clause markers; 4. Properties of the referential system in the *de dicto* domain.

2. FROM DEMONSTRATIVE TO COMPLEMENTIZER

2.1. What needs to be explained

It is a well-known fact that in many languages complementizers are identical with or derived from demonstratives (cf. Noonan, 1985). Why a demonstrative is used in the function of complementizer has not, however, been adequately explained. Lockwood, 1968:222ff. proposes for Germanic that the demonstrative was first the object of the verb 'say' in the main clause, and later became a constituent of the complement clause, becoming thus a complementizer (conjunction in his terminology). Thus there was an evolution from: 'He said that: he will come' to 'He said that he will come'. As evidence for his hypothesis Lockwood provides the following examples from Faroese: (Traugott (in press) gives similar examples from Old English.)

(1) *eg sigi at hann kemur*
'I say that he comes'

(2) *eg sigi tað: hann kemur*
'I say that: he comes' (Lockwood, 1968:223)

Sentence (1) contains complementizer *at*, which derives from demonstrative *tað*, whose full form may be seen in sentence (2). I think that the weakness of this explanation lies in the unmotivated form of the presumable source for (1): It is not clear why there should be a demonstrative in the object position in sentence (2).

2.2. Hypothesis

I would like to propose that the demonstrative is used as a complementizer because it indicates that the following clause belongs to, or should be interpreted as belonging to, the domain *de dicto*. The evidence for this hypothesis will consist of the following:

> Showing that the demonstrative has become an anaphora referring to a proposition, a propositional anaphora, further in the present paper.

- Showing that clauses following the demonstrative belong primarily (in the historical sense) to the domain *de dicto*.
- Showing how an essentially *de dicto* complementizer comes to mark the hypothetical mood.
- A case study of complementation in Mupun in which I will show systematically the development of the function of anaphora into complementizer.

2.3. Evidence

2.3.1. Demonstrative and propositional anaphora

A propositional anaphora refers to a proposition as a whole rather than to only one of the components of a proposition. In English this function is performed by the remote demonstrative 'that', as in the following examples, discussed from a different point of view in Channon, 1980:

(3) 'We should have champagne and caviar at the party after CLS. 'That's (*It's) a good idea'.
'Fred doesn't want to go, and that's (*it's) the problem.' (Channon, 1980:107)

The pronoun 'it' may be used in *de dicto* reference as an anaphora referring to an NP previously mentioned in speech, e.g.:

(4) John bought a car last year. It proved to be a lemon.

The remote demonstrative 'that' has constraints that set it apart from the pronoun 'it'. In particular 'that' is constrained in its use in reference to an NP in the clause, but it is not so constrained in its use as a propositional anaphora, e.g.:

(5) John bought a car last year. That proved to be a disaster.
*That proved to be a lemon.

The remote demonstrative may be used in reference to a nearer of two possible antecedents,[1] e.g.:

(6) John bought a car last year and another car just last week. THAT proved to be a lemon.

Virtually the same situation obtains in other IE languages, where the neutral rather than non-neutral pronoun is used as propositional anaphora, e.g.:

(7) French: *F. ne veut pas aller, mais **ça** ne me derange pas.*
Russian: *F. ne xočet idti, no **éto** (*étot/éta) menja ne volnuet.*
NEG want go but that that(m)/(f) me NEG bother
Polish: *Fred nie chce iść ale **to** (*ten/*ta) mnie nie martwi.*
Fred doesn't want to go, but that doesn't bother me.

2.3.2. Definite article

The purpose of this section is to claim that the definite article has a function linked with the *de dicto* domain.

The primary function of the definite article remains somewhat controversial. The question is whether the definite article marks an NP as a known or as mentioned previously in speech. Greenberg, 1985: 282 states: 'In the case of the [definite] article, besides this anaphoric use, we have rather more frequently reference to what is known from the situational context or general knowledge than speech context.' While Greenberg has provided convincing arguments to show that this claim is true in English, there are equally convincing arguments to show that in some languages the definite article may be used only when a noun has been previously mentioned in speech. The evidence for this claim is provided by the following facts from Mupun. The definite marker in Mupun *nə* is identical with the non-human anaphora. It may occur after any noun, including proper names and toponyms. If it were indeed true that the primary function of the definite is to mark a noun that is known, then we would expect the definite to be used with the first occurrence of a toponym in the text, at least with those toponyms that are significant for a given culture, hence assumed to be known to the speakers and hearers alike. And yet this is not the case. When a toponym occurs for the first time in a text, it does not have a definite article, e.g.:

(8) *yaksə n-yit vom ɗi ɗel n-siam n-jos*
then 1SG-leave Vom there pass 1SG-descend PREP-Jos
'Then I left Vom and went down to Jos.'

After the toponym was mentioned in conversation its subsequent mention in the text may be followed by a definite article, e.g. in a sentence that in the text is separated from the preceding one by five sentences:

(9) *to, lokaci də an n-jos nə*
well time REL 1SG PREP-JOS DEF
'Well, when I was in Jos.'

Compare also the following example, with the toponym 'Rome', without the definite article:

(10) *to, n-bit (1975) ɓe n-dəm n-rom*
well PREP-year CONS 1SG-go PREP-Rome
'OK, in 1975 I went to Rome.'

Four sentences later, the toponym 'Zaria' has a definite article because it has been previously mentioned in speech:

(11) *n-dəm n-kes ɓe wa ba n-dəm dī n-Zaria nə*
1SG-go 1SG-finish COMP return go 1SG-go there PREP-Zaria DEF
'I went, finished [the school] and then returned to Zaria.'

Several sentences after somebody was characterized as German, the following sentence was produced:

(12) *yak sə mu dəm dī n-Germany nə*
then 1PL go there PREP-G. DEF
'Then we went to Germany.'

Compare also the following sentences. In the first, three toponyms are introduced into the discourse, and none of them has a definite article. When a reference is later made to those toponyms they all occur with definite articles:

(13) *pak mo dəm Dortmund, pak mo dəm Essen, pak*
some PL go some PL go some
mo kuma Würzburg.
PL also
'Some went to Dortmund, some went to Essen, some went to Würzburg.'

(14) *to, wen an meme n-but pak nen də mo*
well, 1SG 1SG some PREP-inside some people REL 3PL
dəm Würzburg nə
go DEF
'I was among those who went to Würzburg.'

(15) *wur kə toŋ n-Essen nə ji*
3M COMPL stay PREP-Essen DEF come
'He came from Essen.'

For at least one language, it has been shown that being mentioned previously rather than previous knowledge is the necessary condition for the use of the definite article. In this language the article thus marks the noun that belongs to the *de dicto* domain. I do not have necessary cross language information to assert that in all languages that have a definite article, it will be used to mark a noun mentioned previously in speech, and not necessarily a noun that is known, but not mentioned in the preceding discourse.

There are languages in which there are two definite articles: One to mark a noun that is known and the other to mark a noun that has been mentioned in speech. Thus in Fering (a North-Frisian language) we have the following paradigm:

a maan	'the man'	*at wuf*	'the woman'
di maan	'the man'	*di wuf*	'the woman'

The article *a* refers to a generally known referent, and the article *di* refers to a referent mentioned in a previous or following context (Karen Ebert, p.c.).

2.3.2. Complements of the verba dicendi

The fact that elements introduced by complementizers after verbs of saying belong to the domain of speech is true analytically, i.e. it follows from the fact that the complementizers follow verbs of saying. Additional evidence is provided by the fact that if a language has a complementizer derived from a demonstrative, such a complementizer will mark the complements of the verbs of saying and thinking, while the sentential complements of other verbs may be marked by other complementizers or by other means. The complementizer derived from demonstratives does not carry a modal function when occurring after *verba dicendi*. In Slavic languages the simple form of complementizer (*čto* in Russian, *że* in Polish) after *verba dicendi* does not carry a deontic modality. If deontic modality is intended after *verba dicendi* or other verbs, the complementizer occurs with the particle *by*, e.g. *čto-b(y)* in Russian and *że-by* in Polish. Although in many languages the complementizer used to introduce complements of the *verba dicendi* is also used to introduce other complements, there seems to be little doubt that its primary function was, synchronically and diachronically, to introduce complements of the *verba dicendi*.

The third part of the evidence is provided by the many languages in which complementizers are derived from *verba dicendi*, such as Hausa *cewa* 'saying', Yoruba *pe*, Gã *ake*, and other African languages (cf. Lord, 1976),

English-based creoles (cf. Frajzyngier, 1984). The importance of this argument rests on the fact that it is the verbs of saying rather than some other verbs that were chosen to serve as complementizers. The following sample of languages with complementizers derived from verbs of saying is far from complete, but the fact that the same process has occurred in different families indicates that it is by no means accidental: Kwa languages (Niger-Congo), Hausa (Chadic), Amharic (Semitic), Dargua, Tabasara, Xinalug (Dešeriev, 1959) (Caucasian).

As admittedly fragmentary data show, complementizers derived from demonstratives occur primarily after *verba dicendi* to indicate that what follows belongs to a *de dicto* category.

2.4. Complements of *verba dicendi* as complements of other verbs

It is a fact that demonstratives do not only serve as complementizers after verbs of saying but also after other verbs. There is, however, a difference in the function of the complementizer, partially depending on the verb of the main clause. When the complementizer derived from demonstratives occurs after a verb of saying, it does not carry a modal function. When it occurs after other verbs, it does carry a modal function. Kirsner and Thompson, 1976 noted that after verbs of perception, the complementizer 'that' indicates an indirect evidence, e.g.:

(16) I saw that he was sleeping
cf. I saw him sleeping

Here is an additional illustration of this fact from Polish:

(17) *Powiedziałem że spał*
say-1SG.M.-PAST COMP sleep-3SG.M.-PAST
'I said that he slept.'

(18) *Widziałem że spał*
see-1SG.M.-PAST COMP sleep-3SG.M.-PAST
'I saw that he slept.'

(19) *Widziałem jak spał*
see-1SG.M.-PAST how sleep-3SG.M.-PAST
'I saw him sleeping.'

Although Kirsner and Thompson have observed the function of 'that' they did not explain why it rather than some other complementizer is used to mark the indirect evidence. I would like to propose that the *verba dicendi* complementizer is used to indicate inference because of the strong sense that information obtained through speech is not as reliable as information obtained through direct observation. After *verba dicendi* the complementizer does not carry any information about the epistemic value of the complement clause. The complementizer is associated, however, with verbs of saying, which intrinsically have epistemic value, such that the information obtained through hearsay is less reliable than the information obtained through direct perception (see, hear, feel). The complementizer acquires thus the same epistemic value as the verb that automatically triggers complementizer's presence, i.e. the verb 'say'. The complementizer is now available to serve a function of indicating less than direct evidence with other verbs, including the verbs of perception.

The association between the domain of speech and the hypothetical mood is quite widespread across languages. Verbs of saying are used to indicate less than complete evidence (Frajzyngier, 1985b). In Czech 'doubt in truth' modality is marked by the morpheme *prý* which derives historically from verb *praví* 'he says'; in Slovak the marker of 'doubt in truth' is *vraj*, historically derived from the verb *vraví* 'he says' (cf. Stieber, 1979: 247ff), e.g.:

(20) *On vraj bol v Bratislave*
he was in Bratislava
'Apparently he was in Bratislava.' (Stieber, 1979: 248)

cf.

On bol v Bratislave
'He was in Bratislava.'

Finally, the association between domain of speech and hypothetical is evinced by the fact that in a number of languages an introduction of a hypothetical situation is realized periphrastically by preceding the hypothetical proposition with a phrase equivalent to English 'Let's say: ...'. Further in the paper I will be treating hypothetical mood as an instance of the *de dicto* domain with respect to its semantic properties.

2.5. A case study: Complementizer in Mupun

The evidence for the function of demonstrative as a *de dicto* marker for NPs and clauses was based so far on fragmentary information taken haphazardly from a variety of languages. The purpose of the present section is to provide evidence based on a systematic analysis of relevant phenomena in one language.

2.5.1. The form of the complementizer

I will be concerned here only with one complementizer *nə*, which is phonologically identical with the non-human anaphora and with the definite article discussed earlier. Unlike similar morphemes in other languages, *nə* does not have in contemporary language a deictic function. Thus one cannot use *nə* while pointing at something either close or remote. Its function is thus limited to an NP or a propositional anaphora. As the anaphora for non-human NPs, *nə* can function as subject, object, and prepositional phrase complement, e.g.: (antecedent bold, anaphora underlined)

Subject:

(21) *ama* ***yil*** *də* ***get*** ***n-yam*** ***nə*** *nə* *kə* *kwance*
but world REL PAST PREP-time DEF ANAPH ASSOC quiet
rai met də n-yak sə
life surpass REL PREP-time DEM
'the world of the past had a much quieter life than the present world.'

Object and prepositional phrase:

(22) ***səm*** ***bature*** ***mo*** *an mbə tu nə n-ba*
name European PL 1SG FUT kill ANAPH 1SG-throw away
kə nə
PREP ANAPH
'European names, I would eliminate them, throw them away.'

Prepositional phrase:

(23) *jiraap mo yak* ***am*** *mo loom ji kə nə*
girls PL fetch water 3PL approach come PREP ANAPH
'girls fetch water and they approach with it...'

Recall from a previous discussion that the anaphoric *nə* also functions as the definite marker, e.g.:

(24) *n-naa jiel wur dafuan nə*
1SG-see pity 3M hare DEF
'I pity him, the hare.'

2.5.2. *Anaphora nə as complementizer*

The anaphora occurs as a complementizer after verba dicendi *sat* 'to say', *tal* 'to ask', and also after verbs denoting mental activity, equivalents of 'know', 'think', 'remember', 'recall'. The complementizer *nə* carries neither an epistemic nor a deontic function after these verbs. The deontic value of the complement clause depends to a large degree on the verb of the main clause, e.g.:

(25) *wu sat nə n-nas mo*
3M say COMP 1SG-beat 3PL
'He said that I beat them.' or
'He said that I should beat them.'

(26) *mo sat nə ɖe pa se*
3PL say COMP CONS 3F eat
'They said that she should eat it.'

(27) *wa ɗaar nə ɗe man pa*
3F scream COMP 3FL know 3FL
'She screamed that she knows her.'

(28) *wu suun nə ɗi naa pa*
3M dream 3ML see 3FL
'He dreamed that he saw her.'

(29) *wu ben nə wu pan an*
3M think COMP 3M remember 1SG
'He thinks he remembers me.'

(30) *n-pan nə man wur*
1SG-think COMP know 3M
'I think that I know him.'

(31) *n-man nə ba wur kə baa n-mapun kas*
know COMP NEG 3M PERF return PREP-NEG
'I know that he didn't return to M.'

(32) *n-kak nə a səm n-Mupun-é*
1SG-think COMP COP name PREP-M.-Q
'I think it is a name in Mupun, isn't it?'

The fact that *nə* has no modal function after *verba dicendi* provides evidence that its primary function within a given language is to mark the complement as belonging to the *de dicto* domain. The primacy of this function is further reinforced by the fact that, unlike in Indo-European languages, the interrogative sentences with the main verb *tal* 'to ask' have the same complementizer as indicative sentences with the verb *sat* 'to say'. And the reason they have the same complementizer is that both are verbs of saying. The modality of the complement clause after the verb *tal* is marked by one of several clause final interrogative markers, but it may also be marked by an additional modal complementizer *két* 'whether' (not illustrated here), e.g.:

(33) *mo tal pə an nə n-man pa-e*
3PL ask PREP 1SG COMP 1SG-know 3FL-Q
'They asked me whether I know her.'

(34) *a man nə ta n-kat me gwar si pə*
2M know COMP fall 1SG-meet QUANT man QUANT PREP
swup as fin-on
wash dog 3M-Q
'Can you imagine that I came across a man washing his dog?'

(35) *mo mbə tal pə mis nə nə niwa siak -é*
3PL FUT ask PREP man DEF COMP 3PL.L together-Q
'They will ask the husband: are you together?'

Additional evidence for the function of *nə* as a marker of a *de dicto* complement is provided in the next section.

2.5.3. Complementizer nə as the sole marker of de dicto

Complementizer *nə*, without any modal function, can also occur in sentences whose main verbs cannot be characterized as *verba dicendi*. The importance of this fact for the proposed hypothesis is the following: If it is indeed true that *nə* marks the complement clause as being a *de dicto* category, how does one explain sentences with modality neutral complementizer *nə* but without a verb of saying in the main clause. I would like to propose that such sentences, rather than weakening the hypothesis, provide additional support for it. Consider the following sentences:

(36) *n-sin takarda n-ɣa nə a la a taŋ*
1SG-give book PREP-2M COMP 2M *take* 2M read
'I gave you a book to read.'

(37) *kadə mu cin krismas kes ɓe wu ji kə me*
when 1PL make Christmas finish CONS 3M come ASSOC QUANT
jarida n-an nə n-la n-taŋ
paper PREP-1SG COMP 1SG-take 1SG read
'When we finished celebrating Christmas he brought me a newspaper to read.'

These sentences were interpreted as containing, in the embedded clause, an underlying verb *sat* 'to say'. In order to check the native speakers' intuition with respect to these sentences, I asked for and obtained the following sentence:

(38) *wa cet lua n-an nə n-se*
3F cook meat PREP-1SG COMP 1SG-eat
'She cooked meat for me and told me to eat.'

This sentence cannot be used if there is no actual contact between the person who cooked the meat and the speaker. Thus it cannot be used felicitously if the speaker returns home, finds the meat, but the cook is not there. Sentence (38) is therefore not an equivalent of 'she cooked meat for me to eat' because the felicity of the English clause does not depend on the participants' being in the same place at the same time. Without the complementizer *nə*, there is no requirement of direct contact between the subject of the main clause and the subject of the embedded clause, and the following sentence is grammatical in the situation in which the previous one is ungrammatical:

(39) *wa cet lua n-an n-se*
3F cook meat PREP-1SG 1SG-eat
'She cooked meat for me and I ate it.'

Thus the complementizer *nə* serves as the only marker of the *de dicto* category. Additional evidence for this claim comes from sentences of the structure: NP *nə* S, i.e. sentences without any verb in the main clause. The 'missing' verb is *sat* 'say'. In elicited sentences the verb *sat* is most often present. In conversations, however, the verb *sat* is most often omitted, e.g.:

Elicited:

(40) *n-sat nə i*
1SG-say COMP yes
'I said yes', 'I agreed.'

(41) *wu sat nə i*
3M say yes
'He said yes', 'he agreed.'

(42) *a sat n-wurnə əŋ*
2M PREP-3M COMP yes
'Tell him yes.'

Conversations:

(43) *wur nə i*
'He said yes', 'he agreed.'

(44) *npuun fen nə*
father 1SG COMP
'My father said that...'

(45) *an nə niwa maŋ can nua ji n-mun baa*
1SG COMP 3PL take hoe 3PL come PREP-1PL come
'I told them to take a hoe and come to join us.'

(46) *an nə gwar taŋ me me mbi n-an*
1SG COMP 3ML find QUANT thing PREP-1SG
'I told him that he should find something for me.'

The verb *sat* 'to say' may of course appear in natural conversations, e.g.:

(47) *wur pə sat nə dəm ɗu ɓal kawey*
3M PREP say COMP go 3PL.L marry anyhow
'He will tell them to go and marry anyhow.'

From the syntactic point of view, the sentences with the missing main clause verb are interesting because they cannot be analyzed as cases of simple deletion of the phonetic form of the verb. The pronominal subject in the 'missing' verb clauses does not occur in the preverbal form but rather in the independent form, i.e. the form in which it occurs following prepositions, verbs, and as subject in equational sentences. Sentences without the main clause verb of saying provide one more piece of evidence that the complementizer is used as an independent marker of the *de dicto* category. The presence of the complementizer *nə* is not evoked by the main clause verb.

An additional piece of evidence that *nə* marks a *de dicto* category is provided by the following consideration. The verb *dém* means 'want' and also 'agree'. This polysemy is known to occur in other African languages (Bernd Heine, p.c.). When this verb is followed by the complementizer *nə* it means 'agree'. When *dém* is followed by the deontic complementizer *kə* the verb means 'want', e.g.:

(48) *n-dem nə wa cet mbise n-darap*
1SG-agree COMP 3F cook food PREP-Darap
'I agree that she cook for Darap.'

cf.

(49) *n-dem kə n-war cet mbise dī n-darap*
1SG-want COMP PREP-3F cook food Anaph PREP-Darap
'I want her to cook for Darap.'

2.5.4. Epistemic modality after verba dicendi

Recall that the complementizer *nə* does not have a modal function when it occurs after verbs of saying. An epistemic modality after *verba dicendi* is marked through the use of the marker *paa*, which indicates 'doubt in truth'. The marker is derived most probably from the verb *paa* 'to think'. The modal *paa* has all the characteristics of an auxiliary verb: The first and second person pronouns follow *paa* and precede other verbs in the clause, while third person pronoun precedes *paa*.

The modal *paa* can not be used with the first person subject of the main clause because the speaker cannot doubt the truth of his own proposition (cf. Frajzyngier, 1985b), e.g.:

(50) *a sat nə wu paa mbə yo muan*
2M say COMP 3M FUT go trip
'You said that he will go on a trip (but he may or may not go).'

(51) *n-sat ɣa nə wur mbə yo muan*
1SG-say 2MCOMP
'I told you that he is going on a trip.'

(52) **n-sat ɣa nə wur paa mbə yo muan*
for 'I told you that he is going on a trip but I don't think so.'

If the subject of the embedded clause is first person, then the proposition of the embedded clause marked by the complementizer *paa* is interpreted as false, e.g.:

(53) *wu sat nə a mun paa mu can əɣ nə*
3M say COMP COP 1PL 1PL cut goat DEF
'He said that it was we who slaughtered the goat (but we didn't).'

cf.

(54) *wu sat nə dĩn paa dĩ cin hankuri*
'He said that he was patient (but I have my doubts).'

(55) *wu sat nə a yi paa yi-can əɣ nə*
3M say COMP COP 2F 2F-cut goat DEF
'He said that it was you who slaughtered the goat (but I doubt it).'

More evidence that the modal *paa* indicates doubt in truth is provided by the fact that it cannot be used after the main clause verb *yen* 'to think', e.g.:

(56) **n-yen wu paa siwa təbaa*
1SG-think 3M drink tobacco
for 'I thought that he smoked tobacco.'

The explanation for the ungrammaticality of the above sentence rests in the fact that the verb *yen* 'think' intrinsically indicates doubt in truth. The construction *n-yen -S* 'I think that S' in Mupun as in English is used as a device to mark doubt in truth. It is entirely possible, that using two devices whose primary function is to mark the same semantic category is considered superfluous and therefore sentences such as (54) are ungrammatical.

2.5.5. De dicto and the hypothetical: Complements of verbs of perception

After verbs of perception, such as *náa* 'see', *klə̄ŋ* 'hear', the complementizer *nə̄* indicates that the evidence for the event is indirect, that the event itself has not been observed, e.g.:

(57) *n-naa nə wu ta n-yil*
1SG-see COMP 3M fall PREP-ground
'I saw that he fell down.'

(58) *n-naa nə wu pəsiwa təbaa*
COMP PREP smoke tobacco
'I saw that he smoked tobacco.'

(59) *wu kləŋ nə n-ta n-yil*
3M hear COMP 1SG-fall PREP-ground
'He heard that I fell down.'

Similarly to English (cf. Kirsner and Thompson 1976), the difference between sentences without and sentences with a complementizer is that the former indicate direct evidence, while for the latter the evidence is indirect. Thus the verb *kləŋ* 'hear' indicates only hearsay when followed by the complementizer *nə*.

(60) *wu kləŋ n-taa n-yil*
1SG-fall PREP-ground
'He heard me fall down.'

(61) *wu kləŋ nə n-taa itn-yil*
'He heard that I fell down.'

An indication of the function of *nə̄* after verbs of perception is provided by spontaneous translation of the verb *naa* 'to see' evoked by the presence of the complementizer, viz.:

(62) *n-naa a can əɣ*
1SG-see 2M slaughter goat
'I saw you slaughter a goat.'

(63) *n-naa nə a can əɣ*
'I thought that you slaughtered a goat.'

An additional piece of evidence for the function of *nə* is provided by essentially negative information: The doubt in truth marker *paa* cannot be used as a complementizer with the verbs of perception, hence this functional gap is filled by the complementizer *nə*, e.g.:

(64) **n-naa wu paa ta n-yil*
1SG-see 3M fall PREP-ground
for 'I saw that he fell down.'

(65) **n-naa wu paa pə siwa təbaa*
PREP drink tobacco
for 'I saw that he smoked tobacco.'

(66) **wu klәŋ paa n-ta n-yil*
3M hear 1SG-fall PREP-ground
for 'He heard that I fell down.'

(67) **war klәŋ wur paa can әɣ*
3F hear 3M slaughter goat
for 'She heard that he has slaughtered a goat.'

We see therefore a systematic relationship between the verbs of the main clause, the function of the complementizer, and the modality of the embedded clause. The complementizer *nә* occurring after *verba dicendi* has no modal function. The epistemic modality after such verbs is marked by the modal *paa*. When the complementizer *nә* occurs after other verbs it acquires the function of epistemic modality marker. Modal *paa* cannot be used after *non verba dicendi*. I believe that a similar development of the function of the complementizer derived from demonstrative occurred in other languages as well.

3. RELATIVE CLAUSES

There is a partial or complete overlap in the forms that function as complementizers, definite markers, and relative clause markers. In many languages the forms of these markers are similar to remote demonstratives or neutral pronouns, as the following data from a selection of languages from various families indicate:

Table 1.

Language	Demonstrative	Definite	Complement	Relative
German	das/die/der	das/die/der	dass	das/die/der
Yiddish			vos	vos
English	that	the<that	that	that/wh
Ge'ez	za	Ø	za	za
Amharic	ya	u/w	ya/ala	ya
Beja	ūn/tún	ū/tū	Ø	ū/tū
Mupun	*nә*	*nә*	*nә*	*dә*
Ewe	si/sia	a/lá	be/béna	sì
Toba Batak	na	na	na	
Yurok		ku/k'i		ku/k'i
K'ekchi		li		li
Drehu	la	la	la-ka	

It is tempting to use the notion of *de dicto* domain as a common element that would explain the formal similarity among the three grammatical categories. What follows is then a speculation on the possible connection between the relative clause formation in some languages and the demonstrative, definite, and complementizers after *verba dicendi.*

I would like to consider an analysis whereby, in some languages relative clauses have been conceptualized as a comment interjected into another proposition. With respect to the proposition into which it is interjected, the relative clause is a *de dicto* category. Hence there is the option of marking by the same marker that is used as the complementizer or by the same marker that marks the definite, i.e. by markers that elsewhere mark other *de dicto* categories in the language. If we assume that the relative clause is marked as an interjected proposition with respect to the sentence in which it is embedded, we can explain why it is that the demonstratives occur as relative clause markers predominantly in post-nominal relative clauses (cf. Keenan, 1985). In such sentences, the main proposition has already begun, and it is interrupted by the relative clause, which is essentially a comment on one of the components of the main proposition or a modification of one of the components. In pre-nominal relative clauses, the main proposition will usually start after the relative clause has ended, hence there is no interjection, and thus no motivation to treat any element of the utterance as being more remote, *de dicto*, than the other. In languages in which both pre-nominal and post-nominal relative clauses occur, the post-nominal relative clauses must have the demonstrative preceding them, while the pre-nominal clauses may or may not have the demonstrative, e.g.:

(68) *der Mann, der in seinem Büro arbeitet*
ART man who in his study works
'The man who is working in his study.'

(69) *der in seinem Büro arbeitende Mann*
ART
'The man who is working in his study.' (Keenan, 1985:144)[2]

(70) *ein in seinem Büro arbeitender Mann*
ART(INDEF)
'A man who is working in his study.'

(71) *poika joka tanssi poydalla oli sairas*
boy REL dance on-table was sick
'The boy who danced on the table was sick.'

(72) *poydalla tanssinut poika oli sairas*
'The boy who danced on the table was sick.' (Finnish, Karlsson, 1972:106 ff.)

Relative clauses in Amharic, which are introduced by the morpheme *ya-*, may serve as possible counter-evidence for the lack of demonstratives in prenominal relative. The morpheme *ya-* which at least historically is derived from a demonstrative precedes the prenominal relative clause:

(73) *ya-matta saw*
REL came man
'A/the man who came.' (Cohen, 1936:115)

Since this morpheme is also a marker of the genitive construction, the relative clause in Amharic may be seen as a variant of the genitive construction, with the relative clause being a syntactic equivalent of the 'possessor' phrase, e.g.:

(74) *ya-šum baqlo*
chief mule
'A/the mule of the chief.'

(75) *ya-baqlo əgər*
foot
'The foot of the mule.' (Cohen, 1936:78)

Many Tibeto-Burman languages also have genitive constructions used to form relative clauses (Scott De Lancey, p.c.).

4. DE DICTO REFERENCE SYSTEMS

4.1. Two properties

The existence of two sets of pronouns, one of which refers only to the *de re* objects and the other only to the *de dicto* objects, is the most obvious evidence for the validity of the *de re–de dicto* distinction. The best known examples of the existence of two sets of pronouns are in languages with logophoric systems. Logophoric systems, whether identified as such or not, have been described with various degrees of completeness in Jungraithmayr, 1963/64; Cloarec-Heiss, 1969; Burquest, 1973; Hagège, 1974, who coined the term; Clements, 1975; Ebert, 1979; Hyman and Comrie, 1981; Stanley, 1982;

and Frajzyngier, 1985. As the term was originally used by Hagège, it designated pronouns occurring in the embedded clauses whose referent was the subject of a *verbum dicendi* in the main clause, e.g.:

(76) *wu sat nə dï nas an*
3M say COMP 3MLog beat 1SG
'He$_1$ said that he$_1$ beat me.'

(77) *wu sat nə wu nas an*
3M 3M
'he$_1$ said that he$_2$ beat me.' (Mupun)

A less well-known phenomenon is the existence of a formal distinction between the addressee of a current discourse (a *de re* addressee) and the addressee of a reported discourse (a *de dicto* addressee), e.g.:

(78) *ca, peemu ta kayu laa mu mijiba*
say 2P FUT drive-out man REL stranger
'He said that you (reported speech addressee) will drive the stranger away.'

(79) *ca, ka (*2M*) ta kayu laa mu mijiba*
'He said that you(m.) are going to drive the stranger away.' (Pero, Frajzyngier, 1985)

Since such systems have been described in the references listed, I will take their existence as a proof of the distinction between *de dicto* and *de re* reference and not dwell on it anymore.

4.2. Locative anaphora

In some languages there exists a formal distinction between demonstratives referring to a *de re* location and demonstratives referring to a location mentioned in speech, e.g.:

(80) *wu wa dï*
3M come home there (Anaph.)
'He came back from there.'

(81) *wu wa sə*
3M return there (Deictic) (Mupun)
'He came back from there.'

The *de dicto* demonstrative refers only to a locative argument mentioned in speech. The deictic demonstrative refers only to a location that can be pointed to. Note that (81) with a deictic demonstrative is ungrammatical if referring to a location mentioned in speech. Similarly (80) is ungrammatical if accompanied by some kind of a gesture pointing to a place (for a description of this type of anaphora see Frajzyngier, 1989).

In many languages the locative anaphora is derived from a remote demonstrative:

(82) Put the book here
Put the book there
If you took the book from a box put it back there /*here

(83) *Položi etu knigu syuda*
put this book here
'Put this book here.'

(84) *Položi etu knigu tuda*
there
'Put this book there.'

(85) *Esli ty vzjal knigu iz jaščika tak položi eo obratno tuda/*
if 2M take book from box then put it back there
**sjuda*
here (Russian)
'If you took a book from the box put it back there.'

(86) *Mets cet livre ici*
Mets cet livre là
Si tu as pris le livre d'une boite remettre le là. (French)

The use of the remote rather than the proximate deictic in the anaphoric function is not accidental, as shown by the sample in Table 2:

The fact that in many languages the anaphoric locative is derived from a remote deictic can be explained by metaphoric extension, i.e. in the way in which Greenberg, 1985 explained emergence of the discourse deixis.

4.3. Formal distinctions in the *de dicto* referential systems

In the discussion to follow I consider that the *de dicto* category and the hypothetical mood overlap semantically in that neither of them refers to a domain of reality. As has been pointed out already in many languages, the

Table 2. *Locative demonstratives*

	Proximate	Remote	Anaphoric
English	here	there	there
German	hier	da	da
French	ici	là	là
Spanish	aqui	alla, alli/ahi	alli/ahi
Russian	zdes'	tam	tam (Stative)
	sjuda	tuda	tuda (Movement)
Polish	tutaj	tam	tam
Hausa	nan	can	can

hypothetical mood is encoded as a *de dicto* category. It appears that the number of formal distinctions encoded in the *de re* reference system is different from the number of formal distinctions encoded in the *de dicto* reference system. Typically the *de dicto* reference system will have fewer distinctions than the *de re* reference system. In the following sections I will consider distinctions made within the systems addressee pronouns, interrogative pronouns, and quantifiers.

4.3.1. *Addressees in the de dicto and de re domains*

In many languages the gender of the addressee is formally encoded, e.g.:

(87) *kogo widziałeś*
whom-ACC see-PAST-2M
'Who did you (m.) see?'

(88) *kogo widziałaś*
who-ACC see-PAST-2F
'Whom did you (f.) see?' (Polish)

In a hypothetical discourse, the addressee is always second person masculine, as in the following fragment from Szymborska's 'Pisanie życiorysu' where the poet talks to a hypothetical addressee:

(89) *Pisz tak jakbyś ze sobą nigdy nie*
write-IMPER-SG so as if with REFL never NEG.
rozmawiał i omijał z daleka
talk-2SG-**M**-PAST and avoid-2SG-**M**-PAST from afar
'Write as if you have never talked with yourself, and avoided yourself from afar.'

The sentence as it stands indicates an addressee that could be either masculine or feminine. If Szymborska were to use verbs in the feminine rather than masculine form, the addressee would be interpreted as a concrete woman whose identity happens to be unknown rather than a hypothetical addressee that may be a man or a woman. Compare the following sentences built on the constituents of the line from Szymborska:

(90) *z kim rozmawiałeś a kogo omijałeś*
with whom talk-PAST 2M-SG CONJ who-ACC avoid-PAST-2M-SG
z daleka
from afar
'With whom did you (m.) talk and whom did you (m.) avoid from afar?' (may be interpreted as having a *de dicto* or a *de re* addressee)

(91) *z kim rozmawiałaś a kogo omijałaś*
with whom talk-PAST 2F-SG CONJ who-ACC avoid-PAST-2F-SG
z daleka
from afar
'With whom did you (f.) talk and whom did you (f.) avoid from afar?' (can be interpreted as having only a *de re* addressee)

Striking evidence for the distinction between a *de dicto* reference system and a *de re* reference system exists in Mupun. The language has a formal distinction between the second person masculine and second person feminine singular addressee of an actual speech event, e.g.:

(92) *ɣa pə dem a mi*
2M PREP want COP what
'What do you (m.) want?'

(93) *yi pə dem a mi*
2F PREP want COP what
'What do you (f.) want?'

In a hypothetical event this distinction does not exist, and instead there is only one form for the addressee, second person masculine. In the next four examples a female speaker talks about obviously female participants in hypothetical events, and yet she refers to those participants by second person masculine *a/ka* rather than by second person feminine *yi*, which she would have used were she to talk in the situation with real, rather than hypothetical, addressees of the propositions involved:

(94) *gaskiya, get kadan* ***ka*** *kə ak ba də mo pə*
truly PAST if 2M with pregnancy NEG PAST 3PL PROGR
ɓal ɗik n-ka
marry PREP-2M
'Truly, in the past if you were pregnant they wouldn't marry you.'

(95) *mo yap wur* ***fua*** *mo we mo sei mo man nə*
3PL check breast 2M PL thing PL till 3PL know COMP
ka *nəən ak daŋ sə mo ɓal n* ***ka***
2M lack pregnancy before they marry PREP 2M
'Before they marry you, they will check your breasts, etc., till they are satisfied that you are not pregnant.'

(96) *kat naan get sin anjirem məə n-ɣa məndon ɗak sə i*
if God PAST give placenta ANAPH PREP-2M one only
'If God gave you only one placenta...'

(97) ***a*** *da sian kə sə daŋ*
2M go remove PREP DEM like that
'You go and get an abortion just like that.'

These sentences are not grammatical errors, slips of the tongue, or some other 'exceptional' utterances. Their analyses with other native speakers, confirmed every single one of them, not only as grammatical, but actually as the only possible variant in the context of the conversation.

It appears that in a hypothetical event there is also no number distinction. In the following sentence, the topicalized subject is marked for plural, and it is inherently feminine. And yet the pronominal form preceding the verb is *a*, the second person masculine singular subject pronoun:

(98) *jirap də n-yak sə mo a vwan sar vwan ɗaa*
girls REL PREP-time DEM PL 2M wash hand wash dish
'The girls of nowadays, just wash their hands, wash dishes.' (the modern girls do not want to do anything dirty)

4.3.2. Interrogative pronouns

The distinction between *de re* and *de dicto* reference systems can explain at least one phenomenon that has not been explained so far. It is well known that interrogative pronouns in many languages trigger only one verb 'agreement' while non-interrogative pronouns may trigger more than one agreement, e.g.:

(99) *Kto to kupił*
who it buy-PAST-3M-SG
'Who bought it?'

cf.

**Kto to kupiła*
who it buy-PAST-3F-SG (Polish)

The non-interrogative usage of the 'interrogative' pronoun has the same properties as the interrogative usage, viz., there is only one system of agreement, e.g.:

(100) *Białe plamy jak by kto wapnem*
white stains as if somebody whitewash-INSTR
pochlapatł
splash-PAST-3M-SG
'White stains, as if somebody splashed whitewash all over.' (Polish)

cf.

**Białe plamy jak by kto wapnem*
white stains as if somebody whitewash-INSTR
pochlapała
splash-PAST-3F-SG

If one accepts the distinction between *de dicto* and *de re* reference, the explanation of why the interrogative should have no gender distinction becomes straightforward: *kto* 'who' and *co* 'what' are not identified until the answer is provided. They are thus not *de re* but rather *de dicto* elements. Therefore they have a reduced system of distinctions like other *de dicto* elements in Polish. If, however, an interrogative is used with respect to a specific group of people, i.e. when we know at least one element of the possible answer, then instead of the general interrogative the so-called relative pronouns are used. Thus if one were to address a group of boys and suspected that one of them bought the given object, one would say:

(101) *który* *kupił*
who (M-SG.) buy-PAST-M-SG
'Which one bought (it)?'

Addressing a group of girls in similar circumstances one would say:

(102) *która* *kupiła*
who (F-SG.) buy-PAST-F-SG
'Which one bought (it)?'

The gender distinction is also made in plural pronouns referring to the actual participants, viz. *którzy* (M.PL) and *które* (F.PL). No number distinction is made in interrogative pronouns when the answer is completely unknown.

Invoking the notion of *de dicto* domain we can perhaps explain the often noted but left unexplained syncretism of the interrogative and indefinite pronouns, such as in English clauses:

(103) Watch what you eat
Watch who you talk to

This syncretism is known in many Indoeuropean languages (ex. 100 above in Polish) and was already a feature of Proto-Indoeuropean (cf. Meillet, 1937). But it occurs also in other languages, e.g. in Hungarian, Uto-Aztecan, Chadic, to name just a few of the unrelated families in which the indefinite and interrogative pronouns have an identical form. The indefinite pronouns refer to some person, thing, place, etc. whose further identity is unknown, hence very much an argument belonging to a hypothetical domain, the same domain to which interrogative pronouns belong. The identical coding of the two interrogative and the indefinite pronouns in so many languages suggests that rather than having two different sets, we have only one set, which is used in different syntactic environments, but always in the same function. This conclusion is especially evident where specific questions are encoded by other means along with the interrogative pronouns (cf. Frajzyngier, 1985c).

4.3.3. Plural verb in an interrogative clause

There is a verbal prefix *po-* in Polish. With many verbs this prefix indicates plurality of object and plurality of action, e.g.:

(104) *Piotr otworzył okno*
Peter open-3M-past window
'Peter opened the window.'

(105) *Piotr pootwierał okna*
Peter PL-open-PAST-3M-SG window-PL
'Peter opened up the windows.'

In interrogative sentences the plural form of the verb is felicitous only as an echo question. Thus the following sentence would not be felicitous unless it is preceded by some proposition in which the verbs have the plural form, such as 'X opened up windows, Y opened up doors':

(106) *Co Piotr pootwierał?*
what Peter PL-open-3M-SG
'What did Peter open?'

The analogous question with a singular verb, however, is felicitous in situations in which the plural form is not:

(107) *Co Piotr otworzył*
open-PAST-3M-SG
'What did Peter open?'

A possible explanation of the different felicity conditions for the singular and plural form of the verb in interrogative sentences lies in presuppositions one has to make before asking the question. The important fact is that for a speaker to use the plural form of the verb in an interrogative sentence, he has to assume that the object is plural. The speaker does not have to make any assumptions about the number of the object in order to use the singular form of the verb. The link between interrogative and hypothetical (i.e. *de dicto*) is that in the interrogative we refer to an object whose characteristics are not as fully known as in a *de re* reference.

4.3.4. Quantifiers and de dicto referents

In some languages quantifiers make a distinction between masculine and feminine forms. Thus in Polish an appropriately coded quantifier has to be used with masculine and feminine nouns, or when addressing somebody, e.g.:

(108) *każd-y chlopiec*
every (M) boy
'Every boy.'

każd-a dziewczyna
every (F) girl
'every girl.'

(109) *każd-y z was i każd-a z was*
each (M) PREP you(PL) CONJ each (F) PREP you(PL)
'Every one of you (M) and every one of you (F).'

In a reference to hypothetical persons only the masculine form is used, e.g.:

(110) *dla każdego coś innego*
for everybody-DAT something different
'Something different for everybody.'

A similar situation obtains in German. Ulrike Claudi has drawn my attention to the following perfectly grammatical sentence once used on a tampon package. The quantifier in this sentence is in the masculine form:

(111) *Die Menstruation ist bei **jedem** etwas anders*
DEF menstruation is for everybody (M) a little bit different
'Everybody has a slightly different menstruation.' (Pusch, 1984)

Yet if one were to address a group of girls, one would use the feminine form of the quantifier, *jeder*.

4.3.5. Gender in the de dicto domain in English

I would like to claim that the *de dicto–de re* distinction is/was also encoded in the reference system of English and that, in particular, for many speakers of English the system of reference to the *de dicto* domain is reduced when compared to the system of reference to the *de re* domain. Let us take a typical sentence from contemporary academic English (all underlining mine).

(112) "The reader will find in this superb volume almost anything he/she might wish to know about English grammar and its rules." (Reference Book Review)

And now two typical sentences from academic English of some fifty years ago:

(113) ". . . and in both cases I have given references, in the Notes and Bibliography, which will enable the reader to look into things, and, if he chooses, to arrive at an opinion of his own." (Bloomfield, 1933:VII)

(114) "The ultimate success of the worker in Africa, whether he be trader, settler, missionary, anthropologist, educator, or administrator, depends to a large extent upon his language performance." (Ward, 1937:6).

As examples from Bloomfield and Ward indicate, the system operated and for many speakers still operates in the following way: If a reference is made to a [+human] noun from a *de dicto* domain, and that noun is not inherently feminine, the form used is the third person pronoun 'he'. It is important that the reference is made to an element from the *de dicto* domain rather than to an element that one could consider to be a 'generic'. In recent times we have seen a change, at least in some varieties of English, whereby a reference is made as in the quote from Reference Book Review (ex.112). Whatever was the social motivation for this change, it reflects an analysis that did not take into account the *de dicto–de re* distinction. The sporadic acceptance of this change reflects a small triumph of social pressure over language structure.

5. CONCLUSIONS

I have shown that *de dicto–de re* distinction may be usefully applied to explain several apparently unrelated phenomena in language structure. Invoking this distinction, one can provide a motivated explanation of why definite articles, complementizers after *verba dicendi*, and postnominal relative clauses have similar markers in a number of unrelated languages. Lack of demonstratives as markers of prenominal relative clauses follows naturally from the proposed hypothesis. I have provided an explanation for the use of demonstrative pronouns as complementizers after *verba dicendi*, and their use as inference-only markers after verbs of perception. The explanation implies that a rather abstract notion of reference to an element from the domain of speech emerged independently in a number of unrelated languages. I have shown that in a number of languages there exist two sets of pronouns, one referring to *de re* elements and the other to *de dicto* elements. The set referring to the *de dicto* domain does not encode so many distinctions as the set referring to the domain *de re*.

ABBREVIATIONS

ANAPH	anaphora
ART	article
CONS	consecutive
F	feminine
FL	feminine logophoric
M	masculine
ML	masculine logophoric
PL.L	plural logophoric

ACKNOWLEDGEMENTS

Work on this paper was supported by the NSF Grant BNS-84 18923. I am grateful to Dwight Bolinger, Ulrike Claudi, Karen Ebert, Bernd Heine, John Koontz, and Elizabeth C. Traugott for the close reading of a previous version of this paper and for their insightful comments and additional examples and references.

NOTES

1. The following analysis and example is due to Dwight Bolinger in private correspondence.
2. Although Keenan, op cit. considers sentence (69) to be an instance of the relative clause, this analysis is not shared by other linguists (Ulrike Claudi and Bernd Heine, p.c.). The force of my argument here hinges not on the status of this sentence but on the fact that it represents a pre-nominal rather than a post-nominal modification of a noun by a clause.

REFERENCES

Almkvist, Herman. 1881–1883–1885. *Die Bischari-Sprache. Tu-Bedawie in Nordost-Afrika*. Uppsala: K. Geselschaft der Wissenschaften zu Uppsala.

Anderson, Stephen R., and Edward L. Keenan. 1985. "Deixis." In Shopen 1985, 3:259–308.

Bloomfield, Leonard. 1933. *Language*. New York: Holt.

Burquest, Donald. 1973. A Grammar of Angas. Ph.D. Dissertation, University of California at Los Angeles.
Channon, Robert. 1980. "Anaphoric that: A friend in need". In *Papers from the Parasession on Pronouns and Anaphora*, Jody Kreiman and Almerindo E. Ojeda (eds), 98–109. Chicago: Chicago Linguistic Society.
Clements, George Nicholas. 1975. "The logophoric pronoun in Ewe: Its role in discourse." *Journal of West African Languages* 10:141–177.
Cloarec-Heiss, F. 1969. *Les modalités personelles dans quelques langues oubanguiennes (Discours direct–Discours indirect)*. Liège: SELAF.
Cohen, Marcel. 1936. *Traité de langue amharique*. Paris: Institut d'ethnologie.
Dešeriev, Jurij D. 1959. *Grammatika xinalugskogo jazyka*. Moscow: Akademja Nauk.
Dubois, Jean, Mathé Giacomo, Lois Guespin, Christian Marcellesi, Jean-Baptiste Marcellesi and Jean-Pierre Mevel. 1973. *Dictionnaire de linguistique*. Paris: Larousse.
Ebert, Karen H. 1979. *Sprache und Tradition der Kera (Tschad). Teil III: Grammatik*. Berlin: Reimer.
Frajzyngier, Zygmunt. 1984. "On the origin of *say* and *se* as complementizers in Black English and English-based creoles." *American Speech* 59(3):207–210.
Frajzyngier, Zygmunt. 1985a. "Logophoric systems in Chadic." *Journal of African Languages and Linguistics* 7:23–37.
Frajzyngier, Zygmunt. 1985b. "Truth and the indicative sentence." *Studies in Language* 9:243–254.
Frajzyngier, Zygmunt. 1985c. "Interrogative sentences in Chadic." *Journal of West African Languages* 15(1):57–72.
Frajzyngier, Zygmunt. 1987. "From verb to anaphora." *Lingua* 72:15–28.
Frajzyngier, Zygmunt. 1989. "Three kinds of anaphora." In *Current Progress in African Linguistics*, Isabelle Haik and Laurice Tuller (eds). Amsterdam: Foris.
Greenberg, Joseph. 1985. "Some iconic relationships among place, time, and discourse deixis." In Haiman 1985:271–287.
Hagège, Claude. 1974. "Les pronoms logophoriques." *Bulletin de la Société de Linguistique de Paris* 69:287–310.
Haiman, John. 1985. *Iconicity in Syntax*. Amsterdam: John Benjamins.
Hughes, G.E. and Cresswell, M.J. 1968. *An Introduction to Modal Logic*. London: Methuen.
Hyman, Larry M. and Bernard Comrie. 1981. "Logophoric reference in Gokana." *Journal of African Languages and Linguistics* 3:19–37.
Karlsson, Fred. 1972. "Relative clauses in Finnish." In *The Chicago Which Hunt*. Chicago Linguistic Society, Paul M. Peranteau, Judith N. Levi and Gloria C. Phares (eds), 106–114.
Keenan, Edward L. 1985. "Relative clauses." In Shopen 1985:141–170.
Kirsner, Robert, and Sandra A. Thompson. 1976. "The role of pragmatic inference in semantics: A study of sensory verb complements in English." *Glossa* 10(2):200–240.
Lockwood, W.B. 1968. *Historical German Syntax*. Oxford: The Clarendon Press.
Lord, Carol. 1976. "Evidence for syntactic reanalysis: from verb to complementizer in Kwa." In *Papers from the Parasession on Diachronic Syntax*. Chicago: Chicago Linguistic Society, 179–191.
Lowenstamm, Jean. 1977. "Relative clauses in Yiddish: A case for movement." *Linguistic Analysis* 3(3):197–216.

Meillet, Antoine. 1937. *Introduction à l'étude comparative des langues indo-européennes*. Paris: Hachette.

Moyse-Faurie, Claire. 1983. *Le drehu*. Paris: SELAF.

Noonan, Michael. 1985. "Complementation." In Shopen 2:42–140.

Percival, Keith W. 1981. *A Grammar of the Urbanised Toba-Batak of Medan*. Pacific Linguistics, Series B. Nr. 76.

Pusch, L.F. 1984. *Das Deutsche als Männersprache*. Frankfurt.

Shopen, Timothy, (ed.). 1985. *Language Typology and Syntactic Description*. Cambridge: Cambridge University Press.

Stanley, C. 1982. "Direct and reported speech in Tikar narrative texts." *Studies in African Linguistics* 13:31–52.

Stieber, Zdzislaw. 1979. *Zarys gramatyki porównawczej jezyków stlowiańskich*. Warszawa: Państwowe Wydawnictwo Naukowe.

Szymborska, Wistlawa. 1986. *Ludzie na moście*. Warszawa: Czytelnik.

Traugott, Elizabeth Closs. 1980. "Meaning-change in the development of grammatical markers." *Language Sciences* 2(1):44–61.

Traugott, Elizabeth Closs. 1982. "From propositional to textual and expressive meanings: Some semantic-pragmatic aspects of grammaticalization." In *Perspectives on Historical Linguistics*, Winfred P. Lehmann and Yakov Malkiel (eds), 245–271. Amsterdam: John Benjamins.

Traugott, Elizabeth Closs. (In press). "Old English syntax." In *The Cambridge history of English*, Vol. 1, Richard Hogg (ed.). Cambridge: Cambridge University Press.

Ward, Ida C. 1937. *Practical Suggestions for the Learning of an African Language in the Field*. Oxford: Oxford University Press.

Westermann, Diedrich. 1952. *A study of the Ewe language*. Oxford: Oxford University Press.

Wright, S. and T. Givón. 1987. "The pragmatics of indefinite reference: Quantified text-based studies." *Studies in Language* 11(1):1–33.

The Grammaticalization of Rhetorical Questions in Tamil

Susan C. Herring
California State University, San Bernardino

1. INTRODUCTION*

One of the foremost tenets in diachronic grammaticalization theory today is the notion of *unidirectionality*, according to which change in meaning from less to more grammatical is viewed as a linear and irreversible process. Defined thus in general terms, unidirectionality might appear to be a simple description of, rather than a claim regarding the nature of, the grammaticalization process. However inasmuch as the term is frequently extended to characterize other features of the grammaticalization process which might or might not hold true for all instances in all languages, the use of the label 'unidirectionality' makes a claim which must be demonstrated according to its own merits for each feature proposed.

For example, grammaticalization is widely claimed to be unidirectional with respect to increasing degree of *abstraction*; that is, language users tend to refer to abstract, less accessible concepts in terms of more familiar, concrete ones, and this tendency is one of the factors which motivates the linguistic encoding of new concepts in old forms (cf. Heine, Claudi, & Hünnemeyer, This volume). Such a claim is well-motivated cognitively, and is supported by synchronic and diachronic evidence from a number of languages.

It has also been claimed that grammaticalization involves *semantic bleaching*, or weakening of lexical meaning, and that this process, too, is unidirectional. The validity of this claim is, however, far less evident than that for increasing abstraction, since not all meaning change necessarily involves bleaching, and in numerous instances, as is demonstrated by Traugott and König (This volume), the exact opposite process, that of semantic *strengthening*, may also take place. A more comprehensive view would seem to be that weakening and strengthening are independent processes, either or both of which may potentially be a factor in grammaticalization in any given instance.

Finally, Traugott (1982; 1988) and Traugott & König (This volume) have claimed that grammaticalization is also unidirectional in the sense of increasing *subjectification* or 'speaker involvement'; that is, the extension of meanings encoded by a given lexical or grammatical item is predictably away from objective, referential meaning towards subjective, "speaker-based" attitudes and points of view. Drawing on a model proposed by Halliday and Hasan (1976), Traugott (1982) identifies three functional-semantic components which she labels propositional, textual, and expressive. Her prediction is that when grammaticalization involves a meaning-shift from one functional-semantic component to the other, it will proceed from the propositional (via, optionally, the textual) to the expressive level, but not in the reverse direction. Extensions of this type are accounted for in terms of (among others) the inclusion within a form's "meaning" of some pragmatic nuance which was formerly implicated by context alone. An example cited by Traugott is the diachronic extension of English 'while' from a noun meaning 'period' or 'time' to a temporal connective on the textual level to, ultimately, a concessive conjunction (in the sense of 'although') which encodes the attitude of the speaker towards the proposition (Traugott, 1982:254).

What is not clear is that the process of grammaticalization as a whole is necessarily unidirectional with respect to this characterization, nor indeed, why we might expect that it should be. To begin, the claim that the historical trend in language change has been towards increasing grammatical expression of subjective and pragmatic meanings would seem to imply that at some remote earlier stage such meanings were not expressed, or were expressed with a far lower frequency. This would be an awkward position to maintain, it seems, even aside from the problems inherent in attempting to demonstrate it empirically. Second, the claim that grammaticalization *necessarily* has its roots in the propositional (i.e. local, or lexical) level is at odds with the findings of a growing body of researchers that point to the discourse-pragmatic origins of a number of grammatical elements. Thus Givón (1979) has argued in favor of the diachronic discourse basis of morphological relativizers, causativizers, and other types of clause subordinators in a variety of languages; Hopper (1979, 1982, for Literary Malay) and Herring (1988, for Tamil) have pointed out the possibility of discourse/pragmatic focus elements developing into markers of perfective aspect; and DuBois (1987) attributes the grammaticalization of ergative case-marking systems to functional constraints on the rate and nature of information flow in narrative.

The implications of such claims on the unidirectionality hypothesis are clear: If grammaticalization is defined as the process whereby grammatical elements (be they morphological or syntactic) come into being, then if there is any validity at all to the claims of the proponents of grammar *ex*-discourse, the grammaticalization process cannot be unidirectional in the sense proposed by Traugott. Rather the evidence suggests that autonomous grammatical elements may arise *either* out of individual lexical or already existing grammatical elements on the propositional level, *or* they may take as their source the larger discourse/pragmatic context.[1] Indeed, it is my assertion that, as in the case of semantic bleaching mentioned above, the two processes are essentially independent, and that they are free to interact. Thus, it is theoretically possible that a single grammatical word or affix may have undergone extensions in both directions at different times over the course of its development.

If this position is correct, then important questions immediately arise regarding the nature of the two processes. Do they apply to comparable data cross-linguistically, or do certain grammatical meanings exhibit an affinity for one source component or the other? Do individual languages show a preference for one strategy over the other; that is, are some languages more 'discourse-grammaticalizing', and others more 'lexical-grammaticalizing', or do both kinds of processes operate in all languages to a similar extent? As for the specific mechanisms which drive these processes, a number of mechanisms which account for meaning change in isolated lexical items have been discussed in the literature; e.g. analogy, bleaching, strengthening, metaphor, systems of inference, and so forth. The mechanisms involved in the grammaticalization of discourse functions, however, have yet to be systematically identified and described. Will we find the same, or similar, motivating factors at work, or will it be necessary to postulate other mechanisms which derive not from considerations of meaning but rather from considerations of communicative function? If the latter turns out to be the case, we must confront a methodological issue as well: Since "hard" diachronic evidence of communicative function — especially in the very earliest stages of grammaticalization — is by the very nature of things often excluded, can the process(es) involved be inferred on the basis of synchronic evidence alone? Or should we attempt to devise other methods for getting at discourse-functional factors in language change? I do not propose to address all of these questions, or even any one of them exhaustively, in the present paper. I do hope, however, to shed some light on the nature of the specific mechanisms involved in the grammaticalization of discourse functions. I propose to do this by examining, in depth, a particular instance of discourse/pragmatics-based grammaticalization: That of the grammaticalization of rhetorical questions as markers of clausal subordination in Tamil.

A word about the organization of the remainder of this paper may be useful here. In considering the Tamil evidence, I begin by identifying three rhetorical question types. I then trace what I hypothesize to be the diachronic evolution of these types, from their pragmatic (interactive and expressive) origins (Section 3 and Section 4), to their reanalysis as markers of textual cohesion (Section 4), and ultimately to their grammaticalization as clausal morphology (Section 5). This expository sequence is accompanied by a progressive narrowing of focus: Only two out of the original three rhetorical question types participate in the second and third stages of the above process, and within those two types, a subset of the actual linguistic forms involved have attained fully grammaticalized status. By presenting the material in a sequence iconic with its (hypothesized) historical development, I hope to illustrate the naturalness of the processes involved, and to hint at the contextual richness — and perhaps too, at a certain random element, leading to the grammaticalization of some forms but not of others — which shaped the phenomenon as a whole. For those who prefer the omniscience of hindsight, however, a more focused reading is also possible. Two forms for which clear evidence of grammaticalization will be adduced are the causal conjuction *ē̱ṉṉā*, and the relativizer *-ē*, derived from a WH- word (*ēṉ* 'why') and a tag question marker, respectively. In the general overview of Tamil rhetorical questions presented below, the individual stories of these two forms can also be traced. The final section (Section 6) considers the implications of the Tamil evidence for the unidirectional hypothesis and grammaticalization theory.

2. RHETORICAL QUESTIONS: THE THREE TAMIL TYPES

The data on which this study is based are from Tamil, a Dravidian language with SOV word order and suffixing, agglutinative morphology. Except where indicated otherwise, all of the examples presented here are drawn from a corpus of thirty-five oral narratives which I recorded in Tamil Nadu, India, in 1986–87. These include personal narratives as well as folk tales of various types, as related by both professional storytellers and ordinary adult native speakers. Of special note are two lengthy public performances in the *Villu Pāṭṭu* (lit. 'Bow Song') style, which provide evidence for the interactive basis of rhetorical questions in traditional narrative.

A striking feature of Tamil oral narration (and to a lesser extent, of written narration as well) is the frequent use of rhetorical questions. A rhetorical question is defined here as any utterance which is interrogative in form, but which — as opposed to a genuine, information-seeking question — does not sollicit a response. The three most common rhetorical question types in Tamil[2] are what I refer to as the Classical Rhetorical Question (CRQ), the Thematicizing Rhetorical Question (TRQ), and the Rhetorical Tag Question (RTag), illustrated in examples (1)–(3) below:[3]

(1) *"Pāl kuṭikkāta pūṉai kūṭa irukkum-**ā**?"*
milk drink-NEG cat even be-F3NS-Q
'Is there any cat that doesn't drink milk?!' [CRQ]

(2) *Oru nāḷu puruṣaṉkāraṉ **eṉṉa** ceñcirukkṟāṉ;*
one day husband what do-PERF-PR3MS
'One day, what did the husband do?' [TRQ]

(3) *Inta pañcāyattellām vaippāṅka **illai**, pakkattu ūrile.*
this panjayat&all hold-F3PL TAG next town-LOC
'They hold this panjayat (meeting) and all, right? in the next town.' [RTag]

2.1. CRQs

The first example is typical of the rhetorical question type discussed in classical rhetoric and speech act theory; I refer to this as the Classical Rhetorical Question, or CRQ. An oft-described characteristic of this type is that the surface syntax is conventionally understood to be the opposite of that of the underlying indicative assertion to which it corresponds. That is, a positive question implies a negative assertion, and a negative question, a positive assertion.[4] Thus, in uttering example (1), the speaker expresses the view that there is *no such thing* as a cat that doesn't drink milk. CRQs may also be WH- questions; in such cases, the usual sense of the corresponding assertion is universal (absolute) negation (e.g. '*Where* will you find a cat that doesn't drink milk?!', both in Tamil and in English, normally means 'You *won't* find a cat that doesn't drink milk *anywhere*!').

2.2. TRQs

The question in example (2) establishes a theme (namely, that the husband *did something*), which the narrator must elaborate upon by answering his own question in subsequent clauses. The fact that Thematicizing Rhetorical Questions (TRQs) require further comment is reflected in Schmidt-Radefeldt's phrase "the rhetorical use of question-answer sequences" (1977:378), and in Grésillon's (1981) expression *question-réponse à un seul locuteur*, to refer to essentially the same phenomenon. Theoretically TRQs may be realized as either Yes-no or WH- questions, although as it turns out, virtually all of the TRQs in the Tamil data are WH- questions, an interesting fact in its own right, which can be attributed to pragmatic constraints (cf. Section 4.2 below). In terms of content, the two most frequently encountered TRQs in the Tamil corpus are 'And then what did X do?' and 'And then what happened?'.

There is a variant of the Tamil TRQ which involves the addition, in clause-final position, of the subordinating conjunction *ṉṉā* (the conditional form of the quotative verb *eṉ* 'to say/ask'); a literal translation of *ṉṉā* is 'if (you) say/ask'.[5] Thus, while example (2) is a syntactically independent clause, TRQs followed by *ṉṉā* are formally subordinate to some other (finite) clause. Aside from this formal distinction, the presence or absence of *ṉṉā* does not appear to significantly affect the meaning or function of the TRQ, although from a diachronic perspective, *ṉṉā* will be seen to play a role in the grammaticalization of TRQs as clausal subordinators (cf. Section 5.1). The TRQ + *ṉṉā* construction is illustrated in (4) below:[6]

(4) *Atu vantu varuṣā varuṣam* ***eppaṭi*** *ṉṉā,*
it TOP year-as year how ask-COND
'If (you) ask, "How (is it) year after year?"'

Ṉṉā could also be added on to example (2) above. Indeed TRQs with and without *ṉṉā* appear to be in free variation in oral narration in Modern Tamil.

2.3. RTags

Example (3) is a tag question, formed by the addition of the invariant tag particle *illaiyā* (lit. 'is it not?') to an otherwise declarative utterance. In addition to *illaiyā* (and its phonologically reduced variants, *illai*, *ille*, and *-le*), there are two other important tag question markers in Tamil: The so-called "emphatic" clitic *-ē*, and the imperative (or, the 2nd person past tense form) of the verb *pār* 'to see, look'. These are illustrated in examples (5) and (6):

(5) *Inta aracaṉ kaṇṇai mūṭikkiṭṭiruntāṉ-ē*;
this king eye-ACC close-PROG-P3MS-ē
'The king was keeping his eyes closed, right?'

(6) *Iṉṉoru- anta mutallē kāmatēṉu pacu vacciruntār* ***pāruṅka***.
another that first-LOC Kamadenu cow keep-PERF-P3RS see-IMP
'The other — in the beginning, (he) was the one keeping the Kamadenu cow, right?'

Although there is no syntactic constraint which prohibits the use of any of the Tamil tags with a negative assertion, such uses are rare in these data; again, this can be accounted for pragmatically (cf. Section 4.3). Thus the tag questions considered here overwhelmingly presuppose an affirmative response.

These examples, while representing unrelated types syntactically, are similar in that all are rhetorical (rather than genuine information-seeking) questions, which were uttered in the context of narration. The interpretation of an utterance as a rhetorical rather than a true question is dependent on a complex of features, including the presence of characteristic or otherwise incompatible grammatical elements,[7] intonation, context, and the shared knowledge and perspective of speaker and hearer. In my recorded data, it is generally clear, from the narrators' intonation and the presence or absence of clause-final pauses in oral delivery, which utterances were intended rhetorically and which as true questions (in the case of rhetorical questions, lack of response from the native speaker listeners further supports my assessments). Moreover, all question forms used in professional performances must be construed as serving some other, non-interrogative purpose, since in such contexts the audience is prohibited by convention from participating verbally in the discourse.

3. THE INTERACTIVE BASIS OF RHETORICAL QUESTIONS

Why, then, do narrators — and Tamil narrators more than most — use rhetorical questions when telling a story? I will first consider the most straightforward explanation, which is a pragmatic one: Rhetorical questions, not unlike genuine questions, are intended to stimulate the involvement of the listeners in the story by making a direct appeal to their attention and evaluative processes. Thus a number of scholars following in the recent German pragmatic tradition (cf. Gülich, 1970; Schmidt-Radefeldt, 1977; and Vandeweghe, 1977) characterize rhetorical questions as "appelative" in function:

> Rhetorische Fragen — bei denen der Frage-Charakter mehr oder weniger deutlich ausgeprägt sein kann — lassen sich daher als Appell an die Aufmerksamkeit des Hörers interpretieren. Der Sprecher, der sie verwendet, zeigt, dass er sich ständig der Anwesenheit des Hörers bewusst ist.[8] (Gülich, 1970:229)

Similarly:

> Mit seiner Frage macht der Sprechende S einen Appell an den Hörenden H, und er stellt so eine interpersonale Beziehung her.[9] (Vandeweghe, 1977:279)

However, rhetorical questions differ crucially from questions in general in that not only is no answer expected of the hearer, but the hearer may actually be prevented from answering, due to "particular situational, social or institutional conventions" (Schmidt-Radefeldt, 1977:378) which prescribe to him or her a passive role. One such convention is that which governs oral narration, which is, except in certain exceptional cases (cf. Section 3.1 below), essentially monologic. There are a number of reasons why it is to the advantage of the narrator to discourage extensive listener participation. As Popovici (1981:i5) observes, *le rejet d'un argument ou d'une objection possible implique un dialogue entrevu et évité* ('the rejection of a possible argument or objection implies a dialogue foreseen and avoided'). Dialogue is to be avoided in that it is less predictable and less under the control of a single participant than is a monologue. More serious still, a narrator who gives up the floor to another, no matter how briefly, risks losing it altogether and never finishing his story.

At the same time, it is the task of the narrator to engage and hold the attention of his audience, a task all the more critical in oral narration, where numerous opportunities may arise for the listener to become distracted. The use of rhetorical questioning strategies allows the narrator to address simultaneously both of these conflicting concerns. He poses questions as a means of engaging the attention of the interlocutor. At the same time, rather than risk interruption or derailment by allowing the interlocutor to answer for himself, the narrator constructs a hypothetical listener with whom he "interacts", even speaking at times in this other listener's "voice". Thus a narrator may "answer" his own CRQ by explicitly stating the assertion it implies:

(7) *Avaṉ peyilā pōyṭṭā itai colṟatukku vīṭṭukku*
he fail-ADV go-COND this to-say house-DAT
*varuvāṉ-**ā**? Varamāṭṭāṉ.*
come-F3MS-Q come-NEG-F3MS
'If (a schoolboy) fails (an exam), will he come (straight) home to tell about it? He won't.'

Or, he may imitate a dialogue by means of a TRQ and its response:

(8) *Āka inta poṇṇu* ***e<u>nn</u>a*** *āyirutu; karppamā*
thus this girl what become-PFV-PR3NS pregnant
ākutu inta poṇṇu.
become-PR3NS this girl
'And so what happens to the girl?
She gets pregnant, the girl (does).'

(The implication here is that the listener, unable to contain his or her curiosity, has posed the question.)[10] This hypothetical listener is an idealized listener, in that at any given point in the narration, he knows all that he is supposed to know in order to appreciate the story, and is attentive and eager to receive whatever information follows.[11] Actual listeners are unreliable in these respects, since they may fail in comprehension and attention for a variety of reasons.

3.1. Rhetorical questions in traditional performance narrative

Compelling evidence in support of the abstract ideal listener analysis can be found in the traditional Tamil *Villu Pāṭṭu* storytelling genre.[12] In a *Villu Pāṭṭu* performance, a principal narrator ('A') is assisted by a secondary narrator ('B') and several singer/musicians (whose "narrative" duties are largely restricted to echoing and agreeing with 'A' and 'B'). Of special interest is the role of 'B' in the narrative performance. On the one hand, he may introduce new material into the narrative sequence to a limited extent, either alone or in conjunction with the main narrator (this constitutes one of the "exceptions" referred to earlier to narration as monologue). His primary role, however, is as a physical embodiment of the "ideal listener", whose duty it is to respond to the main narrator at each appropriate moment in an appropriate way. As such, he responds to rhetorical questions by making explicit the (normally unspoken) responses which they conventionally presuppose. Rhetorical questions are extremely common in *Villu Pāṭṭu* performances. Consider example (9) below, which contains four CRQs:

(9) (The wife of the great god Shiva, cursed by her husband, despairs of accomplishing what he has ordered her to do)
A: *"Nilaṅkaḷai cīrtiruttam ceyya nammāl muṭiyum-**ā**?*
B: *Muṭiyātē!*
A: *Pātti kaṭṭa muṭiyum-**ā**?*
B: *Atuvum muṭiyātē!*

A: *Ceṭikaḷai nāṭṭa muṭiyum-**ā***?
B: *Atuvum muṭiyātē!*
A: *Nammāl **e<u>nn</u>a** ceyya muṭiyum?*
B: *Oru kāriyamum naṭakkātē!"*

A: '"Am I capable of domesticating the land?! [Yes-no]
B: (I) can't!
A: Can (I) lay out plots (for cultivation)?! [Yes-no]
B: (I) can't (do) that, either!
A: Can (I) plant plants?! [Yes-no]
B: (I) can't (do) that, either!
A: What will I be able to do?! [WH-]
B: Not a single thing will come out right!"'

In this example, Narrator B responds negatively to affirmatively-phrased CRQs, and with a universal negative to a WH- type CRQ, confirming that this is indeed how the Tamil narrator who makes use of such constructions intends himself to be understood.

Narrator B also responds appropriately to TRQs, not by providing any information, but by encouraging Narrator A to supply the answer himself, as in examples (10) and (11):

(10) A: *Akkā taṅkai ē<u>l</u>upērum **eppaṭi** nīrāṭukki<u>r</u>ār?*
B: ***Eppaṭi?***
A: [*pāṭṭu*] *Avar ku<u>l</u>uttaḷavu nalla taṇṇīrilē...*
ka<u>nn</u>iyarkaḷ vantu nīrāṭa...
vāyaḷavu taṇṇīrilē...
vantu ni<u>n</u>ṟu viḷaiyāṭa...

A: 'How do the seven sisters bathe?
B: How?
A: [sings] Up to their necks in the good water...
the maidens came and bathed...
up to their mouths in the water...
they came and stood playing...'

(11) A: *Aṅkē āṇṭu varukin<u>r</u>ava<u>n</u> **yār***?
B: ***Yār?***
A: *Turiyōta<u>n</u>a<u>n</u>.*

A: 'Who is the one who rules there?
B: Who?
A: Duryodhanan.'

Observe that in the last two examples, it is not the "listener" (Narrator B) who introduces the question, as might have been expected on the basis of the preceding discussion, but rather Narrator A. This is because TRQs also serve an important organizational function, which will be described later on, and which is normally reserved for the principal narrator alone. Thus even in his role as ideal listener, Narrator B cannot be relied upon to ask the right questions at exactly the right time; the wrong question or the wrong timing could derail the flow of Narrator A's narration.

RTags are also common in the *Villu Pāṭṭu*, although they do not elicit an explicit response as frequently as the other two types. When Narrator B does respond, his responses follow the expected pattern of affirming the sentential assertion:

(12) A: *Namma periyār pasṭāṇṭu irukku* ***pāruṅka****, ceṇṭral pasṭāṇṭu.*
B: *Āmā.*
A: *Atukku muṉṉāle piḷāṭpārattile tī peṭṭi vittukkiṭṭu iruntāṉ.*

A: 'There's our Periyar Bus Stand, right? The central bus stand.
B: Yes.
A: In front of it, on the platform, he was selling matches.'

(13) (A young god muses aloud)
A: *"Mantirattilē ciṟantatu malaiyāḷam tāṉ-ē?*
B: *Malaiyāḷa nāṭu tāṉ.*
A: *Nāṉ malaiyāḷam pōka tāṉ vēṇṭum!"*

A: "'(The place where they have) the best enchantments (is) Malaiyāḷam (country), right?
B: (It's) Malaiyāḷam country, indeed.
A: I must go to Malaiyāḷam (country)!'"

The first of these examples contains the polite imperative form *pāruṅka*; the second, the bound suffix *-ē*. Both function here as tags, as shown by the English translations.

Note that in none of these examples do the responses provided by B introduce any new information into the discourse. The impression is of a dialogue, but in fact the range of responses permitted B is quite restricted. The *Villu Pāṭṭu* data provide evidence, therefore, of the validity of the "ideal listener" concept in Tamil oral narration. The value of such a construct is that it allows the narrator to evoke an interactional dynamic, while at the same time maintaining ultimate control of the discourse. Hart (1980) claims that the stylistic device of addressing oneself to some fictional, absent, or inanimate third person audience can be observed, not just in Tamil, but as a pan-Indian tendency dating back to the earliest recorded literary works. Thus the high RQ content in contemporary Tamil narrative may well reflect, to some extent at least, a more traditional interactive narrative strategy.

4. FROM "EXPRESSIVE" TO "TEXTUAL" FUNCTIONS

Let us now consider uses which extend the RQ phenomenon beyond the limits of the interactive domain. In this section, I discuss the expressive pragmatic 'meaning' of each of the basic RQ types, and show how, in the case of TRQs and RTags, expressivity has been largely replaced by textual — by which I intend discourse-organizational — functions. This constitutes a shift which, it will be argued, paves the way for the eventual grammaticalization of a subset of these elements as clause-linking markers.

4.1. Expressive functions of CRQs

If rhetorical questions are interactive in the qualified sense just discussed, they are also expressive, in that each RQ type is associated with a particular stylistic effect. The classical type, as is often pointed out, is a *persuasive* device which characteristically presents the point of view of the speaker as if it were obvious. From the perspective of the addressee, of course, the point may not be obvious in the least, but part of the efficacy of a CRQ is that it is more difficult to refute than an ordinary assertion, in that it *presupposes* the addressee's agreement. In the Tamil narrative corpus, CRQs are also used to scoff ('I can't do with my eyes open what you can do with your eyes closed?!'), boast ('Is there anyone greater than I?!'), express dismay ('What's the use of being a great king if I can't fulfill my mother's dying wish?!'), show amazement ('Is it possible to behold such a forest?!'), and to convey many other expressive nuances as well. These examples appear almost exclusively in *mimetic*, or quoted sections of text.[13] The use of CRQs in quoted dialogue within narrative closely parallels their use in actual conversation. As such, the principle function of CRQs in narration is pragmatic; i.e. to represent a conversational exchange in a more persuasive or expressive fashion.

4.2. Expressive functions of TRQs

In order to illustrate the expressive value of TRQs, it is necessary to take into account not only the question clause but the clause or clauses which follow it in sequence, and which serve as its response. Consider, in this context, example (8) and example (2′) (an expanded version of (2) above):

(8) *Āka inta poṇṇu* ***eṉṉa*** *āyirutu;* *karppamā*
thus this girl what become-PFV-PR3NS pregnant
ākutu *inta poṇṇu.*
become-PR3NS this girl
'And so what happens to the girl? She gets pregnant, the girl (does).'

(2′) *Oru nāḷu puruṣaṉkāraṉ* ***eṉṉa*** *ceñcirukkṟāṉ,*
one day husband what do-PERF-PR3MS
"Nāṉ vēṭṭaikku pōkaṇum" *ṉṉu* *pōyiṭṭāṉ.*
I hunt-DAT go-be-necessary QUOT go-PFV-P3MS
'One day, what did the husband do?
Saying, "I must go hunting", he went off.'

In her analysis of discourse strategies in Romance, Wehr (1984) characterizes question-answer sequences of this type as marked with respect to simple declarative word order by the addition of the pragmatic feature [+SURPRISE]; that is, the information which follows the question is evaluated, by means of this device, as being in some sense unexpected or reaction-worthy. In this schema, the use of a question form functions to create drama by placing the audience in suspense, arousing their curiosity about what is to follow.

These observations would seem to apply to English as well, in that the most straightforward English translations of Tamil TRQ-response sequences tend to convey the impression that the narrator is attempting to interject a suspenseful tone, as in the examples above. Here Tamil differs from English, however, in that (i) the overall frequency of TRQ-response sequences is notably higher in Tamil; (ii) they may be employed even when the events they introduce are in no way dramatic or unexpected; and (iii) their use does not necessarily imply that the speaker evaluates said events as dramatic or unexpected. That is, while the analysis advanced by Wehr may well have been true for Tamil TRQs at an earlier stage in their development, the suspenseful function, possibly through pragmatic unmarking based on frequency of use, has largely given way to a function on the textual level: That of introducing new information[14] into the text in a pragmatically "focused" way. WH-words are especially effective in focusing interest on a particular constituent, a fact which may tie in with the overwhelming predominance of WH- TRQs (rather than the Yes-no type) in Tamil. Thus a more idiomatic translation of

(8) above might be, 'So what happens is, the girl gets pregnant', where a pseudo-cleft construction, rather than a question, translates the Tamil TRQ. As such, the construction serves as an alternative to syntactically more complex *focus constructions*, which in Tamil typically take the form of nominalizations. Viewed in this light, the TRQ and the clause which follows, although syntactically independent, function in the discourse as a single structural unity,[15] an observation supported by prosodic and intonational evidence as well. They resemble topic-comment structures in which the "theme" or "topic" introduced by the TRQ is commented upon in the response; e.g. 'What happens to the girl is, she gets pregnant'; 'One day what the husband did was, he said he had to go hunting, and went off'.

The strategy serves a broader organizational function within the story as a whole by relating entire sequences of short, syntactically independent clauses to a single focus or theme, thereby creating loose structural unities reminiscent of paragraphs in written discourse. In the continuation of (4), given as (4′) below, the narrator goes on to add ten more finite clauses, all of which contribute in some way to the "answer" to the TRQ 'If you ask "How is it year after year?"':

(4′) *Atu vantu varuṣā varuṣam* ***eppaṭi*** *ṉṉā,*
Kīḻattuvalle pasṭ ārampikkum canṭai.
Kīḻattuval ñkiṟatu oru ūr.
Kīḻattuvalle tāṉ pasṭ ārampikkum.
Campantillāma..pasṭ canṭai anta hariccaṉs pōṭavē māṭṭāñka.
Inta tēvaruñka tāṉ pōṭuvāñka.
Avañka eṉṉamāvatu colluvāñka.
Ivañka uṭaṉē pōy, avañka itule..añcu āṟu pēr pōy veṭṭiṭuvāñka.
Veṭṭiṉa uṭaṉē, avañka vantu koñca pēttai veṭṭuvāñka.
Ivañka vantu koñca koñca kūṭa pēttai veṭṭuvāñka.
Ippaṭi tāṉ varuṣā varuṣam, april mācam, karekṭṭā inta canṭai naṭanturum.

'If (you) ask, "**How** (is it) year after year?" (=How it is year after year is,) the fighting starts in Kīḻattuval.
Kīḻattuval's a town.
It starts first in Kīḻattuval.
For no reason...the Harijans never start fighting first.
It's the Devars who start (it).
They (the Harijans) say something or the other.

And then they (the Devars) immediately go over...five or six people go and cut (them) up.
As soon as they do that, (the Harijans), they cut a few people.
They only cut a few people.
The fighting takes place like this, year after year, exactly in the month of April.'

Here the repetition of the adverbial *varuṣā varuṣam* 'year after year' in the last clause effectively brackets off the TRQ and the ten clauses which follow as a single cohesive unit within the discourse.

TRQs, as mentioned above, are more frequent in oral than in written narration, and we are now in a position to account for this distribution. As a device which may be employed to create structural cohesion while at the same time preserving a straightforward paratactic "one clause at a time" (Pawley and Syder, 1977) mode of presentation, TRQ-response sequences are well suited to the demands of on-line oral narrative production, which tends to prefer loose sequences of finite clauses to more complex embedded constructions. Formulaic expressions such as 'And then what happened?', 'And then what did he do?' presumably require a minimum of processing in the narrator's consciousness, allowing more time in which to organize his thoughts and plan what he is going to say next (Chafe, 1980). At the same time, because of their open-endedness as question forms, they help to insure that the audience will remain attentive until the speaker has succeeded in formulating his next utterances.

The extent to which this strategy is productive can be seen in the following example, an excerpt from an informal oral retelling of a mythological tale. Note the narrator's heavy use of TRQs in organizing (and reorganizing) the linear presentation of his ideas:

(14) *Āṉā anta ūrile, payaṅkara pañcam.*
Cāppiṭuratukku kūṭa oṉṉum kiṭaiyātu makkaḷukku.
Āṉā rājāvukku veṟṟi viḻā koṇṭāṭuṟāṉka.
Koṇṭāṭuratu ṉṉā...cāppāṭu maṭṭilum rājāvukku ***eppaṭi*** *varutu* ***ṉṉā****,*
oru iṭattil iruntu oru muṉivar vantu cāppāṭu kuṭuttu viṭuvāru rājāvukkāka.
Oru arai vayiṟu cāppāṭu ille; arici ille.
Avvaḷavu pañcam.
Ēṉ ṉā *caṇṭai pōṭṭatuṉāle, irukkiṟa...paṇamellām celavaḻiccu pōccu.*
Appa muṉivar kuṭuttuviṭum pōtu, iṭaiyilē anta cāppāṭa...inta...
rājāvōṭa āḷuṅka koṇṭṭu varṟāka.

Varum pōtu..iṭaiyile ***eṉṉa*** *paṉṟāṅka tiruṭaṅka;*
anta cāppāṭellām piṭuṅki cāppiṭaṟāṅka.
Avaṅka ***ēṉ*** *piṭuṅki cāppiṭṭāṅka* ***ṉṉā****,*
avaṅkaḷukku cāppiṭaṟatukku oṉṉum ille.
Ataṉāle avaṅka piṭuṅki cāppiṭaṟāṅka.

'But in that town, (there's) a terrible famine.
There isn't anything at all for the people to eat.
But they're holding a victory celebration for the king.
(How they're) celebrating is... **how** does a serving of food come for the king?
A sage comes from someplace and donates food for the king.
(There's) not even half a belly-full of food; (there's) no rice.
(That's) how much famine.
Why? The money they had all got spent in waging war.
Then when that sage donates (the food), in the meantime the food (was)...
the kings' men bring it back.
As they're bringing (it back)...in the meantime **what** do (some) thieves do?
They snatch up the food and eat it.
Why do they snatch it up and eat it?
They don't have anything to eat.
So they snatch it up and eat it.

The repeated use of rhetorical questions in this section of discourse may sound odd or even incoherent to native speakers of English, since it is difficult to ascribe an expressive interpretation to what is not a particularly dramatic sequence of events (nor is the sequence of central importance for the story as a whole). If, however, we change the TRQs in the English translation to pseudo-cleft constructions, as in (14′), it is possible to appreciate something of the cohesive function which they serve in the original Tamil:

(14′) 'But in that town, (there's) a terrible famine.
There isn't anything at all for the people to eat.
But they're holding a victory celebration for the king.
(How they're) celebrating is...
how a serving of food comes for the king is,
a sage comes from someplace and donates food for the king.
(There's) not even half a belly-full of food; (there's) no rice.

(That's) how much famine.
(The reason) why is (because) the money they had all got spent in waging war.
Then when that sage donates (the food), in the meantime the food...
the kings' men bring it back.
As they're bringing (it back)...in the meantime what (some) thieves do is,
they snatch up the food and eat it.
(The reason) why they snatch it up and eat it is,
they don't have anything to eat.
So they snatch it up and eat it.

Clearly we have moved here beyond the realm of expressivity to the organization and presentation of the discourse itself; or, to employ Traugott's terminology in a somewhat broader sense, from the "expressive" to the "textual" level.

4.3. Expressive functions of RTags

In the same way that CRQs are persuasive, and TRQs (in some languages at least, and probably originally in Tamil as well) suspenseful, a narrator's use of rhetorical tag questions evokes solidarity with the listener by presupposing the listener's knowledge of the information thus tagged, thereby including both listener and speaker within the informed sphere of those capable of fully appreciating the significance of the narrated information.[16] As in the case of CRQs, the listener need not in actual fact be familiar with the information thus evaluated, or he may not have the particular information in mind at the time, such that the RTag serves as well to bring it to the foreground of his consciousness.

RTags draw on two types of "common" knowledge: That which is external, and that which is internal to the narrative. The former typically includes (i) shared cultural knowledge, as reflected in the use of the term 'panjayat' (the popular form of village government in India) in the RTag in example (3); (ii) shared point of view (especially if there is a close social or interpersonal relationship between speaker and listener); and (iii) knowledge, both general and specific, that the speaker has reason to believe — or chooses to represent as though he believed — is shared by the listener. Narrative-internal knowledge is information that was either specifically mentioned in, or can be inferred from, the previous discourse; this is reflected in examples (5) and (6).

Beyond this use, which is essentially pragmatic, RTags have a textual function in Tamil, which is again one of clause-linking. An important characteristic of RTags is that they are anaphoric; that is, they refer back, either to the discourse, or to previous experience of a more general nature. As such, they are frequently used to specify and retrieve referents which are old information, i.e. in cases where the narrator wishes to predicate something new of these referents. Such referents are typically positive and definite; hence the absence in the data of RTags with negative propositions. The "retrieval and predication" function of RTags becomes clear once we examine the examples given in isolation above along with the clauses which follow them immediately in the discourse:

(3′) *Inta pañcāyattellām vaippāṅka **illai**, pakkattu ūrile.*
this panjayat&all hold-F3PL TAG next town-LOC
Eṅka appā pōkāma irukkum pōtu ivaṉ pōyiṭuvāṉ.
our father go-NEG be time he go-PFV-F3MS
'They hold this panjayat (meeting) and all, right? In the next town. When my father couldn't go, this (boy) would go (in his place).'

(5′) *Inta aracaṉ kaṇṇai mūṭikkiṭṭiruntāṉ-**ē**;*
this king eye-ACC close-PROG-P3MS-TAG
ivaṉum kaṇṇai tiṟantu pākkuṟāṉ.
he-also eye-ACC open see-PR3MS
'The king was keeping his eyes closed, right?
He too opened his eyes and saw (them).'

(6′) *Iṉṉoru- anta mutallē kāmatēṉu pacu vacciruntār$_i$* ***pāruṅka**.*
another that first-LOC Kamadenu cow keep-PERF-P3RS see-IMP.
Oru muṉivar$_i$.
a sage.
Avar$_i$ visvāmittirarai viruntukku kūppiṭuvār oru nāḷ.
he Vishvamitra-ACC feast-DAT call-F3R one day
'The other- in the beginning [i.e. of the story], (he$_i$) was the one keeping the Kamadenu cow, right?' A sage$_i$.
He$_i$ invited Vishvamitra to dinner one day.'

In each of these examples, the situation referred to in the RTag clause is old or otherwise accessible information; the assertion in the second clause is new information. As in the case of TRQs and the clauses which follow them, it is possible to speak of a loose structural unity between the RTag and its following predication, a unity reinforced in many cases by prosody and intonational contour. Functionally, sequences of RTag+clause may replace more complex embedded *relative clause constructions*, especially in the spoken language. Compare, for example, the loose paratactic version in (3′) above with the version in (15), which contains an embedded (participial) relative clause construction modifying the nominal head 'panjayat' (note: 'FAJP' = 'Future Adjectival Participal'):

(15) *Eñka appā* ***pakkattu ūrile vaikkum pañcāyattukku***
our father next town-LOC hold-FAJP panjayat-DAT
pōkāma irukkum pōtu, ivaṉ pōyiṭuvāṉ.
go-NEG be time he go-PFV-F3MS
'When my father couldn't go **to the panjayat (meeting) which (they) hold in the next town**, this (boy) would go (in his place).'

There are a number of advantages which the tag strategy has over the participial strategy. By preserving the iconic order of the two clauses, the RTag version not only avoids the necessity of embedding, but it also eliminates the need to indicate case relations (in the example above, the dative indicating GOAL) on the nominal head; that is, the paratactic version is non-specific as to the thematic relationship between the arguments of the two clauses. The linking of clauses by means of RTags is a strategy, therefore, which facilitates the presentation of information with a minimum of encoding complexity.

5. THE GRAMMATICALIZED STATUS OF RQ ELEMENTS

These observations regarding the textual functions of TRQs and RTags are of interest in their own right, and merit further consideration within the realm of discourse analysis. For the purposes of the present discussion, what is to be noted is that the discourse-organizational use of RQs represents a shift in function away from the basic RQ strategy defined above. We might hesitate to claim that grammaticalization has taken place, however, since we are not left with new autonomous grammatical markers, but rather with two highly specific (albeit extremely productive) *construction types*. We might predict, nevertheless, that if the constructions were to grammaticalize further, it would be as clause-connecting elements of some type, given the evident trend towards the combining of two finite utterances into one.

In fact, this prediction turns out to be correct. The WH- elements *ē<u>n</u>* 'why', *e<u>nn</u>a* 'what', and *eppaṭi* 'how' (either alone, or in combination with the conditional conjunction *<u>nn</u>ā*), show evidence of grammaticalizing away from TRQ constructions into autonomous conjunctions. As for RTags, while all three of the Tamil tags presented here can function as informal relativizers, as examples (3′), (5′), and (6′) demonstrate, the particle *-ē* has taken on many of the features of a formal relativizing particle as well. These developments are considered in greater detail below.

5.1. From TRQ to conjunction

There is a qualitative shift from the discourse-organizational use of TRQs described above to the use of the conjunction *ē<u>nn</u>ā* (*ē<u>n</u>* 'why' + *<u>nn</u>ā*) in the following sentence:

(16) *Ava<u>n</u> iṅkē illai* ***ē<u>nn</u>ā*** *ava<u>n</u> ūrukku pō<u>n</u>ā<u>n</u>.*
he here NEG CONJ he town-DAT go-P3MS
'He is not here because he went to his village'.

In purely syntactic terms, this shift involves the displacement of the WH-word *ē<u>n</u>* from its usual clause-second position to the end of the clause, where it attaches to the subordinating conjunction *<u>nn</u>ā*. (Compare, for example, (16) above with the TRQ-response focus construction: *Ava<u>n</u>* ***ē<u>n</u>*** *inkē illai* (***<u>nn</u>ā***), *ava<u>n</u> ūrukku pō<u>n</u>ā<u>n</u>* 'Why he isn't here is, he went to his village'.) A further fact regarding the compound conjunction *ē<u>nn</u>ā* is that it may be analyzed as belonging exclusively to the second, but not the first clause in the sequence, as evidenced by the fact that

Ava<u>n</u> iṅkē illai* ***ē<u>nn</u>ā.*
*'He isn't there because.'

is not a complete grammatical utterance, while

Ē<u>nn</u>ā *ava<u>n</u> ūrukku pō<u>n</u>ā<u>n</u>.*
*'Because he went to his village.'

is fully grammatical in Tamil. In sentence-initial position, *ē<u>nn</u>ā* functions analogously with sentence-initial conjunctions such as *ata<u>n</u>āle* 'therefore', *ā<u>n</u>ā* 'but', and *iruntālum* 'nevertheless' (the latter two also deriving from conditional forms):

Ata<u>n</u>āle *ava<u>n</u> ūrukku pō<u>n</u>ā<u>n</u>.*
'Therefore he went to his village.'

Āṉā *avaṉ ūrukku pōṉāṉ.*
'But he went to his village.'
Iruntālum *avaṉ ūrukku pōṉāṉ.*
'Nevertheless, he went to his village.'

It also groups with this class of elements semantically; in particular, 'because' (REASON) and 'therefore' (CAUSE) express closely related logical concepts.

A further argument for the grammaticalized status of expressions such as *ēṉṉā* involves intonation and prosody. (In the case of *ēṉṉā*, phonological reduction is also involved; i.e. a sequence of three alveolar nasals is reduced to two, in keeping with the phonotactic rules of the language.) WH- words in Tamil typically exhibit a high, rising intonation with an optional drop in pitch at the end. The intonation of the subordinator *ṉṉā*, on the other hand, falls from the high to the middle range; i.e. to signal a non-final clause boundary. When, however, the two are combined as in example (16), *ēṉṉā* tends to be pronounced with a high, *level* intonation, leading directly into the following clause. The two strategies can be contrasted graphically as in (16a) and (16b):

(16a) *Avaṉ* ***ēṉ*** *inkē illai* ***ṉṉā****, avaṉ ūrukku pōṉāṉ.*
he why here NEG SUBD he town-DAT go-P3MS
'Why he isn't here is, he went to his village'.

(16b) *Avaṉ iṅkē illai* ***ēṉṉā*** *avaṉ ūrukku pōṉāṉ.*
he here NEG CONJ he town-DAT go-P3MS
'He's not here because he went to his village'.

The intonational characteristics of *ēṉṉā* are similar to those for other two-syllable sentence-initial conjunctions, such as *āṉā* 'but' and *āka* 'therefore'.

These same criteria allow us to establish the word *ēṉ* alone as a coordinating conjunction (with the same functional value as *ēṉṉā*), as in the following example:

(17) *Tērle naṭṭu pōlṭṭu ellām cariyā irukkā ṉṉu,*
chariot-LOC nut bolt all okay be-PR3NS-Q QUOT
ēṉ *aṭutta nāḷ tēr ōṭṭaṇum-ē.*
CONJ next day chariot drive-be-necessary-TAG
ivar tāṉ pākkaṇum atellām.
he EMPH look-be-necessary that-all
'(He checks to see) if the nuts and bolts on the chariot are all okay, *because* the next day he has to drive the chariot, right?
He has to take care of all that stuff himself'.

Thus *ṉṉā* is, strictly speaking, not an essential ingredient in WH- conjunctions, although it is more often present than not.

So far, we have been dealing almost exclusively with *ēṉ*; however, a similar shift can be seen to have taken place with two other WH- elements, *eṉṉa* 'what' and *eppaṭi* 'how', which combine with *ṉṉā* to produce the conjunctions *eṉṉaṉṉā* and *eppaṭiṉṉā*. Although they exhibit the same syntactic and prosodic properties as *ēṉṉā*, it is more difficult to ascribe to them distinct semantic labels. Indeed, they may sometimes be used interchangeably, or in place of *ēṉṉā*. This fact suggests that their lexical identity (i.e. as distinct WH-words) may be weakening, even as their grammatical meaning (as coordinating conjunctions) is strengthened.

Finally, it may be mentioned that the written language, which is generally more conservative than the spoken language, recognizes two of these conjunctions, *ēṉṉā* and *eṉṉaṉṉā*, as unitary grammatical entities. In Written Tamil they appear as single words, viz. *ēṉeṉṟāl*, from *ēṉ* + *eṉṟāl* (written form of *ṉṉā*), and *eṉṉaveṉṟāl*, from *eṉṉa* + *eṉṟāl*, with the glide *-v-* inserted according to a regular morphophonemic process. All of this evidence — syntactic, prosodic, and orthographic — argues in favor of treating these elements as fully grammaticalized conjunctions in Modern Tamil.

5.2. From RTag to relativizer

Turning now to rhetorical tag questions (RTags), recall that a sequence made up of a clause containing a tag (*-ē*, *illai(yā)*, or *pāruṅka*) plus the clause or clauses which follow may function as an informal relativizing construction in Tamil. Examples of this are concatenated utterances of the type: 'The king was standing there keeping his eyes closed, right? He too opened his eyes and saw them', which may be contrasted with embedded relative clause constructions, e.g. 'The king, who was standing there keeping his eyes closed, also opened his eyes and saw them'. Of the three Tamil tags described here, *-ē* alone has achieved the status of a full-fledged grammatical relativizer. This status is attested by a number of facts, not the least of which is that it has been classified as such by at least one native grammarian. Annamalai (1980) explicitly refers to *-ē* marked constructions of the sort we have been discussing as "tag relative clauses", which he notes are "almost like two consequent sentences in a discourse" (1980:291). The tag RC is one of three relative clause types which he identifies for Tamil; the other two are the "participial RC" and the "pronominal RC". The so-called "pronominal RC" (a calque from a Sanskrit construction) is not of interest here, but it may be observed that Annamalai's examples of tag and participial RCs, which I reproduce below, correspond exactly to the distinction made here between informal paratactic and formal embedded relativizing constructions, as illustrated in examples (3′) and (15) above (note: PAjP = 'Past Adjectival Participle'):

(18a) *Nēttu oru payyaṉ vantāṉ-ē avaṉ iṇṇekkum*
yesterday a boy come-P3MS-TAG he today-also
vantāṉ.
come-P3MS
'A boy came yesterday, you know, he came today also'.

(18b) *Nēttu vanta payyaṉ iṇṇekkum vantāṉ.*
yesterday came-PAJP boy today-also come-P3MS
'The boy who came yesterday came today also'.

Further arguments can be made for the grammaticalized status of *-ē*. Syntactically speaking, its role has shifted from that of a clause-final particle to a particle which may relate an attribute to a nominal head within a clause. This is illustrated in the following example, taken from a contemporary Tamil short story:[17]

(19) *Nāṉ pōy **avaḷ niṉṟiruntāḷ-ē** anta iṭattil*
I go she stand-PERF-P3FS-TAG that place-LOC
atē mātiri niṉṟu kaṭalai veṟittu pārkkiṟēṉ.
that-EMPH way stand ocean-ACC stare look-PR1S
'I went and stood in the place **where she had stood**, and stared at the ocean in the same way'. (lit. 'I went and in the she had stood-*ē* place in the same way stood and stared at the ocean').

Here the finite clause 'she had stood' modifies the noun phrase 'that place', with the suffix *-ē* indicating the subordinate relationship of the former to the latter; i.e. *-ē* translates the English relative pronoun 'where'. We may further observe that the relativized clause is entirely embedded within, rather than simply preceding, the matrix clause. Behavior of this sort is associated with the participial RC type, but not with the tag type, which tends to preserve the order 'old information'-'new information', and to present information one clause at a time. This fact alone indicates that *-ē* has undergone a qualitative shift in function in the direction of increased grammatical autonomy.

Like relative pronouns in English, *-ē* may also stand in for the nominal head, in the sense of 'that which', 'the one who', '(the place) where', etc. Thus the heroine in another Tamil short story[18] who, having just been robbed, responds to her husband's inquiry as to what was stolen with:

(20) *"Cañkili, mōtaram, vāṭc, paṇam, nīṅka kuṭutt-iruntīṅkaḷ-ē..."*
chain ring watch money you(resp) give-PERF-P2R-REL
'(Your) chain, ring, watch, money... what you gave (me)!

is clearly not commenting on the husband's past action of giving, but rather on that which was given. A similar usage is illustrated in the oral example below:

(21) *"Nāṉ appō coṉṉēṉ-ē uṅkaḷukku puriñcatā?"*
I then say-P1S-REL you-DAT be-understood-P3NS-Q
'Do you understand (now) what I said then?'

Here what is relevant is not the fact that the speaker of the utterance said something previously, but rather what was said, which had been misunderstood by the addressee at the time.

As in the case of WH- conjunctions, prosodic cues provide additional support for the grammaticalized status of *-ē*. In example (21) above, there is no break between *coṉṉēṉē* and *uṅkaḷukku*, whereas if we were to literally interpret the first half as a tag question, we would expect either a pause or deceleration at that juncture. Moreover, the utterance is characterized by a single, rather than a two-part, intonation contour. While normal intonation for the tag *-ē* is rising-falling, the intonation for (21) is mid-high and level throughout, rising only at the end of the sentence to signal the Yes-no question. On the basis of this and the other types of evidence mentioned, it is clear that the suffix *-ē* must be accorded the status of a full-fledged relativizer.

6. FROM MORE OR LESS PRAGMATIC: IMPLICATIONS FOR A THEORY OF GRAMMATICALIZATION

These observations on the grammaticalization of TRQs and RTags in Tamil lend support to Givón's claim (1979) that "[subordinated] constructions ar[i]se diachronically, via the process of syntacticization, from looser, conjoined, paratactic constructions" (p.222). The RQ strategies examined here can be characterized as moving from what Givón calls a 'pragmatic' towards a more 'syntactic' mode of communication (cf. Table 1).

Table 1 *The pragmatic vs. the syntactic mode of communication (adapted from Givón 1979:223)*

Pragmatic Mode	Syntactic Mode
·loose conjunction	·tight subordination
·topic-comment structure	·subject-predicate structure
·slow rate of delivery under several intonation contours	·fast rate of delivery under a single intonation contour
·no use of grammatical morphology	·elaborate use of grammatical morphology

The 'pragmatic mode' roughly characterizes the discourse-organizational use of RQs described in Section 4, which relies, as we have seen, on loose topic-comment structures delivered under separate intonation contours and conjoined primarily by virtue of their juxtaposition in the narrative sequence. In contrast, elements such as *ē̱ṉṉā* and *-ē* subordinate one clause to another, unite pairs of clauses under a single intonation contour, and have themselves evolved into grammatical morphology — in short, display features of the 'syntactic mode'. As Givón himself cautions, these labels represent but two poles at the extremes of a continuum; there exist numerous intermediate possibilities (particularly with regard to intonation), and more than one 'stage' may be attested simultaneously at any given point in the history of a language. Thus the Tamil data provide evidence for the view that grammatical elements develop as means of encoding basic discourse-pragmatic functions, such as focus, topic-comment, anaphora, and attribution. Given the primacy of these concerns in oral communication, it indeed seems to be the case, as DuBois (1987) claims, that "grammar codes best what speakers do most".

To summarize, the direction of development which best accounts for the Tamil data described here takes as its point of departure the interactive use of rhetorical questions in narration, i.e. to evoke listener involvement in the events of the story. I have suggested that the narrator's desire to maintain control of the discourse results in the constraining of the listener's right to respond, a fact which appears to have contributed critically to the conventionalization of the strategy at the expense of its interactive value. At the same time, each RQ type has its own expressive character: The persuasive force of the CRQ, the suspenseful nature of the TRQ, the use of RTags to create an aura of complicity. As the latter two types begin to develop textual functions based on their cataphoric and anaphoric natures, respectively, increased usage inevitably results in *pragmatic unmarking*, or the gradual diminishing of their expressive impact. Via a reanalysis on the textual level, TRQs and RTags develop as cohesive devices in tandem with the clauses which they introduce. This, in turn, leads to their ever-increasing specialization as grammatical markers of conjunction and subordination. By the time they arrive at the final stage, the question forms have lost their marked, stylistic value; they are no longer interpreted as questions on any level. The process is gradual, however, and it is less appropriate to speak of discrete "stages" than it is of points along a continuum which allow for considerable synchronic overlap of function.

Thus we may speak of an overall extension of the function of TRQs and RTags, from the pragmatic (interactive/expressive) level to the textual (organizational) level to autonomous clause-level grammar. If this analysis is correct, it is evidence that the process of grammaticalization, defined in general terms as the means by which new grammatical elements come into being, is not 'unidirectional' in the sense proposed by Traugott. That is, subjective, pragmatic-based meanings are not always late concomitants of grammaticalization; rather, as we have seen, they may constitute the very roots of grammar.

In concluding, I return to the questions raised at the outset of this paper. While a great deal more research is clearly necessary before we can venture any conclusions as to the relative importance of discourse-grammaticalizing, as opposed to lexical-grammaticalizing, strategies in the languages of the world, or even within a particular language, it is likely that discourse-based grammaticalization will be found to play a more important role than has been suspected up until now. Given the level of sophistication achieved in the field of historical semantics as opposed to the relative newness and lack of a consistent methodology which, unfortunately, has characterized most studies of discourse-related phenomena to date, it is only natural that we, as linguists, should have focused most on what we can talk about most easily; e.g. the study of change in meaning of individual words. Yet the fact that natural language use is necessarily situated in the context of some larger discourse means that it is subject to manipulation for discourse-pragmatic ends. In some cases, such usage may facilitate a shift in meaning and/or function of the form or forms involved, as in the example given here of the grammaticalization of rhetorical questions. Unfortunately, concrete indications of context are typically lacking in the written records which constitute the basis for historical reconstruction, with the result that factors which might have been crucially influential may not figure in our analyses at all.

Given this limitation, I believe that we are justified, to a limited extent at least, in applying diachronic methods to synchronic data. What makes this approach feasible is the fact (supported by a growing body of evidence) that language change is not discrete, but rather progresses along a continuum, with old usages co-existing alongside of new ones. It is for this reason that we are able to observe, or at least infer, the progression of stages from the evidence in Modern Tamil: RQ forms may still function (to some degree, at least) interactively, and varying degrees of syntacticization are evidenced in the narrative data base examined here. An obvious advantage of the method of "synchronic reconstruction" is that it enables us to study phenomena to which we might not have access otherwise. As I have noted, there is reason to believe that most discourse-based grammaticalization falls into this category.

What of the mechanisms which drive discourse-based grammaticalization? On the basis of observations made for Tamil, we may cite the following three processes: *Pragmatic unmarking*, or the process whereby a stylistically or expressively-marked usage loses its marked value as a result of frequent use; *reanalysis* of function, e.g. from one functional/semantic component to the other; and, in the sense employed by Givón, *syntacticization* of loosely conjoined structures into syntactically unified ones. Although further research will no doubt expand and refine this list, there is good reason to believe that each of these processes represents a general, underlying force in language change.

Processes traditionally associated with semantic change are also involved in the grammaticalization of Tamil rhetorical questions: *Bleaching* of lexical meaning (i.e. of WH- words), and corresponding *strengthening* of grammatical meaning, as well as increasing *abstraction* away from the immediate context of face-to-face interaction in the direction of grammatical autonomy. Finally, to return to the original point of controversy, it can be argued that the shift to rhetorical from interrogative question meaning, which presumably must have preceded the developments discussed here, is a type of *subjectification*, in the sense intended by Traugott. Thus the history of the conjunctions *ēn̲n̲ā*, etc. and the relativizer *-ē* may be said to involve both subjectification — in the original extension of function from true to rhetorical questions — and de-subjectification, in the grammaticalization of pragmatic devices as autonomous clause-linking elements. This supports the hypothesis that subjectification is a bi-directional process.

Since all known human languages have strategies for forming questions, it is likely that the rhetorical question is a universal phenomenon as well. I would not be surprised if a correlation were discovered in other, unrelated languages between the use of rhetorical questioning strategies and grammatical subordination; the evolution of the former into the latter is well-motivated in terms of basic communicative functions which speakers of all languages share. Clearly, there is a need to integrate discourse-functional approaches of this type with the methods and insights of those researchers whose principal concern has been with lexically-driven meaning change. Yet before this can be achieved, the existence of functional influences, and their potential importance to the study of grammaticalization, must first gain wider acceptance. I have presented an analysis which reveals the ways in which functional influences may operate, both synchronically and over time, within a particular language. At the very least, the evidence is highly suggestive of an alternative course of development, and as such merits closer consideration within the domain of grammaticalization studies.

ABBREVIATIONS

F3ns	Future 3e person neuter singular
Pr3ms	Present 3e person masculine singular
F3pl	Future 3e person plural
P3ms	Past 3e person masculine singular
P3rs	Past 3e person respectful singular
F3ms	Future 3e person masculine singular
Pr3ns	Present 3e person neuter singular
F3r	Future 3e person respectful
FAjP	Future adjectival participle
SUBD	Subordinator
PAjP	Past adjectival participle
P1s	Past 1e person singular
P3ns	Past 3e person neuter singular

ACKNOWLEDGEMENTS

* An earlier version of this paper was presented at the Tenth Annual South Asian Languages Analysis Roundtable at the University of Washington, July 10-13, 1988. Thanks are due to Suzanne Fleischman, Talmy Givón, Bernd Heine, Eric Pederson, Harold Schiffman, and Elizabeth Traugott for their helpful comments on a revised, later version. Any problems that remain, either of fact or of interpretation, are entirely my own responsibility.

NOTES

1. In contrasting individual lexical elements with the larger discourse/pragmatic context, I do not mean to suggest that the two are isolatable in actual usage: Natural language use is always framed in a broader functional context, and discourse strategies (at least, of the type we are concerned with here) necessarily make use of individual words. The point I wish to emphasize is that grammaticalization — a process traditionally viewed as affecting the internal semantic structure of individual words — may also operate on discourse-based strategies or construction types, in which the individual identities of the words or morphemes are subordinated to the functional identity of the device as a whole.

2. This list is not intended to be exhaustive; other rhetorical question types and sub-types may be identified for Tamil, although I will not undertake to do so here.

3. The examples in this paper (with the exception of examples (19) and (20), which are transliterated directly from the written Tamil) are presented in phonemic transcription, standardized to minimize individual and dialectical variations in pronunciation, while still preserving characteristic Spoken Tamil forms. The system of transliteration is the same as that used in the **Tamil Lexicon** (University of Madras, 1982) and other modern references. Note should be made of the following diacritics: Underdashes indicate alveolar phonemes, with the exception of *ḻ*, which is a retroflex continuant. Overdashes indicate length for vowels, and the velar nasal *n̄*. The other diacritics used — a single dot under retroflex sounds, and *ñ* for the palatal nasal — are standard.

4. That this need not necessarily be the case, however, is indicated by Pope (1976:61, n. 13) who cites J. Ross's example: 'Do we need this raise, after all?'. In this utterance both the form of the question and its corresponding asssertion (e.g. 'After all, we need this raise') are positive. A similar example from the Tamil narrative corpus is the following, the response of some loyal servants to a request from their princess:

   Nī etu colṟiyō ceyṟōmā?
   'Whatever you say (to do), will we do it?'
   (='Of course. We will do whatever you say.')

   The existence of 'double positive' CRQs in no way affects the present analysis.

5. Readers unfamiliar with Tamil should note that the clausal subordinator *ṉṉā*, from Written Tamil *eṉṟāl* ('say + COND'), is not related to the WH- words *eṉṉa* 'what' or *ēṉ* 'why'. Nor should the compound conjunction *ēṉṉā* (*ēṉ* + *ṉṉā*) 'because' (discussed in Section 5) be confused with *eṉṉa* 'what'. Aside from being distinguished by vowel length, which is phonemic in Tamil, the two words have distinct derivational histories, the latter having existed in its current form since the time of the earliest written records, while the former is a relatively recent compound derived from a WH- word and an inflected form of the verb *eṉ* 'to say'.

6. Note that in example (4) there is no finite verb in the surface realization of the clause "embedded" by *ṉṉā*. Clauses with "deleted" or zero predicates constitute acceptable finite utterances under certain pragmatic conditions in Tamil (cf. Herring, 1989).

7. Characteristically rhetorical elements include adverbial phrases such as *varuṣā varuṣam* 'year after year' in example (4), which are pragmatically odd in genuine questions, in that they assert new information. (If such utterances are analyzed as *narrative* in function,

however, then the oddness disappears.) An example of an otherwise incompatible grammatical element is the adverb *kūṭa* 'even' in example (1), which normally would not appear in a genuine question of affirmative structure, in that it presupposes a negative response. For a discussion of similar elements in other languages, cf. Schmidt-Radefeldt (1977) for English and German; Pope (1976) for English; and Grésillon (1981) for German and French.

8. 'Rhetorical questions — the interrogative character of which may be more or less clearly marked — may be interpreted as an appeal to the attention of the hearer. The speaker who uses them demonstrates that he is continuously aware of the hearer's presence' (Gülich, 1970:229).

9. 'By means of his question, speaker S makes an appeal to hearer H, and thereby establishes an interpersonal connection' (Vandeweghe, 1977:279).

10. The implication that the listener has posed the question may also be made explicit. In place of *ṉṉā*, which has been effectively bleached of its literal meaning 'if (you) ask', the expression *ṉṉu coṉṉā*, lit. 'if (you) ask, saying...', appears several times in the corpus, in contexts where it can only be construed rhetorically, e.g.:

Avar eṉṉa paṇṇuvār ***ṉṉu coṉṉā***,
he what do-F3RS QUOT say-COND
kaṭai ellām eṭuttu vaittiṭṭu, oru oṉpatu maṇikku mēle avar varuvār.
wares all take store one nine o'clock after he come-F3RS
'What does he do, (you) ask? Taking up and storing his wares, he comes (to the temple) after nine o'clock.'

11. The notion of "ideal listener" evoked here is adapted from Fillmore's (1981) "ideal reader",

> who knows, at each point in the text, everything that the text presupposes at that point, and who does not know, but is prepared to receive and understand, what the text introduces at that point (p.253).

12. For a discussion of the *Villu Pāṭṭu* genre in its cultural context, cf. Blackburn (1988).

13. In this respect, CRQs differ crucially from TRQs and RTags, which most typically occur in *diegetic*, or narrative portions of text. This distribution may well be responsible for the fact that TRQs and RTags have extended clause-linking functions, while CRQs do not. That is, unlike CRQs, TRQs and RTags are directly involved in relating the sequential events of the narrative.

14. The term 'information' is used here in a broad sense, to include both nominal reference and verbal assertion (cf. Herring, 1989).

15. Similarly, Schmidt-Radefeldt, in describing "the rhetorical use of question-answer sequences" in German and English, comments:

> On the strength of textual-pragmatic coherence (that the same speaker asks a question and answers it all at once) such utterances end up by being one complex declarative sentence (1977:379).

16. A similar analysis is developed by Östman (1981) for the English tag 'you know'.

17. From "Enkō, Yārō, Yārukkākavō..." by Jeyakāntan. In **Guru Pīṭam**. Madurai: Meenakshi Puttaka Nilaiyam, 1971.

18. "Ammā Mantapam" by Sujātā. In **Ciṟukatai E̱ḻutuvatu Eppaṭi**. Madurai: Meenakshi Puttaka Nilaiyam, 1975.

REFERENCES

Annamalai, E. 1980. "Some syntactic differences between spoken and written Tamil." In *South Asian Languages: Structure, Convergence and Diglossia*, Bh. Krishnamurti (ed.), 289–93. New Delhi: Motilal Banarsidass.

Blackburn, Stuart H. 1988. *Singing of Birth and Death: Texts in Performance*. Philadelphia: University of Pennsylvania Press.

Chafe, Wallace L. 1980. "The deployment of consciousness in the production of a narrative." In *The Pear Stories: Cognitive, Cultural, and Linguistic Aspects of Narrative Production*, W. Chafe (ed.), 9–50. Norwood: Ablex.

DuBois, John W. 1987. "The discourse basis of ergativity." *Language* 63(4). 805–55.

Fillmore, Charles J. 1981. "Ideal readers and real readers." In *Analyzing Discourse: Text and Talk*, D. Tannen (ed.), 248–270. Washington, D.C.: Georgetown University Press.

Givón, Talmy. 1979. *On Understanding Grammar.* New York: Academic Press.

Grésillon, Almuth. 1981. "Interrogation et interlocution." *Documentation et Recherche en Linguistique Allemande Contemporaine, Vincennes (D.R.L.A.V.)* 25. 61–75.

Gülich, Elisabeth. 1970. *Makrosyntax der Gliederungssignale im gesprochenen Französisch.* München: Wilhelm Fink.

Halliday, M.A.K. and Ruqaiya Hasan. 1976. *Cohesion in Spoken and Written English.* London: Longman.

Hart, George L. 1980. The Indian Audience: Folklore and Beyond. University of California, Berkeley, ms.

Herring, Susan C. 1988. "Aspect as a discourse category in Tamil." *Berkeley Linguistic Society* 14. 280–292. University of California, Berkeley.

Herring, Susan C. 1989. "Accounting for verbless sentences in Tamil narrative: A discourse-functionalist approach." Paper presented at the 11th South Asian Languages Analysis Roundtable, University of Wisconsin, Madison.

Hopper, Paul J. 1979. "Some observations on the typology of focus and aspect in narrative language." *Studies in Language* 3(1): 37–64.

Hopper, Paul J. 1982. "Aspect between discourse and grammar." In *Tense-Aspect: Between Semantics and Pragmatics*, P. Hopper (ed.), 3–18. Amsterdam: John Benjamins.

Östman, Jan-Ola. 1981. *"You Know": A Discourse-Functional Study.* Amsterdam: John Benjamins.

Pawley, Andrew and Frances Syder. 1977. The One Clause at a Time Hypothesis. University of Auckland, ms.

Pope, Emily N. 1976. *Questions and Answers in English.* The Hague Paris: Mouton.

Popovici, Vasile. 1981. "Dialogues rhétoriques." *Degrés* 28: 11–16.

Schmidt-Radefeldt, Jürgen. 1977. "On so-called 'rhetorical' questions." *Journal of Pragmatics* 1(4).

Traugott, Elizabeth Closs. 1982. "From propositional to textual and expressive meanings: Some semantic-pragmatic aspects of grammaticalization." In *Perspectives on*

Historical Linguistics, Winfred P. Lehmann and Yakov Malkiel (eds), Amsterdam: John Benjamins.

Traugott, Elizabeth Closs. 1988. "Pragmatic strengthening and grammaticalization." *Berkeley Linguistic Society* 14. 406–416. University of California, Berkeley.

Vandeweghe, Willy. 1977. "Fragen und ihre Funktionen. Versuch einer Typologie auf pragmatischer Basis." *Semantik und Pragmatik: Akten des 11. Linguistischen Kolloquiums, Aachen* 1976. 277–286.

Wehr, Barbara. 1984. *Diskurs-Strategien im Romanischen.* Tübingen: Gunter Narr.

Some Grammaticalization Changes in Estonian and their Implications

Lyle Campbell
Louisiana State University

1. INTRODUCTION

In this paper I am concerned with grammaticalizations in two areas of Estonian grammar, with possible explanations for some of the changes, and with their implications for theories of grammatical change in general. One is the rise of a new category of modality in verbs (*kaudne kõneviis*); the other is the development of question markers. While much work on grammaticalization is of the top-down variety — aimed at the 'big picture' with a broad brush and bold strokes —, such work has been criticized by some for what they perceive to be lack of rigor. This paper is of the bottom-up type, beginning with these concrete cases and examining their implications for theoretical claims, i.e. for what they have to say about some of the broad strokes.[1]

2. MODUS OBLIQUUS

Balto-Finnic languages have a number of participial constructions for subordinate clauses of various sorts, and some of these have changed in Estonian (and Livonian, as well) to create what is traditionally called 'Modus Obliquus' forms. I begin by giving a thumbnail sketch of the change, followed by concrete examples and more specific considerations.

The change involves two alternative 'complement' structures with roughly the same meaning; it deals with the cases of speech-act (SAV) or mental-state (MSV) main verbs (*verba sentiendi et dicendi*).

In Stage 1, two constructions are available:

a. Main verb [SAV/MSV] ... *et*[complement] ... Finite verb
b. Main verb [SAV/MSV] ... non-finite verb-ACTIVE.PARTCP

In Stage 2, three constructions become available, (a), (b), and:

c. Main verb [SAV/MSV] *et* Verb-ACTIVE.PARTCP

At this point the Verb-ACTIVE.PARTICIPLE of (c) was reinterpreted as a finite verb form, called *Modus Obliquus*, associated with 'reported' speech, with an 'evidential' function, where the speaker has not experienced the event personally or does not wish to take responsibility for the accuracy of the report — called 'indirect' in this paper (called 'inferential' by Comrie, 1981:125).

In Stage 3, the reinterpreted Verb-ACTIVE.PARTICIPLE, now Verb-MODUS.OBLIQUUS, came to be employed also in main clauses.

For a more detailed exposition, it will be helpful to begin, not with Estonian, but with the corresponding constructions in Finnish, a closely related language which illustrates the state of affairs before the change took place. Finnish has the two original constructions (a. and b. above) with SAVs and MSVs, in both the 'present' and 'past', as in 1–4:

(1) *kuul-i-n, että hän puhu-u sii-tä*
hear-PAST-I that he speak-3.PRES.INDICATIVE it-about
'I heard that he is speaking about it.'

(2) *kuul-i-n häne-n puhu-van sii-tä*
hear-PAST-I he-SG.GEN speak-PRES.PARTCP it-about
(same meaning as (1))

(3) *poika sano-i, että isä käv-i koto-na*
boy say-PAST that father visit-PAST home-in
'The boy said that his father visited home.'

(4) *poika sano-i isä-n käy-neen koto-na*
boy say-PAST father-SG.GEN visit-PAST.PARTCP home-in
(Same meaning as (3))

The participle constructions are also often employed in clauses which bear the sense of 'reported speech' or 'non-commitment':

(5) *hän näky-y asu-van siellä*
he appear-3.PRES.INDICATIVE live-PRES.PARTCP there
'It seems that he lives there'/'he seems to live there.'

(6) *hän kuulu-u asu-neen siellä*
he is.heard-3.PRES.INDICATIVE live-PAST.PARTCP there
'They say that he has lived there'/'it is said that he lived there.'

The Estonian equivalents are:

(7) *sai kuul-da, et seal üks mees ela-b*
got hear-INF that there one.NOM man.NOM live-3.PRES.INDICATIVE
'She came to hear/she heard that a man lives there.'

(8) *sai kuul-da seal ühe mehe ela-vat*
got hear-INF there one.GEN man.GEN live-PRES.PARTCP
'He came to hear / he heard (of) a man's living there.'

The innovative construction, with no Finnish counterpart, is seen in:

(9) *sai kuul-da, (et) seal üks mees ela-vat*
got hear-INF that there one.NOM man.NOM live-MODUS.OBLIQUUS
'He came to hear/he heard that (they say) a man lives there.'

(10) *isa ütles poja-le, (et) ta sõit-vat*
father said boy-to (that) he travel-MODUS.OBL
homme linna
tommorrow town.into
'The father told the boy to travel to town tomorrow.'

Later, the *Modus Obliquus* forms (henceforth labelled 'indirect', INDIR) were extended, occurring also in main clauses:

(11) *ta tege-vat töö-d*
he.NOM do-PRES.INDIR work-PARTV
'They say he is working.'

Forms with the former past participle are more common:

(12) *ta tei-nud töö-d*
he.NOM do-PAST.INDIR work-PARTV
'They say he worked'/'he worked, so they say.'

(13) *naabri* *perenaine* *ole-vat* *linna*
neighbor.GEN lady.NOM is-PRES.INDIRECT town.into
sõit-nud
travel-PAST-PARTCP
'They say the neighbor lady (lady of the house) has travelled to town.'

Thus, Estonian has created an 'indirect' modality marker employed with finite verbs from a former participle construction. The 'indirect' (*Modus Obliquus*) forms came to be employed also in main clauses.[2]

3. EXPLANATIONS

I now turn to proposed explanations of the Estonian changes. While in recent years historical syntax has received much attention, there remains considerable controversy with respect to the potential for explanation of syntactic change, as seen in quotes from a recent book on historical syntax:

> Nowadays it is often questioned whether explanation of linguistic change, and particularly syntactic change, is possible at all. (Gerritsen, 1984:114)

> The longer I deal with linguistics the more certain I am that language is a simple phenomenon and that all true explanations of language phenomena are equally simple. (Mańczak, 1984:242)

The truth must lie somewhere between these two extremes. Several 'traditional' explanations for the origin of the Estonian *Modus Obliquus* have been offered, and it is instructive to consider these — they suggest that explanation in this case is neither simple nor impossible. One is Grünthal's (1941), based on a presumed ellipsis of the main verb (SAV or MSV), where it is assumed that (14b), for example, derives from (14a):

(14a) *naaber* *ütle-b* *ost-vat* *kolm hobust*
neighbor.NOM says buy-PRES.PARTCP three horses
'The neighbor says he is buying three horses.'

(14b) *naaber* *ost-vat* *kolm hobust*
neighbor.NOM buy-INDIR three horses
'They say the neighbor is buying three horses.'

Grünthal believed that the main verb, 'say' in this case (as in (14a)), was understood, self-evident, and could therefore be left out (as in (14b)). The documented stages of the change, however, do not support this interpretation, and in any case, the semantic route from, for example, "the neighbor says he ..." to "they say/reportedly the neighbor ..." is not at all self-evident.

Kettunen's (1924) explanation was that the *Modus Obliquus* had developed from the participle in subordinate clauses and then gradually the main verb was lost. While Kettunen's proposal might seem sensible, the most widely accepted proposed explanation appears to be Ikola's (1953) of 'contamination', a mixture or confusion of the two constructions, (a) and (b) above, to produce (c), the 'contamination' (blending) of the *et* complement and the participial constructions. In this view, clauses with the *et* complement conjunction require a finite verb; thus, the participle, when it occurred with *et* in the 'blended' construction (as in (c) above), was taken to be a finite verb form. Such a view, however, hardly accounts for the grammatical function or semantics acquired by this former participle which became a finite verb form, the new *Modus Obliquus* ('indirect'). More to the point, since this new construction (*et* ... Verb-*vat* [Present] or *et* ... Verb-*nud* [Past]) occurred only after speech-act and mental-state verbs, a sense of 'reported speech' or 'noncommitment' was attributed to the participle, even before the change, as is seen even in the case of the Finnish examples with SAVs and MSVs (cf. (4)–(6); Hakulinen and Leino, 1987).[3]

As an alternative to Ikola's widely-accepted 'contamination' explanation, it is hypothesized that because the participles after SAVs and MSVs already had an 'indirect' sense, these participles grammaticalized the 'reported speech' function. This, in turn, permitted the reinterpreted former participles, now 'indirect' modality, to be used in contexts otherwise requiring a finite verb form, including in contexts as main verbs. This proposal may be similar to Kettunen's explanation, though with more emphasis on the discourse function. The seeds of this hypothesis are seen in Hakulinen and Leino's (1987) discourse account of developments in Finnish participial constructions.

Naturally, here, as in the case of most other changes in Balto-Finnic languages, we are not to be spared proposed external explanations. On the one hand, some have imagined Baltic (Latvian and Lithuanian) influence. Latvian and Lithuanian both have a similar phenomenon, the so-called 'relative mood', which bears the suffix *-ot* and indicates that the speaker doubts the truth of the statement or does not assume responsibility for its truth. However, Baltic's *Modus Obliquus* appears, rather, to be best explained as the result of Estonian and Livonian influence. (See Thomason and Kaufman, 1988:243–4.) On the other hand, others see influence from the German 'conjunctive' (subjunctive), used in reported-speech contexts (cf. discussion in

Ikola, 1953:43; Hakulinen and Leino, 1987; Laanest, 1982:238–40). It is true that German has had considerable influence on Estonian and Livonian. The ultimate explanation, then, may need to be broad enough to include multiple causation, 'grammaticalization' of an internally motivated, already available, 'reported speech' sense, spurred on by the existence of such a grammatical category (conjunctive) in German, a language which has had much influence on Estonian.

The questions are, then: 1. Did the form/structure appear first (through 'contamination') and then later acquire its particular meaning (as in Ikola's position)? 2. Did the function already exist in the discourse context, permitting — perhaps urging — an independent form for signaling this function to develop (similar to Hakulinen and Leino's position 1987; cf. Kettunen's opinion)? 3. Is the *Modus Obliquus* due to language contact? Or, 4. Is its origin perhaps due to a combination of these factors, say all of 1–3? It cannot be solely due to German (or Baltic) influence, since the semantic seeds are present in the corresponding Finnish constructions, which were not so influenced by these languages, and it clearly developed from native morphological material, not borrowed forms. It cannot be due to the form alone, since the participial complement is used also with other verbs (non-SAVs and non-MSVs), where it has maintained its original form and meaning. Thus, of the proposals available, the most promising is the discourse explanation (2), or multiple causation (4), which also encompasses (2).

4. QUESTION PARTICLES

The second example deals with a series of changes in question markers, especially in yes-no questions in Estonian. Old Estonian lost the Proto-Balto-Finnic interrogative suffix *-*ko* (cf. Finnish: *tule-t-ko huomenna?* [come-you-Q tomorrow?] 'Are you coming tomorrow?'). This was replaced first with the question particle *es*, illustrated in Older Estonian (from 1696 New Testament, Alvre, 1976:345):

(15) *Nüüd es tee uSSute*
now Q you.PL believe.you.PL
'Now do you believe?'

(16) *MiSt es minna Seddä peä tundma*
it.from Q I.NOM it should know.INF
'How should I know that?'

In earlier times, this particle was a clitic/suffix; it developed in the following way. First, the modern Estonian particles (independent words), such as *es* 'question particle' and *ep* 'emphasis', were once bound forms, which became 'decliticized' — or 'lexicalized' in Alvre's (1976:345) terms — at roughly the same time, due in part to phonological developments. Final vowels were lost (apocopated). However, when the clitics *-*pa* 'emphatic' and *-*(ko)-s* '(question)-informal speech, [note: -*s* is a pan-Balto-Finnic 'clitic' used to signal informal speech, casualness] were attached, the final root vowel was no longer in word-final position and so was protected from apocope, e.g.: *keltä* 'from whom?'>*kelt*, but *keltä-s*>*keltes*; *päällä* 'on (top of)'>*pääll*, but *päällä-pä*>*päällä-p*. Apocope applied, as expected, to the clitic -*pä*, giving -*p*; vowel harmony was lost; and non-initial *ä* changed to *e*, ultimately yielding *peallep*. This vowel-loss rule left many apocopated stems, with less common alternant forms ending in a -V when the clitics were attached. Given the frequency and salience of the apocopated stems, these forms with attached clitics were ripe for reinterpretation. The morpheme boundary was reinterpreted; the V was considered to be part of the clitic: *kelte-s*>*kelt-es*; *peale-p*>*peal-ep*. With vowel harmony lost, there was no longer evidence that -*es* and -*ep* were phonologically dependent upon other words, rather than independent (though unstressed) particles. They were reinterpreted, lexicalized as specific lexemes, as independent words. (Cf. Ariste, 1973; Alvre, 1976.)

The 'decliticization' which created the new 'affirmative adverb' *ep* as an independent word, like the new question word *es*, also goes against the expected unidirectional change from independent word to clitic/affix (cf. Ariste, 1973; Alvre, 1976 for details), discussed below. Therefore, it is worth citing Ariste's (1973:37) abstract with regard to the creation of this independent word:

> Estonian has an affirmative adverb *ep* 'yes, indeed, just so, then', which is unknown in the other Balto-Finnic languages. This adverb ... has developed from the unproductive affirmative suffix -*p*, -*ap*, -*pä*, Finnish -*pa*, -*pä*. Such words as *sestap, sestep* 'therefore indeed', *miksep* 'why then', *siisap, siisep* 'right/just (so)', *seep* or *see'p* (*see on*) 'that is it indeed', the modern bearers of the Estonian language have unlinked [zergliedert] metanalytically, that is, falsely: *sest ep*, *miks ep*, *siis ep*, *see ep*. After this suffix was lexicalized, the word *ep* could change its syntactic position and precede the affirmed words: *see ep* → *ep see*. (My translation, LC.)

The original value of the clitic -*s* was to signal 'informal' speech, and was with great frequency attached to the Balto-Finnic question suffix. The vowel was optionally lost in certain Balto-Finnic languages, as in the informal question suffix, *-ks*, in colloquial Finnish, which itself became optional in Estonian, leaving the alternation of *-ko-s*, *-ks* and *-s* as signals of questions (particularly for informal questions). Alvre (1981:30) explains the remaining residue of *-ks* in Estonian as follows:

> The remnants of the Estonian *ks*-type are not especially numerous. The spread of the question word *kas* has had a disintegrating effect on this category. The suffix *-*kos*, which extends back to Proto-Balto-Finnic, has shortened to *ks* in the separate development of Estonian. The same path of evolution is presently current in the Finnish language, where in the colloquial language *vieläks* 'still?', *onks* 'is [it]?', *oliks* 'was [it]?', etc. compete with the standard language shapes *vieläkö(s)*, *onko(s)*, *oliko(s)*, etc. (My translation, LC.)

Thus, this question particle (*es*) in Estonian ultimately derives from a suffix signaling informal speech (*-s*), which became independent and came to be used in conformity to Wackernagel's principle of clitics in sentence second position. (See Alvre, 1976, 1981; Nevis, 1984, 1985a, 1985b:111–3, 1988, In press.)

Later, the Estonian *es* 'question particle' (now archaic and dialectal) was again replaced, this time by *kas*, illustrated in:

(17) *kas ta tuli?*
Q he came
'Did he come?'

(18) *kas ta ei tulnud?*
Q he NEG came
'Didn't he come?'

It has been documented through the careful investigation of Estonian historical documents that this particle developed from what was originally a postposition *ka(:)s* 'with' (e.g. *mehe ka(:)s* [man.GEN with] 'with the man'), which later gave rise to adverbs meaning 'also, and', e.g.: Are you going with > are you going also > and/also are you going > Q are you going? It is from this sense that this question particle eventually arose, e.g. from sentences such as, 'and [kas], are you going', the *kas* acquired a sense and function of introducing questions (cf. Alvre, 1976, 1983; Nevis, 1988, In press for details).

Initially, questions introduced with *kas* could appear only in the affirmative; there were no examples with negation. Later, this restriction disappeared and *kas* came to be employed regularly also with negative verbs, as for example in (18). (For details, see Alvre, 1983; Nevis, 1984, 1985a, In press.)

5. IMPLICATIONS

Whatever the ultimate explanation for these grammatical changes, they are clear and well-documented, with implications for a number of general claims about grammatical change. It is to these that I now turn. While some of these are of much less interest than others, they illustrate the approach being advocated here, to consider what these concrete examples have to say about various claims concerning grammatical change.

1. Syntactic change affects main clauses before subordinate clauses; the converse does not occur. This claim, or close paraphrases thereof, has been made by several scholars, starting with Biener, 1922a, 1922b (compare Givón, 1971, 1984; Lightfoot, 1981:228, etc.).[4] The general idea involved is the belief that change starts in main clauses and may or may not ultimately come to affect subordinate clauses, but that it never (or usually does not, in a weaker version) begin in subordinate clauses, later reaching main clauses. In its strong version, this claim is clearly falsified by the Estonian *Modus Obliquus* example, where the change from participle to 'indirect' finite verb clearly began first in lower verbs and later appears in main clauses.

2. Related to the first claim, but not stated so generally, is: "The more dependent the SUB-clause is semantically/pragmatically on the MAIN-clause, the less likely are independently-expressed TAM [tense-aspect-modality] markers to appear in the SUB-clause. The uncoded TAM categories of the SUB-clause may then be inferred, in some systematic fashion, from semantic or pragmatic information given in the main clause or in the discourse context" (Givón, 1984:315). Again, the Estonian *Modus Obliquus* ('indirect') goes against this claim, in that a TAM category developed — became expressed independently — in subordinate clauses, in spite of (or perhaps because it was aided by) its predictability in this context.

Nevertheless, there appears to be value to both these claims. That is, in general, subordinate clauses do contain fewer morpho-syntactic contrasts than main clauses, suggesting that on the whole fewer changes would begin in subordinate clauses, since main clauses would normally also already have most of the essential morpho-syntactic trappings of the subordinates, plus additional things not found in lower clauses. With respect to the second claim, the foreground-background distinction (while somewhat imprecise) plays an important role. Subordinate clauses and irrealis TAM categories tend to correlate in discourse with 'backgrounded' material (cf. Givón, 1984:288). This being the case, it is not so surprising that the Estonian 'indirect' (an irrealis form) should have developed in subordinate clauses.

3. Changes in structure may affect the syntax of grammatical relations before the morphology that encodes them, with the result that morphology may reflect a previous syntactic situation (cf. Anderson, 1980; Comrie, 1980; Givón, 1971, 1984; Heine et al., This volume, etc.), or in Givón's (1984:34) words, "diachronic change in syntax often removes a particular structure from its original functional domain — while at least initially leaving the structure itself relatively intact." Heine et al. (This volume) express it as, "Since conceptual shift precedes morphosyntactic and phonological shift, the result is asymmetry between meaning and form ... languages ... show examples of morphemes or constructions which have acquired a new meaning or function although they still retain the old morphosyntax." This claim appears to hold for our Estonian *Modus Obliquus* example. While the morphological form, the participle (*-vat* or *-nud*), remains unchanged, its grammatical status is completely reinterpreted in these constructions. However, the development of the question particle *es* from a bound 'clitic' *-s* would seem to go against the thrust of this claim; surely the 'decliticization' — change in morphological status — took place before the form was reinterpreted as a question marker to be employed in second position.[5]

4. The extension of the grammatical function of a morphological marker proceeds by the removal of conditions on the rules that assign the marker (Harris, 1985:382–4; cf. also Plank, 1980). This claim would appear to be related to the last one; the Estonian changes appear to conform. The extension of the *-vat* and *-nud* participles to *Modus Obliquus* status is reflected in removal of the constraint first that they should not appear after the *et* complement conjunction, then later, that they should not appear in main clauses. Similarly, the earlier constraint against *kas* questions in negative clauses was later removed.

5. The earlier restriction against *kas* in negative sentences conforms to Givón's (1975:94) and Disterheft's (1980:114) claims that syntactic change may be actualized in affirmative clauses before negative ones; the converse does not occur.

6. A weaker sort of claim is that grammatical morphemes usually (always?) eventually arise out of lexical words through semantic bleaching and phonological reduction (cf. Bybee and Pagliuca, 1987; Givón, 1984:48; Langacker, 1977; etc.) While in general there can be no quarrel with this claim, it is nevertheless the case that the examples considered here do not come from lexical items, but rather from the (re)grammaticalization of participles, bound clitics, and postpositionals. Perhaps more room should be allowed

for the origin of new grammatical morphemes from other, not-so-lexical resources, as well.

7. There is a very widely accepted claim with something like the following form: In language change, independent words tend to lose their boundaries, cliticize, and/or become bound morphemes; the reverse does not happen (or is very rare indeed) — bound morphemes do not (do only rarely) split and become independent elements (cf. Comrie, 1980; Givón, 1971, 1984; Langacker, 1977, etc.). Again, few would want to quibble with this claim, at least not in its weaker form. Nevertheless, in the development of the question particle *es*, Estonian has done exactly what is not supposed to be done (or done only very infrequently), reanalyzing a suffix and separating it off as an independent form. Since this is an important point, perhaps surprising to some supporters of the claim, it is worth pointing out that other examples of 'decliticization' (or 'upgrading' in Nevis' terminology), while not frequent, are reasonably well-known (cf. Janda, 1981; Nevis, 1984, 1985a, 1985b, 1988, In press).

8. Langacker (1977:66) claims that there is a general tendency in language, revealed in grammatical change, to bring morpheme boundaries into line with syllable boundaries. While at some level there may be something to this claim, Balto-Finnic languages abound in morphological changes which establish morpheme boundaries at odds with syllable boundaries. The origin of the Estonian question particle *es* is a case in point. From forms such as *pää-llä-s* 'on top of' [syllables *pääl.läs*], the development of an independent *es* is hardly to be expected from Estonian syllable structure, though morpheme structure may well hold clues in this case.

9. A claim that one can infer from some writings goes something like this: When a language changes from postposed to preposed grammatical elements, the preposed elements are usually drawn from pre-exisitng elements which had different functions; when, on the other hand, a language changes from preposed to postposed, it often uses the same elements in the same functions (compare M. Harris 1978, A. Harris 1985). Should this claim have any measure of validity, the development of the Estonian sentence-initial question particle *kas* from the postposition **kans[s]aX* 'with' might prove to be an example.

6. CONCLUSIONS

I hope that the phenomena considered in this paper, together with their implications for claims about grammatical change, has illustrated the value of the bottom-up approach.

ACKNOWLEDGEMENTS

This material is based upon work supported by the National Science Foundation under Grant No. BNS8712240; any opinions, findings, and conclusions or recommendations expressed in this publication are those of the author and do not necessarily reflect the views of the National Science Foundation.

NOTES

1. While there are a variety of definitions for grammaticalization about, I intend my use of the term to include not only change from lexical status to more grammatical, but also the creation of new grammatical elements from already existing ones (cf. Kuryłowicz, 1965:52).
2. Auli Hakulinen (personal communication) has expressed reservations concerning the discussion of 'main' and 'subordinate' clauses in treatments of Balto-Finnic non-finite participial forms, since on the surface the participle appears as a constituent of the main (and only) clause, and not obviously as a subordinate clause. While this is important to keep in mind, apparently the theories considered here (both formal and functional) do consider non-finite participials to be non-main clauses (cf. particularly their treatments of preposed relative clauses without finite verb forms), at least with respect to their claims about the nature and directions of grammatical change, which is my main concern with these examples in this paper.
3. Some of these examples, though clearly not all, illustrate the kind of "complex clauses" which are "obligatorily *irrealis* in their modality" (Givón, 1984:286), discussed later in this paper.
4. In this context Lightfoot (1981:227), discussing Givón's ideas and relating them to Emonds' notion of structure-preserving root transformations, concludes essentially the same thing:

   It will follow ... that non-structure-preserving innovations will enter the language first as root transformations, affecting just root sentences, and only later percolating through the grammar to affect the phrase structure rules and thus the structures in embedded clauses.
5. Balto-Finnic offers a more telling exception; clearly changes in the form can precede and trigger changes in the syntax, as can be seen in the well-known and related example of Finnish participial embedded clauses (cf. Anttila, 1972; Breckenridge and Hakulinen, 1976; Hakulinen and Leino, 1987; Ikola, 1959; Svensson, 1983; Timberlake, 1977). Briefly, historically Finnish had constructions equivalent to the following examples, which are presented in their modern form for ease of understanding except for the crucial information about case endings, which later changed:

   (1) *näin poja-m juokse-va-m*
   saw.I boy-SG.ACC run-PRES.PARTCP-SG.ACC
   'I saw that the boy runs/I saw the boy running.'

   (2) *näin poja-t juokse-va-t*
   saw.I boy-PL.ACC run-PRES.PARTCP-PL.ACC
   'I saw that the boys run/I saw the boys running.'

However, with the sound change of *-*m*>-*n*, the 'singular accusative' and the 'singular genitive' became homophonous, both -*n*. The construction was reinterpreted from a main verb with its direct object and a participial attribute, both in the accusative case, to a verb with a participial complement, with the noun as a genitive subject of the participial complement, i.e.:

(3) *näin poja-n juokse-van*
saw.I boy-SG.GEN run-PRES.PARTCP
(Same meaning as (1))

This grammatical change is seen clearly with plurals, when one contrasts (2) with (4):

(4) *näin poik-i-en juokse-van*
saw.I boy-PL-GEN run-PRES.PARTCP
(Same meaning as (2))

Thus, the morphological change both preceded and triggered the syntactic change in this case, showing that the claim cannot be framed in the strongest possible form.

REFERENCES

Alvre, Paul. 1976. "Vana kirjakeele küsisõnu" [Old standard Estonian question words]. *Keel ja Kirjandus* 19:343–50.

Alvre, Paul. 1981. "*Veelaks*-tüüp kirjakeeles ja murdeis" [The *Veelaks* 'still?' type in the standard language and in the dialects]. *Keel ja Kirjandus* 24:24–30.

Alvre, Paul. 1983. "Zur Herkunft der Wörter *kas* und *teps* in der estnischen Sprache." *Soviet Finno-Ugric Studies* 19(2):81–89.

Anderson, Stephen R. 1980. "On the development of morphology from syntax." In *Historical Morphology*, Jacek Fisiak (ed.), 51–70. Mouton: The Hague.

Anttila, Raimo. 1972. *An Introduction to Historical and Comparative Linguistics*. New York: Macmillan.

Ariste, Paul. 1973. "*Eesti rõhumäärsõna ep*" [The affirmative adverb *ep* in Estonian]. *Journal de la Société Finno-ougrienne* 72:33–7. Helsinki: Suomalais-Ugrilainen Seura.

Biener, Clemens. 1922a. "Zur Methode der Untersuchungen über deutsche Wortstellung." *Zeitschrift für deutsches Altertum und deutsche Literatur* 59:127–44.

Biener, Clemens. 1922b. "Wie ist die neuhochdeutsche Regel über die Stellung des Verbums entstanden?" *Zeitschrift für deutsches Altertum und deutsche Literatur* 59:165–79.

Breckenridge, Janet and Auli Hakulinen. 1976. "Cycle and after." In *Papers from the Parasession on Diachronic Syntax*, Sanford B. Steever, Carol A. Walker, and Salikoko S. Mufwene (eds), 50–68. Chicago: Chicago Linguistic Society.

Bybee, Joan L. and William Pagliuca. 1987. "The evolution of future meaning." In *Papers from the 7th International Conference on Historical Linguistics*, Anna G. Ramat, Onofriu Carruba and Giuliano Bernini (eds), 109–22. Amsterdam: John Benjamins.

Comrie, Bernard. 1980. "Morphology and word order reconstruction: Problems and Prospects." *Historical Morphology*, Jacek Fisiak (ed.), 83–96. The Hague: Mouton.

Comrie, Bernard. 1981. *The Languages of the Soviet Union*. Cambridge: Cambridge University Press.

Disterheft, Dorothy. 1980. *The Syntactic Development of the Infinitive in Indo-European*. Columbus, Ohio: Slavica.

Gerritsen, Marinel. 1984. "Divergent word order developments in Germanic languages: A description and a tentative explanation." *Historical syntax*, Jacek Fisiak (ed.), 107–36. Berlin: Mouton.

Givón, Talmy. 1971. "Historical syntax and synchronic morphology: An archaeologist's field trip." *Chicago Linguistic Society* 7:394–415.

Givón, Talmy. 1984. *Syntax: A Functional-typological Introduction, Vol. I*. Amsterdam: John Benjamins.

Greenberg, Joseph H. 1963. "Some universals of grammar with particular reference to the order of meaningful elements." In *Universals of Language*, Joseph H. Greenberg (ed.), 73–113. Cambridge, Mass: MIT Press.

Grünthal, W. 1941. *Itämerensuomalaisten kielten yksikön nominatiivi objektin edustajana aktiivin yhteydessä*. [The nominative singular of Balto-Finnic languages as representative of the object in active contexts.] Helsinki.

Hakulinen, Auli and Pentti Leino. 1987. "Finnish participial construction from a discourse point of view." *Ural-Altaische Jahrbücher* 59:35–43.

Hale, Kenneth. 1973. "Deep-surface canonical disparities in relation to analysis & change: An Australian example." In *Current Trends in Linguistics*, Thomas Sebeok (ed.), 11:401–458. The Hague: Mouton.

Harris, Alice C. 1985. *Diachronic Syntax: The Kartvelian Case*. New York: Academic Press [Syntax and Semantics 18].

Harris, Martin B. 1978. *The Evolution of French Syntax: A Comparative Approach*. London: Longman.

Heine, Bernd, Ulrike Claudi and Friederike Hünnemeyer. This volume. "From cognition to grammar: Evidence from African languages."

Ikola, Osmo. 1953. "Viron ja Liivin modus obliquuksen historiaa." [On the history of the oblique mode of Estonian and Livonian.] *Suomi* 106(4). Helsinki: Suomalaisen Kirjallisuuden Seura.

Ikola, Osmo. 1959. "Eräistä suomen syntaktisista siirtymistä." [On certain Finnish syntactic changes.] *Suomen Kielen Seuran Vuosikirja* 1:39–60. Helsinki.

Janda, Richard. 1981. "A case of liberation from morphology to syntax: The fate of the English genitive-marker *-(e)s*." *Syntactic change. Natural Language Studies* 25:59–114.

Kettunen, Lauri. 1924. *Lauseliikmed eesti keeles*. [Constitutent Structure in Estonian.] Tartu.

Kuryłowicz, Jerzy. 1965. "The evolution of grammatical categories." *Esquisses Linguistiques II*, J. Kuryłowicz, 38–54. Munich: Fink.

Laanest, Arvo. 1982. *Einführung in die ostseefinnischen Sprachen*. Hamburg: Buske Verlag.

Langacker, Ronald W. 1977. "Syntactic reanalysis." In *Mechanisms of Syntactic Change*, Charles N. Li (ed.), 59–139. Austin: University of Texas Press.

Lightfoot, David. 1981. "Explaining syntactic change." In *Explanation in Linguistics*, N. Hornstein and D. Lightfoot (eds). London: Longman.

Mańczak, Witold. 1984. "*If I was* instead of *if I were*." In *Historical Syntax*, Jacek Fisiak (ed.), 237–46. Berlin: Mouton.

Nevis, Joel A. 1984. "A non-endoclitic in Estonian." *Lingua* 64:209–24.

Nevis, Joel A. 1985a. "Language-external evidence for clitics as words: Lappish particle clitics." *Chicago Linguistic Society* 21:289–305.
Nevis, Joel A. 1985b. Finnish Particle Clitics and General Clitic Theory. Ann Arbor: University Microfilms International. Ohio State University Ph.D. dissertation.
Nevis, Joel A. 1988. "On the development of the clitic postposition category in Estonian. *Finnish-Ugrische Forschungen* 68:171–97.
Nevis, Joel A. In press. "Decliticization in Old Estonian." *Ohio State University Working Papers in Linguistics.*
Plank, Frans. 1980. "Encoding grammatical relations: Acceptable and unacceptable non-distinctness." In *Historical Morphology*, Jacek Fisiak (ed.), 289–326. The Hague: Mouton.
Svensson, Pirkko Forsman. 1983. *Satsmotsvarigheter i Finsk prosa under 1600-talet: Participialkonstruktionen och därmed synonyma icke-finita uttryck i jämförelse med språkbruket före och efter 1600-talet.* Helsinki: Suomalaisen Kirjallisuuden Seura.
Thomason, Sarah G. and Terrence Kaufman. 1988. *Language Contact, Creolization, and Genetic Linguistics.* Berkeley: University of California Press.
Timberlake, Alan. 1977. "Reanalysis and actualization in syntactic change." In *Mechanisms of Syntactic Change*, Charles N. Li (ed.), 141–77. Austin: University of Texas press.

The Last Stages of Grammatical Elements: Contractive and Expansive Desemanticization

Joseph H. Greenberg
Stanford University

The present study resumes and expands some of the topics discussed in Greenberg (1978) on the stages of the definite article and Greenberg (1981) which is devoted to two additional instances of Stage III articles, Nilo-Saharan *k*- and Penutian -*s*.[1]

I will be concerned with the final stages of these and certain other grammaticalized elements. Here, as in the earlier stages one finds concomitant phonological, semantic and distributional changes. Phonologically there is a tendency to reduction. Semantically, investigators have often mentioned desemanticization or loss of meaning. This is a complex phenomenon which cannot be separated from what are here called distributional characteristics, that is, the range of environments in which the item occurs. One tendency is for contraction to the point at which it is found in fossilized form in only a few lexical forms. We can then say that it is lexicalized in the sense that synchronically it is a part of the host morpheme. We may also say that it is desemanticized in the sense that it can no longer be assigned a meaning. Another alternative is for it to expand its distribution, initially by semantically motivated extensions, but in an increasingly arbitrary way so that its meaning becomes highly disjunctive and even a prototypical definition cannot be readily formulated. In a quite different way, then, than with contractive lexicalization, increasing extension leads to zero intension, so that the item has become desemanticized. There is, however, with expansive lexicalization a further possibility, namely its reinterpretation in a new function. In all cases known to me the new meaning is grammatical. We may call this process regrammaticalization.

More concretely I propose to study, even if only in a preliminary fashion, some phenomena whose consideration derives quite naturally from earlier work on the development of the definite article. This usually originates from a demonstrative, and the later stages of such an article as found in a number of languages I have called the Stage II and Stage III article.

One topic I will discuss concerns further developments of the anaphoric pronoun. As is well known the anaphoric pronoun in almost all instances derives from a demonstrative just as does the article. In the instance of the Romance languages the anaphoric pronoun and the article both derive from the same distance demonstrative *ille*.[2] I shall outline some instances in which the anaphoric pronoun goes through stages reasonably comparable to that of the definite article although this is of less frequent occurrence than in the case of the article. Moreover, in its final stages it may undergo significant reinterpretation, which I believe goes beyond what is usually called reanalysis in discussions of grammaticalization.

Along with this we find a typical sort of variation which for want of a better term I shall call random variability and which is once more quite comparable to that of the Stage III article, for example, Nilo-Saharan *k*-. The development of third stage articles from the beginnings of a definite article in a demonstrative takes a long period of time. For example, in the historically attested case of Aramaic we can trace the development of a suffixed *-ā* through the later stages of the article over a period of approximately 3,000 years. Yet its origin in a demonstrative *-ā*<*-hā*, accepted by Semitists on comparative grounds, precedes our earliest written records of the language. During such a long period most languages will break up into separate dialects and languages several times. The phenomenon here called random distribution is encountered when such languages or dialects are compared.

A well attested instance is Nilo-Saharan *k*- which is found almost exclusively in nouns.[3] What I here call random variability takes the following forms. If we call the form with prefixed *k* the articulated form and the one without it the unarticulated, then we may summarize the sort of phenomena encountered as follows:

1. The same dialect or language sometimes shows the articulated and non-articulated form of the same stem in free variation.[4]
2. Even among closely related languages of the same subgroup we frequently find the articulated form in one and the non-articulated in the other.
3. More broadly within the same linguistic stock there is hardly a form which does not show some variation among the languages in this regard so that comparativists reconstruct both forms as original

and as variants in the ancestral language. The contribution of diachronic typology is to show how these variants arise in the process of grammaticalization particularly in its later stages.

4. Finally one may note that certain languages seem in general to prefer either the articulated or non-articulated form. Thus in the Nilotic languages, a subbranch of Nilo-Saharan, the Western Nilotic languages such as Dinka and Shilluk show initial *k-* much less frequently than Eastern Nilotic languages. For example in the word for 'cow' Shilluk (West Nilotic) has singular *dheaŋ* whereas Masai (East Nilotic) has *(en)-ki-teŋ* in which *en-* is a new second stage article.

It will be shown that this sort of random variability is found in later stages of other grammatical forms. Moreover, basically similar alternations are found in variants of phonological origin, e.g. in the breakdown of vowel harmonic systems. Whereas for grammatical formatives the variation will be that between presence and absence of the element, in phonological cases it will rather be the choice between two phonological alternants which are no longer phonologically conditioned in any clear way. In at least one well known instance, so called moveable *s-* of Indo-European, which appears initially in a random fashion on roots beginning with an unvoiced stop, liquid or nasal, opinions are divided as to whether the origin is phonological, as the outcome of word-sandhi, or whether it is morphological. As with grammatical items, there is the possibility of interpretation of phonological items as having a grammatical significance, e.g. umlauting in German. This might be called grammaticalization from below. It is, compared to the grammaticalization of lexical items, relatively infrequent and often a subsidiary method which accompanies others of the more common type. Nevertheless, its properties as compared to that of grammaticalization of the more usual type are I believe well worth exploring. This is not attempted here.

In general I think it will be fruitful to consider within the same basic frame of grammaticalization, processes of development of grammatical elements from all sources. These will include the origin of grammatical elements from morphemes of more concrete meaning by semantic change, the grammaticalization of variants of phonological origin and the third major source, reanalysis with morpheme boundary shift. An example of the latter is the German neuter plural in *-er* in which the $r<{}^*z$, a variant of *s* arising by the operation of Verner's law, was formerly the formative of *s*-stems which was reinterpreted as a plural marker after the loss of final vowels had produced an unmarked plural.

Finally a somewhat speculative attempt will be made to help explain the phenomenon of random variation whether in phonology or grammar which I believe are similar in their sociolinguistic complications regarding language variation.

As a point of departure, I will briefly recapitulate the particular points in Greenberg (1978) which have a bearing on the present argument. A definite article which almost always derives from a distance or unmarked demonstrative may go through two further stages which I have called the Stage II and Stage III article. A Stage II article arises from the usual definite article by adding, roughly speaking, the uses of the indefinite article thus combining the uses of both.[5] Along with this there is incorporation of the article in the noun giving rise to a prefixed or suffixed article. Because of the high frequency of combined definite and indefinite uses it becomes the "normal" form of the noun and the one that is usually elicited when an investigator asks for the lexical equivalent of a noun in his or her own language. However at this stage, unarticulated forms still survive in functional, or sometimes conventionalized alternations resulting from the analogical spread of originally purely functional distinctions.

On the one hand, the non-articulated form typically survives in forms which are automatically definite and therefore did not require articles in the first stage. Among these are common nouns, which when used as proper names of either persons or place will frequently show the unarticulated form, vocatives, and nouns with demonstrative modifiers. On the other hand, we find generic uses such as the incorporated noun object, nominal predication, dependent genitives in compounds and adverbial, particularly locative, uses e.g. 'at home', 'on foot'.

Stage III is defined by the absence of functional contrasts such as those still found in Stage II. At this point the articulated form will spread to virtually all nouns, or less commonly, the articulated variant will be ousted everywhere by the non-articulated variant. Thus, in regard to the Bantu pre-prefixes, which are to be interpreted as Stage II articles, and which are common in East Africa, there are instances in which in genetically closely related languages one has retained the pre-prefix and the other has lost it. Thus Bisa, a Bantu language of Zambia, has retained it, while Ila, a member of the same Bantu subgroup and also spoken in Zambia, has lost it, e.g. Bisa *u-mwezi*, Ila *mweze* 'moon'.

It should be emphasized that this whole sequence of events is a gradual process, and that each stage presents a cluster of characteristics which are to be viewed as prototypes.

There are two basic classes of instances. If the language to begin with had noun classes and the demonstratives, which become articles, are also classifying elements that belong to the same system, then the process becomes one of renewal of a class system the inherited markers of which had become phonetically eroded.[6]

Where there was no system of nominal classifications and the new markers do not introduce one, we simply find the articulated as the normal form of a considerable number or of virtually all nouns. There is in this case the possiblity of reeinterpretation of the articulated form and the attribution to it of new functions.

The most common and grammatically significant new function is that since, in fact it exists on virtually all nouns, it becomes a sign of nominality and becomes a productive morpheme which derives nouns from verbs and from adjectives in languages in which adjectives when predicated are to be considered a special subclass of stative verbs.

A far less frequent and occasional function is that of distinguishing homonyms through the use of the articulated versus the non-articulated forms. Another sporadic use is that of distinguishing singularity from plurality or, more likely, singulative from collective. In the case of Nilo-Saharan, this occurs in individual instances in some languages, e.g. Kanuri *k-am* 'person', *am* 'people'. There are some languages, however, in the Eastern subgroup of Nilotic in which this is a fairly common formation, e.g. Karimojong *(e)ki-leŋ* 'knife'; *(ŋi)leŋia*. I believe that a likely basis for this usage, which is also found in sporadic instances with Penutian *-s*, is that the collective is very much like the generic in that it is viewed as a unity and often requires additional grammatical mechanisms to distinguish units as against the undivided whole.[7]

We now turn to the question of possible further stages of the anaphoric pronoun which might parallel that of the article. I have by now found several instances in Amerind languages as well as in Northeastern Asia of a very similar sequence of events in the development of the anaphoric pronoun which show a fairly obvious similarity to later stages of the article.

I shall treat briefly one of these examples and only as it appears in Chibchan-Paezan where it develops from *i*, the common third person singular anaphoric, generally as a bound form, prefixed as a possessive on the noun and the subject or object on the verb.[8] We will be concerned here with developments as verb object and as possessive. As a verb object it sometimes comes to be used as indefinite specific in the following way. It will appear on transitive verbs where there is no overt object but will be absent if the object is present. Thus in a narrative we might have something like 'He came, he ate and he went away'. In a language of this sort, a pronominal object which might be glossed as 'something' is expressed by a third person marker. If, on the contrary, the narrative account proceeded as follows: 'He came, he ate beans and went away', then no pronominal object would appear on the verb 'to eat'.

In Itonama, a Chibchan language of Bolivia, this stage is clearly illustrated in Camp and Liccardi (1967) in which *i-* is described as an unspecified object. There are in this language, in addition to ordinary objects, a whole series of incorporated objects, mostly body parts. When none of these is present then *i-* is compulsory, e.g. *mas-t?it?ye* 'cut the arm' (literally arm-cut), *chas-dotye* 'grain-pound' versus *i-t?it?ye* 'to cut' (unspecified object) and *i-dotye* 'to pound' (unspecified object). For Bribri, a language of the Talamanca branch of Chibchan spoken in Costa Rica, Lehmann (1920:285) describes a similar situation. "When no object is mentioned the verb has *i-*." There are still other Chibchan languages for which this usage holds, which are not discussed here. The next development is that, since *i-* can only be used with transitive verbs, it becomes a derivational element which transitivizes intransitive verbs. The mechanism involved here is essentially similar to the reinterpretation of the Stage III article as a nominalizer. In Warrau, a Paezan language of Venezuela, the *i-* prefix functions not only as a transitivizer but also as a causative (Barral, 1957:92), e.g. *miki* 'see', *imiki* 'show'. This is, of course, a common situation with regard to transitivizers. In English 'hang' (tr.) may be paraphrased as 'cause to hang (intr.)'.

The same marker *i-* prefixed to nouns, originally as third person inalienable possessor, goes through a different though analogous course of change. After his description of Bribri *i-* as an indicator of indefinite object, Lehmann goes on to cite, for the same language, its development, generally in body part nouns, to a generalized meaning. He cites a similar development of *i-* in Rama in which, as he states it, "*i-* before the noun indicates a general form *i-ŋut* his, her face = face in general" (ibid.). Here we have a change to general indefinite rather than specific indefinite, i.e. 'anybody's face' rather than 'someone's face.'

Whereas I have not noted any instances in regard to *i-* in the verb of random variation across or within dialects or languages, this does happen in regard to the noun.[9] For example, in Chibchan there are a number of instances in which forms with the *i* prefix are reinterpreted as belonging to the stem so that *i-ba* simply means 'blood' and *i-ta* 'hand'. For definite third person possessor one rather finds *a-*, e.g. *a-ba* 'his/her blood' with a marker *a-* which is widespread in Chibchan-Paezan and always marks third person definite possessor (Greenberg, 1987:286). On comparative grounds it must be more recent than *i-*. We frequently find cognates across languages in which some languages have *i-* and others do not. For example, corresponding to Chibchan *iba* 'blood' is Murire (Guaymi subgroup) *bea*, Estrella (Talamanca group, Costa Rica) *pe* and Mura, a Paezan language of Brazil *be* all with the meaning 'blood'. For Timucuan, a Paezan outlier in Florida, Gatschet (1880:485) gives the variant forms *chini* and *ichini* for 'nose'. This is a widespread Chibchan-Paezan root which occurs elsewhere without *i-*, e.g. Gayon (Jirajara subgroup of Paezan) *kin* 'nose'.

In two different word lists of Boruca, a Chibchan language of the Talamanca subgroup in Costa Rica reported in Lehmann (1920:346–8), those of Thiel and Valentini, one finds instances in which body part forms have been recorded with *i-* in one writer and without *i-* in the other, e.g. Valentini *ikasa*, Thiel *kasa* 'tooth', but Valentini *uran*, Thiel *iuran* 'flesh'. Although such material should obviously be treated with caution, it is nevertheless striking that what is historically the third person possessive should have been elicited in a sporadic way as the equivalent of Spanish terms such as *diente*, *carne* whereas where possessive prefixes are found it is usually the first person singular which occurs.

The fossilization of a third person which has become indefinite in meaning might also be expected in kin-terms which are the other large class of inalienably possessed nouns. Many American Indian languages treat them as verbs with relational meaning. However in Timucua a whole series of kin-terms have their general form in *i-* to which may be added possessive suffixes, clearly an innovation though derived from inherited pronominals, e.g. *iti* 'father'; *iti-na* 'my father'; *isa* 'mother'; *itora* 'grandfather'; *itele* 'father's brother'; *-isale* 'mother's sister'; *yame* 'brother-in-law' (Gatschet 1880:485). For Rama, Lehmann cites *i-tuuŋ* with the meaning 'someone's father, a father in general' (1920:422).

A typologically similar development to that of Chibchan *i-* is found in Algic and Salish *m-*. Here it seems from the start to have been an indefinite pronoun. With regard to the verb, Boas in his discussion of Thompson River Salish (1898:30) describes a stage which is parallel to that already described in regard to Chibchan *i-*. In Thompson River from *xwe-* to look', for example, we have, *xwe-əm* meaning 'to look at an unspecified object'. This contrasts with *xwe-es* 'to look at it' i.e. a definite object. It reflects the ambiguous position of the specific indefinite that whereas it becomes a transitivizer in Chibchan-Paezan, in many Salishan languages *-m* rather indicates the intransitive. We can see that the contrast with the definite object in Salish easily leads to generalization of the indefinite specific object form to an intransitivizer.

As a possessive prefixed to the noun, *m-* in Algic and Salish gives rise to developments which are extremely close to that of Chibchan-Paezan *i-*. In all the Algic languages *m-* appears as a marker of impersonal possessive on nouns often in fossilized form so that it becomes part of the stem. When thus desemanticized such a form as 'somebody's hand' comes to mean 'a human hand' or 'hand' in the abstract. There is random variation across languages between forms with and without *m-*. Michelson (1938:103) states that "it is a well-known fact that in Proto-Algonquian times stems with initial **m-* have non-initial cognates lacking this *m-*." In her comparisons within Algic (Algonkian, Wiyot, Yurok) Haas (1958) freely allows forms with and without *m-* in body part terms in her comparison.

In Salishan languages *m-* appears in fossilized form on a number of body-parts. Kuipers (1967:116) notes in his grammar of Squamish "m- a prefix on body parts." In instances like Upper Chehalis *ma-qs-n* 'nose' *ma-* is clearly a prefix since *-qs-* here and elsewhere in Salish is a suffix meaning 'nose' and *-n* is found in body parts. All this is quite like Algonkian but in Salish *m-* survives in only a small number of lexical items and always in fossilized form.[10]

If we consider the foregoing examples, we can see that there are two extremes to what has simply been called desemantization in regard to meaning, and fossilization, that is, absorption into other historically distinct morphemes, from the morphosyntactic point of view. At one end we have what might be called shrinkage or contractive desemanticization and at the other end expansive desemanticization.

In instances like the *m-* in body part terms in Salishan or the *i* of kinterms in Timucua, only a few examples are left and we have as it were the "accident" that a disproportionate set of body parts or kinterms have the item in question. In both instances a non-historically oriented treatment, that of Kuipers in Squamish and Gatschet in Timucua, cannot help but notice an element which is certainly non-productive and marginal synchronically but is susceptible to historical-comparative explanation. At the other extreme are instances like *k-* on nouns in some Nilo-Saharan languages in which, if one were to attempt a definition of it synchronically one would have a highly disjunctive definition which would cover a very large number of instances, not unlike an attempt to define the meaning of gender classes in languages like Sanskrit and Latin. This latter type is ripe for regrammaticalization though of course it need not occur.

The other characteristic that all of the examples cited have in common is what has been called here random distribution within and across related languages and dialects.

An interesting case is that of Chibchan-Paezan **-kwa.* In Greenberg (1987:298–299), there is a brief discussion of which the following is a somewhat expanded and emended version. A full study could easily be of monographic proportion. It is well-known from grammaticalization studies that an element that becomes grammaticalized can also continue in ungrammaticalized form, e.g. Latin *habere* 'to have', which continues as a verb in Romance languages (French *avoir*; Italian *avere* etc.), and as future suffix in grammaticalized form (e.g. French *aimer-a*, Italian *amer-à* 'he/she will love').

In the case of Chibchan-Paezan **-kwa*, it appears that a noun which designated round objects and whose original meaning was an independent noun, can still be found in Terraba (Talamanca group) *gwa* 'egg' and Cuna *kwa-kwa* 'nut' and perhaps in other Chibchan languages. In the Cuna form *-kwa* has been suffixed as it is to a large number of nouns in that language.

We may distinguish two lines of development. One is that, in accordance with a common Chibchan-Paezan pattern, it participates in superordinate compounds, just as for example the word for 'water', *li, ri, ni* is in many Chibchan languages suffixed to words indicating liquids. The other type of development is as a numeral classifier. In the first of these functions it undergoes expansive desemanticization and in some instances regrammaticalization; in the latter instance, as a numeral classifier, after becoming the general classifier, with the loss of the classifier system, it survives in some languages in a restrictively desemanticized fashion, fossilized on certain numerals.

These two types of development are treated here successively. In some languages like Chibchan proper it is largely confined to certain objects perceived as round, and usually small. Examples are *up-kwa* 'eye'; *pihi-gwa* 'hole'; *fa-gua* 'star'. However even here it shows a tendency to spread to other nouns, e.g. *kip-kwa* 'place'. We find once more random variation cross-linguistically, e.g. corresponding to *up-kwa* 'eye' in Rama we find *up* 'eye, fruit, round thing'. In some languages it has spread very far indeed. For example, Holmer (1952:54) says regarding *-kwa* "It is the most common suffix in Cuna and at the same time typical of a whole group of languages including Chibcha." The same writer states:

> -kwa has actually such a wide variety of meanings that we consider it a general formation of concrete nouns. Originally it was (as in the related languages of the Talamanca group) restricted to names of a certain class of small objects which are found to have related or identical names in the different languages of the Indians such as stone, egg, nut, bud, flower, star... (Holmer, 1946:188)

Already in Cuna we find signs of semantic reinterpretation, one being to form singulatives from collectives, e.g. *wini* 'beads', *win-kwa* 'a single bead' and a diminutive function, e.g. *machi-kwa* 'boy'. A more productive reinterpretation is as that of agent noun, e.g. *ope-kwa* 'a bather' (Holmer, 1952:55) and abstract qualitites from adjectival roots, e.g. *sipu-kwa* 'white, whiteness'.

In certain Chibchan languages we find the reinterpretation as a verbal noun dominant, e.g. Millcayac, a Paezan language of Argentina, in which *gue* forms verbal nouns, e.g. *cheri* 'to give', *cherigwe* 'gift', *pi-na* 'to die', *pigue* 'death' (Valdivia, 1943).

As a numeral classifier it appears in some languages with round objects but often in more extended uses as a more general classifier. For example in Cuna it can also appear with persons as in *tule pakke-kwa* 'person four-classifier'. Its general significance is also detectible in the fairly widespread interrogative 'how many', Cuna *pi-kwa*, Chibcha *fi-gwa*, Binticua *bi-ga*, Boruncа *bi-k* (Chibchan subgroup of Chibchan-Paezan only).

In some languages in which the numeral classifier system no longer functions it survives only in fossilized form with certain numerals, e.g. Kagaba (Aruaco subgroup of Chibchan in Columbia) *mai-gwa* 'three'; *ku-gwa* 'seven'; *abi-gwa* 'eight'; *aita-gwa* 'nine' and *u-gua* 'ten'. With the word for 'three' cf. Margua *meia* and, with *-gwa* fossilized as *-g*, Paya *mai-g*; with 'seven' compare Margua *kuki*, and with 'eight' Margua *avi*.

Numeral classifiers, articles and indefinite objects are of course by no means the only grammatical elements which undergo desemanticization. Whether all do is a question I am not prepared to answer. Other examples of desemanticization are diminutives (e.g. in Romance) and honorifics. To illustrate the former there are numerous instances in Romance languages in which the Latin diminutive in *-l-* ~ *-cul-* (the former alternant with first and second declension nouns and the latter with the third, fourth and fifth declension) survives in one Romance language in the diminutive forms and in another not with diminutive meaning, e.g. French *soleil* < *soliculus* vs. Italian *sole*, both meaning 'sun' as against French *frère* and Italian *fratello* 'brother'.

As an example of an honorific we may take Japanese *o-* prefixed to nouns. While still having a distinct honorific meaning it has in a number of nouns become desemanticized so that *ocha* is now the ordinary word for 'tea' and *okome* for 'rice'.

The case of the Latin diminutive is more complex than set forth above and I believe these complications are typical of derivational elements. The diminutive mentioned above was already fossilized in some instances in Latin and sometimes with meanings differing from that of diminutive, e.g. *puella* 'girl' <*puer-la* 'puer' = 'boy'; *stella* 'star' (cf. Greek *astēr*) and *osculum* 'kiss' cf. *os* 'mouth'.

In the case of derivational elements the framework of desemanticization is generally more complex and would be a subject for special treatment. The process here affects not the element as a whole but rather in each individual occurrence with a stem there are found separate and idiosyncratic semantic changes. Where, as with the Semitic derived forms of the verb, forms are held together in the form of a distinct paradigm, the class may survive indefinitely as a more and more conventionalized morphological subclass. On the other hand it is in danger of simply disappearing as has happened in all forms of colloquial Arabic with the fourth, originally causative, conjugation or of merging with others via analogical processes, e.g. with the Semitic 'intensive' (Arabic class II) in Amharic where it now coincides with the original underived form of the verb while inheriting some morphological features of the original 'intensive' conjugation.

Another possibility for derivational elements is incorporation into the inflectional system. Here we have a parallel to lexicalization but the morpheme into which the derivational item is incorporated is inflectional. Thus the Latin inceptive suffix *-sc-* after desemanticization became a part of the inflectional endings of certain classes of verbs in Romance languages, e.g. Italian *fini-sco* 'I finish', but *fini-amo* 'we finish'. The details differ for the various Romance languages. For, example in French *finissons* it is incorporated whereas for Italian *finiamo* it is not. As with other derivational elements we find that this is an extended process. Thus in Latin it is already fossilized in *crescere* 'to grow', Italian *crescere*, and French *croître* in which it has been lexicalized rather than incorporated into the inflectional system, a process that begins in Vulgar Latin. In the initial portion of this paper it was stated that in the breakdown of vowel harmony systems, one finds distributions across languages and dialects similar to that of morphological elements. Vowel harmony systems break down either by merger (e.g. Aliutor, a dialect of Koryak) or simply by disregard of the rules, often through external influence (e.g. Iranicized Uzbek).

An example of the latter type is the group of East Mongolian languages.

In the western group which includes Classical Mongolian as well as Buryat, Khalka and others, there is a system of back-front vowel harmony which is stem-driven. By this is meant that the stem has constant vowels but the affixes have back and front variants which harmonize with the vowel or vowels of the stem. One such alternating pair is *a* (back harmony) versus *e* (front harmony). The results for a series of affixes with former *a*~*e* alternation is shown in the following table:

Table 1. *Inflectional affixes in four East Mongolian languages*

	Baoan	Dagur	Dunsian	Monguor
Plural	le	—	la	—
Ablative	se	se	se	dza
Locative	ra	aare	—	re
Instrum.	gale	gala	—	—
Comitat.	—	—	le	la
Causative	ge	gaa, gee	ga	ga, ge
Past Part.	sang	sen	sen	dzan

We have seen that random distribution as defined here is basically similar in morphology and phonology. How are we to envision this process from the sociolinguistic point of view? I think that we should consider that for every individual instance variants, idiosyncratically distributed across small groups, or even individuals, existed in the ancestral speech community.

Within each group that later became a distinct language or subgroup there was a particular distribution, of course, subject to later analogic changes and sometimes with an inherited preference for one form or the other. We may compare these with 'founder' groups of the population geneticists.

The ensuing results simply do not fit either the conventional family tree or any modification of it based on areal considerations. However, it only affects a very small part of the total linguistic structures involved.

The topic being considered here is, of course, a very large one and my conclusions are at best tentative. However, if it will direct the interest of linguists interested in grammaticalization to a more detailed study and analysis of the last stages of the process, it will have accomplished its purpose.

NOTES

1. I am indebted to Bernd Heine and Elizabeth Traugott for valuable criticisms and suggestions regarding the present paper.

2. However in Sardinian both the article and the anaphoric pronoun developed from Latin *ipse* 'self'.

3. For details see Greenberg (1981). The *k*- under discussion here is always prefixed, is followed by a vowel before consonant stems and is distinct from the widely attested *k* plural which often contrasts with a *t* singular. By a separate development from its original demonstrative meaning, *k*- also occurs in some of the languages prefixed to the verb to indicate third person.

4. I use the term free variation when a particular source gives both forms as variants. No doubt sociolinguistic investigation would show that the distribution of variants involve individual preferences, and generational and social class differences, but such information is not provided in the sources.

5. I have hypothesized that the starting point of the Stage II article is the indefinite specific use later expanded to the indefinite non-specific. This is because the indefinite specific allows for an ambiguous interpretation which could lead to the usage of the Stage II article which includes all the basic uses of the indefinite article in a language like English. In at least one language, Bemba, there is an article with both definite and specific indefinite uses but which is not employed for the non-specific indefinite. I have noted that in English there are occasions on which the speaker uses the definite article on the assumption that the hearer shares the identification with him but that the assumption turns out to be incorrect leading to a specifying (which) question by the hearer. This problem requires further research. It is noteworthy that Stage II articles only occur in languages which have no indefinite article and are particularly frequent in Africa, an area in which indefinite articles are uncommon.

6. It is possible for languages with noun classes, of which gender classes can be considered a subtype, to develop a second or third stage article which does not distinguish class, e.g. Aramaic *-a*, or for a language without noun classes to develop second or third stage articles which distinguish noun classes, e.g. Maasai, a Nilo-Saharan language which developed a set of Stage II articles which indicate sex gender.

7. I am indebted to Keith Denning for this suggestion.

8. This section as well as those on Algonkian and Salish *m* and Chibchan-Paezan *kwa* are expanded versions of the discussions in Greenberg (1987:56–7, 280–1, 284, 298–9).

9. However, there may be examples of the random survival of *i*- on verbs both transitive and intransitive in Timucuan. Gatschet (1880:485) describes *i*- as a verbal prefix. Among the examples are *iparu* 'swallow'; *ikiti* 'insult'; *ichuki* 'throw away, spill' but also intransitives such as *ikwaso* 'to scream'. Very striking in the present connection is the example *iriboso* 'to flood something'.

10. Comparison with the process discussed in this paper by which a third person pronoun ultimately becomes a transitivizer has an obvious bearing on the much discussed question of Tok Pisin and other Oceanic creoles that use *-im* as a transitivizer. I believe it strengthens the case for substrate influence since the process itself takes a long time and is most likely to have derived from the influence of languages which had already gone through it. I have not myself investigated the historical origin of markers of transitivity in Melanesian languages.

REFERENCES

Barral, Basilio de. 1957. *Diccionario Guarao-Español Español-Guarao*. Caracas: Sucre.

Boas, Franz. 1898. "NtlakyapamuQ. Twelfth report on the northwestern tribes of Canada." In *Annual Reports of the British Association for the Advancement of Science*, 27–36.

Camp, Elizabeth and Millicent Liccardi. 1967. *Vocabularios Bolivianos 6*. Riberalta, Beni, Bolivia: Summer Institute of Linguistics.

Gatschet, Albert A. 1880. "The Timucua language." *Proceedings of the American Philosophical Society* 18:465–502.

Greenberg, Joseph H. 1978. "How does a language acquire gender markers?" In *Universals of Human Language III*, Joseph H. Greenberg, Charles A. Ferguson, and Edith Moravcsik (eds), 47–82. Stanford: Stanford University Press.

Greenberg, Joseph H. 1981. "Nilo-Saharan movable *-k* as a stage III article (with a Penutian parallel)." *Journal of African Languages and Linguistics* 3:105–112.

Greenberg, Joseph H. 1987. *Language in the Americas*. Stanford: Stanford University Press.

Haas, Mary. 1958. "Algonkian-Ritwan: The end of a controversy." *International Journal of American Linguistics* 24:159–73.

Holmer, Nils Magnus. 1946. "Outline of a Cuna grammar." *International Journal of American Linguistics* 12:185–97.

Holmer, Nils Magnus. 1952. *Ethno-linguistic Cuna Dictionary with Indices and References to a Critical and Comparative Cuna Grammar and the Grammatical Sketch in Cuna Chrestomathy*. Goteborg: Ethnografiska Museet.

Kuipers, Aert H. 1967. *The Squamish Language*. The Hague: Mouton.

Lehmann, Walter. 1920. *Zentralamerika*. Berlin: Reimer.

Michelson, Truman. 1938. "Algonquian notes." *International Journal of American Linguistics* 9:103–12.

Valdivia, Luis de. 1943. *Los Textos Millcayac del P. Luis de Valdivia con Vocabulario Español-Allentiac-Millcayac por Fernando Marquez Miranda*. La Plata: Universidad de La Plata.

Substrates, Calquing and Grammaticalization in Melanesian Pidgin

Roger M. Keesing
Department of Anthropology
The Australian National University

1. INTRODUCTION[1]

Melanesian Pidgin has been widely recognized as unusual, in the worldwide spectrum of pidgins and creoles, in the degree of syntactic expansion and stabilization attained despite the fact that, until recently, it remained primarily a plantation *lingua franca* acquired by adults. Melanesian Pidgin incorporates grammatical devices such as transitivity-markers and mechanisms for embedding relative clauses not found in "true creoles" (Bickerton, 1981, 1984) — not to mention the contact jargons antecedent to them. While this has been taken by such scholars as Bickerton and Mufwene (1986) to imply that Melanesian Pidgin has a history different from those of well-known northern hemisphere pidgins and creoles, the special nature of that history, and its linguistic consequences, remain poorly understood.

In a recent book (Keesing, 1988), I argue that the obscurities that shroud this sociolinguistic and linguistic history are partly a result of the enshrining of the New Guinea dialect, Tok Pisin, as the canonical form of Melanesian Pidgin, and the consequence that the Vanuatu (New Hebridean) and Solomons dialects of pidgin remain poorly documented and little known to the international linguistic community. It is these dialects, I argue, that encode and preserve the most critical linguistic evidence of how pidgin in the Pacific acquired its distinctive degree of expansion and stabilization. Moreover, in the Solomons and Vanuatu, the relationship between pidgin and the languages natively spoken by those who have historically been its primary speakers remains in view. Tok Pisin obscures these developmental processes, because:

1. A century ago, the plantation system of German New Guinea was cut off (by the imposition of political barriers) from a vast regional pidgin speech-community that incorporated much of the central and southwestern Pacific and Queensland.[2]
2. Thus cut off from the regional pidgin speech-community, Tok Pisin was extensively relexified (from indigenous Bismarck Archipelago languages, and to a minimal degree, from German); the original regional pidgin lexicon was derived almost entirely from English and from nautical pidgin(s) of northern hemisphere origin (*save*, *pikanini*, etc.).
3. Tok Pisin, in being transplanted from the area where Pacific pidgin developed, acquired a set of substrate languages very different from those whose speakers had been the primary contributors to that initial development.

The question of substrate languages is crucial. Although Pacific pidgin was used as a regional lingua franca across vast stretches of ocean — and it was for thirty crucial formative years primarily a lingua franca of shipboard communication, not plantation life — almost all of the Islanders who participated in its development were speakers of Oceanic Austronesian languages. Most were speakers of languages that apparently fall into a single subgroup of Oceanic (which I will call Eastern Oceanic, or EO), marked by conservatism in preserving Proto-Oceanic grammatical patterns.[3]

Pidgin in the Pacific acquired a remarkable degree of grammatical elaboration partly because, from the 1840s onward, Islanders took the lexical resources of English and nautical jargon and progressively hammered them into grammatical designs common, at an abstract level, to their native languages. In doing so — and in keeping an evolving code accessible to superstrate speakers — they drew massively on universal-based faculties of simplification, and followed paths of minimal markedness/universality. Hence, incorporating substrate patterns into an emerging pidgin is, as Goodman (1985), Mufwene (1986), Mühlhäusler (1987) and others have noted, in no way incompatible with universalist theory or the impress of superstrate patterns: It is the interplay between the three that generates the kinds of phenomena I will examine.

What makes Solomons Pijin and Vanuatu (New Hebrides) Bislama so much more revealing of this dialectical process than Tok Pisin is, firstly, that they clearly incorporate quite specific grammatical patterns common to Eastern Oceanic Austronesian substrate languages; and secondly, that the bending processes that historically shaped Pacific pidgin are still going on. The Solomons and Vanuatu dialects are still connected to particular subgroups of EO languages.[4] Out of the resources available in the pidgin of the 1890s — by which time Melanesian Pidgin had acquired most of its present grammatical resources — patterns congruent with particular sets of substrate languages have been selected. We find evidence of this process in the divergence between the Solomons and New Hebridean dialects since the end of the Labor Trade separated the two speech communities (ca. 1905), and in regional differences in the pidgin of older speakers within each country. Speakers who acquired Pidgin as young adults demonstrably calque Pidgin onto their native languages, lexically and grammatically.

The unusual degree of grammatical elaboration in Melanesian Pidgin, in contrast to other documented pidgins, is primarily the product of a process whereby lexical elements from the superstrate language and nautical jargon were equated with grammatical elements in Oceanic Austronesian languages: A process underway for almost 150 years. Evidence of this process is encoded in a grammatical statigraphy of Melanesian Pidgin dialects, a stratigraphy we can establish on both distributional and textual grounds. Patterns common to all three major dialects of Pidgin and attested in the nineteenth-century texts must have been incorporated a century ago, when Tok Pisin was separated from the other two dialects; patterns common to Solomons Pijin and Bislama must have been incorporated by the turn of the century, when the Labor Trade ended.

Let me be more explicit at the outset about the relevance of Melanesian Pidgin to a developing understanding of the grammaticalization process. Melanesian Pidgin has undergone processes of grammaticalization fundamentally similar to those being documented for natural languages (as Sankoff, Mühlhäusler and others have shown for Tok Pisin). But this, I argue, is not the main mechanism whereby Melanesian Pidgin has acquired a syntactic complexity far beyond that documented for other pidgins. Where the substrate languages whose speakers play the main part in the development of a pidgin are sufficiently closely related to have a common basic grammatical pattern (as is the case with the Eastern Oceanic Austronesian languages), lexical items (or stylistic variants, such as resumptive pronouns) in the lexifying superstrate language can be equated directly with grammatical elements common to substrate languages. It is this process, parallel and complementary to grammaticalization in a strict sense, that I will illustrate in the sections to follow.

2. TRANSITIVE MARKING

The transitive suffix *-im* in Melanesian Pidgin has been widely recognized as a grammatical pattern anomalous in the spectrum of pidgins/creoles. The "-um" form sporadically used in northern hemisphere jargons was almost certainly introduced to the Pacific, through the usages of nautical jargon and perhaps a developing New South Wales pidgin used in white-Aboriginal communication. What is interesting is what happened to this form when it reached the Pacific, and why. In almost all EO languages of the central Pacific, the semantic role relationship of agent to patient (and secondarily, to goal or stimulus) is marked with a transitive suffix (reconstructed for POC as **-i*, and manifest in most EO languages as *-Ci-*) attached to verb roots (Pawley, 1973, Pawley and Reid, 1979). Once available to Pacific Islanders, "-um" was apparently quickly equated with the transitive marker in substrate languages, hence became a grammatical element by a direct borrowing and calquing. Although there is no phonological counterpart to the nasal element in "-um" in Oceanic transitive suffixes, the form otherwise fits perfectly into an Oceanic pattern.[5] Hawaiians encountered by Dana (1840) in San Diego in 1835 are recorded as using *lock him up chest*. By 1844, *me like um man belongen noder place* ('I like foreigners') is recorded in Fiji, from a Fijian who had travelled widely on trading ships (Erskine, 1853:461). In 1852, *Oh, by, by Riko catch 'im putty 'im in calaboose* ('Riko will capture him and put him in jail') is recorded in the Cook Islands (Lamont, 1867:98).[7] From Tanna (southern New Hebrides) in 1869, we have two separate texts in which "make him" (*mek-im*) is recorded (Keesing 1988, Chapter 4).

Textual and distributional evidence indicates that the lexicon of the Melanesian Pidgin of the Labor Trade (mid 1880s) already included a substantial set of verbs, marked as transitive, which represent significant innovations, as reanalyses of or extrapolations from the English source words. The innovations are both semantic and morphological; they occur in all three daughter dialects (I here use Solomons Pijin orthographic renderings):

kas-im	'to reach (a place), to obtain (s.t.)' (from English "catch").
lukaot-im	'to find (s.t.) by searching'
kapsaet-im	'to pour out contents of (s.t.)' (from English "capsize").
lus-im	'to leave (a place)' (from English "lose").
win-im	'to exceed (s.t.), to beat (s.o.)' (from English "win").

The transitive suffix in Melanesian Pidgin operates in exactly the same way as the transitive suffix in EO languages: It marks the relationship to a direct object NP (canonically in the semantic role of patient); and like the transitive suffix in many of the EO languages, it incorporates a zero-marked third-person reference, as in:

mi no luk-im
'I didn't see it/him'(SIP),

except where it is followed by a pronoun, as in:

mi no luk-im olketa
'I didn't see them'.

3. PREPOSITIONAL VERBS

A further pattern not only underlines the direct correspondence between Pidgin *-im* and the Oceanic transitive suffix, but makes strikingly clear that it was Islanders, not English-speakers, who were the primary agents in the incorporation of transitive-marking into Pacific Pidgin. This pattern occurs both in Solomons Pijin and, to somewhat lesser degree, in Bislama.[8] A widespread pattern in Oceanic languages, clearly preserved in the EO languages of Vanuatu and the southeastern Solomons, is the use of what have been called "prepositional verbs." What had at one time been second verbs in compound verbal constructions have become detached, such that they function semantically and syntactically as prepositions, but morphologically retain the structure of transitive verbs (in being marked with transitive-suffixes and/or bound clitic object pronouns). Kwaio, a Southeast Solomonic language of Malaita on which I have worked extensively (Keesing, 1975, 1985), will serve to illustrate. In Kwaio, transitivity is marked either by the transitive suffix *-Ci-a* (where *-a* is a clitic 'it' pronoun) or by the pronominal element (*-a*) alone.

fe'e-ni-a	'with (s.o.)'
fono-si-a	'against (s.o., s.t.)'
folo-si-a	'across (s.t.)'
fa'a-si-a	'away from (s.o. or a place)'
suri-a	'around, beside, on top of' (and metaphorically, 'because of, about')
'ani-a	'with (an instrument)'
'usi-a	'against (s.o., s.t.)'
dari-a	'attaining a destination (s.o., a place)'

In some cases, the roots are still used as verbs, stative or active (*fono* is 'be blocked', *folo* is 'be across', *dari-a* is 'find (s.t.)'). In others, the verbal use has disappeared. A quite similar set of prepositional verbs in the To'aba'ita language of northern Malaita is discussed by Lichtenberk (This volume). Lichtenberk also discusses the way some of these prepositional verbs (in Kwaio, *suri-a* and *fa'a-si-a*) serve as complementizers in Malaita languages.

In Solomons Pijin, a set of prepositional verbs corresponds directly, in morphology, syntactic function, and semantics, to the prepositional verbs pervasive in substrate languages of the southeastern Solomons, and particularly, of Malaita:[9]

wet-em	'with (s.o.)' [often *weit-em* or *wit-im*]
agens-em	'against (s.o., s.t.)'
abaot-em	'about, around (s.t.)'
koros-im	'across (s.t.)'
antap-em	'on top of (s.o., s.t.),
raon-em	'around'
kas-em	'attaining a destination (s.o., a place)'

In Bislama, only *wet-im* 'with (s.o.)' is common, but *agens-em* and *kas-em* have been recorded as prepositional verbs.[10]

The occurrence of these prepositional verbs in the two dialects of Melanesian Pidgin that most directly preserve the lexical and syntactic structures of the pidgin of the Labor Trade is striking evidence both of the nineteenth-century origin of these patterns and of the close correspondence between Melanesian Pidgin and the grammars of EO languages. The prepositional verbs in the two closely-related Pidgin dialects transparently represent a grammatical pattern based directly on constructions of substrate languages, in the creation of which Europeans could have played no direct part — even though the lexical elements came ultimately from English.

4. THE CALQUING PROCESS: THE CASE OF *KAM* AND *GO*

The process whereby lexical borrowings from English acquire grammatical functions corresponding to those in substrate languages through calquing can be illustrated by some of the uses to which the English verbs "come" and "go" have been put in Melanesian Pidgin dialects.

As basic verbs that would have been part of a core English vocabulary used in giving orders and expressing intentions to "the natives," "come" and "go," not surprisingly, turn up in Pacific jargon from the texts of the 1840s onward. In 1852, for example, recorded in the Cook Islands (Lamont, 1867:96), we find *me likey go Carifona; ship he no go.*

"Come" and "go" also serve as auxiliary verbs in English, at least in colloquial registers: Thus, "come and do it" or "go and fetch it" become "come do it" and "go fetch it." We get a collusion here between superstrate patterns and common substrate patterns in Oceanic languages, where such actions are commonly rendered with serial verb constructions.[11] We find even in the early texts evidence of both "come" and "go" (*kam* and *go*) being used by Islanders in serial constructions, in ways transparent to both substrate and superstrate speakers.

Thus we find, in 1844 in Fiji, *You come see me* (Erskine, 1853:461). In 1850, in the Loyalties, we find:

> Great fool Uea man, steal little thing he no want, big ship come and kill him (Erskine 1853:347) ('Uea men are great fools in stealing things they don't want; a big ship will come and kill them'; note the relative clause 'that he doesn't want'.)

What is recorded as "come and kill him" was probably *kam kil-im*. In 1854, on Kosrae in the eastern Carolines, we have *every kanaka: big island, small island, all go and kill every man board ship* (Hezel, 1983:114). In 1869, in the southern New Hebrides, we find *Plenty man come hear you make him bokis sing* (Paton, 1894:77).[12]

Such constructions, using *kam* and *go* as first verbs in serial verb constructions, are common in all three contemporary dialects of Melanesian Pidgin. Some examples from a text in Solomons Pijin recorded from an elderly speaker of Maringe (Santa Isabel)[13] will serve to illustrate:

olketa kam faet aotsaet long ples blong mifala long Baolo
they come fight outside LOC place POSS us LOC Baolo
'They came and fought off (the shore) at our place at Baolo.'

mifala kam luk-im olketa pulande nao
we come see-TRS them be plentiful PRF
'We came and saw that there were lots of them.'

olketa Diapane go nao, olketa go luk-im
PL Japanese go PRF they go see-TRS
'The Japanese went, went and saw

tu-fala endi long rot ia
two-ADJ end LOC road DEM
'the two ends of the road.'

olketa kam dorop-em baum, baum, baum
they come drop-TRS bomb bomb bomb
'They came and dropped bomb after bomb.'

We could go on to ask whether a Maringe speaker or a Kwaio speaker of Solomons Pijin could go further, in equating *go* and *kam* in such serial constructions with verbal auxiliaries or other verbal particles in their native languages — thereby possibly giving them a grammatical force and/or a specific semantic import not transparent to English speakers (or, perhaps, to one another). Could *kam* be equated by a Maringe speaker with one kind of grammatical element and by a Kwaio speaker with a different grammatical element, on the basis of calquing? I will return to these questions.

Another pattern found in both Bislama and Tok Pisin is the use of *kam* and *go* in serial-clausal constructions that express deictic-directional meanings. Thus, in Tok Pisin (Givón 1987):

i wokabaut i go 'he went away (from a reference point)'
em karim i kam 'she brings it (toward a reference point)'.

The rendering of such constructions in Solomons Pijin points particularly clearly to the impress of EO substrate languages. In Oceanic languages generally, and pervasively in the EO languages of the zone where Pacific pidgin underwent its major development, two directionals, used postverbally, serve to express the meanings "hither" and "thither": What are reconstructed for PEO as **mai* and **watu* (these are apparently derived from lexical verbs 'come' and 'go', hence historically represent grammaticalizations in Oceanic). Thus, in Kwaio we find *ngari-a mai* 'bring it' and *ngari-a kau* 'take it (away)', lit. "convey it hither" and "convey it thither." In Solomons Pijin, *kam* is systematically used where *mai* is used in substrate languages, and *go* is systematically used where reflexes of **watu*, such as Kwaio *kau*, are used:

tek-em kam 'bring it'
tek-em go 'take it (away)'

Older speakers use these particles in ways that correspond exactly to patterns in their native languages. Thus for Kwaio speakers

ori-si-a mai
ask-TRS-it hither
'ask about it'

is rendered in Pidgin as:

ask-em kam.

Two fragments from my texts from Kwaio speakers who learned Pijin in prewar plantation contexts will serve to illustrate how such forms are used in discourse:[14]

hem-i stop-em go long sam-fala pepa
he plug-TRS DEI with some-ADJ paper
'He plugged it up with some paper.'

mifala seke nao ma 'efofilen i mekenois kamu nao
we check PRF and airplane it buzz DEI PRF
'We checked, and an airplane was buzzing toward us.'

A further attestation of the impress of the EO substrate on Melanesian Pidgin in the incorporation of *go* is a pattern where the verb *go*, reduplicated, serves to indicate the passage of time in a narrative, a pattern widespread in the EO languages of Vanuatu and the Solomons. We find it in Kwaio *leeleka* (where *leka* is 'go'). In Kwaio as in other Oceanic languages, reduplication of a verb usually indicates repetition or continuation of the act described by the verb. An extract from a text will illustrate *leka* 'go' used in both these ways:

leeleka leeleka leeleka ma ga'i-nau ma
go-go go-go go-go and mother-my and
'And as time went on, my mother and

ma'a a-gu 'agaa'a gala taataunga'i ma
father POSS-me them2[15] they2 work(RED) and
my father worked and

gala leeleka naa fonunga ma gala leeleka naa
they2 go(RED) LOC feast and they2 go(RED) LOC
they'd go to feasts and they'd go to

boni-na makete ma ogulaa ma na ku naanai 'ifi
event-it market and gathering and me I stay home
markets and gatherings, and I'd stay at home.'

Melanesian Pidgin dialects all use this device of *go-go* to indicate the passage of time, as in a fragment from a text from an old Lau (Malaita) speaker of Solomons Pijin:

olketa lukat-em mifala, go-go olketa kas-em sam-fala ...
they search-TRS us go-go they catch-TRS some-ADJ
'They searched for us, and eventually caught some (people) ...'

In Lau, *lea* is 'go' and *lelea* indicates the passage of time: *lelea ka sui* is 'when it is finished' (Fox, 1974:116).

Another text fragment from the same Lau speaker shows *go* (as well as *kam*) in serial verb constructions and *go-go* as marker of time elapsing:

oraete olketa kamu nao olketa kamu ofen-em olketa bokis
OK they come PRF they come open-TRS PLU box
'Then they came and they opened all the boxes,

infikis, tekeaot evri kaleko ia, goo-go i finisi
investigate take out each garment DEM go-go it be finished
investigated, took out every piece of cloth, until it was finished,

olketa go torou-em long faea
they go throw-TRS LOC fire
they went and threw (them) on the fire.'

Many northern and central Vanuatu languages use exactly the same device. Thus in Epi, *ba* is 'go' and *bababa...* indicates the passage of time in a narrative (Darrell Tryon, personal communication). Not surprisingly, Vanuatu Bislama uses *go-go-go* in exactly the same fashion as Solomons Pijin.

Note that there are two processes involved in the way *kam* and *go* have been incorporated into Pijin, one of which involves lexical equivalences and the other of which involves grammaticalization, at least to some degree. In fitting the lexical verbs derived from English "come" and "go" into serial verb constructions corresponding to those in substrate languages, Islanders have needed to do no reanalysis. The verbs 'come' and 'go' are fitted into the same slots in Pidgin that they occupy in Island speakers' first languages. The same is true for the use of *go-go-go* to mark the passage of time in narrative, even though the semantic connection between physical movement and the passage of time in the substrate languages is metaphorically based. Once *go* has been equated with a lexical verb 'go', no further semantic reanalysis is needed: The semantic connection already exists.

In the case of the postverbal directionals, however, the EO 'hither' and 'thither' forms are not lexical verbs for 'come' and 'go'. Hence, a metaphor-based extension of the semantics of *kam* and *go* was required in order for Solomons Pijin to adopt these as equivalents to **mai* and **watu* forms. The further exemplifications I will give of the calquing process include both direct transfers based on lexical equivalence and more indirect ones involving reanalyses or extensions that parallel (although short-cut) grammaticalization processes in the development of natural languages.

5. PREVERBAL PARTICLES MARKING ASPECT/MOOD/ MODALITY

We find further compelling evidence of the more direct paths toward lexicalization and grammaticalization if we examine the aspect-markers of Solomons Pijin and Bislama in relation to those of substrate languages. I will look most closely at Solomons Pijin, for which my data are richest, and in particular at the relationship between the substrate languages of Malaita and Pijin.

In EO languages, tense and aspect are not extensively marked. However, verb phrases in EO languages characteristically have preverbal and postverbal slots filled by particles marking aspect, mood, and modality. These particles may be free or bound to subject-marking pronouns or verbs. Documentary and distributional evidence indicates that lexical elements drawn from English — "by and by," "just," "might," "now," etc. — were by the 1880s being grammaticalized in Melanesian Pidgin as equivalent to Oceanic markers of aspect/modality/mood. In some cases, the transfer of lexical material into Oceanic grammatical slots required greater reanalysis by Islanders: In all three Melanesian Pidgin dialects, *ating* (derived from English "I think," but analyzed by Islanders as monomorphemic) is used as a preverbal particle indicating 'maybe, probably' (often used interchangeably with *maet* ("might").

Baabae (or its short form *bae*) is characteristically not a future tense marker, but rather a marker of irrealis or non-accomplished mode, corresponding in function to a particle reconstructed for PEO (Pawley, 1972). Whereas English speakers have consistently used it in clause-initial position as a temporal adverb, there has been a pull, from the 1880s onward, to bring *bae* into the verb phrase as a grammatical marker, and to use to it express irrealis meanings as well as establish a future time-frame. In many EO languages, markers of mode (dubitive, irrealis, etc.) that canonically fit within the verb phrase can be fronted for emphasis; this is an option used frequently for both *bae* and *maet* in Bislama and Solomons Pijin, one which allows superstrate and substrate speakers to meet in the middle, as it were, while using different grammatical analyses.[16]

The Pidgin of the Queensland Labor Trade apparently incorporated a range of elements available as verbal particles. Which ones were used, and the grammatical force assigned to them, depended in part on the use of particles in the speakers' particular substrate languages. A fully adequate degree of mutual intelligibility could apparently be achieved through speakers of particular substrate languages using these markers of aspect, modality and mood in ways corresponding to those of their native languages: The indigenous languages are close enough in this regard that it seems that little semantic content would be lost in the process.

The process can be illustrated with the particle *des* (or *tes* or *das*), from English "just." The *des* form is manifest both in texts from the late nineteenth-century Labor Trade (recorded, of course, as "just") and in contemporary texts from older speakers of Vanuatu Bislama and Solomons Pijin. For Bislama, Charpentier has pointed out close correspondences with substrate languages. Thus, to take Charpentier's (1979: 353) example from Vetmbao (South Malekula) and Bislama:

naji nga-mandrxa mun
him he-ASP drink[17]
'He just drank.'

em i tes trink
him he ASP drink[18]

A Solomons example will show the same pattern of correspondence, where the form taken from English "just" has acquired grammatical force as an aspect marker. In Kwaio, the particle *bi'i*, fitting between the subject-marking pronoun[19] and the verb, marks the action of the verb that follows as having taken place in the immediate past.

ngai e bi'i aga-si-a
him he just see-TRS-it
'He just saw it.'

Both Kwaio speakers from whom I elicited Pijin equivalents of some 400 Kwaio sentences[20] consistently gave *das* or *tes* as the Pijin equivalent. Thus:

hem i tes luk-im
him he just see-TRS
'He just saw it.'

Given that English "just" fits into a similar preverbal position and that such markers are common in Atlantic creoles, is there any evidence that Kwaio speakers are indeed using *tes*[21] as equivalent to *bi'i?* Here we need to look first at the marking of irrealis/non-accomplished mode in Kwaio.

The Kwaio future marker is *ta-* (with allomorphs *te-* and *to-*), prefixed to the subject-marking pronouns.

gila ta-la leka
them FUT-they go
'They will go.'

The Solomons Pijin equivalent I elicited was

olketa bae i go
them FUT 3PRS go
'They will go.'

This pattern of equating *ta-* with *bae/baebae* is consistent throughout a very large corpus, to mark both a probable future event and the irrealis status of the event described. A second Kwaio speaker gave exactly the same equivalences throughout.

In Kwaio, the irrealis/future marking particle can be conjoined with *bi'i*, with a semantic import not predictable from the two forms used separately. It indicates that the action of the verb will take place in a short time. Both Kwaio speakers from whom I elicited Pijin equivalents used *baebae* and *das/tes* together to express these meanings:

ta-goru bi'i aga-si-a
FUT-weINCL just see-TRANS-it
'We'll see it in a while.'

bae iumi das luk-im
FUT weINCL just see-TRANS

Such detailed correspondences make it inescapably clear that Kwaio speakers use these preverbal markers of aspect/mood/modality in ways that directly follow the grammar of their native language, using — in effect — formulas of equivalence between the two languages. Yet at the same time, the resources for doing so constitute part of the pidgin linguistic system dating back to the nineteenth century. The evidence that Kwaio speakers are calquing on their native language in using verbal particles in Solomons Pijin goes further. In my large corpus,[22] the entire set of Kwaio particles marking the time-frame of the verb, some of which are preverbal and some postverbal, corresponds in their Solomons Pijin usage to a set of particles derived from English but carrying exactly the same import as the Kwaio particles, and placed in exactly the same slots. I will shortly examine another appropriation of *kam* and *go* by Kwaio speakers of Solomons Pijin that further illustrates how English-derived lexical forms can be given grammatical force through direct calquing onto grammatical elements in substrate languages.

The lexical elements of the pidgin of the late nineteenth century Labor Trade were fitted into the aspect-marking system of New Hebridean languages in a somewhat different way. In EO languages of the northern and central New Hebrides, whose speakers were numerically preponderant in the main period of the Labor Trade, a durative aspect marker indicating that an act is in progress is common. The Bislama of Vanuatu has incorporated *stap*, which in other contexts is a verb meaning 'stay, be present, exist', as a durative aspect marker:

iej i-ndang-lualua na-ndam (Nasiariana, Malekula)
he he-DUR-dig ART-yam
'He's in the process of digging yams.'

naji ng-u-xoel dram (Vetmbao, Malekula)
he he-DUR-dig yam
'He's in the process of digging yams.'

em *i stap pik-im yam*
him he DUR dig-TRS yam
'He's in the process of digging yams.' (Charpentier, 1979:351)

la lo retireti na lolo vanua (Tangoa)
they DUR talk (RED) LOC inside village
'They are having a discussion in the village.'

oli stap toktok inside long velej
they DUR tok(RED) inside LOC village
'They are having a discussion in the village.' (Camden, 1979:100–101)

In Southeastern Solomonic languages such marking of durative aspect is not generally found. In Solomons Pijin *stap* is common as a verb but does not occur as a durative aspect marker.[23] In the Malaita languages, to indicate that an action is underway, one can either use a temporal or use a perfect-marking particle after the verb — a marker that indicates either that action of the verb has commenced or that it has been completed. It is to this particle in the Malaita languages, and the corresponding form incorporated into Solomons Pijin, that we now turn.

6. POSTVERBAL PERFECT-MARKING PARTICLES

Textual evidence and contemporary usages in Bislama indicate that *nao* (derived from English "now") was being used in the pidgin of the Labor Trade as a temporal adverb. In Bislama, it continues to function in this way:

mi mi slip nao 'maintenant, moi je dors' (Charpentier, 1979:360).

In Solomons Pijin, *nao* has come to serve as an aspect marker, corresponding to forms universal in Malaita languages — forms which characteristically resemble *nao* phonologically, in having nVV (or nVCV) shapes (see Simons 1986). These perfect markers, occurring in a postverbal slot within the VP, serve to articulate a state at a reference time (the time of the speech event) to an earlier state or event, to indicate that the two are essentially and inseparably connected, and to focus attention on the present state. In addition to indicating that an act has been completed or (with stative verbs) that a state has come into being, they serve to mark prospective perfects (i.e., that the action is underway), and hence are used where northern and central Vanuatu languages would use durative aspect marking. Some examples from Malaita languages will serve to illustrate:

'Are'are (Geerts, 1970:75):
e siko no'o
it be finished PRF
'It is finished.'

e tara'ae no'o
he start PRF
'He has started.'[24]

Kwara'ae (Deck, 1934:38):

ka sui na'a
it be finished PRF
'It is finished.'

nia leka na'a
he go PRF
'He has gone.'

Lau (Ivens, 1934:73):

e sui na
it be finished PRF
'It is finished.'

e lea na
he go PRF
'He has gone.'

Kwaio (see Keesing, 1985):

(ngai) e leka no'o
him he go PRF
'He has gone.'

gala age-a no'o
they2 do-it PRF
'They have done it./They are doing it now.'

e 'akwa no'o
he run away PRF
'She has run away.'

e mou no'o
it be broken PRF
'It's broken.'

For such sentences, speakers of Solomons Pijin use:

hem-i go nao	'He has gone.'
hem-i finis nao	'It is finished.'
hem-i ranawe nao	'She has run away.'
tufala-i du-im nao	'They have done it/are doing it now.'
hem-i birek nao	'It's broken.'

The direct correspondence between *nao* and the postverbal perfect-marking particles in the Malaita languages has been noted and documented by Simons (1986). I have argued that with this standardization of a perfect marker in Solomons Pijin has come the virtual disappearance of *bin* — regularly used as a marker of completed action in regional dialects of Bislama as well as Tok Pisin, and attested widely in nineteenth-century texts.

Simons also notes that in the Malaita languages, the perfect marker or an allomorph of it is used after a noun or focal pronoun to topicalize or foreground it. Thus, in Kwaio:

gila no'o la age-a
them TOP they do-it
'They're the ones who did it.'

ngai ne-e aga-si-a
him TOP-he see-TRS-it
'He's the one who saw it. (Here *ne-* is an allomorph of *no'o*).'

Simons notes that *nao* is used in Solomons Pijin in an identical manner:

hem nao i save
him TOP he know
'He's the one who knows.'

olketa waeteman nao i save wak-em
PLU European TOP he able do-TRS
'It's the Europeans who know how to do it.'

This example is striking in two respects. Presumably, the use of nVV as a topicalizing particle in Malaita languages derives historically from its use as a perfect marker, through the kind of grammaticalization processes explored in these volumes.[25] Hence, the use of *nao* in Pijin to correspond to nVV in both its grammatical slots — as perfect-marker and as topicalizer — represents the kind of shortcut to grammaticalization through direct calquing with which I am concerned in a clear and striking way. Secondly, the path to this calquing was facilitated by a phonological correspondence between a lexical form available in the superstrate language, "now," and the particle in substrate languages with which it was equated.

I have suggested that speakers of particular Solomons languages can, as it were, go beyond the limits of a common code in calquing available Pijin forms onto particular grammatically-salient forms in their native languages — a process I illustrated with the use of *bae ... tes* constructions by Kwaio speakers. We need to look more closely at this phenomenon, since it implies that — like speakers of Chinook Jargon as documented by Silverstein (1972) — speakers of a common code may be using different grammars. In doing so, we shall return to *kam* and *go*, in their role as preverbal auxiliaries.

7. *KAM* AND *GO* AS AUXILIARIES

I shall look first at two Kwaio forms which function as auxiliaries within the verb phrase (neither one is a verb in its own right: They fit into the slot between SRP and verb characteristically occupied by aspect markers). In Kwaio, *kee* usually serves in narrative to indicate the sequential relationship between acts described in successive clauses. *Kee* before an active verb indicates that the act described in the previous clause preceded the act marked with the auxiliary. The two Kwaio speakers in their sixties from whom I elicited Pijin equivalents of Kwaio sentences used *go* (or a reduplicated *gogo*) as equivalent to *kee*, with absolute regularity.

Kwaio:
e kee nigi lolo'o me-'e bi'i leka folo-si-a
he AUX arrive on top and-he just go across-TRS-it
'Then he arrived up there and went across (it).'

Pijin:

hem-i gogo kas-im antafu ana hem-i tas go koros-im
he AUX reach-TRS on top and he just go across-TRS

Note the pervasive pattern of calquing here, in which virtually all the morphemes in the two sentences directly correspond (including the final prepositional verb; note also the calquing of *tas* on *bi'i*).[26]

Kwaio:
ta'a la kee kwai-ri la'u a-i
people they AUX report more LOC-it
'Then the people reported about that as well.'

Pijin:
olketa pipol olketa-i go taleaot long hem moa
PLU people they AUX report LOC it more
'Then the people reported about that as well.'

Kwaio:
alata gila leka mola[27] *gila kee a'a-ri-a 'inoi*
time they go just they AUX carry-TRS-it taro-shoots
'When they set off, they were carrying taro shoots.'

Pijin:
taem olketa go nao olketa go kar-em 'inoi long taro
time they go PRF they AUX carry-TRS shoot GEN taro

The Kwaio form *me'e*, preceding an active verb, also operates as an auxiliary in narrative, to convey meanings that in English would be expressed by "went ahead and ...." The two Kwaio speakers used *kam* as an auxiliary corresponding to *me'e*, with complete regularity.

Kwaio:
gila me'e fane naa 'ue la'akau
they AUX ascend LOC vine DEM
'And then they went ahead and climbed that rattan vine.'

Pijin:
anaa olketa kam koafu long des-fala robu
and they AUX ascend LOC DEM-ADJ vine
'And then they went ahead and climbed that vine.'

Kwaio:
rua solodia gala me'e ula i suri-a
two police they2 AUX stand LOC beside-him
'Two policemen would then stand flanking him.'

Pijin:
tu-fala solodia tufala kam sten weit-em
two-ADJ police they2 AUX stand with-TRS
'Two policemen would then stand flanking him.'

The striking correspondences shown in these paired sentences, where in most cases there is a morpheme-by-morpheme correspondence between the Kwaio and Pijin, is manifest throughout the corpus: I have examined these parallels elsewhere in some detail (Keesing, 1986, 1987, 1988, Chapter 13).

What is important here is that although calquing by Kwaio speakers gives their uses of *kam* and *go* a measure of grammatical as well as lexical force, these forms need not have precisely the same force for speakers of other Solomons languages who use these forms. Let me turn to a Solomons Austronesian language very distantly related to Kwaio,[29] Maringe, spoken on Santa Isabel. I have illustrated above Pijin sentences produced by a Maringe speaker which use *kam* and *go* as auxiliaries in serial verb constructions:

kam faet
kam luk-im
go luk-im
kam dorop-im baum

For Maringe, our only grammatical data come from a forthcoming sketch grammar by Geoffrey White, the introduction to his dictionary (White, Forthcoming). White gives no information about serial verb constructions, but he gives two exemplifying sentences in which the verb *tei* 'go' appears as the first element in compound verbs:

na tei apu noda ...?
FUT go bathe we ...
'Shall we go bathe ...?'

tei rughe ba-go belo gno
go beat PSBL-you drum DEM
'Why don't you go beat the drum over there?'

Tei here is the common verb for 'go'. Although there are no examples given by White in which the common verb *mei* 'come' is used in serial constructions, we may guess that it is used in the same way as *tei.*

When Maringe speakers use *kam* and *go* in Solomons Pijin, they are presumably using a grammatical system in which these forms function as the initial verbs in serial verb sequences. When Kwaio speakers use the same forms preceding other verbs, they have both a different semantic import and a greater grammatical significance: They appear to be homonymous with the verbs 'come' and 'go' (as, too, are the directionals *kam* and *go*, used postverbally as equivalent to *mai* and *kau* in Kwaio). The connections between these forms that led to their incorporation into different grammatical categories are, of course, exactly the sorts of metaphoric connections whose role in grammaticalization is explored in a number of the papers in these volumes.

The point of all this is that a Melanesian Pidgin grammatical element derived from an English lexical form may have acquired this grammatical force not through the usual chain of grammaticalization but through a direct calquing onto a substrate pattern. The semantic bleaching (if there is any) takes place, as it were, in the very process of borrowing. The point can be clarified with reference to *nao* as perfect-marker and topicalizer. The gradual grammaticalization process whereby, in the history of Cristobal-Malaita languages, a perfect-marking particle became used as topicalizing particle did not have to be paralleled by a similar metaphor-based grammaticalization process in Pijin. Once *nao* in the pidgin of the Labor Trade was equated with nVV as perfect marker, which in itself required little bending, it could be transferred directly into the topicalization slot.

Another example from Solomons Pijin may further clarify this process. In Malaitan and other Southeast Solomonic languages, relationships in space are expressed through inalienably possessed nouns, treated grammatically as if they were body-parts (or other parts-to-wholes): "The underneath of the house," "(at) the back-part of the tree" (to express 'behind the tree'), etc. Not surprisingly, relationships in time are treated in the same way: Metaphorically, being in front of or behind is used to express 'before' or 'after'. Thus in Kwaio, *na'o-na 'ifi* 'in front of the house', and *na'o-na omea* 'before the mortuary feast'; and *buri-na 'ai* 'behind the tree' and *buri-na afolonga* 'after the wedding feast'. The incorporation of "behind" into a developing Pacific Pidgin followed the same ("natural") metaphoric path. Thus, in the Solomons Pijin of older Malaita speakers, *bihaen long haos* 'behind the house' and *bihaen long faet* 'after the fight'. In nineteenth-century Melanesian Pidgin *fastaem* was adopted from English "first time" (in such constructions as *mi go fastaem, yu go bihaen*). Solomons Pijin adopted *fastaem* for 'before' (*fastaem long faet* 'before the fight'). Strikingly, this chain of connection being set into motion, Solomons Pijin (at least as used by older Malaita speakers) adopted *fastaem* as a spatial marker: *fastaem long haos* 'the front of the house'. Here we get a reversal of the normal sequence whereby spatial meanings become metaphorically extended to temporal meanings, a reversal made possible by the already-existing connections in substrate languages. What matters is clearly not the direction of the original grammaticalization in substrate languages, but the existence of a semantic bridge across which a borrowed form can move through the calquing process.[30]

Further illumination can come from the prepositional verb 'with'. In adopting the lexical form "with" from English, but adding the transitive suffix *-im* and using it as a prepositional verb, New Hebrideans and Solomon Islanders in Queensland were in a sense grammaticalizing a lexical form. But it was a very different grammaticalization process, and a less circuitous one, than the process whereby in Oceanic languages prepositional verbs evolved from second verbs in serial verb constructions. Similarly, fitting English "go" into a series of slots — as marker of passing-time and a directional as well as a lexical verb — Solomon Islanders were short-cutting rather than recapitulating the grammaticalization process whereby the lexical verb "go" spread through these slots in the evolution of Oceanic Austronesian languages.

The way Kwaio speakers use *go* as equivalent to their auxiliary *kee*, and use *kam* as equivalent to their auxiliary *me'e*, serves further to illustrate the point. I have been unable to find, in other Southeast Solomonic languages, clear evidence of the grammaticalization process whereby these Kwaio auxiliaries developed. It is possible that they, or at least *me'e*, developed from lexical verbs which have subsequently lost their verbal senses. Perhaps *kee*, indicating that the events described in the clause followed those recounted in the preceding clause, is derived from a future/irrealis marker *ka/ke* common in Southeast Solomon languages. Whatever the historical derivation of these auxiliaries, the calquing whereby *go* was equated with *kee* and *kam* was equated with *me'e* did not require the same grammaticalization sequence — although as I have noted, it did require a metaphoric extension of the lexical senses of *go* and *kam*.

It should come as no surprise, since Silverstein's important work on Chinook Jargon (1972), that throughout this process, speakers of English (and other European languages) have brought to their encounter with Pacific pidgin relatively different grammatical systems, and applied to pidgin quite different grammatical analyses.

Once the core structures of Oceanic syntax had been incorporated into the developing pidgin of the Pacific, a process which (judging by distributional evidence and textual records) had effectively taken place by a century ago, the lexical resources of the superstrate language provided the means for further local elaborations. When the original vast and dispersed Pacific Pidgin speech community began to separate into regional speech communities isolated from one another by colonial politics, forms such as "come" and "go" and "stop"[31] could develop in different ways, being mapped onto grammatical patterns broadly common to particular subgroups of substrate languages. Thus, after the separation of New Hebridean and Solomons pidgin speech communities at the beginning of this century and the establishment of internal plantation systems, we find the standardization of *stap* as a durative aspect-marker in Bislama and *nao* as a perfect marker in Solomons Pijin. As recent work by Darrell Tryon and Jean-Michel Charpentier in Vanuatu and my own work in the Solomons shows, even *within* the now-separated national speech communities, there are striking regional variations, some of which seem to go back to the late nineteenth century. The pidgins of the two countries, still very similar, so closely follow the grammatical and semantic patterns of substrate languages, often on a morpheme-to-morpheme basis, that speakers of pidgin can calque directly onto their native languages. As I have illustrated here (and in Keesing, 1988 and Forthcoming), this calquing process then allows a further fine-tuning of pidgin grammar to the particular syntactic patterns and discourse strategies of speakers' first languages.

8. CONCLUSIONS

The syntactic expansion, stabilization and regularization of Melanesian Pidgin dialects has undoubtedly entailed grammaticalization, in a fairly narrow sense. Lexical forms in an early jargon have been transformed into grammatical elements in Pidgin dialects. The scenarios I proposed differ from those advanced by Sankoff (1980)[32] and Mühlhäusler (1980) partly in placing most of these expansions squarely in the nineteenth century rather than the twentieth: Most of them are reflected in all three dialects of Melanesian Pidgin, hence must have already have taken place by the time the Tok Pisin lineage was separated by German political intervention a century ago (see Keesing, 1988, Chap. 5); most appear in nineteenth-century texts. The scenarios I propose differ as well in seeing these expansions as directly connected to the grammatical patterns broadly common to the Oceanic Austronesian languages of the zone where nineteenth-century Pacific pidgin evolved. These connections have been obscured from view in New Guinea, where Tok Pisin has acquired a new and very different array of substrate languages.

The grammaticalization of preverbal markers of tense, mode, aspect and mood out of lexical forms such as "by and by" and "might" and "I think," discussed above, will serve to illustrate. Pulling these forms into verb phrases as grammatical markers clearly required some of the processes of grammaticalization on which other papers in these volumes are focused. However, the existence of corresponding grammatical forms and patterns in substrate languages — ones that have often not been apparent to Tok Pisin specialists — would seem to have led to some shortcuts in the grammaticalization process that would not have been possible if a simple jargon had progressively developed into a creole without mapping onto a relatively uniform substrate pattern. To take another example, discussed by Mühlhäusler (1980), using the transitive suffix to generate causative forms (*hot-im* 'heat it', etc.) in Melanesian Pidgin dialects required some grammatical generalization; but *contra* Mühlhäusler, this pattern of forming causatives was already extensively developed in EO languages.[33] It did not have to be invented, drawing on universal faculties of language expansion, as Mühlhäusler infers.

I have sought to show that where speakers of substrate languages, in a situation of sustained interlingual communication such as that which prevailed in the Pacific, are analyzing the lexical resources of a superstrate language in terms of their own grammars, the processes of grammaticalization that operate in natural languages can be complemented by still more direct pathways to grammatical forms. For Malaita speakers, once *nao* had been calqued onto the perfect marker, it could be used as a topicalization marker with virtually no reanalysis, semantic or syntactic.

Melanesian Pidgin, as Bickerton and many others have realized, constitutes a rare and special case, but one deeply revealing of the faculties enabling language-learning, language simplification, language elaboration, and grammaticalization processes, both indirect and direct.

ABBREVIATIONS

ADJ	adjective
ART	article
DEIC	deictic
PRF	perfective
PSBL	possibility
TRS	transitive suffix

NOTES

1. I am indebted to Elizabeth Traugott and Bernd Heine for particularly valuable suggestions for revision of the original conference paper, and to fellow participants in the conference, particularly Zygmunt Frajzyngier, Talmy Givón, Charles Li, Frank Lichtenberk, Ger Reesink, and Gillian Sankoff, and to Christine Jourdan, for helpful discussion.
2. *Contra* Mühlhäusler (1976, 1978; Mosel and Mühlhäusler, 1982; cf. Salisbury, 1967), I argue (1988, Chapter 5) that the pidgin used in Samoa and parts of the Bismarcks until the late 1880s was essentially the same as the pidgin being used at the same time in the recruiting areas of the New Hebrides and the Solomons, and in Queensland.
3. And innovations apparently assignable to Proto-Eastern Oceanic. The problems of Oceanic subgrouping, and the tentative nature of the Eastern Oceanic subgroup in relation to Southeast Solomonic languages, are discussed in Keesing, 1988, Chapter 6. In relation to the arguments of my book, and this paper, the question on which this subgrouping problem mainly rests — whether the patterns that seemingly define the putative EO subgroup may be shared retentions from POC or some interstage language — is irrelevant. It is the grammatical commonalities, not their time depth, that matter for these purposes. On Oceanic grammar and EO languages, see Pawley, 1972 and 1973.
4. By this I mean that Pidgin is still a second language for most speakers, and that their first languages are the same EO languages that historically shaped the development of southwestern Pacific pidgin; in contrast, Tok Pisin historically acquired a new set of substratum languages, beginning at the turn of this century.
5. A nice example of this occurs in Pohnpeian (in the eastern Carolines in Micronesia, an area where Pacific pidgin disappeared over a century ago) where *-im* in the form *kik-im* ('kick s.o.') is treated as an allomorph of the Oceanic transitive suffix.
6. Modern Solomons Pijin would use *mi laek-em man blong nara ples.*

7. In the Solomons Pijin of older speakers, *ou, baebae Riko kas-em, put -um long kalabus* would be quite acceptable. The form derived from "calaboose" is one of a very substantial number of lexical items widespread in Pacific Pidgin by the 1870s, and documented in all the regional dialects of Melanesian Pidgin.

8. But not in Tok Pisin, a distributional pattern that suggests a post-1890 incorporation into the pidgin of the Labor Trade. However, it is possible that prepositional verbs were in use a century ago but disappeared in New Guinea Pidgin because the support from substrate languages had been lost in the process of transplantation.

9. As I show in Keesing (1988, Chap. 11), speakers of Malaita languages have been the dominant component of the Solomons labor force for well over a century, on the plantations of Queensland, Fiji, New Caledonia and Samoa, and later, in internal Solomons plantations.

10. Terry Crowley, personal communication, Jan. 1988.

11. See e.g. Crowley 1984; examples from Maringe are given in a later section.

12. Mühlhäusler (1980) claims that until 1880, a developing Melanesian Pidgin had such a simple syntax that formation of periphrastic causatives was impossible. This 1869 text shows such a causative construction more than a decade earlier than Mühlhäusler's claim would allow.

13. Provided to me by Geoffrey White.

14. Substantial extracts from these texts have been published in Keesing (1986, 1987, and 1988).

15. I have analyzed elsewhere (Keesing, 1986, 1988, Forthcoming) in detail the close correspondence between Melanesian Pidgin pronominal systems and those of substrate (and particularly EO) languages. Here, I give only glosses of pronouns, to avoid the need for lengthy explanation.

16. See Silverstein (1972) for an analysis of this process in Chinook Jargon.

17. FP here designates a focal pronoun, fitting into the subject NP slot (and usually syntactically optional); SRP designates a subject-referencing pronoun, an obligatory subject-pronominal element in the verb phrase, marked for person and number.

18. See Keesing (1988, Chaps. 9 and 10) for a sustained argument that the so-called "predicate-marker" in Melanesian Pidgin dialects is a pronoun, and corresponds directly to the subject-marking pronominal elements in EO languages — obligatory subject constituents of verbal clauses — represented in Vetmbao by a clitic prefixed to the verb and in the examples from Malaita languages that follow, by such independent pronominal forms as *e* and *gala*.

19. See Keesing (1985) and, for Oceanic, Keesing (1988, Chap. 6).

20. The sentences were the exemplifying ones given in my Kwaio grammar (Keesing, 1985). See f.n. 22.

21. Or *des* or *das*.

22. More than four hundred Kwaio sentences, from my *Kwaio Grammar* (1985), almost all of them originally taken from texts, for which equivalents in Pijin were elicited from middle-aged Kwaio men, independently (and a year apart).

23. In Tok Pisin, *stap* used as a durative marker occurs as a second verb in clausal serial

constructions — a further alternative analysis of the lexical resources of the Melanesian Pidgin of the 1880s. Thus *em bruk-im i stap* 'He keeps breaking it' (Givón, 1987).

24. In the Oceanic pattern, no distinction is made between 'he', 'she' or 'it', but I have made such distinctions according to context in glossing the morphemes.

25. It it not strictly relevant for present purposes to propose an analysis of this development in Malaita languages. However, Heine (personal communication, 1 January 1989) comments that "in some Niger-Congo languages of Nigeria (Nupe, Gwari), a verb 'take' has been grammaticalized as a kind of perfective marker on the one hand and a completive focus ("foregrounding") marker on the other. This appears to be similar to the situation in Kwaio: it would seem that the topicalizer has sort of a focus/cleft function."

26. The only difference between the two sentences is the use of *kas-im* 'reach' as a transitive verb in Solomons Pijin, where Kwaio uses an intransitive 'arrive'.

27. The Kwaio postverbal *mola*, which in many contexts is best glossed as 'just' or 'only', sometimes serves in narrative as a perfect-marking particle, as it does here.

28. The use of the Solomons Pijin prepositional verb *weit-em* 'with (him)' as corresponding to the Kwaio prepositional verb *suri-a* 'alongside (him)' again is striking, and was used by both speakers.

29. See Ross (1986).

30. Heine (personal communication) suggests that "the development of first time (>*fastaem*) from a temporal to a spatial marker among older Malaita speakers might form one of the rare counter-examples to the unidirectionality principle of grammaticalization." The point bears pondering. The case suggests to me that it is precisely where such calquing is operating that we might expect such "counter-examples."

31. Commonly used in working class British (and Australian) English to mean 'stay, be at a place'.

32. Which includes papers by Sankoff (1977), Sankoff and Brown (1976) and Sankoff and Laberge (1973).

33. See Keesing (1988, pp. 124–27).

REFERENCES

Bickerton, D. 1981. *Roots of Language*. Ann Arbor, MI: Karoma Publishers.

Bickerton, D. 1984. "The language bioprogram hypothesis." *Brain and Behavior Sciences* 7:173–221.

Camden, W. 1979. "Parallels in structure of lexicon and syntax between New Hebrides Bislama and the South Santo language as spoken at Tangoa." In *Papers in Pidgin and Creole Linguistics* 2. Canberra: Australian National University [Pacific Linguistics A–57].

Charpentier, J.-M. 1979. Le Bislama(n): Pidgin des Nouvelles-Hébrides. Paris: SELAF.

Clark, R. 1979. "In search of Beach-la-Mar: Towards a history of Pacific Pidgin English." *Te Reo* 22/23:3–66.

Crowley, T. 1984. "Serial verbs in Paamese." Paper presented at the Fourth International Conference on Austronesian Linguistics, Suva.

Dana, R.H. 1840. *Two Years Before the Mast.* New York: Harper.

Deck, N. 1934. *Grammar of the Language Spoken by the Kwara'ae People of Mala, British Solomon Islands.* Journal of the Polynesian Society reprint No.5, from Vols. 42–43.

Erskine, J.E. 1853. *Journal of a Cruise Among the Islands of the Western Pacific.* London: J.Murray.

Fox, C.E. 1974. *Lau Dictionary.* Canberra: Pacific Linguistics [Pacific Linguistics C–25].

Geerts, P. 1970. *'Are'are Dictionary.* Canberra: Pacific Linguistics [Pacific Linguistics C-14].

Givón, T. 1987. Serial Verbs and the Mental Reality of 'Event'. Final Project Report to the National Endowment for the Humanities.

Goodman, M. 1985. Review of D. Bickerton, *Roots of Language, International Journal of American Linguistics* 51(1):109–137.

Hezel, F..1983. *The First Taint of Civilization: A History of the Caroline and Marshall Islands in Pre-Colonial Days, 1521–1885.* Honolulu: University of Hawaii Center for Pacific and Asian Studies, University of Hawaii [Pacific Islands Monograph Series, No.1].

Ivens, W.G. 1934. *A Vocabulary of the Lau Language, Big Mala, Solomon Islands.* Journal of the Polynesian Society Supplement, Memoir No.11. Wellington: Polynesian Society.

Keesing, R. 1975. *Kwaio Dictionary.* Canberra: Australian National University [Pacific Linguistics C–35].

Keesing, R. 1985. *Kwaio Grammar.* Canberra: Australian National University [Pacific Linguistics B–88].

Keesing, R. 1986. "Subject pronouns and tense-marking in southeast Solomonic languages and Solomons Pijin: Grounds for substratomania?" In *Papers in Pidgin and Creole Linguistics* 4, S. Romaine et al. (eds), 97–132. Canberra: Australian National University [Pacific Linguistics A–72].

Keesing, R. 1987. "Pijin calquing on Kwaio: A test case." In *A World of Language: Festschrift for Prof. S. A Wurm*, D. Laycock and W. Winter (eds), 335–360. Canberra: Australian National University [Pacific Linguistics C–100].

Keesing, R. 1988. *Melanesian Pidgin and the Oceanic Substrate.* Stanford, CA: Stanford University Press.

Keesing, R. Forthcoming. "Melanesian Pidgin and Oceanic syntax: Further evidence from Solomons languages." To appear in *Proceedings of Fifth International Congress on Austronesian Linguistics, Te Reo.*

Lamont, E.H. 1867. *Wild Life Among the Pacific Islanders.* London: Hurst and Beckett.

Lichtenberk, F. Volume I. "On the gradualness of grammaticalization."

Mosel, U. 1980. *Tolai and Tok Pisin: The Influence of the Substratum on the Development of New Guinea Pidgin.* Canberra: The Australian National University [Pacific Linguistics B–73].

Mosel, U. and P. Mühlhäusler. 1982. "New evidence for a Samoan origin of Tok Pisin." *Journal of Pacific History* 17(3–4):166–175.

Mufwene, S.S. 1986. "The universalist and substrate hypotheses complement one another." In *Substrata Versus Universals in Creole Genesis*, P. Muysken and N. Smith (eds). Amsterdam/Philadelphia: John Benjamins.

Mühlhäusler, P. 1976. "Samoan plantation Pidgin English and the origin of New Guinea Pidgin: An introduction." *Journal of Pacific History* 11(2):122–125.

Mühlhäusler, P. 1978. "Samoan Plantation English and the origin of New Guinea Pidgin." *Papers in Pidgin and Creole Linguistics* 1. Canberra: Australian National University [Pacific Linguistics A-54].

Mühlhäusler, P. 1980. "Structural expansion and the process of creolization." In *Theoretical Orientations in Creole Studies*, A. Valdman and A. Highfield (eds). New York: Academic Press.

Mühlhäusler, P. 1981. "The development of the category of number in Tok Pisin." In *Generative Studies on Creole Languages*, P. Muysken (ed.). Dordrecht: Foris Publications.

Mühlhäusler, P. 1985a. "External development of Tok Pisin." In *Handbook of Tok Pisin (New Guinea Pidgin)*, S.A. Wurm and P. Mühlhäusler (eds). Canberra: Australian National University [Pacific Linguistics C–70].

Mühlhäusler, P. 1985b. "Internal development of Tok Pisin." In *Handbook of Tok Pisin (New Guinea Pidgin)*, S.A. Wurm and P. Mühlhäusler (eds). Canberra: Australian National University [Pacific Linguistics C–70].

Mühlhäusler, P. 1987. *Pidgin and Creole Languages*. London: Basil Blackwell.

Paton, G. 1895. *Letters and Sketches form the New Hebrides*. London: Hodder and Stoughton.

Pawley, A. 1972. "On the internal relationships of Eastern Oceanic languages." In *Studies in Oceanic Culture History*, Vol. 3, R.C. Green and M. Kelly (eds). *Pacific Anthropological Records* 13:1–142. Honolulu: Bernice P. Bishop Museum.

Pawley, A. 1973. "Some problems in proto-Oceanic grammar." *Oceanic Linguistics* 12:103–188.

Pawley, A. and L.A. Reid. 1979. "The evolution of transitive constructions in Austronesian." In *Austronesian Studies: Papers from the Second Eastern Conference on Austronesian Languages*, P.B. Naylor (ed.), 103–130. Ann Arbor, MI: University of Michigan.

Ross, M. 1986. "A genetic grouping of Oceanic languages in Bougainville and the Western Solomons." In *Proceedings of the Fourth International Conference on Austronesian Linguistics*, P. Geraghty, L. Carrington, and S.A. Wurm (eds). Canberra: Australian National University [Pacific Linguistics C–94].

Salisbury, R. 1967. "Pidgin's respectable past." *New Guinea* 2(2):44–48.

Sankoff, G. 1977. "Variability and explanation in language and culture: Cliticization in New Guinea Tok Pisin." In *Linguistics and Anthropology*, M. Saville-Troike (ed.). Washington D.C.: Georgetown University Press (Reprinted in Sankoff, 1980).

Sankoff, G. 1980. *The Social Life of Language*. Philadelphia: University of Pennsylvania Press.

Sankoff, G. and P. Brown. 1976. "The origins of syntax in discourse: A case study of Tok Pisin relatives." *Language* 52:631–666 (Reprinted in Sankoff, 1980).

Sankoff, G. and S. Laberge. 1973. "On the acquisition of native speakers by a language." *Kivung* 6:32–47 (Reprinted in Sankoff, 1980).

Silverstein, M. 1972. "Chinook jargon: Language contact and the problem of multi-level generative systems." *Language* 48:378-406;596–625.

Simons, L. 1986. "Malaitan influence on two grammatical particles in Solomon Islands Pijin." In *Papers in Pidgin and Creole Linguistics*, No.4, S. Romaine et al. (eds). Canberra: Australian National University [Pacific Linguistics A–72].

White, G. Forthcoming. *Dictionary of Cheke Holo (Maringe)*. Canberra: Australian National University [Pacific Linguistics, In press].

Volume I

Index of languages

Volume I

Index of names

Volume I

Index of subjects

Q

R

S

T

In the TYPOLOGICAL STUDIES IN LANGUAGE (TSL) series the following volumes have been published thus far and will be published during 1991:

1. HOPPER, Paul (ed.): *TENSE-ASPECT: BETWEEN SEMANTICS & PRAGMATICS.* Amsterdam/Philadelphia, 1982.
2. HAIMAN, John & Pam MUNRO (eds): *PROCEEDINGS OF A SYMPOSIUM ON SWITCH REFERENCE, Winnipeg, May 1981.* Amsterdam/Philadelphia, 1983.
3. GIVÓN, T. (ed.): *TOPIC CONTINUITY IN DISCOURSE: A QUANTITATIVE CROSS-LANGUAGE STUDY.* Amsterdam/Philadelphia, 1983.
4. CHISHOLM, William, Louis T. MILIC & John GREPPIN (eds): *INTERROGATIVITY: A COLLOQUIUM ON THE GRAMMAR, TYPOLOGY AND PRAGMATICS OF QUESTIONS IN SEVEN DIVERSE LANGUAGES, Cleveland, Ohio, October 5th 1981 - May 3rd 1982.* Amsterdam/Philadelphia, 1984.
5. RUTHERFORD, William E. (ed.): *LANGUAGE UNIVERSALS AND SECOND LANGUAGE ACQUISITION.* Amsterdam/Philadelphia, 1984. 2nd edition 1987.
6. HAIMAN, John (ed.): *ICONICITY IN SYNTAX. Proceedings of a Symposium on Iconicity in Syntax, Stanford, June 24-6, 1983.* Amsterdam/Philadelphia, 1985.
7. CRAIG, Colette (ed.): *NOUN CLASSES AND CATEGORIZATION. Proceedings of a Symposium on Categorization and Noun Classification, Eugene, Ore. October 1983.* Amsterdam/Philadelphia, 1986.
8. SLOBIN, Dan I. & Karl ZIMMER (eds): *STUDIES IN TURKISH LINGUISTICS.* Amsterdam/Philadelphia, 1986.
9. BYBEE, Joan L.: *Morphology. A Study of the Relation between Meaning and Form.* Amsterdam/Philadelphia, 1985.
10. RANSOM, Evelyn: *Complementation: its Meanings and Forms.* Amsterdam/Philadelphia, 1986.
11. TOMLIN, Russ (ed.): *COHERENCE AND GROUNDING IN DISCOURSE.* Outcome of a Symposium on -, Eugene, Ore, June 1984. Amsterdam/Philadelphia, 1987.
12. NEDJALKOV, Vladimir P. (ed.): *TYPOLOGY OF RESULTATIVE CONSTRUCTIONS.* Translated from the original Russian edition publ. by "Nauka", Leningrad, 1983, English translation edited by Bernard Comrie. Amsterdam/Philadelphia, 1988.
14. HINDS, John, Senko MAYNARD & Shoichi IWASAKI (eds): *PERSPECTIVES ON TOPICALIZATION: The Case of Japanese 'WA'.* Amsterdam/Philadelphia, 1987.
15. AUSTIN, Peter (ed.): *COMPLEX SENTENCE CONSTRUCTIONS IN AUSTRALIAN LANGUAGES.* Amsterdam/Philadelphia, 1987.
16. SHIBATANI, Masayoshi (ed.): *PASSIVE AND VOICE.* Amsterdam/Philadelphia, 1988.
17. HAMMOND, Michael, Edith A. MORAVCSIK & Jessica R. WIRTH (eds): *STUDIES IN SYNTACTIC TYPOLOGY.* Amsterdam/Philadelphia, 1988.
18. HAIMAN, John & Sandra A. THOMPSON (eds): *CLAUSE COMBINING IN GRAMMAR AND DISCOURSE.* Amsterdam/Philadelphia, 1988.
19. TRAUGOTT, Elizabeth C. & Bernd HEINE (eds): *APPROACHES TO GRAMMATICALIZATION. 2 volumes.* Amsterdam/Philadelphia, 1991.
20. CROFT, William, Keith DENNING & Suzanne KEMMER (eds): *STUDIES IN TYPOLOGY AND DIACHRONY. Papers presented to Joseph H. Greenberg on his 75th birthday.* Amsterdam/Philadelphia, 1990.
21. DOWNING, Pamela, Susan D. LIMA & Michael NOONAN (eds): *THE LINGUISTICS OF LITERACY.* Amsterdam/Philadelphia, 1991. n.y.p.
22. PAYNE, Doris (ed.): *PRAGMATICS OF WORD ORDER FLEXIBILITY.* Amsterdam/Philadelphia, 1991. n.y.p.